Legacy Resource Management Program
Project 05-194

ERDC/CERL M-06-2
August 2006

The Built Environment of Cold War Era Servicewomen

Dawn A. Morrison and Susan I. Enscore

Construction Engineering Research Laboratory
U.S. Army Engineer Research and Development Center
2902 Newmark Drive
Champaign, IL 61826-9005

Prepared for Legacy Resource Management Program
              Arlington, VA 22202
       Under W31RYO31415903 and W31RYO51119492

Abstract: Although women have served in defense of our country since the American Revolutionary War, women were not given full military status until World War II. Providing full military status to women had repercussions for the built environment of the country's military installations, especially as the government mandated a gender-segregated military. It required a reconsideration of both the spatial organization and the design protocols used in constructing and/or rehabilitating military infrastructure, specifically as related to the housing, training, and workspaces of military women. This reconsideration led to ever-evolving regulations and standard operating procedures throughout the course of the Cold War concerning this matter, reflecting the military's immediate needs, as well as changing societal norms regarding gender.

This project provides a service-wide historical context for how the accommodation of service women during the Cold War impacted the military's built environment. This historical context is based on archival research, oral histories, and an examination of historic photographs, plan maps, architectural drawings, and other associated primary documents.

DISCLAIMER: The contents of this report are not to be used for advertising, publication, or promotional purposes. Citation of trade names does not constitute an official endorsement or approval of the use of such commercial products. All product names and trademarks cited are the property of their respective owners. The findings of this report are not to be construed as an official Department of the Army position unless so designated by other authorized documents.

DESTROY THIS REPORT WHEN NO LONGER NEEDED. DO NOT RETURN IT TO THE ORIGINATOR.

Contents

Figures v

Preface x

Acknowledgements xi

Acronyms xii

1 Introduction 1
    A date with destiny 1
    Objective and regulations 6
    Methodology 7

2 World War II: Free a Man to Fight 14
    Policy 17
    Women's Area Layout 19
    Recreational Facilities 24
    Mess Halls 26
    Detention Facilities 30
    Housing Policy 31
    Housing Design 37
    Latrines 46
    Laundry Facilities 48
    Luggage Rooms 50
    Fire Escapes 52
    Lounges, Date Rooms, and Kitchens 54
    Beauty Shops 56
    Training 58

3 Post-War Period Integration: A Permanent Role for Women 63
    Policy 63
    Women's Armed Services Integration Act 65
    Housing Design 70
    Training 74

4 The Korean War and the 1950s: Recruitment and Retention 76
    Policy and Utilization Studies 77
    Housing Standards 81
    Housing Design 85
    Color Schemes 93
    Support Facilities 95
    Training 97

5 Vietnam and the 1960s: Typewriter Soldiers	**101**
Quality of Life and Housing Studies	103
Housing Design	109
Tri-Service Design	112
DoD Minimum Housing Standards	114
Training	116
6 All Volunteer Force and the 1970s: Typewriter Soldiers No More	**117**
All-Volunteer Force	117
Women's Roles and Expansion	119
Policy	123
Military Occupation Specialties	125
Equal Treatment	126
Housing Policy	129
Housing Design	134
New Barracks Designs	137
Detention Facilities	143
Equipment	144
Training	144
7 Police Actions and the 1980s: All But Combat	**151**
Refining Women's Roles	152
Housing and Facility Design	155
Training	157
8 Conclusion: This Man's Army No More	**159**
Bibliography	**165**
Appendix A: List of Plans and Drawings	**179**
Administrative Data	180
Building Data	197
Housing/Sleeping Data	216
Restroom Facilities Data	249
Appendix B: Copies of Plans and Drawings	**289**
Report Documentation Page	**290**

Figures

Figure 1. Fort Des Moines, women in the field in their tents, WWII (WIMSA, Vertical Photo File, Collection of Howard Bright). 11

Figure 2. Camp Lee Training Center, Black WACs, Company B, First Battalion, in dayroom, 9 September 1949 (WAC Museum, Vertical Files, File: Segregation). 13

Figure 3. WWII cartoon by Chesney (WIMSA). 16

Figure 4. Plan for establishing WAAC area, 1942. 19

Figure 5. Layout for one WAAC company, 1943 (USACEHQ). 20

Figure 6. Fort Des Moines, WAC barracks row showing privacy fencing, WWII (WIMSA, Vertical Photo File, Collection of Kris Morrison). 20

Figure 7. Outdoor private space for WACs, Gulfport Army Air Base, May 1945 (WIMSA, Vertical Photo File, Collection of Doris Mamolen). 21

Figure 8. White Sands Missile Range, WAC barracks, exterior patio furniture, 1965 (WAC Museum, Vertical Files, File: Housing Enlisted Survey of 1964-65). 22

Figure 9. Fort Des Moines, WAC barracks sign, WWII (WIMSA, Vertical Photo File, Collection of Donna Porter). 22

Figure 10. WAC area building, Camp Lejuene, 1943 (WIMSA, Document File, Collection of Lyla Spelbring). 24

Figure 11. WAC archery practice (note tiny picket fence), Harlingen Army Gunnery School, TX, 25 April 1945 (WIMSA, Vertical Photo File, Collection of Dorothy V. Clement). 25

Figure 12. Fort Lee WACs playing volleyball in front of barracks, 1952 (WAC Museum, Vertical Files, File: Athletics V-a-5). 25

Figure 13. Men and women leaving the post chapel during WWII, Fort Custer, MI (WIMSA, Vertical Photo File, Collection of Ann Zimmerman). 26

Figure 14. Camp Lee, WAC Mess Hall with attached benches, 1949 (WAC Museum, Vertical Files, File: Firsts V-a-14). 28

Figure 15. Fort Des Moines, Mess Hall with stools, 1943 (WIMSA, Vertical Photo File, Collection of Donna Porter). 28

Figure 16. Mess Hall with chairs, Naval Air Technical Training Center, Norman, OK, 1943 (WIMSA, Vertical Photo File, Collection of Margaret Holman). 29

Figure 17. Consolidated mess, Camp Crowder, MO, WWII (Camp Crowder Museum). 30

Figure 18. WAVES barracks locker, Naval Air Technical Training Center, Memphis, 1944 (WIMSA, Vertical Photo File, Collection of Margaret Holman). 33

Figure 19. WAVES using ironing room in barracks, WWII (WIMSA, Vertical Photo File, Collection of Elaine Krieter Engh). 33

Figure 20. WAVES recreation room in barracks, NAS Seattle, 1944-45. In booklet WAVES: U.S. Naval Air Station, Seattle, Washington, nd. (WIMSA, Document File, Unknown donor #164). 34

Figure 21. Camp Lejuene, Women Marine barracks upstairs lounge "off-limits to men," 1944 (WIMSA, Vertical Photo File, Unknown donor). 35

Figure 22. Women's Squad Bay interior with dressers and photos, Camp Lejuene, 1944 (WIMSA, Vertical Photo File, Unknown donor). 35

Figure 23. WAC company dayroom with easy chairs and other furnishings, Camp Lee Training Center (WAC Museum, Vertical Files, File: Dayrooms V-a-24). 37

Figure 24. WAVES four-person barracks cubicle, NAS Seattle, 1944-45. In booklet WAVES: U.S. Naval Air Station, Seattle, Washington, nd. (WIMSA, Document File, Unknown donor #164).. 38

Figure 25. Open bay converted to cubicles with partitions, 1943 (NARA). 38

Figure 26. Naval WAVES barracks with bunk beds and lockers, Air Technical Training Center, Norman, OK, 1944 (WIMSA, Vertical Photo File, Collection of Margaret Holman). 39

Figure 27. WAVES Lounge, NAS Seattle, 1944-45. In booklet WAVES: U.S. Naval Air Station, Seattle, WA, nd. (WIMSA, Document File, Unknown donor #164). 40

Figure 28. Enlisted WAVES barracks showing lounge, 1943 (NARA). 41

Figure 29. Enlisted WAVES barracks showing toilet stall doors and laundry facilities, 1943 (NARA). 41

Figure 30. WAVES Detachment wrapped in shower curtains, Shoemaker, CA, 1945. In Waves, United States Navy, 1950s (WIMSA, Document File, Collection of Ruth Smith #4437). 42

Figure 31. Plan of mobilization type WAAC barracks with bunks for 75 women, 1942 (USACEHQ). 43

Figure 32., AAF WAC Detachment laundry facilities, Eagle Pass, TX, Army Air Field, 1944 (WIMSA, Document File, Collection of Violet Rodgers #1537). 44

Figure 33. WAC Date Room interior, Will Rogers Field, July 43- Sept 44 (WIMSA, Vertical Photo File, Collection of Doris Mamolen). 45

Figure 34. Women Marine barracks showing dressers and personal items, Camp Lejuene, 1945 (WIMSA, Vertical Photo File, Unknown donor). 46

Figure 35. Conversion of male barracks bath facilities for female use, 1943 (USACEHQ). 47

Figure 36. Provision of bathtubs for WAACs, 1942 (USACEHQ). 48

Figure 37. Women Marines washing and ironing in barracks, Camp Lejuene, 1944 (WIMSA, Vertical Photo File, Unknown donor). 49

Figure 38. WACS with luggage, Fort Des Moines, WWII (WIMSA, Vertical Photo File, Collection of Kris Morrison). 50

Figure 39. WAVES recruits stowing suitcases in racks, US Naval Training Center, Bainbridge, MD, 1956. From yearbook "The Portal" for Company 15 (WIMSA, Document File, Collection of Doris Brown #4642). 51

Figure 40. Plan for luggage room, WAVES barracks, 1943 (NARA). 51

Figure 41. WAACS uniforms with narrow skirts and heeled shoes, Fort Devens, January 24, 1943 (WIMSA, Document File, Collection of Lois Bowen). 52

Figure 42. WAC barracks area showing fire escape stairs, Fort Des Moines, 1942 (WIMSA, Vertical Photo File, Collection of Ruth Sparacio). 53

Figure 43. Plan for fire escape stairs, 1943 (NARA). 53

Figure 44. Layout of date room (note men's bathroom off the lobby), 1946 (USACEHQ). 55

Figure 45. Plan for small lounge kitchen (on right), 1951 (USACEHQ). 55

Figure 46. WAVES beauty shop, Naval Air Technical Training Center, Norman, OK, 1943 (WIMSA, Vertical Photo File, Collection of Margaret Holman). 56

Figure 47. Beauty Shop in Recreation building, 1942 (USACEHQ). 57

Figure 48. WACs at machine gun training, Harlingen Army Gunnery School, TX, WWII (WIMSA, Vertical Photo File, Collection of Dorothy V. Clement). 58

Figure 49. WAVES Aviation Machinist Training, WWII (WIMSA, Vertical Photo File, Collection of National Archives, Photo 86-WWT-60-8) 59

Figure 50. WAC MPs, Fort Des Moines, WWII (WIMSA, Vertical Photo File, Collection of Howard Bright). 60

Figure 51. WAVES at work on engine maintenance, Naval Air Station Banana River, FL, 30 August 1944 (NARA, RG 80-G Box 758, 244460). 60

Figure 52. WAVES packing parachutes, Naval Air Station Banana River, FL, 30 Aug. 1944 (NARA, RG 80-G Box 758, 244458). 61

Figure 53. Obstacle course at an Army Air Corps base, 1943 (WIMSA, Document File, Unknown donor #4674). 61

Figure 54. WACs read the Women's Armed Services Integration Act at the Pentagon, Washington, DC, June 1948 (RG 111 SC, Box 371, Photo 300881, NARA, College Park, MD). 66

Figure 55. Hotel-type housing plan for enlisted WACs with two-person rooms, 1946 (USACEHQ). 71

Figure 56. Apartment-type barracks for higher grade enlisted WACs with two-bedroom suites, 1946 (USACEHQ). 72

Figure 57. Barracks layout showing rudimentary partitions between bunks, 1952 (NARA). 73

Figure 58. WAVES recruits arriving for training, U.S. Naval Training Center, Bainbridge, MD, 1956. From yearbook "The Portal" for Company 15 (WIMSA, Document File, Collection of Doris Brown #4642). 79

Figure 59. Additional barracks facilities provided for women, including privacy considerations in bathrooms, 1954 (USACEHQ). 86

Figure 60. WAC barrack kitchenette, Ft. McClellan, 1954 (WAC Museum, Vertical Files, File: Inspections of Construction VI-A-13). 87

Figure 61. WAC Training Center at Fort McClellan, AL, mid-1950s (WAC Museum, Vertical Files, File: Activation VI-A-1). 88

Figure 62. Typical Enlisted Women's barracks under construction at WAC Training Center, Fort McClellan, 1953 (WAC Museum, Vertical Files, File: Construction VI-A-13). 88

Figure 63. Basic trainee barracks interior, WAC Center, Fort McClellan, 1955 (WAC Museum, Vertical Files, File: UA WAC School – Facilities/Buildings/Grounds VI-A-17). 89

Figure 64. Two-person officer suite, WAC Center, Fort McClellan, 1955 (WAC Museum, Vertical Files: File: UA WAC School – Facilities/Buildings/Grounds VI-A-17). 90

Figure 65. WAC Center Commander's living room, Fort McClellan (WAC Museum, Vertical Files, File: UA WAC School – Facilities/Buildings/Grounds VI-A-17). 90

Figure 66. Senior officers quarters at WAC Center, Fort McClellan (WAC Museum, Vertical Files, File: UA WAC School – Facilities/Buildings/Grounds VI-A-17). 91

Figure 67. Plan for Navy BOQ with bath for every two rooms, 1953 (NARA). 92

Figure 68. Two-person junior officer BOQ suite with bedrooms flanking a shared living room and bath (second bedroom not shown), similar to the Fort Knox design, 1954 (NARA). 93

Figure 69. WAC barracks with pastel painting, White Sands, 1965 (WAC Museum, Vertical Files, File: Housing Enlisted Survey of 1964-65). 95

Figure 70. Dance at WAC Service Club #1, Fort McClellan. Club had TV room, music room, reading room, game room, snack bar, craft and hobby shop (WAC Museum, Vertical Files, File: Facilities/Buildings/Grounds VI-A-17).. 96

Figure 71. Hobby shop with yarn and loom at Fort Lee, VA (WAC Museum, Vertical Files, File: Crafts V-b-17)... 96

Figure 72. WAVES Town Club powder room, Naval Air Training Base, Pensacola, FL, WWII (WIMSA, Document File, Collection of Blanche Schultz #3464, in *The Naval Air Training Bases, Pensacola, Florida Thru World War II,* 1945)... 97

Figure 73. Plan showing powder room in service club/post exchange building, 1966 (USACEHQ)... 97

Figure 74. Class in restaurant etiquette for "Individual Standards & Social Concepts" course, Fort Lee, VA (WAC Museum, Vertical Files, File: Enlisted Permanent Party Training V-a-27)... 98

Figure 75. Headquarters of the U.S. Women's Army Corps Center, Fort McClellan, AL, 1971 (WIMSA, Document File, Collection of Christine Henry #4780). 99

Figure 76. WAC Classroom, Fort McClellan (WAC Museum, Vertical files, File: UA WAC School – Facilities/Buildings/Grounds VI-A-17). 99

Figure 77. WACS march past barracks, Fort McClellan, 1654 (WAC Museum, Vertical Files, File: UA WAC School – Facilities/Buildings/Grounds VI-A-17)......................................100

Figure 78. WAC "typewriter soldiers" alongside men, Fort Custer, MI, WWII (WIMSA, Vertical Photo File, Collection of Ann Zimmerman)..102

Figure 79. Austere WM recruit barracks at Parris Island, SC, 1967. In *Marine Corps Recruit Depot Yearbook, Platoon 4B* (WIMSA, Document File, Collection of Ellie Lopez #4167)..108

Figure 80. Gender-neutral motel type BOQ concept sketch, 1967 (NARA)......................... 111

Figure 81. Bathrooms, kitchens, and lounges, Tri-Service Enlisted Women's Barracks, 1955 (Fort Myer). 113

Figure 82. Recreation and visitor facilities Tri-Service Enlisted Women's Barracks, 1955 (Fort Myer)..114

Figure 83. Enlisted Women's center-hall type barracks concept sketch, 1967 (USACEHQ). 115

Figure 84. Chesney cartoon (WIMSA). 130

Figure 85. Motel type housing with exterior room doors (USACEHQ)................................134

Figure 86. Tri-Service design for motel type Officer's quarters, 1962 (USACEHQ). 137

Figure 87. Navy high-rise enlisted quarters influenced by 1962 Tri-Service designs, 1975 (NARA)..138

Figure 88. Interior of barracks showing old-style open squad bay (note irons under bunks), 1973 (WAC Museum, Vertical Files, File: US WAC Center Barracks/Dayrooms VI-A-17). 139

Figure 89. Navy/Marine version of three-man rooms with bath, 1975 (NARA). 139

Figure 90. Metal bunks and lockers at Parris Island, 1967. In *Marine Corps Recruit Depot Yearbook, Platoon 4B* (WIMSA, Document File, Collection of Ellie Lopez #4167)..........................140

Figure 91. Women Marines doing laundry, Parris Island, 1967. In *Marine Corps Recruit Depot Yearbook, Platoon 4B* (WIMSA, Document File, Collection of Ellie Lopez #4167). 141

Figure 92. WAC double room showing personal touches, White Sands Missile Range, 1965 (WAC Museum, Vertical Files, File: Housing Enlisted Survey of 1964-65)...........................142

Figure 93. Gender-integrated basic combat training, Fort Jackson, SC (Courtesy of Fort Jackson, U.S. Army). 146

Figure 94. WACs receive training in hair care and cosmetics, U.S. Army Training Center, Fort Jackson, 1977. In Company book for *Women's Army Corps (WAC) Company A, 18th Battalion, 5th Brigade* (WIMSA, Document File, Collection of William Polcsa #4637). 147

Figure 95. WACs on obstacle course, Fort McClellan, AL, 1977. In yearbook from *WAC Basic Training Battalion Training Brigade*, 1977 (WIMSA, Document File, donor unknown #4674)...150

Figure 96. Two double-room/shared bath design (NARA). 156

Figure 97. Gymnasium plan from 1969 showing gender differences in bathroom facilities (NARA). 156

Figure 98. 15 S&T Battalion gender-segregated training, Fort Hood, TX, 1983 (1st CAV Museum, Fort Hood). 157

Figure 99. U.S. Army servicewomen, King Fahd International Airport, Saudi Arabia, January 1991 (WIMSA, Vertical File, Collection of Lorraine Souza). 160

Preface

This study was conducted for the DoD Legacy Resource Management Program under Military Interdepartmental Purchase Requests (MIPRs) 97/0100/701/A/W31RYO31415903 and 97/0100/701/A/W31RYO51119492, "Built Environment of Cold War Era Servicewomen," dated 21 May 2003 and 4 April 2005. The technical monitors were Claire Henline and Brian Lione of the DoD Legacy Resource Management Program Office, Washington, DC.

The work was performed by the Land and Heritage Conservation Branch (CN-C) of the Installations Division (CN), Construction Engineering Research Laboratory (CERL). The project manager and secondary author was Dr. Susan I. Enscore. The historian and primary author was Dr. Dawn A. Morrison. Research assistants Vincent J. Spencer and Timothy W. Scovic provided architectural support. Dr. Lucy A. Whalley is Chief, CEERD-CN-C, and Dr. John T. Bandy is Chief, CEERD-CN. The associated Technical Director is Dr. William D. Severinghaus, CEERD-CV-T. The Director of CERL is Dr. Ilker Adziguel.

CERL is an element of the U.S. Army Engineer Research and Development Center (ERDC), U.S. Army Corps of Engineers. The Commander of ERDC is COL Richard B. Jenkins and the Director of ERDC is Dr. James R. Houston.

Acknowledgements

The wealth of information contained in this report would not have been possible without the help and support of many people. The authors wish to thank the following individuals and organizations' general staff for their assistance with this effort. First and foremost, four repositories provided the vast majority of the photographs, plans, and architectural drawings that highlight the text. Their staff remained engaged and resourceful through the course of several extended stays by our research team. In no particular order, we express our thanks to Britta K. Granrud and Dr. Judith Bellafaire at the Women in Military Service for America Memorial Foundation, Inc.; Ms. Amy Hill, U.S. Army Women's Museum; Dr. Regina Akers at the Naval Historical Center, Operational Archives; the staff of the Cartographic and Architectural Records Branch at the National Archives and Records Administration, Archives II; and Dr. William Baldwin and Dr. John Lonnquest at the U.S. Army Corps of Engineers Office of History. In addition, Dr. Regina Akers at the Naval Historical Center, Operational Archives gave a large amount of her time to guide our research efforts during our visits there. Staff at the Air Force Historical Research Agency, the Marine Corps Historical Center, and the Naval Historical Foundation Library also provided assistance.

We would also like to thank Mr. Peter Boice, Mr. Brian Lione, Ms. Claire Henline, and Dr. Julie Schablitsky at the Legacy Resource Management Program. Their unflagging support for this project has been invaluable.

Acronyms

AAF	Army Air Forces
AVF	All-Volunteer Force
BOQ	Bachelor Officers' Quarters
DACOWITS	Defense Advisory Council on Women in the Services
DoD	Department of Defense
ERDC-CERL	Engineer Research and Development Center-Construction Engineering Research Laboratory
FY	Fiscal Year
ICBM	Intercontinental Ballistic Missile
MOOTW	Military Operations Other Than War
MOS	Military Occupational Specialties
MP	Military Police
NARA	National Archives and Records Administration
NAS	Naval Air Station
NCO	Non-Commissioned Officer
NHPA	National Historic Preservation Act of 1966
NRHP	National Register of Historic Places
OCONUS	outside the continental United States
ROTC	Reserve Officers' Training Corps
TRADOC	Training and Doctrine Command
USAF	United States Air Force
USACEHQ	U.S. Army Corps of Engineers, Headquarters History Office
WAAC	Women's Army Auxiliary Corps (a precursor to WAC)
WAC	Women's Army Corps
WAF	Women's Air Force
WAVES	Women Accepted for Volunteer Emergency Service (Navy)
WIMSA	Women in Military Service for America (Memorial Foundation, Inc.)
WM	Women Marines
WOQ	Women's Officers Quarters

1 Introduction

A date with destiny

In 1942, Oveta Culp Hobby, Director of the Women's Army Auxiliary Corps, addressed the inaugural class of women attending the Army's first female military training center at Fort Des Moines, Iowa: "You have taken off silk and put on khaki. You have a debt to democracy and a date with destiny."[1] Also in 1942, folklore has it that the portrait of Archibald Henderson, former 5th Commandant of the Marine Corps, "crashed from the wall to the buffet the evening that Major General Commandant Thomas Holcomb announced his decision to recruit women into the Corps."[2] To be sure, reactions ran the gamut at the thought of women in the military, even though in 1942, women were admitted only into the military reserves or auxiliary.

In World War II, the manpower shortage was quickly becoming more acute than that experienced during World War I. In response, the country began recruiting women to take over the clerical, administrative, and telephone operators jobs (i.e., traditional female occupations) from able-bodied men who could then be sent to the front lines overseas. This initial recruitment was not what caused controversy and dissention, as the country had experienced this before during World War I when the Navy and the Marine Corps recruited a corps of women reservists to provide clerical and telephone services in order to compensate for manpower shortages. Controversy began when it quickly became clear that freeing a man to fight soon made it necessary for called upon America's women to take on non-traditional jobs, such as drivers, mechanics, air traffic controllers, and parachute packers. Indeed, the *man*-power shortage was so extreme that,

---

[1] "WAACS: First Women Soldiers Join Army," *Life* (September 7, 1942), 75.

[2] Col. Mary V. Stremlow, *Free a Marine to Fight: Women Marines in World War II*, World War II Commemorative Series Pamphlet (Washington, DC: Marine Corps Historical Center, 1994), 1.

unlike in World War I where approximately 12,500 women served in the reserves, almost 250,000 women served during World War II.[3]

Also unlike the previous war, discussions leading up to the admission of women into the reserves in 1942 raised the issue of directly enlisting women and granting them full military status. The significance of full military status meant that women would be subject to military protocol, regulations, command, and customs. They would undergo boot camp, training, wear a uniform, and adhere to strict military customs. But, they would also receive rank, pay, and benefits. Altogether, it was the combination of these three things—performing non-traditional jobs, the sheer volume of women who would be involved in the effort, and the prospect (and eventual reality in 1943) of full military status—that provoked strong, and at times extreme, reactions from the American people in the early 1940s.

The reaction of the American people would once again run the gamut when, at the successful conclusion of World War II, the government proposed and began debating whether or not to make women a permanent part of the new military structure. The short-lived alliance between the United States, the United Kingdom and the Soviet Union soon gave way to the spread of communism and the start of the Cold War.[4] The advent of the Cold War and America's new-found role as a superpower necessitated a new military philosophy that provided for a large permanent military, rather than the country's previous practice of maintaining a core permanent military and mobilizing and demobilizing the larger populace in times of need. In defining America's new military structure it was realized that should the country ever go to war again, the military would have to rely on women just as it did during World War II. Thus, as the final argument went, it behooved the military to retain a small corps of trained military women as part of the regular force. This decision granting women permanent status in the regular military, in turn, ushered in a new round

---

[3] These statistics do not include women who served in the Army, Navy, or Civilian Nurse Corps; close to 23,000 nurses served during World War I, and close to 200,000 in World War II. Statistics derived from the education webpage on the Women in Military Service for America Memorial Foundation, Inc. website: http://womensmemorial.org, and "Significant Events in the History of Women Marines," *Marines* (June 1988): 3, Reference File—Report on Progress of Women in the Marine Corps (1988), Washington Navy Yards, Marine Corps Historical Center Archives, Washington, DC.

[4] It is commonly accepted that the Cold War began in 1946 with Winston Churchill's "Iron Curtain" speech, and ends with the fall of the Berlin Wall in 1989. See United States Army, *Cultural Resources Management*, DA PAM 200-4 (Washington, DC: Department of the Army, 1998).

of social debate on the role of women in society, similar to that which had occurred during World War II. The larger social debate over gender roles was mirrored within the military subculture and became a recurring, and sometimes contentious, debate that persisted throughout the Cold War in response to women's changing and ever expanding role in the military.

The social ramifications of admitting women into the military and granting them full status, and the history of women in the military, are subjects that have been well-covered by historians, veterans, and military enthusiasts.[5] Although the history of servicewomen has been well documented, little attention, if any, has been paid to their physical accommodation in the military. There is an old saying that "an Army moves on its stomach." Granted that this is certainly true, it is important to note that before an Army can move anywhere, it has to be organized and trained. Thus, before an Army moves on its stomach, what must be acknowledged is that an Army develops *in place*. The result of this is a network of built environments in the form of military installations, training centers, and other assorted facilities, all of which embody the ideology, traditions, practices and necessities of a constantly evolving military.

Moreover, understanding that social mores are often writ large in the built environment, the physical accommodation of servicewomen—in terms of housing, work, training, and leisure—throughout their history reflects the influence of prevailing social attitudes toward the role of women, both in the military and in society at large. The confluence of social attitudes toward women, and evolving military ideology, traditions, practices, and necessity, uniquely impacted the built environment of our country's military landscapes over the course of the Cold War. In large part, this impact resulted from the government's mandate for a gender-segregated military. This mandate required a reconsideration of both the spatial organization and the design protocols used in constructing and/or rehabilitating military infrastructure, specifically as related to the housing, training, and

---

[5] See Maj. Gen. Jeanne Holm, USAF (Ret.), *Women in the Military: An Unfinished Revolution* (Novato, CA: Presido Press, 1982); Stremlow, *Free a Marine*; Col. Mary V. Stremlow, *A History of the Women Marines, 1946-1977* (Washington, DC: History and Museums Division, Headquarters, U.S. Marine Corps, 1986); Susan H. Godson, *Serving Proudly: A History Of Women in the U.S. Navy* (Annapolis, MD: Naval Institute Press, 2001); Bettie J. Morden, *The Women's Army Corps, 1945-1978*, 2d ed. (Washington, DC: Center of Military History, U.S. Army, 2000); Mattie E. Treadwell, *The Women's Army Corps*, U.S. Army in World War II, Special Studies (Washington, DC: Department of the Army, Office of the Chief of Military History, 1954).

workspaces of military women. This reconsideration led to ever-evolving regulations and design criteria throughout the Cold War—changes that directly reflected the military's immediate needs and the changing societal norms regarding gender and gender roles.

Initially, physically accommodating women in the military followed, at least in principle, a mantra of "separate but better."[6] Implementing this principle required new design plans for both new construction and for retrofitting and converting existing barracks; support facilities; and work, training, and leisure areas. From World War II through the beginning of the Cold War, regulations were enacted that significantly altered the built environment of military installations, from the spatial organization of structures and facilities (e.g., placing at least 150 feet between female and male barracks), to the structural design of buildings (e.g., increased square footage per individual), to the interior design of buildings (e.g., installing partitioning devices between sleeping areas).

Further, two major themes were recurrent throughout the historical continuum of accommodating women in the military: privacy and protection. These two themes, in turn, significantly influenced design development throughout its evolution. Various design considerations included interior design issues concerned with meeting the perceived needs of women in terms of privacy and added amenities. Design considerations also included external measures focused on providing protection for the women in terms of segregating them from the men and from military activities designated inappropriate for women (e.g., combat training). In short;

> "... [A]ll of the services tended to treat enlisted women like immature girls in a boarding school, away from home for the first time. In part, this was a reflection of the military's traditional attitudes toward enlisted personnel, which was by habit paternalistic, and in part a reflection of our cultural attitudes toward women...but whatever the motivation, there was an

---

[6] Diane Shaw Wasch, Perry Bush, Keith Landreth, and James Glass, *World War II and the U.S. Army Mobilization Program: A History of 700 and 800 Series Cantonment Construction*, edited by Arlene R. Kriv (Washington, DC: U.S. Department of Defense, Legacy Resource Management Program and U.S. Department of the Interior, National Park Service, 1988).

> ever present, almost prudish concern for protecting military women's virtue, chastity, and reputation—individually and collectively."[7]

This attitude toward women became more "modern" over the course of the Cold War, spurred on in large part by the attitude of servicewomen themselves. As Maj. Ann Wright, who served in Grenada for three months with the XVIII Airborne Corps's International Law Team, stated, "One does not join the military to lead a sheltered and protected life."[8] Shifts in the military's attitude toward women also mirrored larger social trends in American society regarding women's roles. The result was continuously evolving gender-based regulations that mandated different requirements for the accommodation of female personnel. Modified regulations reflected the changing role of women as they were gradually integrated into more areas of the military. These regulations in turn impacted the built environment of America's military installations, whether through the relaxation of (or modifications to) the spatial organization requirements, changes in structural requirements of buildings, or incorporation of new training spaces for women's evolving roles. These regulations eventually progressed into one standard for both men and women in terms of physical accommodations for housing, training, working, and leisure (although many of these activities were still segregated).

By the end of the Cold War, the physical imprint of women in the military could be seen throughout America's military installations, making it likely that buildings, structures, and physical elements associated specifically with Cold War Era servicewomen still exist. These aspects of the built environment are potentially eligible as historic properties and cultural resources, reflecting not only the specific subculture of women in American society, but also the physical manifestation of Cold War culture and societal norms as they pertained to the specific subgroup of women. However, little, if any, attention has been focused on understanding the history or development of these potentially unique resources.

---

[7] Holm, *Women in the Military*, 68-69.

[8] Quoted in Holm, *Women in the Military*, 405.

Objective and regulations

It is the purpose of this study to examine the built environment of Servicewomen, its history, and its evolution over the course of the Cold War. This project will result in the creation and dissemination of an historic context to be used by all branches of the military in identifying and evaluating aspects of historic buildings, landscapes, and properties associated with Cold War Era servicewomen. Properties associated with the built environment of Cold War Era servicewomen may be eligible as historic properties and cultural resources reflecting not only the specific subculture of women in American society, but also the physical manifestation of Cold War culture as it applies to women. As such, these properties fall under the auspices of the National Historic Preservation Act of 1966 (NHPA), as amended. The NHPA provides requirements for consideration of historic properties by Federal agencies. Section 106 of the NHPA requires Federal agencies to take into account the effects of any undertaking on historic properties and consult with preservation agencies regarding these effects and possible mitigating actions before spending federal funds on the undertaking. Historic properties are those properties that are either listed in, or are eligible for listing in, the National Register of Historic Places (NRHP). Section 110 of the NHPA requires installations and commands to develop and implement plans for the identification, management, and nomination of cultural resources.

Under NHPA, the Department of Defense (DoD) is mandated to inventory, examine, and assess the potential eligibility to the NRHP of historic properties associated with women in the military during the Cold War. A service-wide historic context to be used in evaluating aspects of the built environment associated with Cold War era servicewomen is necessary in fulfilling this mandate. The context will enhance the preservation and management of Cold War resources by facilitating installation compliance with NHPA in two ways: by providing (1) a valuable tool that can be used DoD-wide therefore reducing individual compliance efforts, and (2) support for future mitigation efforts, reducing the need for case-by-case research.

This report augments recent and ongoing projects such as the Navy Cold War context, the Air Force Cold War context, and the Unaccompanied Personnel Housing Cold War context, as it is the only study to focus on gender issues impacting cultural resources. Prior to this effort, no such study or historic context existed. A broad range of literature was available concerning the history and experiences of women serving in the various branches of the military, but none of these studies specifically dealt with the built environment of military installations or the physical manifestation and repercussions of accommodating Cold War era servicewomen. This study rectifies this absence by drawing from existing literature, as well as other sources, and compiling a service-wide historic context specifically concerned with how the accommodation of servicewomen during the Cold War impacted the military's built environment.

Methodology

In preparing this historic context for understanding how the addition of women as active duty soldiers affected the design of facilities on military installations during the Cold War period, the authors first conducted a literature review. Much has been written about the subject of women in the military, both by academics and laymen alike, resulting in a large body of secondary literature on the subject. This literature was used to form a general overview and background for the research. No study has yet provided a serious or focused treatment of the built environment created to accommodate the presence of women in the military. As commonly happens, the built environment in which we conduct our day-to-day lives is largely relegated to the background. Most people do not stop to think about the details, decisions, and processes involved in creating the built environment with which they interact daily, or through which they navigate their everyday lives. As a consequence, it is often neglected in historical recollection and analysis. Such is largely the case with the body of literature concerning women in the military. Although studies exist that mention or even discuss barracks, support facilities, and/or training, work, and leisure spaces, the attention paid to such subjects is brief and woefully lacking in detail. At the same time, it is this built environment that has the potential to provide physical, tangible, and direct links to the history of women in the military.

To compensate for the lack of secondary sources dealing directly with the built environment of Cold War Era servicewomen, the authors relied on primary documents obtained through archival research. This archival research was conducted at appropriate repositories including: Air Force Historical Research Agency, Maxwell Air Force Base, Montgomery, AL; Marine Corps Historical Center, Washington Navy Yard, Washington, DC; National Archives and Records Administration (NARA), College Park, MD; Naval Historical Center, Washington Navy Yard, Washington, DC; Naval

Historical Foundation Library, Washington Navy Yard, Washington, DC; U.S. Army Corps of Engineers (USACEHQ), Headquarters History Office, Alexandria, VA; U.S. Army Women's Museum (WAC Museum), Fort Lee, VA; Women in Military Service for America Memorial Foundation, Inc. (WIMSA), Arlington, VA; University of Illinois, Urbana-Champaign library, Urbana, IL; and U.S. Army Corps of Engineers, ERDC-CERL technical library, Champaign, IL.

Primary sources included government documents in the form of memoranda, letters, studies, regulations, and reports that focused on issues pertaining to the accommodation of women, including construction mandates and gender-based regulations. Military building plans (proposed, tentative, and definitive) were also a significant source of data for this report. Historic photographs and plan maps also offered a great wealth of information. The authors used all of these sources in a reiterative process of analysis and evaluation to determine not only what was built, and how and where it was built, but by whom, how, and why were the decisions made and the designs drafted.

The scope of this study covered the Cold War Era, from the end of World War II through the destruction of the Berlin Wall, roughly 1946 through 1989. To this end, the context is organized by the major benchmarks of the Cold War, beginning with World War II, covering the 1948 Integration Act transition period, the Korean War and the 1950s, the Vietnam War and the 1960s, the All-Volunteer Force and the 1970s, and, lastly, the Police Actions of the 1980s.

This study provides a historical overview of women in the military focusing on the evolution of policies and regulations pertaining to women, the larger social movements in American society and how these impacted women in the military, and larger military trends that contributed to the development of women's roles in the military. Of particular interest in compiling this overview is discerning the origins and thought processes that influenced and eventually dictated the shape that the military's built environment would take insofar as accommodating women was concerned. It was the intent of this research to focus on all facilities of a tangible, built nature that were constructed and/or modified for women on military installations during the Cold War period.

What quickly became evident in the research was that the primary emphasis of the built environment of servicewomen centered on the barracks complexes. It was in the barracks that the most modifications were made to accommodate women, and it was on the construction of new barracks for women that the most money was spent in accommodating women. Thus, even though this study intended to encompass all facilities constructed or modified for women on military installations, the bulk of this study deals with barracks complexes. That said, design plans for barracks constructed or modified after the early 1970s were not specifically addressed in the research under the broader context of the late Cold War (1970s and 1980s). These design plans were not available at the various archival facilities visited, as they are still retained at the individual installations.[9] Research, however, indicated that by the late 1970s, designs were standardized for gender-integrated housing, and thus were no longer specific to servicewomen alone. In addition, some buildings constructed earlier may be still standing and the installation may retain the drawings.

Furthermore, given the broad spectrum of the subject matter, by necessity, certain subjects and aspects of the built environment of Cold War Era servicewomen received little, if any, treatment. These subjects, with explanation for why they were not covered, included the following:

Coast Guard. Except during times of war, when the Coast Guard falls under the command of the Navy, the Coast Guard is not part of the Department of Defense, and therefore is outside the limits of this study. However, it is worthwhile to note that despite falling outside of the DoD, the Coast Guard faced essentially similar situations as the remaining service branches did in accommodating women, especially the Navy. It likewise shared many commonalities with the other services in its solution to the physical accommodation of women. Thus, while this study is a DoD-wide historic context, it may still be useful and applicable to cultural resource managers in the Coast Guard.

Nursing components. While closely aligned in several regards with servicewomen, the Army and Navy Nursing Corps, although historically pre-

---

[9] Obtaining and analyzing these building plans is proposed to be conducted as part of the second phase of this research, pending funding. Phase II focuses on compiling case studies at various military installations in order to demonstrate implementation of this historic context as part of NHPA compliance.

dominantly female, were not strictly female staffed.[10] Both the Army and Navy Nurse Corps, established by Congress in 1901 and 1908, respectively, have a distinct history that predates the enlistment of women in the regular military. While this history often parallels the history and development of servicewomen, it is unique in its own right, specifically with regard to the physical accommodation and training of the nursing corps. Nurses were often housed in off-base facilities and were provided a housing allowance; training and education was provided by private (nonmilitary) schools; and work was conducted in non-gender differentiated hospitals or medical environments. When nurses served on military posts, in the field, or with combat units, their physical accommodations were not much different from standard Theater of Operations construction built for men—the only difference being that their tents were usually separated from the men with signs posted warning and prohibiting males from entering the area.[11]

Military academies. Military academies began admitting women in 1976, following a Congressional mandate (P.L. 94-106) that the military open its academies and service schools to women. Physically accommodating women at the academies, at least in housing them and providing restroom facilities, of course necessitated a change in the built environment. However, this study does not specifically address the issue of the physical accommodation of women at the academies as it is felt that this is a subject that merits its own study. The built environment of military academies is a distinct environment substantially different from the military installation environment, and it is the military installation environment that is the focus of this study.

Ships and submarines. The built environment of ships and submarines, while of course necessitating physical changes to accommodate servicewomen, is a distinct and unique environment substantially different from that of military installations, and therefore warrants its own separate study.

---

[10] Men were accepted into the Army and Air Force Nurse Corps beginning in 1955, and into the Navy Nurse Corps in 1965.

[11] See Godson, *Serving Proudly,* for history of Navy Nurse Corps; and Elizabeth A. Shields (ed.), *Highlights of the History of the Army Nurse Corps* (Washington, DC: U.S. Army Center of Military History, 1981) and Judith A. Bellafaire, *The Army Nurse Corps in World War II* (Washington, DC: Center for Military History, 1993) for history of Army Nurse Corps.

Child care facilities. Although child care facilities may be initially attributed to the presence of women in the military—particularly after the policy of separating pregnant women from service was discontinued in the 1970s—childcare facilities are not solely the product of physically accommodating servicewomen. Servicemen with families also have need of these facilities.

Theater of operations designs. Women have served outside the continental United States (OCONUS) and in active theaters of operation, thus necessitating their physical accommodation in such settings. However, in these instances, their accommodations appeared to largely adhere to standard Theater of Operations designs (Figure 1), with only a few exceptions, and with the only distinction being the physical segregation of their tents/structures from men with posted signs, fences, or sentries to keep male personnel out. Further, when stationed in other countries, for example during World War II and Vietnam, when not housed in Theater of Operations construction, women were usually housed in local, nonmilitary facilities.

Figure 1. Fort Des Moines, women in the field in their tents, WWII (WIMSA, Vertical Photo File, Collection of Howard Bright).

Racially segregated facilities (before desegregation). Although not specifically ignored in this study, facilities for black servicewomen were not differentiated from facilities for women in general. On July 26, 1948, Harry Truman signed Executive Order 9981 establishing the President's

Committee on Equality of Treatment and Opportunity in the Armed Services, which mandated integration for both men and women. Prior to this, only the Army provided segregated and separate facilities for black servicewomen, which by all accounts were duplicative of facilities provided for white servicewomen (Figure 2; compare with Figure 23). Black Women Accepted for Volunteer Emergency Service (WAVES) enlisting in the Navy were fully integrated from 1942, primarily because the Navy did not actively recruit black women and thus there were never enough black WAVES to justify separate accommodations.[12] The first black women did not enlist in the Marine Corps until 1949.[13]

Finally, even though there are four distinct service branches in America's military, this study does not treat each branch in a comprehensive individual manner. Separate treatment of each branch was not necessary in order to provide a comprehensive service-wide history. Although each branch's history is certainly unique, in terms of the history of women, there are sufficient corollaries and parallels between the branches to negate the need for comprehensive individual histories. In fact, practically from the beginning in World War II, the Women's Directors for each branch recognized that they each faced similar problems and obstacles, and thus felt that collaborating would be a more efficient means of accomplishing the end

---

[12] In July 1945, there were only 72 black enlisted women and 2 black officers out of 78,000 WAVES. See Debra L. Newman, "The Propaganda and the Truth: Black Women and World War II," *Minerva* 4, no. 4 (Winter 1986), 87.

[13] For further reading on the experience of blacks and minorities in the military, see, for personal recollections, Eleanor Stoddard, "One Woman's War: The Story of Joan Campbell, Member of the Women's Army Corps, World War II, April 1943 – September 1945," *Minerva* 4, no. 1 (Spring 1986): 122-156; idem, "The Education of Margaret Jackson: Member of the Women's Army Corps, September 1943 – March 1946," *Minerva* 9, no. 4 (Winter 1991): 56-77; and Tiffany Wallace, "Corps Woman is WWII Veteran," *Engineer Update, USACE* 16, no. 8 (August 1992), Box 131, General Files; Folder 130-2-1: Corps Woman is WWII Veteran, U.S. Army Corps of Engineers History Office Archives, Alexandria, VA. For a bibliography of additional resources, see Regina T. Akers, comp, "Select Bibliography on Blacks and Women in the United States Military During the Twentieth Century," Reference File—Women Marines: (2 of 2) Brochures/Publications, Washington Navy Yards, Marine Corps Historical Center Archives, Washington, DC. And, for general articles, see Newman, "The Propaganda and the Truth"; Capt. Ellen R. Willis, "Segregation in the WAC," (Fort McClellan, AL: WAC School and Center, May 21, 1963), Student Study Files (1003-12 Permanent), WAC Museum Archives, Ft. Lee, VA.; Regina T. Akers, "Negro WACS and WAVES, 1942-1945: Some Notable Differences (Draft)," (Unpublished paper, November 16, 1990), Vertical Files: WWII African American Women, Washington Navy Yards, Naval Historical Foundation Library, Washington, DC; and Grendel Howard, "Carrying Forth A Tradition," *Soldiers* 40, no. 2 (February 1985), Collection no. 3547, Women in Military Service for America Memorial Foundation, Inc. Archives, Washington, DC.

Figure 2. Camp Lee Training Center, Black WACs, Company B, First Battalion, in dayroom, 9 September 1949 (WAC Museum, Vertical Files, File: Segregation).

goals. "They eventually formalized this relationship as a special subcommittee of the Joint Army/Navy Personnel Board and met regularly to discuss matters of mutual concern. A major policy affecting women was seldom adopted by one of the services until all had the opportunity to consider it. Through the cooperation of this group, identical policies were usually developed and announced jointly. This spirit of cooperation and friendship existed until the directors' offices were abolished in the mid-1970s."[14] Thus, generalizations can be made about events and policies happening in one branch for which information is not readily available based on what was happening in the other branches. As such, details are not always broken down by each service branch, but only where noteworthy or where there are differences between the branches.

---

[14] Holm, *Women in the Military*, 39.

2 World War II: Free a Man to Fight

World War II, although not technically considered part of the Cold War, is an important starting point for this study. By the end of World War II nearly 450,000 women had served in American's military and, except for those who served as nurses, these women served in programs that had literally started from scratch in 1942.[15] By 1946, when the Cold War began, the decision had been made not to demobilize the women's programs as the country realized a permanent need for women in the regular peacetime military. To organize and establish women's roles in the new military structure, planners relied upon the policies and regulations developed and lessons learned during the war as a starting point. Simply, military planners did not have a blank slate to work from in establishing and defining the women's programs for a postwar force. It was the programs established during the war and the original foundation they provided that set the tone for how servicewomen would be accommodated, both literally and figuratively, over the course of the Cold War.

Within a year of America's entry into World War II, the country faced a serious manpower crisis, both in the military and industry. Out of necessity, women were deemed the best solution to this crisis and by the end of 1943, "nearly half the workers in civilian industry and nearly a third in war industry" were women, in addition to the thousands of women who enlisted in the military.[16] While in retrospect, Rosie the Riveter and her military sisters—the WACs, WAVES, and WMs[17]—hold a revered and highly respected position in our cultural memory, during the war they posed a serious challenge to social norms. These women pushed at the boundary of gender equality and in doing so called into question existing notions regarding social differentiation. As a *Life* magazine editorial observed,

---

[15] Holm, *Women in the Military*, 100.

[16] "Manpower: An Army of 7,500,000 Men With Draft of 18-Year-Olds is First Step in Solution," *Life* (October 26, 1942): 30.

[17] WAC: Women's Army Corps (WAAC: Women's Army Auxiliary Corps was a pre-cursor to the WAC); WAVES: Women Accepted for Voluntary Emergency Service (Navy); WM: Women Marines, also referred to as Women Reserves during World War II (Marine Corps).

> "Let us face the fact that the status of women in America, which was changing fast enough before the war, is changing with lightning speed during it....[Yet] social equality does not mean the end of social differentiation, nor of chivalry, for these stem from nature. It means merely that American women, as a class, even more than men, have a lot to learn about the responsibilities of all-around citizenship and their role in the modern world."[18]

In other words, American society was willing to allow women to perform in new and untraditional roles out of necessity (as long as they took on the social responsibilities associated with those roles), but society was not ready or willing to allow the demise of social differentiation between the genders. The concern over social differentiation was heightened even more when it came to women serving in the military. A large portion of society was opposed to, and even scandalized at the prospect for fear that military women would lose their femininity.[19] There was no question that women could perform many of the military jobs that men were doing, thereby freeing the men for the frontlines; the concern was that the women, in doing so, would jeopardize their morality and sense of propriety.[20] In 1930s and 1940s America, "respectable" women rarely worked outside of the home except in traditionally female roles (e.g., nurses, teachers, or secretaries), they lived with their family or in a proper boarding facility until married, and dates were chaperoned. A woman's primary role, according to society, was as a wife, mother, and homemaker. Asking her to not just work outside the home and perhaps take on a nontraditional job, but to join the military, which included basic training, living in military camps or other environments, associating with military men, and being exposed to crude, unpleasant war business was, for a significant part of society, like

---

[18] "American Women: Draft Them? Too Bad We Can't Draft Their Grandmothers," *Life* (January 29, 1945): 28.

[19] See Godson, *Serving Proudly*, 110.

[20] A letter written by Robert Gerard to the editor of *Life* in the September 28, 1942 issue proclaimed: "the Women's Army is the most foolish undertaking this country has ever attempted." The writer felt that women could certainly be of use to the military, but that the country should do as they did in World War I, rather than actually enlist women, thereby avoiding having to train women in camps. The writer felt that "such a system did away with maintenance of camps, and the undesirable things that might go with them."

asking a nun to work in a brothel. To say the least, there were real concerns for her social welfare and reputation.[21]

Still, there was no question that America needed its women to serve their country in those desperate times. Thus, the military's needs were tempered by these societal standards and gender expectations, and this set the tone for the policies and practices that the military would establish for servicewomen right from the start (Figure 3).

Figure 3. WWII cartoon by Chesney (WIMSA).

---

[21] See Mindy Pomper (producer/director), *Free a Man to Fight! Women Soldiers of World War II*, Falls Church, VA: Landmark Media, Inc., 1999. Women interviewed for the documentary recalled how male relatives and friends, including men who were in the military themselves, reacted negatively, some even refusing to talk to them anymore when the women joined the military, because the men were so scandalized.

Policy

The original policy regarding women in the Army, Navy, and Marine Corps stated that women would be governed by the same laws and regulations established for the men, except where physical or psychological differences necessitated.[22] The intent was to treat men and women equally so as to prevent dissention or disgruntlement in the ranks. However, military leaders of all services soon learned what the Army did: "While all authorities were agreed that equal treatment must be given to men and women in the Army, it was soon apparent that *equal* did not mean *identical* in every case. The Army was thus faced with the problem of what styles of garments, though not identical with those of men, gave equal comfort, fit, and military appearance; what medications and surgery, although not identical, promoted equally good health; what standards of conduct, well-being, recreation, and training would enable the military service to answer to the American public for the women in its keeping as conscientiously as it customarily did for the men."[23]

Despite the original intent of military authorities to have men and women governed by one policy, the exceptions necessitated by physical and so-called psychological differences quickly appeared. Among the exceptions, women were assigned only to duties where physical strength and endurance requirements were "within those of the average woman," and as long as the environment and working conditions were suitable for women. If the environment and working conditions were not suitable, governing procedures could be varied in order to ensure the "health, morale and general well-being" of women.[24] Indeed, War Department Circular 289—the first official publication of regulations for WACs—listed the differences instituted to existing Army Regulations for women, including the following:

---

[22] See Treadwell, *Women's Army Corps*; G.C. Marshall (Chief of Staff, War Department), *Women's Army Corps Regulations*, Circular No. 289 (Washington, DC: Government Printing Office, 1943): 2, USAF Collection, 247.911, 1 Nov 1943 – 10 Feb 1944, IRIS No. 5228512, Air Force Historical Research Agency, Maxwell AFB, Montgomery, AL; and Commandant, U.S. Marine Corps [Memo to All Commanding Officers of Posts and Stations where Marine Corps Women's Reservists are to be employed and All Officers, Marine Corps Women's Reserves], "Marine Corps Women's Reserve General Policies, pertaining to," November 25, 1943, Reference File—Women Marines: WWII Regulations, Washington Navy Yards, Marine Corps Historical Center Archives, Washington, DC (hereafter cited as Commandant, U.S. Marine Corps, "MCWR General Policies").

[23] Treadwell, *Women's Army Corps*, xii.

[24] Marshall, *Women's Army Corps Regulations*, 2.

"1. WAC units would contain only women and be commanded by WAC officers, exactly as men's units were composed of and commanded by men.

2. WACs would not be confined in the same building with men, except a hospital.

3. WAC messes would not be combined with men's messes except with War Department approval. [This policy was repealed almost immediately.]

4. WACs would not be used in 'restaurants or cafeterias in service clubs, guest houses, officers' clubs or messes.' [Such assignments were ordinarily not authorized for any military personnel.]

5. WAC officers would not be promoted to the grade of colonel. [By Act of Congress.]

6. WACs would not command men unless specifically ordered to do so. [By Act of Congress.]

7. WACs would not be employed as physicians or nurses. [By Act of Congress, to avoid infringing on existing organizations.]

8. WAC officers would be appointed only from officer candidate school graduates, and officer candidates would be selected only from women already in the Corps.

9. Enlistment standards would differ from men's in the age and citizenship requirements set by Congress, and in a different physical examination; venereal disease was also disqualifying, and women with dependent children were ineligible.

10. Discharge was mandatory for minors [by act of Congress]; authority was included for discharge for pregnancy."[25]

Women's Area Layout

As a result of these new policies, and influenced by societal standards, women received different treatment and several amenities not received by the men, particularly in terms of their physical accommodations. Not only were women to be housed separately from the men in their own barracks, but policy dictated that the women be segregated as far from the men's barracks as possible while still allowing for a reasonable walking distance between the barracks and where women worked (Figure 4 and Figure 5). Since women usually worked for the company or command headquarters, leaders urged that their housing be established near this area. For the Army, policy specifically dictated that that there be a minimum of 150 feet, or at the very least an intervening structure between the male and female barracks.[26] Irrespective of where female barracks were established, fencing was often placed around the barracks complex as an additional measure of privacy, protection, and segregation from the men (Figure 6).

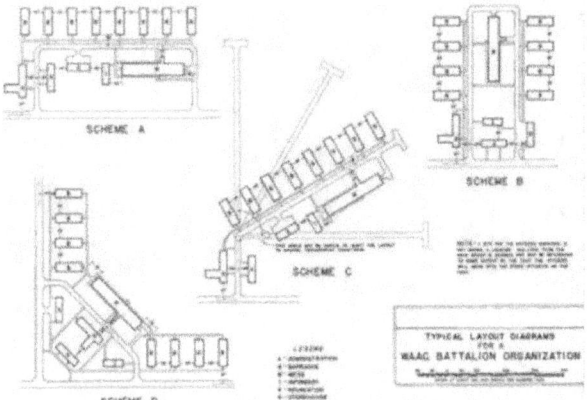

Figure 4. Plan for establishing WAAC area, 1942.

---

[25] Marshall, *Women's Army Corps Regulations*; see also Treadwell, *Women's Army Corps*, 264.

[26] Secretary of War, *Circular No. 325, Amendments* (Washington, DC: War Department, December 14, 1943), WAC Museum Archives, Ft. Lee, VA, 2; see also Treadwell, *Women's Army Corps*, 515.

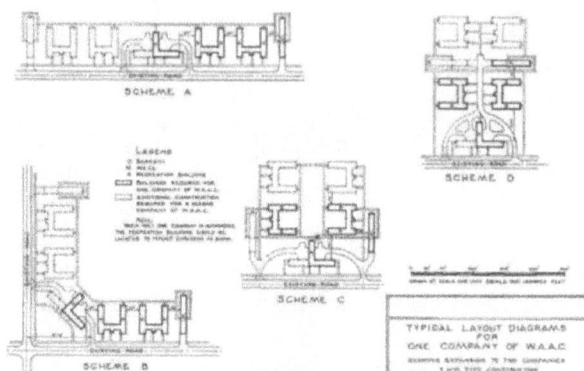

Figure 5. Layout for one WAAC company, 1943 (USACEHQ).

Figure 6. Fort Des Moines, WAC barracks row showing privacy fencing, WWII (WIMSA, Vertical Photo File, Collection of Kris Morrison).

As Col. Stremlow, former Director of the Women Marines, noted, "Discreetly, a fence hid from public view the dainty unmentionables drying on the clothes line while at the same time providing a spot for sunbathing" (Figure 7 and Figure 8).[27] Of course, as a tangible barrier to men, fencing

---

[27] Stremlow, *History of the Women Marines*, 142.

did not always work as intended. Former WAVES Director, Jean Palmer, recalled how, in Hawaii, "the Marine Corps built a stockade around their women's quarters but that the men were scaling it and causing a lot of trouble—it was a challenge to be met by any good, tough marine," but how the Navy commander had built "a white, two-foot picket fence around the WAVE quarters," and had no problem with the men invading the area (Figure 9; see also Figure 11 for a short picket fence around the barracks in the background).[28]

Figure 7. Outdoor private space for WACs, Gulfport Army Air Base, May 1945 (WIMSA, Vertical Photo File, Collection of Doris Mamolen).

---

[28] Holm, *Women in the Military*, 94.

Figure 8. White Sands Missile Range, WAC barracks, exterior patio furniture, 1965 (WAC Museum, Vertical Files, File: Housing Enlisted Survey of 1964-65).

Figure 9. Fort Des Moines, WAC barracks sign, WWII (WIMSA, Vertical Photo File, Collection of Donna Porter).

Also for the protection of the women, it was encouraged that a women's area be established that met as many, if not all, of their needs within one area (see Figures 4 and 5 for examples). The Commandant of the Marine Corps, in a 1943 memo, stated that if it was at all possible and if there were enough women to warrant it, women should have their own post exchange, uniform shop, and recreation hall or hostess house "where they may meet and entertain guests in proper surroundings."[29] Of course, more often than not, cost restrictions and limited building supplies made it impossible for the services to provide completely separate areas and facilities for women at every installation where women were stationed. Still, many places did manage to provide fully contained women's areas. For example, the Army created five separate training camps for women,[30] WAVES had their own area in Hawaii, while the Marine Corps established a women's area at Camp Lejeune, New River, North Carolina. Camp Lejeune offered a quintessential example of a completely contained women's area, as both officers and enlisted women who trained at Camp Lejeune were confined to that area. The area included, in addition to the red brick barracks that housed the women, classrooms, administration buildings (Figure 10), movie theater, post exchange, uniform and tailor shops, laundry, dispensary, chapel, and a service club "complete with five bowling alleys, reception room, soda fountain, library, and ping-pong and dance room."[31]

---

[29] Commandant, U.S. Marine Corps "MCWR General Policies," 1-2.

[30] The first at Fort Des Moines, Iowa; the second at Daytona Beach, Florida; the third at Fort Oglethorpe, Georgia; the fourth at Fort Devens, Massachusetts; and the fifth at Camp Ruston, Louisiana (originally built as a POW camp).

[31] Lt. Louise Stewart, USMCR, "Women in Uniform," *Sea Power* 3, no. 11 (November 1943), Vertical Files: Women in the Military, 1940-1949, Washington Navy Yards, Naval Historical Foundation Library, Washington, DC, 61.

Figure 10. WAC area building, Camp Lejuene, 1943
(WIMSA, Document File, Collection of Lyla Spelbring).

Recreational Facilities

Where completely contained and outfitted women's areas were not possible, military leaders urged that arrangements be made for women to occasionally have "exclusive use" of sports facilities, as it was deemed unfitting for the women to engage in coed sports.[32] Recreation programs of all kinds were deemed necessary to improve the morale and effectiveness of the women (Figure 11 and Figure 12).[33]

---

[32] Commandant, U.S. Marine Corps "MCWR General Policies," 1-2.

[33] W.M. Techteler (Assistant Chief of Naval Personnel) [Memo to Chief of Naval Air Technical Training], "Women's Reserve Policies; clarification of," May 25, 1945, Box 3, WAVES, Folder: (I-23) Future Planning (1943-1947), Washington Navy Yards, Naval Historical Center Archives, Washington, DC, 1.

Figure 11. WAC archery practice (note tiny picket fence), Harlingen Army Gunnery School, TX, 25 April 1945 (WIMSA, Vertical Photo File, Collection of Dorothy V. Clement).

Figure 12. Fort Lee WACs playing volleyball in front of barracks, 1952 (WAC Museum, Vertical Files, File: Athletics V-a-5).

Most installations found that expanded recreational facilities were needed once servicewomen arrived, not only to accommodate the women, but more interestingly, to accommodate the increased number of men who stayed on base to use them instead of going offpost for recreation. Because women tended to stay on base rather than venture into the surrounding areas during their leisure time, as the men typically did, the men began spending more time on post using the recreational facilities as a means of meeting the women. Joy Bright Hancock, first Director of the WAVES, noted how "dances, organized picnics, athletics, and chapel attendance increased greatly," where women were stationed (Figure 13).[34]

Figure 13. Men and women leaving the post chapel during WWII, Fort Custer, MI (WIMSA, Vertical Photo File, Collection of Ann Zimmerman).

Mess Halls

Mess halls were another facility type that, in the majority, was shared between men and women, even though official policy originally intended for the women to have their own segregated messes.[35] Research uncovered

---

[34] Joy Bright Hancock, *Lady in the Navy: A Personal Reminiscence* (Annapolis MD: Naval Institute Press, 1972), 178-79. Captain Hancock recounts a story told to her by a Navy Chaplain who reported that the men's attendance at church rose significantly with the arrival of the women as it was one of the only places were the men could actually, physically sit next to the women.

[35] Marshall, *Women's Army Corps Regulations*, 3.

only a few instances where segregated mess halls for women were constructed and that was at the WAC training centers. These mess halls were substantially similar to the facilities built for men; however, several adjustments were made in order to accommodate differences between men and women. "These included duckboards to limit the depth of sinks to a woman's reach, shelves and wheeled carriers to minimize lifting and bending, and similar mechanical contrivances to make it possible for women to manage heavy equipment designed for men."[36] Outside of these training centers, it was quickly found impractical to have segregated mess halls, and thus the official policy was changed to allow for consolidated messes. Although consolidated, the modified policy did reflect one change that specifically accommodated women, and that was with regard to seating. The standard design for mess halls included long tables with attached benches (Figure 14). It quickly became apparent, however, that this would not do for the women, since there was no "lady-like" method for climbing over a bench while wearing a skirt. As a result, picnic style tables were soon replaced with detached benches or, more preferably, stools or chairs (Figure 15 and Figure 16).[37]

---

[36] Treadwell, *Women's Army Corps*, 525. Note: Duckboards are raised wooden slats for standing in areas with wet floors.

[37] Ibid., 515-16; Secretary of War, *Circular No. 307, Amendments* (Washington, DC: War Department, July 19, 1944), WAC Museum Archives, Ft. Lee, VA.

Figure 14. Camp Lee, WAC Mess Hall with attached benches, 1949
(WAC Museum, Vertical Files, File: Firsts V-a-14).

Figure 15. Fort Des Moines, Mess Hall with stools, 1943
(WIMSA, Vertical Photo File, Collection of Donna Porter).

Figure 16. Mess Hall with chairs, Naval Air Technical Training Center, Norman, OK, 1943 (WIMSA, Vertical Photo File, Collection of Margaret Holman).

Mess halls offer a good example of how the military made adjustments to physically accommodate women. Despite the military's intention of segregating and sequestering the women from the men in all possible circumstances, the reality of limited supplies and building materials prevailed. Certain facilities, such as mess halls and post exchanges, could be consolidated with only minimal modifications needed to accommodate women, such as adding restroom facilities, and substituting stools for attached benches. Modifying existing facilities was found to be far more cost effective than constructing a separate facility for women, especially since many installations rarely had enough women stationed to warrant individual facilities (Figure 17; note unattached benches that can be pulled out).

Figure 17. Consolidated mess, Camp Crowder, MO, WWII (Camp Crowder Museum).

Detention Facilities

Not every facility could be shared or consolidated. One such facility was brigs or post prisons. Official policy for all branches of the service specifically prohibited the arrest or confinement of its female members in any building (other than a hospital) in which male officers or enlisted men were being held under arrest or confinement.[38] Not only were existing brigs and post prisons off limits for use by women, but none of the services even contemplated providing separate brigs or post prisons for the women. Instead, women were confined to quarters, or "other appropriate buildings suitable for such purpose."[39] The reasoning behind this policy

---

[38] Marshall, *Women's Army Corps Regulations*, 3; "Analyses of Building and Fixtures for 700 EW Barracks, Fort Myer," circa 1960s, Ft. Lee 228-01, WHC-378, Folder—Housing, Misc Reports (1965-67), WAC Museum Archives, Ft. Lee, VA, 144.

[39] Marshall, *Women's Army Corps Regulations*, 3; Commandant, U.S. Marine Corps (Director, Marine Corps Women's Reserve) to Assistants for Women's Reserve via Commanding Officers, "Marine Corps Women's Reserve, matters affecting," May 19, 1944, Reference File—Women Marines: WWII Regulations, Washington Navy Yards, Marine Corps Historical Center Archives, Washington, DC, 2; Stremlow, *Free a Marine to Fight*, 30; Randall Jacobs (Chief of Naval Personnel) to All Continental Shore Stations, "General Policies Pertaining to the Women's Reserve," Women's Reserve Circular Letter No. 1-43, April 30, 1943, Box 3, WAVES, Folder: (I-31) Historical—Women's Reserve Circular Letters (1943-1946), Washington Navy Yards, Naval Historical Center Archives, Washington, DC, 3.

was that rather than build women's quarters in brigs (considered an undesirable option), barracks could be constructed so that there were one or more small rooms where prisoners could be kept under guard.[40] Typically, the room set aside for this purpose "was sparsely furnished, had a door with a small window, and could be locked from the passageway."[41]

The policy concerning confinement and arrest was significantly driven by gender norms of the time. As the Chief of Naval Personnel stated, "discipline for men and women will vary because of different standards prevailing in non-military circles." For example, women were more severely punished than men for drunkenness and/or disturbing the peace because of public opinions on how women should behave.[42] This double standard also applied to the public's attitude on confining women, versus confining men. That is, "there always existed a reluctance to confine women," and while those convicted of civil crimes could be sent to civilian prisons, "women who rated confinement as a result of a court martial were more apt to be restricted to the barracks and fined—a punishment that did not require posting a guard."[43] In short, not only was society reluctant to subject women to severe punishment, but for those that were punished, the strict security provided by brigs was deemed largely unnecessary as women were considered to be less violent and non-threatening.

Housing Policy

Women's housing was another type of facility that, in the 1940s, could not be shared or consolidated with men. Unlike brigs and post prisons, however, providing housing facilities for servicewomen was mandatory and required either the modification of existing facilities or the construction of new facilities specifically designed for women. Providing housing for servicewomen posed a unique challenge for military planners. Societal perceptions on gender norms and what was, and was not, appropriate for women at the time meant that the government could not simply put women in barracks constructed for men. At the same time, military doctrine proclaimed that women should not receive preferential treatment so

---

[40] Commandant, U.S. Marine Corps, "Marine Corps Women's Reserve," 2.

[41] Stremlow, *History of the Women Marines*, 144.

[42] See Jacobs, "General Policies Pertaining to the Women's Reserve," 3.

[43] Stremlow, *History of the Women Marines*, 144.

as to avoid discontent among the ranks. Resolving these two seemingly opposed directives would result in a policy-driven built environment that set the tone for how women would be accommodated in the military for decades to come.

In 1943, the Navy adopted an official policy on the non-preferential treatment of women, which proclaimed the importance of establishing "the principle that women do not ask for special privilege."[44] However, this policy also conceded that "for their efficiency women need some conveniences which may not be necessary for men who are being trained to live on board ship. For example, quarters should not be so congested that women can achieve no privacy. Women spend more time in their rooms than is apt to be true of enlisted men and allowance should be made for this fact. For permanent quarters it will probably be wise to allow more than the minimum cubic footage allowed by the Bureau of Medicine and Surgery, not to pamper the women but to keep them at maximum efficiency."[45] The Navy further believed that women were "more definitely influenced by their immediate surroundings," and as such providing extra amenities such as "lining the walls and ceilings of barracks and painting them with light cheerful colors, installing cubicles, providing larger lockers or extra stowage space, installing adequate laundry facilities, providing attractive lounges, both for out-of-uniform relaxation and the reception of guests," translated to "increased efficiency, higher morale and fewer discipline cases" (Figure 18; note larger lockers—more storage, portable partitions, room for "feminine" touches, Figure 19, Figure 20).[46]

---

[44] Jacobs, "General Policies Pertaining to the Women's Reserve," 2.
[45] Ibid.
[46] Techteler, "Women's Reserve Policies," 2.

Figure 18. WAVES barracks locker, Naval Air Technical Training Center, Memphis, 1944 (WIMSA, Vertical Photo File, Collection of Margaret Holman).

Figure 19. WAVES using ironing room in barracks, WWII (WIMSA, Vertical Photo File, Collection of Elaine Krieter Engh).

Figure 20. WAVES recreation room in barracks, NAS Seattle, 1944-45.
In booklet WAVES: U.S. Naval Air Station, Seattle, Washington, nd.
(WIMSA, Document File, Unknown donor #164).

In 1943, the Marine Corps established similar official policy, stating, "while women do not ask for special privileges, for their efficiency they need conveniences and considerations unnecessary for men; such as, more privacy in quarters, different facilities for laundering, and a somewhat varying recreational program. Women should have some lounging space that is private (Figure 21). This is highly essential, and if no other building is available, it is suggested that temporarily a barracks room or portion thereof be converted for this purpose, even though some overcrowding in their quarters may result."[47] Just as in the Navy, Marine Corps leadership believed that because the women spent significantly more time in their barracks, they were more concerned with and impacted by their surroundings. Consequently, the Women's Director, Colonel Streeter, insisted that women received extra amenities in their barracks such as a guest lounge furnished with comfortable chairs, sofa, record player, piano and/or board games, a sewing room, hair dryers, refrigerators and cooking equipment.[48] Women Marines were also allowed to dress up their barracks by painting them (sometimes with pastel paint), or with personal items such as bedspreads, stuffed animals, and personal photos. Further, "dressers were

---

[47] Commandant, U.S. Marine Corps "MCWR General Policies," 1.
[48] Stremlow, *History of the Women Marines*, 141.

lined up to provide a little privacy, shower curtains were hung, and doors closed off toilet stalls" (Figure 22).[49]

Figure 21. Camp Lejuene, Women Marine barracks upstairs lounge "off-limits to men," 1944 (WIMSA, Vertical Photo File, Unknown donor).

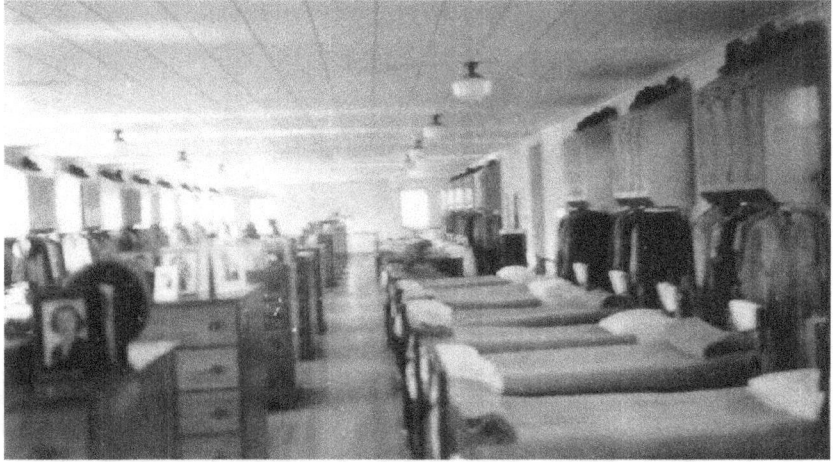

Figure 22. Women's Squad Bay interior with dressers and photos, Camp Lejuene, 1944 (WIMSA, Vertical Photo File, Unknown donor).

---

[49] Stremlow, *Free a Marine to Fight*, 29.

In the Army, the official stance on preferential treatment was that men and women should be treated differently only where physical or psychological differences necessitated. Where housing was specifically concerned, Army policy held that the standards for the WAC approximate those for the men except where gender differences mandated changes and adjustments. As such, "the modifications deemed necessary to convert Army barracks for female use were, in general, those essential to personal safety, segregation from men, and those required to adapt the sanitation facilities for use of women."[50] Amenities initially extended to the WACs thus included window shades for privacy, bed sheets (because "the Surgeon General expressed the opinion that sanitation problems peculiar to women" made it easier to launder sheets than blankets), plumbing modifications that included "not only the elimination of certain fixtures, but the provision of others believed needed for feminine hygiene, such as two bathtubs per 150 women," and partitioned shower and toilet stalls, as well as shower curtains.[51] The Army required WAC latrines to be located inside or attached to the barracks, and if not, a covered walkway connecting the latrine to the barracks was required.[52] WACs were also often provided with laundry rooms, and dayrooms "equipped with books, records, easy chairs, radios and usually bright curtains and other colorful furnishings" (Figure 23).[53]

---

[50] Office of the Director, WAC, "Background on Enlisted Housing," prepared for WSA Conference, November 1964, Ft. Lee 228-01, WHC-377, Folder—Housing, Enlisted/Officer (General) (1957-63), WAC Museum Archives, Ft. Lee, VA.

[51] Treadwell, *Women's Army Corps*, 515.

[52] Secretary of War, *Circular No. 325*, 3.

[53] "The Women's Army Corps: Fact Sheet," December 1, 1945, in J. Sewell Papers, 168.7172-2 1907 – Jul 1957, IRIS No. 1041204, Air Force Historical Research Agency, Maxwell AFB, Montgomery, AL, 23.

Figure 23. WAC company dayroom with easy chairs and other furnishings, Camp Lee Training Center (WAC Museum, Vertical Files, File: Dayrooms V-a-24).

Housing Design

Regardless of what language or justification was used, and despite proclamations of non-preferential treatment, when it came to housing servicewomen, all of the services adopted the mantra that women should receive "separate but better" facilities.[54] This was evident from the initial planning stages. The Navy, for example, tasked Captain Hancock with aiding in the development of housing plans, and she dug out an old, but approved, male barracks design that divided the open squad bay into two- and four-person cubicles (Figure 24 and Figure 25).[55] In the original development of this plan, the Bureau of Medicine and Surgery had "recommended that the usual open-dormitory spaces be divided into cubicles in the interest of privacy for the occupants, as well as the prevention and spread of communicable, particularly respiratory, diseases."[56] While this plan was never implemented for the men, Women's Reserve leaders were successful in having it implemented for the women, although in some places WAVES were still quartered in traditional open bay squad rooms. Still, as one

---

[54] Wasch, et al., *World War II and the U.S. Army Mobilization Program*, 22.

[55] Susan H. Godson, "Capt. Joy Bright Hancock: Builder of the Co-Ed Navy," *The Retired Officer* (December 1982): 15-17, Box 2, RG Women in Aviation: WAVES folder, Washington Navy Yards, Naval Aviation Office Archives, Washington, DC, 16; Hancock, *Lady in the Navy*, 173-74.

[56] Hancock, *Lady in the Navy*, 173-4; see also Department of the Navy, Naval Historical Center, "World War II Era WAVES—Quarters & Meals," Online Library of Selected Images: People-Topics—Women & The U.S. Navy, http://www.history.navy.mil/photos/prs-tpic/females/wvw2-qf.htm, February 18, 2001, (hereafter cited as Department of the Navy, NHS, "World War II Era WAVES").

source noted, "whatever the housing, the double-decked bunk bed was a ubiquitous feature" (Figure 26).[57]

Figure 24. WAVES four-person barracks cubicle, NAS Seattle, 1944-45. In booklet WAVES: U.S. Naval Air Station, Seattle, Washington, nd. (WIMSA, Document File, Unknown donor #164).

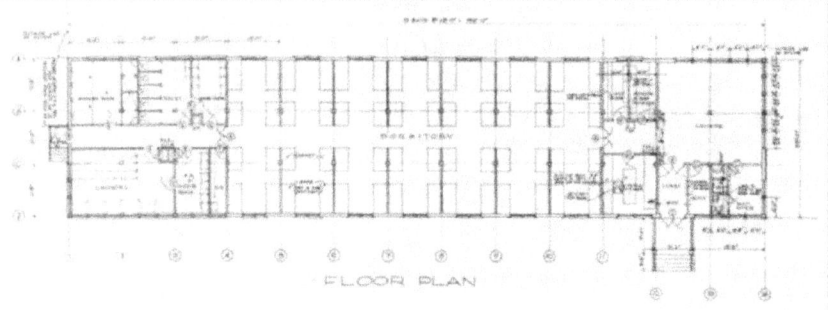

Figure 25. Open bay converted to cubicles with partitions, 1943 (NARA).

---

[57] Department of the Navy, NHS, "World War II Era WAVES."

Figure 26. Naval WAVES barracks with bunk beds and lockers, Air Technical Training Center, Norman, OK, 1944 (WIMSA, Vertical Photo File, Collection of Margaret Holman).

The success of the Women's Reserve leaders in housing women in cubicles was due in large part to the Navy's recognition that women were far less transitory than men in terms of station assignments. Not only were women more likely to spend their leisure time in the barracks, but women also tended to be stationed at one post for a significantly longer period of time. Men's barracks, for all intents and purposes, had a revolving door in terms of actual time spent in the barracks as well as time assigned to an individual station. The permanent nature in the assignment of women also justified further modifications to building plans that provided amenities not afforded the men. At Captain Hancock's urging, doors were hung on toilet stalls, partitions erected in the showers, limited cooking facilities (where practicable), refrigerators, laundry facilities, and irons were provided, as well as more stowage space and a lounge for receiving guests (Figure 27, Figure 28, Figure 29, and Figure 30). Similar to the Marines, WAVES were also allowed to hang curtains, and decorate their cubicles with bed spreads, rugs, pillows, and the like in order to provide a homier atmosphere.[58] As the Bureau of Naval Personnel explained, "these features were called for not as special factors or coddling but because they made the women more efficient members of the organization."[59]

Figure 27. WAVES Lounge, NAS Seattle, 1944-45.
In booklet WAVES: U.S. Naval Air Station, Seattle, WA, nd.
(WIMSA, Document File, Unknown donor #164).

---

[58] Hancock, *Lady in the Navy*, 173-4; Godson, *Serving Proudly*, 121; Treadwell, *Women's Army Corps*, 520; see also Godson, "Capt. Joy Bright Hancock," 16.

[59] Treadwell, *Women's Army Corps*, 520.

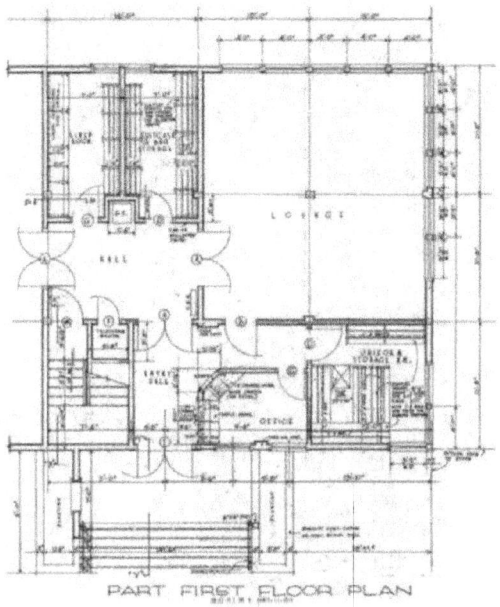

Figure 28. Enlisted WAVES barracks showing lounge, 1943 (NARA).

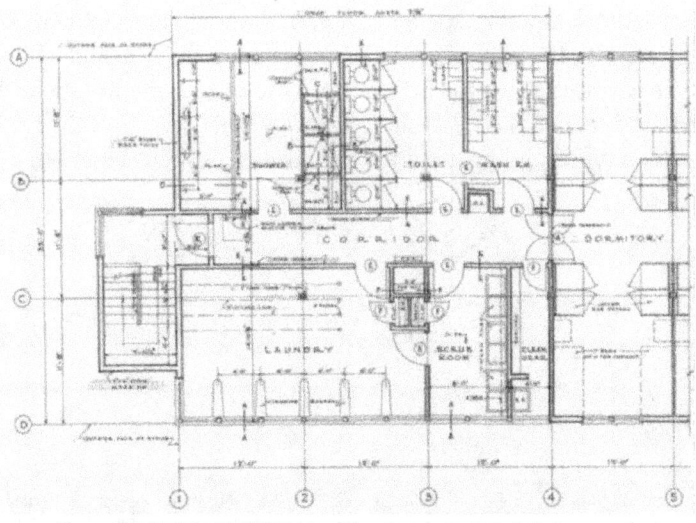

Figure 29. Enlisted WAVES barracks showing toilet stall doors and laundry facilities, 1943 (NARA).

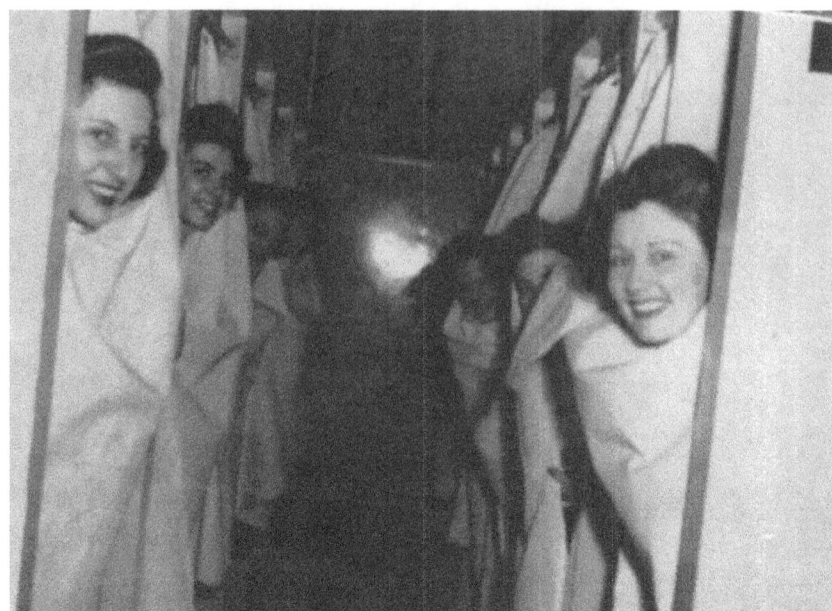

Figure 30. WAVES Detachment wrapped in shower curtains, Shoemaker, CA, 1945. In Waves, United States Navy, 1950s (WIMSA, Document File, Collection of Ruth Smith #4437).

Original recommendations for housing women in the Army called for room-type dormitories, akin to that proposed by the Navy. Financial and time restrictions, however, meant that WACs were housed in modified regular barracks. In some cases, WACs were housed in Theater of Operations type barracks as well as Prisoner of War encampments (such was the case at Camp Ruston, LA).[60] At first, new construction was of the two-story mobilization type building designed to house 75 women (Figure 31).

---

[60] "Presentation of Merits of Four Plans for Inclusion of Women, Other than those of the Medical Department in the Postwar Military Establishment," January 1946, Ft. Lee 228-01, WHC-310, Folder—Four Plans for a Women's Corps (1946), WAC Museum Archives, Ft. Lee, VA., 4-5 of Appendix I.

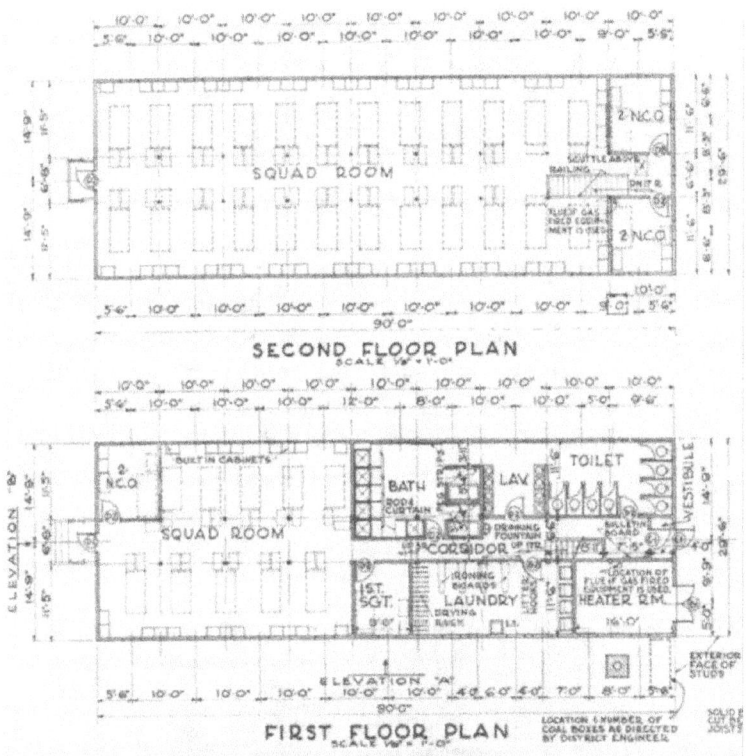

Figure 31. Plan of mobilization type WAAC barracks with bunks for 75 women, 1942 (USACEHQ).

As the war progressed and supplies tightened, new construction was of the temporary Theater of Operations type buildings.[61] In the end, the only thing that WAC housing had in common with the Navy so far as floor and room layouts were concerned was the use of bunk beds. Indeed, the trend in WAC housing involved a series of "successive compromises with expediency," that resulted in a "gradual reduction of standards."[62] The Army may have started with good intentions in terms of housing the women, but women did not initially fare as well as men in terms of personal space. Women started with a space allowance of 50 square feet (not including support facilities, such as latrines, storage, etc.), whereas the men were given 60 square feet per individual. Due to a miscalculation by the Chief of

---

[61] Office of the Director, WAC, "Background on Enlisted Housing."

[62] Treadwell, *Women's Army Corps*, 516-17.

Engineers, however, this space allocation was further reduced to 42.5 square feet for woman for converted buildings and 45 square feet for new construction.[63] By the end of 1943, however, Oveta Culp Hobby, the WAC Director, asked for and eventually secured an increase in square footage per woman to 60 feet, which removed the need for double-decked bunks and allowed more space for clothing.[64]

Even though the men received more square footage in their living space, women fared better in terms of the amenities provided to them in their barracks. Similar to the Navy, latrines were furnished with doors, partitions and shower curtains, with one latrine per every ten women; laundry facilities were also provided at the rate of one tub, one ironing board, and "adequate drying racks," as well as duck boards provided for every twenty women (Figure 32).[65] WACs were further provided with hairdressing facilities, limited cooking equipment, storage facilities, day rooms and date rooms, as well as being allowed to decorate their barracks with personal items (Figure 33).

Figure 32., AAF WAC Detachment laundry facilities, Eagle Pass, TX, Army Air Field, 1944 (WIMSA, Document File, Collection of Violet Rodgers #1537).

---

[63] Ibid., 516-17; and Office of the Director, WAC, "Background on Enlisted Housing."

[64] Treadwell, *Women's Army Corps*, 520.

[65] Secretary of War, *Circular No. 325*, 3.

Figure 33. WAC Date Room interior, Will Rogers Field, July 43- Sept 44 (WIMSA, Vertical Photo File, Collection of Doris Mamolen).

Housing standards in the Marine Corps were a compromise between those established for WAVES and WACs. Although living conditions varied from installation to installation, Women Marines were typically housed in open squad bays, outfitted with double metal bunks, lockers, locker boxes, and wooden dressers, a "concession to the women" that normally had to be shared (Figure 34). However, "much ingenuity went into the arrangement of the furniture to form cubicles, thereby assuring a measure of privacy to several occupants."[66] In terms of amenities, Women Marines received many of the same things as WAVES and WACs, such as large laundry rooms, modified latrines, recreation rooms, lounges or squad rooms, Venetian blinds, and so on. Women Marines were also allowed to decorate their bunk space with personal items, although unlike the other service branches, "to keep some semblance of order, the company regulations specified how many items per dresser, and how many stuffed dolls by size per bunk."[67]

---

[66] Stremlow, *History of the Women Marines*, 142.

[67] Stewart, "Women in Uniform," 63; and Stremlow, *History of the Women Marines*, 142.

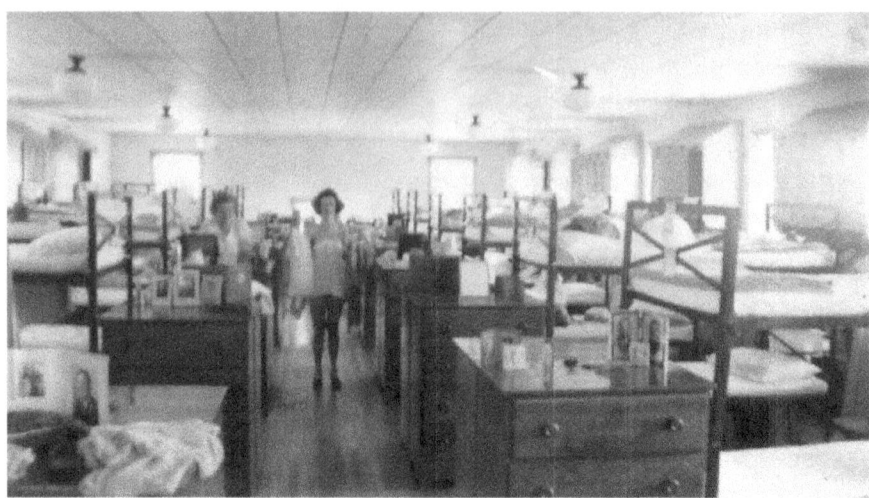

Figure 34. Women Marine barracks showing dressers and personal items, Camp Lejuene, 1945 (WIMSA, Vertical Photo File, Unknown donor).

All in all, housing standards among the various women's branches were driven by the same philosophy of providing women with the best accommodations that money and supplies could provide. The Navy was able to provide the best accommodations, specifically in terms of privacy, perhaps simply because the bulk of WAVES were stationed on the East coast in and around Washington, DC. This high concentration of women made new construction feasible. Women Marines and WACs, on the other hand, were more dispersed throughout the country to individual installations and camps, and thus their lower numbers typically did not justify the cost of new construction. As a result, they often had to make due with modified barracks and/or compromised standards. Mess halls were a clear example of this—as stated previously, military leaders optimally desired that women have their own, segregated mess hall, but reality and practicality meant compromise, which resulted in consolidated mess halls.

Latrines

Even though the women may have received less square footage or reduced privacy standards than those initially intended for them, they certainly fared exceptionally well with regard to amenities. In fact, most of the provided amenities were similar across all the branches, and were significant to the built environment insofar as they were not typically provided to the men. Although many of these amenities have been mentioned already, some deserve further attention and explanation. In particular, latrines were often at the top of the list of what needed to be modified both in converting male barracks, and in drafting new designs for women. Where possible, the ratio between latrine facilities and individual women was lower than that for the men—not only did the number of latrine facilities need to be increased, but latrine design needed to be modified to accommodate women. Male latrines consisted of gang showers, open commodes, and urinals. In 1940s America, most "proper" women had no idea what a male bathroom looked like, and thus were shocked the first time they saw one in their barracks. That is, when women were first enlisted in the military, because time was of the essence, they were quite often placed in barracks that had not yet been fully converted for their use (Figure 35; note modifications written on plan). According to one story, a group of women, upon entering an unconverted male latrine, and having never seen or heard of a urinal, thought it was for washing undergarments, or for use as a planter.[68]

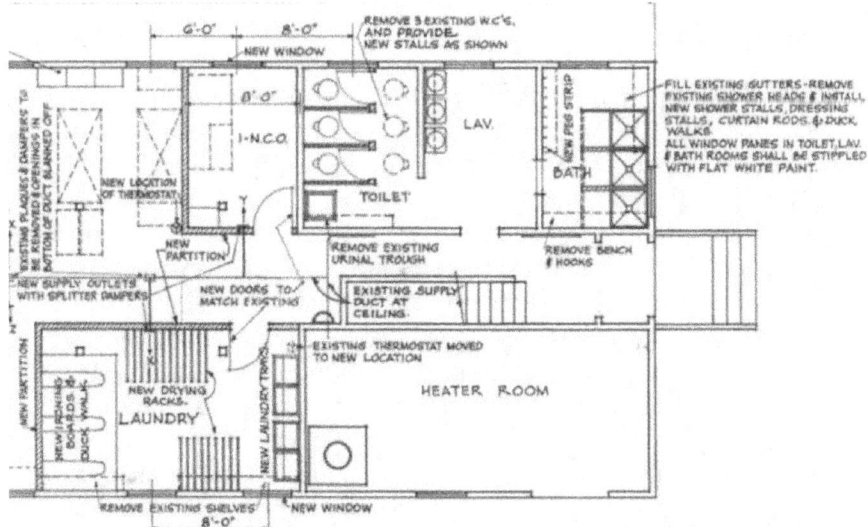

Figure 35. Conversion of male barracks bath facilities for female use, 1943 (USACEHQ).

Further, privacy and modesty were two essential aspects of proper female decorum at the time, which resulted in a very negative reaction to the gang showers and open toilet areas. "It was almost unthinkable to a woman to use a commode in open view of others or to strip naked and shower in

[68] Pomper, *Free a Man to Fight*.

front of other women."⁶⁹ In response, latrines were modified by installing partitions and doors on the toilets, converting gang showers into individual cubicles with shower curtains, as well as quite often private dressing areas. Additionally, bathtubs were often provided for the women (Figure 36; note privacy curtains for shower and bathtub).

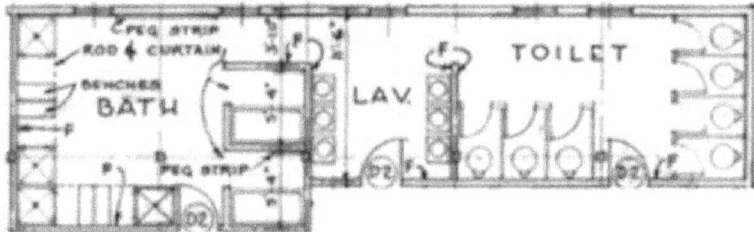

Figure 36. Provision of bathtubs for WAACs, 1942 (USACEHQ).

Laundry Facilities

Laundry facilities were another amenity not provided to the men. In all service branches, the men's laundry was done for them at base facilities, whereas the quality of material used in the women's uniforms was not durable enough to survive the "brutal process" used to launder male uniforms.⁷⁰ Even if women could have used base facilities, social custom at the time dictated that women do their own laundry; indeed, several accounts indicated that the women preferred doing it themselves.⁷¹ In fact, civilian psychologists studying the WAC found that the "lack of opportunity to launder and iron her shirt for the next day" proved a greater hazard to morale than "any lack of movies, camp shows, and pinball machines," and that "a woman's grooming was vitally connected not only with her morale but with her health and actually with her conduct."⁷² Thus, women asked for laundry tubs, ironing boards, and electrical outlets, and when the ones they received were not enough, they demanded more. In the Marine Corps,

---

⁶⁹ Holm, *Women in the Military*, 61.

⁷⁰ Ibid.; see also Edna Hill Schultz, "Free a Marine to Fight," *Naval History* 17, no. 1 (February 2003): 46-49, Reference File—Women Marines: Newspaper Clippings—WWII, Washington Navy Yards, Marine Corps Historical Center Archives, Washington, DC, 47, and Stremlow, *History of the Women Marines*, 141-42.

⁷¹ Holm, *Women in the Military*, 61 and Stremlow, *History of the Women Marines*, 141-42.

⁷² Treadwell, *Women's Army Corps*, 67.

for example, "It had to be explained that women, as opposed to men, do not send personal clothing to commercial laundries and therefore needed more washing machines, dryers, and ironing boards than government specifications allowed."[73] This resulted in barracks having a laundry room either within the building or directly adjacent to it, such as was the case at Camp Lejeune.[74] Typically, laundry rooms contained, in addition to laundry tubs and ironing boards, drying racks and duckboards for underneath the ironing boards, which were authorized after several women received severe shocks from standing on the wet concrete while ironing (Figure 37).[75] Further, engineers not only had to install additional electrical outlets in the laundry rooms, but also spent time replacing fuses as most women brought their own irons with them "in numbers which so frequently blew out barracks fuses that their use had to be limited."[76]

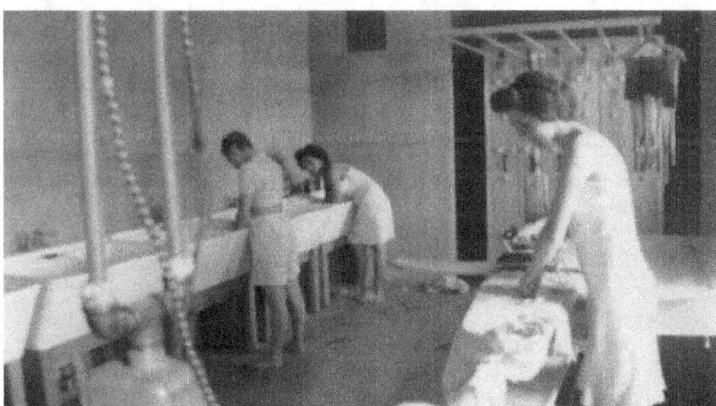

Figure 37. Women Marines washing and ironing in barracks, Camp Lejuene, 1944 (WIMSA, Vertical Photo File, Unknown donor).

---

[73] Stremlow, *History of the Women Marines*, 141-42.

[74] Schultz, "Free a Marine to Fight," 47. The washhouse was adjacent to the women's compound, and was described thus: "There were no washing machines or dryers, just a series of deep washtubs, 'Irish ukuleles' (washboards), and hand wringers. To dry the clothes, we hung them out on lines behind our barracks or, in case of inclement weather, draped them onto a series of metal rods that slid into a heated space. There were ironing boards and irons in the squad room."

[75] Treadwell, *Women's Army Corps*, 515. In the Army, one tub and one ironing board were allotted for each twenty women.

[76] "Camp Facilities for Females" Memo, 21 August 1944, Box X-115-19 "Military Theaters of Operations SWPA, General Operations—Women-Camp Facilities for Females," U.S. Army Corps of Engineers History Office Archives. Alexandria, VA.; *Building the Navy's Bases in World War II: History of the Bureau of Yards and Docks and the Civil Engineers Corps, 1940-1946*, Vol. 1 (Washington: GPO, 1947), 289; see also Treadwell, *Women's Army Corps*, 67, and Holm, *Women in the Military*, 61.

Luggage Rooms

Female barracks also differed from male barracks in that they contained luggage rooms rather than ammo and weapon storage rooms. Official policy prohibited women from carrying a sidearm or using other weapons, thus eliminating the need for these rooms in their barracks. Conversely, women were not issued duffel bags and were thus required to provide their own luggage (Figure 38).

Figure 38. WACS with luggage, Fort Des Moines, WWII (WIMSA, Vertical Photo File, Collection of Kris Morrison).

As a result, luggage rooms replaced ammo and weapons rooms, and two square feet of luggage storage space was authorized for each woman, as long as space and funds were available to make the modification (Figure 39 and Figure 40). Since most women's units only required 330 square feet for company supply, while male barracks designs provided 1,037 square feet for supply and combat equipment, the space was usually available and the cost of conversion was negligible.[77]

---

[77] Treadwell, *Women's Army Corps*, 516.

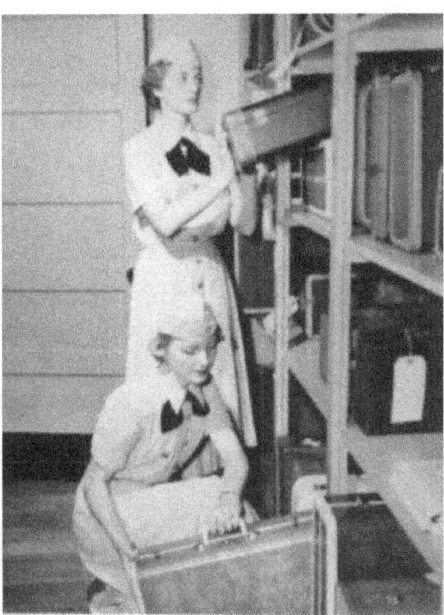

Figure 39. WAVES recruits stowing suitcases in racks, US Naval Training Center, Bainbridge, MD, 1956. From yearbook "The Portal" for Company 15 (WIMSA, Document File, Collection of Doris Brown #4642).

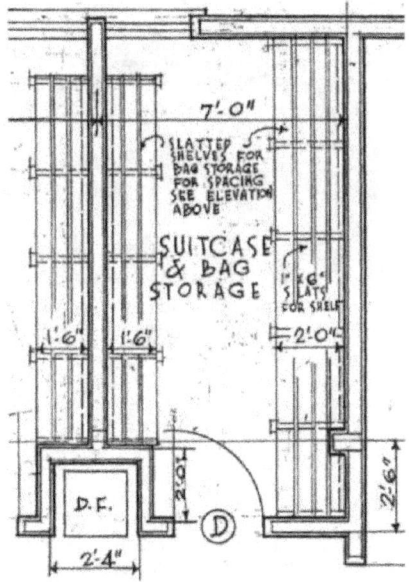

Figure 40. Plan for luggage room, WAVES barracks, 1943 (NARA).

Fire Escapes

Another simple modification made to male barracks designs concerned fire escapes. Typical designs provided ladders for buildings over two stories; however the women's uniforms and heeled shoes often made using these ladders difficult. (Women were required to wear modestly heeled shoes and fitted skirts—Figure 41.) As a result, "it was found that women in the WAC service uniform, with its narrow skirts, had difficulty in jumping from windows to the standard fire escape ladders, and fire stairs were ordered substituted on two-story barracks" (Figure 42 and Figure 43).[78]

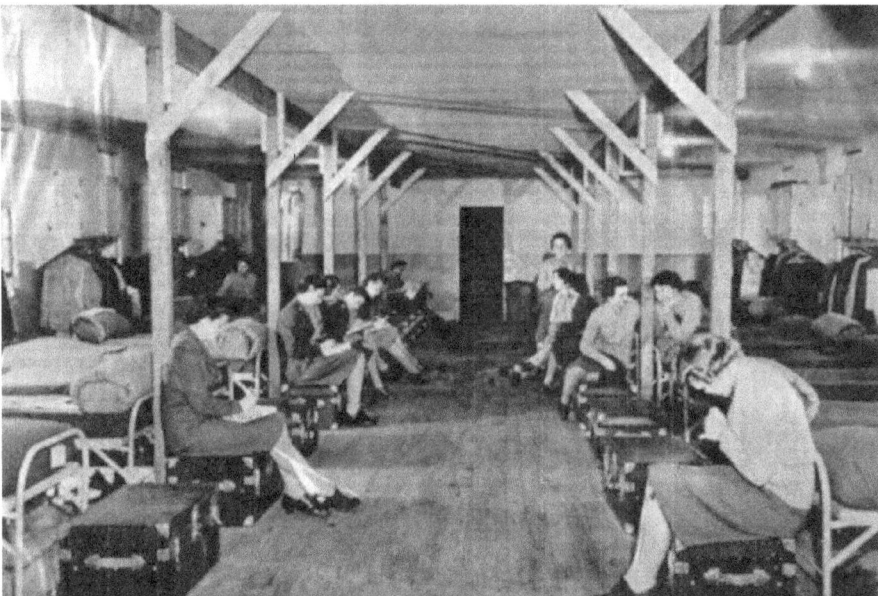

Figure 41. WAACS uniforms with narrow skirts and heeled shoes, Fort Devens, January 24, 1943 (WIMSA, Document File, Collection of Lois Bowen).

---

[78] Ibid, 515; see also Secretary of War, *Circular No. 325*, 3.

Figure 42. WAC barracks area showing fire escape stairs, Fort Des Moines, 1942 (WIMSA, Vertical Photo File, Collection of Ruth Sparacio).

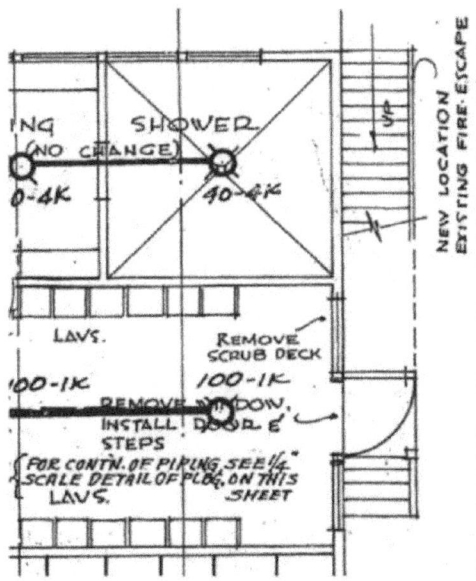

Figure 43. Plan for fire escape stairs, 1943 (NARA).

Lounges, Date Rooms, and Kitchens

Date rooms and kitchens were other amenities not provided to the men. Social custom at the time regarding dating called for women to entertain male guests in their homes, usually under the chaperoning presence of family. At the very least, men were expected to pick their dates up at their home and pass family inspection. Societal expectations mandated that this tradition be facilitated within the confines of the military. "This meant providing a place to entertain [the women's] dates in a wholesome, family-like atmosphere without invading the privacy of the women who wanted to sit around reading, sewing, or just rapping."[79] The solution was to provide two lounges or dayrooms in the barracks, one informal and private for the women only, and the other to serve as a date room. Date rooms were typically located by the front entrance to the barracks, near the administration room, while the private lounge was often located on an upper floor. Date rooms also had male lavatories (toilet and sink) installed adjacent to them (Figure 44). Likewise, kitchen equipment was often provided in one of the lounges (Figure 45). The justification for this amenity stemmed from the fact that women spent more time and entertained in their barracks, rather than frequent local establishments, but they also often preferred their own cooking over the heavy food provided at the mess halls.

---

[79] Holm, *Women in the Military*, 61.

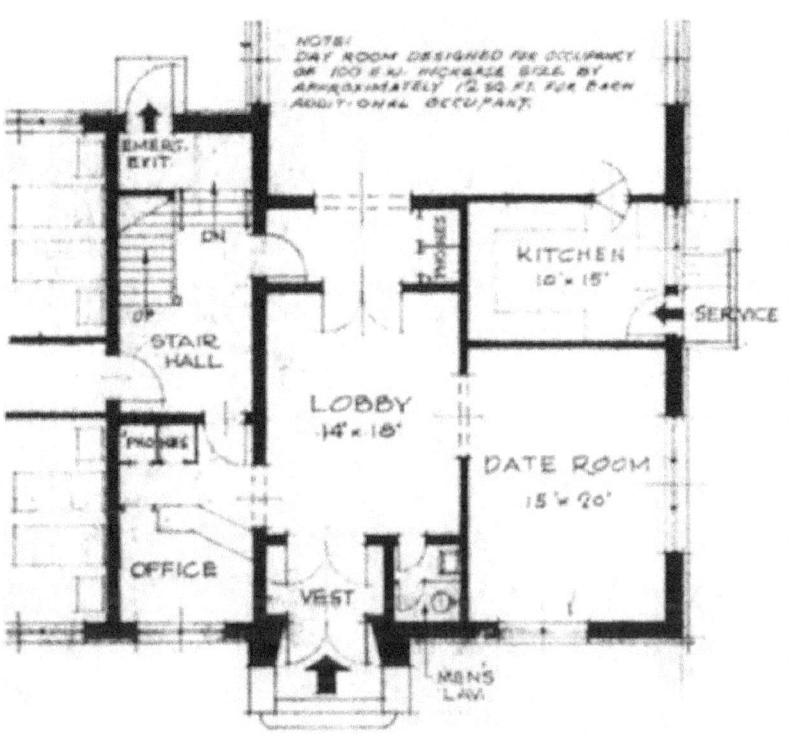

Figure 44. Layout of date room (note men's bathroom off the lobby), 1946 (USACEHQ).

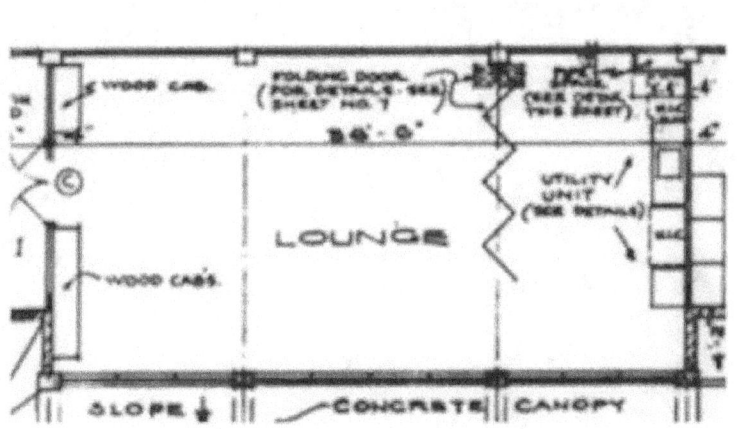

Figure 45. Plan for small lounge kitchen (on right), 1951 (USACEHQ).

Beauty Shops

Another common facility that installation commanders had to provide was a beauty shop (Figure 46 and Figure 47). Each branch had regulations concerning appearance and hair styles. At first, women were expected to make use of local facilities, thereby saving the military from having to provide them. This approach did not work, though, as military schedules were often at odds with the scheduled business hours of local salons. As a result, in the Army at least, a directive was approved by the Chief of Engineers that "authorized partitioning off part of the WAC dayrooms and the installation of water connections, if the unit could equip and operate the shop."[80] Eventually, beauty shops were established as part of the company grouping and located in the post exchange.

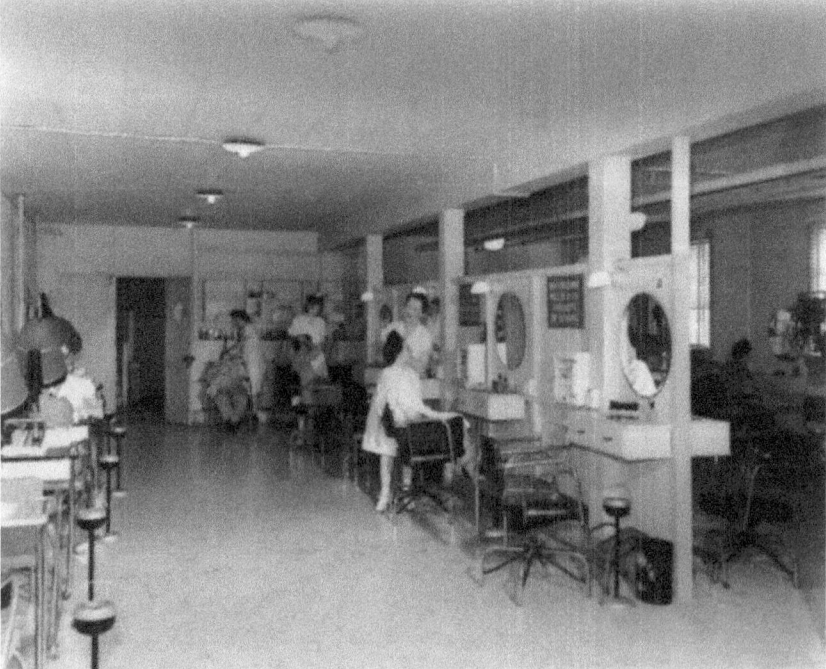

Figure 46. WAVES beauty shop, Naval Air Technical Training Center, Norman, OK, 1943 (WIMSA, Vertical Photo File, Collection of Margaret Holman).

---

[80] Treadwell, *Women's Army Corps*, 522.

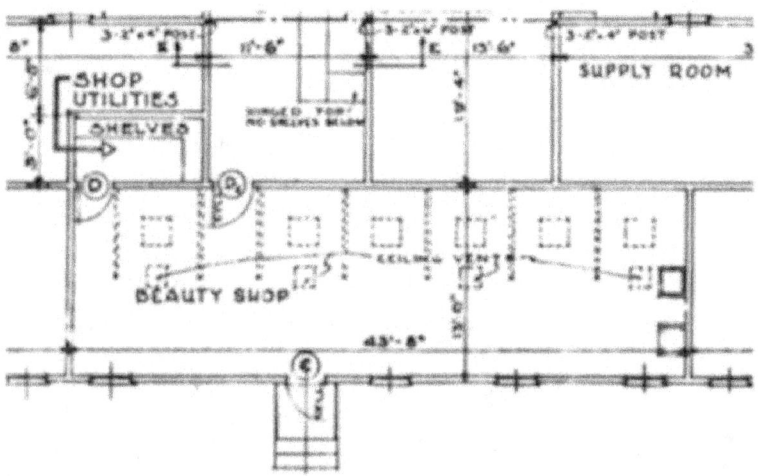

Figure 47. Beauty Shop in Recreation building, 1942 (USACEHQ).

Outside of the barracks, installation commanders had to make certain modifications to other facilities to physically accommodate servicewomen. At a minimum, latrine facilities had to be provided in all buildings designated for coed use, such as post exchanges, chapels, athletic facilities, and so forth. As Captain Joy Hancock found:

> [T]he problem of providing toilet facilities often proved to be a stumbling block when plans for receiving a contingent of WAVES were under way. For example, a commanding officer of an air station would say, 'We want to have the WAVES, but hangars, storerooms and other facilities are not equipped with toilets for women.' Fortunately, early in the WAVES program, I found an answer...With the aid of an ole-time male chief petty officer, they had solved the problem by installing a peg on the outside of the toilet facility and posting a sign, 'Before entering here, hang up your hat.' It worked [and] the solving of this small problem meant that the immediate assignment of women to those stations not having additional toilet

facilities need not be halted until they could be made available."[81]

Training

One area where installation commanders had an easier time was in the provision of training facilities. Although society had "carefully cherished notions that 'proper' young ladies must be trained in segregated facilities," all of the services were quick to allow for coed education in their training classes.[82] Or, in lieu of actual coed classes, at the very least, gender-segregated classes used the same facilities on a time share basis (Figure 48 and Figure 49).

Figure 48. WACs at machine gun training, Harlingen Army Gunnery School, TX, WWII (WIMSA, Vertical Photo File, Collection of Dorothy V. Clement).

---

[81] Hancock, *Lady in the Navy*, 176-77.
[82] Godson, "Capt. Joy Bright Hancock," 16.

Figure 49. WAVES Aviation Machinist Training, WWII
(WIMSA, Vertical Photo File, Collection of National Archives, Photo 86-WWT-60-8).

The rationale for breaking with societal standards in this regard, aside from saving the military money, was that it ensured the efficient replacement of men by women insofar as "it was felt that undergoing the same training along with the men averted what would otherwise be a transition period when women reported to stations and worked with men on the same jobs" (Figure 50, Figure 51, and Figure 52).[83]

---

[83] Joy B. Hancock, Women's Reserve Section, Training Division to the Administration, Training Division, "Material on the Women's Reserve Section for inclusion in the Secretary of the Navy's Annual Report and the Annual Reports of the Bureaus and Offices for the Fiscal Year 1943," August 12, 1943, WNY, RG Women in Aviation: WAVES Folder, Washington Navy Yards, Naval Aviation Office Archives, Washington, DC, 1.

Figure 50. WAC MPs, Fort Des Moines, WWII
(WIMSA, Vertical Photo File, Collection of Howard Bright).

Figure 51. WAVES at work on engine maintenance, Naval Air Station Banana River, FL,
30 August 1944 (NARA, RG 80-G Box 758, 244460).

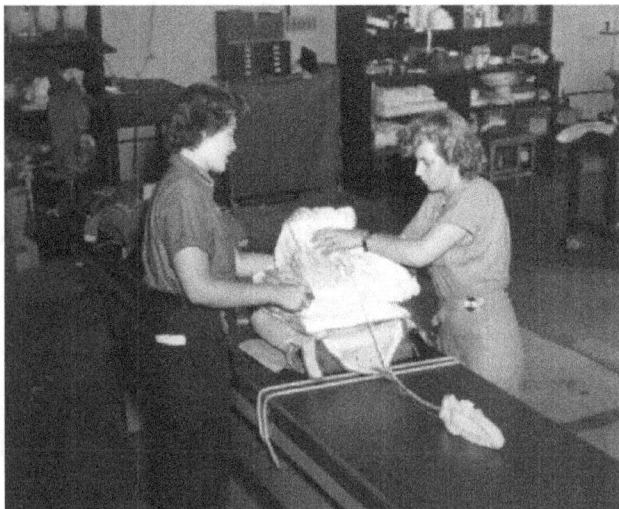

Figure 52. WAVES packing parachutes, Naval Air Station Banana River, FL, 30 Aug. 1944 (NARA, RG 80-G Box 758, 244458).

As for physical training, while women had calisthenics and recreational programs, they were not required to perform on the obstacle courses or other physical training mandated for the men. There is photographic evidence, however, that in some cases women were asked to tackle certain aspects of the obstacle course, even though official policy exempted them from this aspect of physical training (Figure 53).

Figure 53. Obstacle course at an Army Air Corps base, 1943 (WIMSA, Document File, Unknown donor #4674).

By the end of World War II, the presence of women in military service definitely left a tangible imprint on the built environment of America's installations. The policies established and implemented during the war set in place standards and practices that would be carried forth into the post war era. More importantly, the experience of physically accommodating servicewomen during the war was analyzed for lessons learned as the country prepared for a major philosophical and paradigmatic shift in its military posture.

3 Post-War Period Integration: A Permanent Role for Women

Prior to World War II, America engaged in a process of mobilization and demobilization during times of war, maintaining only a small military during times of peace. Following Allied victory, a war-weary public again expected military demobilization, which did occur to a certain extent. Before the war, America had also adopted an isolationist approach to world politics. The result of America's involvement in World War II, however, not only ended this isolationist stance, but prevented full-scale demobilization. At the end of the war, there were approximately 12 million Americans in the armed forces, including more than 300,000 women (including nurses), and by 1948, this number had dropped to a permanent force of 1.4 million.[84] The use of atomic weapons to win the war established America as a superpower. With this power came responsibility in the form of ongoing military commitments throughout the world as a result of the war, including the occupation of Japan and Germany. Combined with the advent of the Cold War, these factors forced the country to adopt a new military paradigm that involved maintaining a permanent military force capable of being deployed at a moment's notice. To support the new paradigm, the government created the Department of Defense, organized the Air Force as a separate military branch in 1947, and for the first time in American history, in 1948, instituted a peacetime draft.

Policy

As contentious as establishing a permanent force was to the American public, even more contentious was the issue of whether or not women would be a part of that permanent force. The original legislation allowing women to enlist in the military treated their service as temporary and called for women to be demobilized within six months of the resolution of hostilities. Women, however, were performing in critical roles that facili-

---

[84] Following the end of World War I, America demobilized roughly 3.2 million people and retained a standing regular volunteer force of approximately 19,000 officers and 205,000 enlisted men. See *American Military History*, Army Historical Series, Center of Military History, Washington, DC: Center of Military History, United States Army, 1989 [online version: http://www.army.mil/cmh/books/AMH/amh-toc.htm; updated April 25, 2001].

tated both the demobilization process and the efficient running of the stateside military.[85] This fact, along with recent memories of the personnel shortages that caused women to be enlisted in the first place, led some military leaders, with General Eisenhower at the forefront, to consider a role for women in the permanent force. Those leaders realized that should America ever have to mobilize for war again, it would no doubt require the service of women to succeed. Not everyone in the country agreed with General Eisenhower's stance, including many other military leaders. For example, Brig. Gen. Gerald C. Thomas, Marine Corps Director of Plans and Policies, stated, "The opinion generally held by the Marine Corps is that women have no proper place or function in the regular service in peacetime. The American tradition is that a woman's place is in the home...women do not take kindly to military regulation. During the war they have accepted the regulations imposed on them, but hereafter the problem of enforcing discipline alone would be a headache."[86]

It was not just the men who opposed women in the military. In the discussion of the post-war retention of women, many high-ranking women were against it as well. They felt the military was not prepared to accommodate women adequately. Rather, their experience showed them that the military expected the women "to make the entire adjustment to men's standards of dress, privacy, cleanliness, and recreation," because otherwise it would be seen as favoritism or special privilege. "The early directors were worried over the possible long-term effects of women's attempts to adjust to the rigid male environment and did not care to assume the responsibility for what they apparently feared would be a masculinizing experience for the young women involved."[87] Similarly, "there was, and continued to be, a general reluctance at all service levels to accept as valid, or equally compelling, the special needs and concerns of women, accompanied by a tendency to treat those needs as frivolous or not worth the bother," and as

---

[85] Holm, *Women in the Military*, 100. In the Navy alone, WAVES comprised more than half of the Navy Department headquarters personnel in Washington, DC, 70 percent of the Bureau of Naval Personnel, two-thirds of the enlisted personnel in the Chief of Naval Operations' Office, and 18 percent of the total stateside naval personnel at shore establishments.

[86] Quoted in Holm, *Women in the Military*, 107.

[87] Holm, *Women in the Military*, 103.

such the concern was that women were expected "to adjust and to conform to the rules laid down *by men for men.*"[88]

Of particular concern in how the military treated women was the issue of housing. A discussion paper prepared by the Army on whether or not the WAC should be retained, listed housing in its section on current problems. It cited a 1945 Surgeon General report stating that the lack of privacy in barracks affected the mental and physical health of women, and impaired their job efficiency.[89] The Surgeon General's report found that WACs were suffering alarming rates of fatigue, and among its findings as to why, stated, "the type of housing proved to have a direct relationship to fatigue, with those who slept in rooms being considerably less fatigued than those who were in barracks."[90] The report found this was because two-or four-person rooms were well-ventilated, and the women who lived in them were generally able to choose their own roommates who had similar working hours, thus resulting in similar sleeping habits and congeniality. A desire for better living conditions and more privacy was not unique to the women, though, as the Army's report found that enlisted men were also critical of housing conditions and expressed a desire for improvement.[91]

Women's Armed Services Integration Act

In spite of the opposition posed by the public as well as high-ranking military officials (including several of the former directors of the women's programs) the Women's Armed Services Integration Act (P.L. 625, 80th Congress) passed by a vote of 206 to 133, and was signed into law by President Truman on June 12, 1948 (Figure 54). Its primary purpose was to lessen the need for a peacetime draft, provide a trained corps of women as a basic reservoir for future expansion in time of national emergency, and improve efficiency and economy by utilizing women in those jobs for which they were better suited than men. Although women were granted a permanent place in the military, the Act included many special provisions that signifi-

---

[88] Ibid., 104.

[89] "Presentation of Merits of Four Plans," 7, The Surgeon General's report can be found in Appendix I of this document; see also Treadwell, *Women's Army Corps*, 628.

[90] Treadwell, *Women's Army Corps*, 628.

[91] "Presentation of Merits of Four Plans," 9.

cantly limited the scope of their role, and for all intents and purposes made full integration practically impossible.

Figure 54. WACs read the Women's Armed Services Integration Act at the Pentagon, Washington, DC, June 1948 (RG 111 SC, Box 371, Photo 300881, NARA, College Park, MD).

Specifically, the Act established separate women's corps in each service and put in place the following policies which would guide military service for women until the late 1960s:

1. women could constitute no more than 2 percent of the total force, with the number of women officers being no more than 10 percent of that 2 percent;
2. promotion potential was capped with Lieutenant Colonel or Commander being the highest permanent rank obtainable (the directors of the WACs, WAVES, WAFs[92], and Women Marines were temporarily promoted to Colonel or Captain);
3. women were barred from serving on Navy vessels and on combat aircraft engaged in combat missions;

---

[92] WAF stands for Women's Air Force, established with the separation of the Air Force from the Army.

4. women were denied spousal benefits (unless their husbands depended on them for more than 50 percent of their support);
5. women were precluded from having authority over men, and had separate promotion lists from the men;
6. the minimum enlistment age was set at 18, with parental consent required for women under the age of 21 (men could enlist at age 17 and only required parental consent if they were under age 18); and
7. authorized a blanket authority for discharging any female "under circumstances and in accordance with regulations proscribed by the President."[93] (In 1951, the President signed Executive Order 10240 authorizing the services to discharge any woman who became pregnant or became a parent through adoption or marriage. This blanket authority for discharge did not apply to the men.)

As sexist as the provisions of this Act may seem by today's standards, "this law accurately reflected the prevailing cultural attitudes of the postwar period concerning women's roles and legal status. To have completely integrated them into the armed forces in 1948 with fully equal status would have been totally out of character with that stage in the evolution of women's roles in American society. It would simply never have occurred to those who were most directly involved."[94]

The passage of the Act presented military leaders, in particular the Women's Directors, with the challenge of establishing and defining policies and procedures to organize and guide the women's programs for each of the services. All of the policies, regulations, guidelines, and practices established during World War II were predicated on the belief that women were a temporary fixture and would be demobilized at the end of the war. Thus, while the experiences of World War II certainly presented a foundation upon which to build, military leaders needed to assess which of the policies and procedures would adequately serve for a peacetime women's program, which needed to be modified, as well as what, if any, new policies needed to be established. In the Navy, this was the task of the Eberstadt

---

[93] See Women's Research and Education Institute, *Chronology of Significant Legal & Policy Changes Affecting Women in the Military: 1947-2003* (Washington DC: Women's Research and Education Institute, 2003), available online at http://www.wrei.org/projects/wiu/index.htm, and Holm, *Women in the Military*, 119-127 for discussion of the Act.

[94] Holm, *Women in the Military*, 127.

Committee, which determined that there were "special morale and discipline problems," such as housing and fraternization for which new policy applicable to a peacetime force would be required.[95]

In general, the personnel policies developed by each service continued the practice established during the war of governing men and women alike with no preferential treatment. Still, wartime experience demonstrated that there were certain factors more important to the morale of women than men, such as privacy in unit housing, unit messes, fashionable looking uniforms, group status, an assignment that kept the person busy, and non-fraternization. Regulations concerning each of these as applied to women were in turn developed. In terms of the assignment and training of women, the official policy across all the branches mirrored that of the Marine Corps (which was the most reluctant of all the services to accept women), which prescribed that women would be assigned to and trained for duties in accordance with the requirements of the Marine Corps and their qualification for such duty be determined in accordance with the standards prescribed for male personnel in similar assignments.[96] However, wartime experience also demonstrated that despite the intention of equal treatment, certain considerations must be taken into account in the assignment and training of women: women were not assigned to combat duty; women should not be assigned to duties requiring more than the normal physical strength of a woman; and women must be assigned where separate and suitable housing could be provided.[97] In 1949, the military began intensive studies to determine what jobs met these requirements and thus were suitable for women, both in time of emergency and during peacetime.[98]

---

[95] Matthew Radom (Consultant), "Points discussed at Mayflower Hotel with heads of Women's Services," September 10, 1948, Box 2, WAVES, Folder: (I-21) Eberstadt Committee (1948), Washington Navy Yards, Naval Historical Center Archives, Washington, DC, 1.

[96] R.D. Lyons and Steven Marcus, "The Women Marines: 11th Anniversary," *Leatherneck* 37, no. 2 (February 1954): 14-30, Collection no. 1704 (Margaret Stinson), Women in Military Service for America Memorial Foundation, Inc. Archives, Washington, DC, 16.

[97] Capt. Joy Bright Hancock to Admiral Sprague, "Conference with Mr. Random of the Eberstadt Committee," September 14, 1948, Box 2, WAVES, Folder: (I-21) Eberstadt Committee (1948), Washington Navy Yards, Naval Historical Center Archives, Washington, DC, 1.

[98] U.S. Women's Army Corps School, *Role of the WAC: History, Organization, and Function of the U.S. Women's Army Corps*, Special Text 35-150 (Fort McClellan, AL: Office of Doctrine, Literature, Plans and Programs, 1972), Collection no. 4814 (Wendy Wadinger), Women in Military Service for America Memorial Foundation, Inc. Archives, Washington, DC, 18.

It was housing and the physical accommodation of women, however, that became one of the paramount issues in developing policy for servicewomen. It also became one of the biggest obstacles in the utilization of women as each branch adopted a policy that in effect stated that women could not be assigned to a station in groups of less than 50, nor where there was not adequate housing available for them. In the Air Force, which as a new service branch had the most flexibility in developing policy, official policy pertaining to WAF stated that:

> [E]nlisted WAF will be housed in designated buildings located and equipped with adequate facilities to provide group privacy and supervision. Enlisted WAF normally will not be assigned to an installation in groups of less than 50. When assignment of a smaller group is considered necessary, request for administrative instructions will be forwarded to Headquarters USAF. WAF commissioned officers and warrant officers will be housed in women officers' quarters when available and adequate."[99]

The Air Force further proscribed that separate mess halls would not be provided unless they were "required by local conditions and specifically authorized by the wing, base, or installation commander."[100]

The other service branches, for the most part, modified existing housing policy, in some cases relaxing particular regulations while in other cases instituting new and stricter regulations. The Army, for example, relaxed its regulation calling for a minimum of 150 feet between male and female barracks, instead dictating that WAC barracks be "a reasonable distance" from male barracks, as well as within walking distance of the workplace. Defining what constituted a "reasonable distance" was left up to the local post engineer. The restriction could, however, be waived by the post commander, often at the urging of the WAC commander and/or staff adviser, if "an opportunity arose for obtaining a newer or a larger building for a

---

[99] *Military Personnel: Assignment and Administration of WAF Personnel*, AFR 35-44 (Washington, DC: Department of the Air Force, 1949), USAF Collection, 168.12035-44 October 25, 1949, Air Force Historical Research Agency, Maxwell AFB, Montgomery, AL, 2.

[100] *Military Personnel: Assignment and Administration of WAF Personnel*, 2.

WAC detachment, whether the building was next door or across the street from a male unit."[101] Conversely, regulations got stricter, at least on paper, regarding minimum housing standards to be afforded servicewomen, specifically as related to the consistent provision of space allowances, amenities, and privacy.

Factors driving the call for improved housing stemmed from two sources, namely societal expectations and the perceived impacts of housing on women's health and welfare. At end of World War II, WAC Director Colonel Hobby, noted in her final report that the Army would have to provide suitable living standards with a greater degree of privacy if it wished to attract and retain women of high ability.[102] Colonel Hobby specifically referenced the Surgeon General's report in support of her argument, stating that better housing would also improve the efficiency and effectiveness of the women. Colonel Hobby's final report resonated with all WAC authorities, and echoed the final reports from other military leaders. A Colonel from the Army Air Force summarized the Air WAC experience thus: "From the standpoint of hindsight...it would seem that one of the major aspects of the WAC program which might have been improved, in the initial planning stages, was the housing program. Field experience indicated that drab or flimsy wartime housing had a greater effect on WAC efficiency and morale than anyone had anticipated."[103]

Housing Design

In response, all services began planning barracks with two- to four-person cubicles or rooms.[104] At the forefront of such design plans were those drawn up by the G-4 Division and the Chief of Engineers for the Army, which incorporated all the hopeful policy and thinking going on across the service branches. The G-4 plans envisioned hotel-type housing where enlisted women would each have 120 square feet (the wartime officer allowance) and share two-person rooms. Each barracks would be furnished with a kitchen, dayroom, date room (with male lavatory), storage facility,

---

[101] Morden, *Women's Army Corps*, 196-202.

[102] Office of the Director, WAC, "Background on Enlisted Housing," 2 and Treadwell, *Women's Army Corps*, 754-55.

[103] Quoted in Treadwell, *Women's Army Corps*, 754-55.

[104] Hancock, "Conference with Mr. Random of the Eberstadt Committee," 7.

and "bountiful latrine facilities, including bathtubs" (Figure 55). These plans also provided greater privacy and comforts with age and promotion. Enlisted women who attained the first three grades were to have two-bedroom apartments with living room, kitchen, and bath for every four women (Figure 56). Enlisted women at training centers were to have 90 square feet per person (recalling that 42.5 to 60 square feet was the standard during the war), window shades, hairdressing facilities, dayroom, date room, storage room, and adequate laundry facilities.[105]

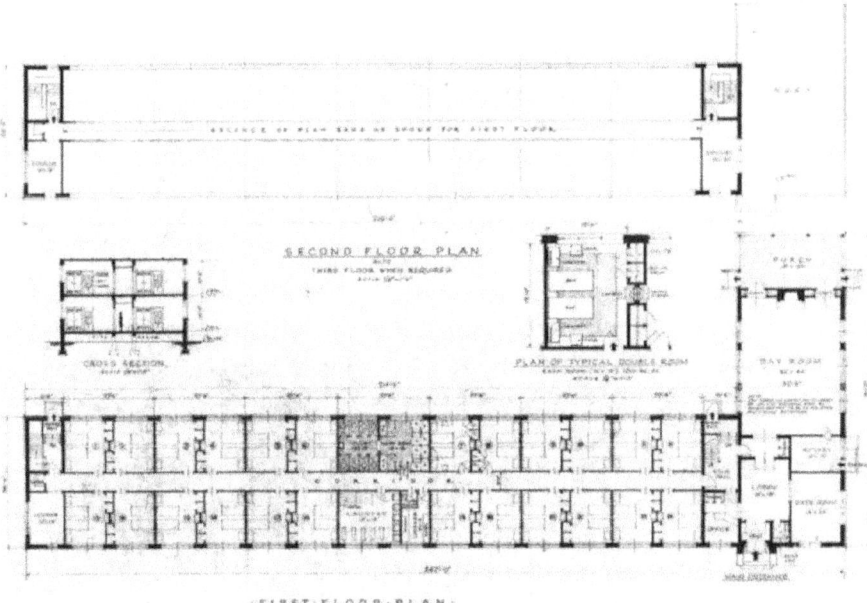

Figure 55. Hotel-type housing plan for enlisted WACs with two-person rooms, 1946 (USACEHQ).

---

[105] Treadwell, *Women's Army Corps*, 524-25; Office of the Director, WAC, "Background on Enlisted Housing," 2.

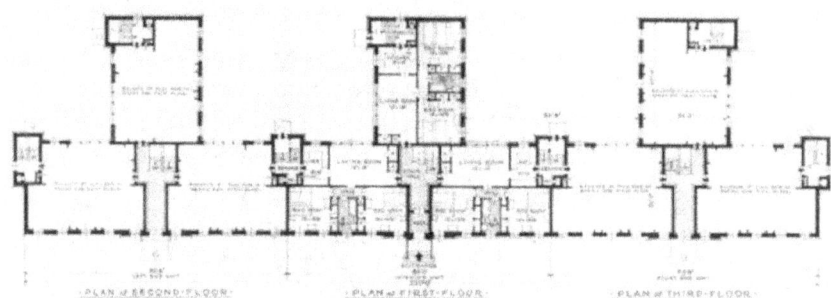

Figure 56. Apartment-type barracks for higher grade enlisted WACs with two-bedroom suites, 1946 (USACEHQ).

For all enlisted women, these plans were more than adequate in providing privacy and those amenities deemed necessary for women. The intent behind the G-4 plans was to provide women who made the military a career with "a semblance of home life" as it was expected that these women would never marry or have children if they remained in the military. Unfortunately for the women, the G-4 plans were never implemented as there was no need for new construction following the war.[106] The plans did, however, serve to crystallize and capture in print the prevailing thought at the time on how women should be accommodated, building on plans and policies that had been implemented during World War II. Although these plans were not translated into new construction, they did serve to influence the modification of existing structures.

For example, at Camp Lee, Virginia, the first Army training center established for the WACs, the one-story buildings contained orderly, supply or day rooms, while the two-story buildings functioned as either barracks or classrooms. Barracks for basic recruits were organized with approximately 45 cots, footlockers, and steel wall lockers per floor along with two small rooms reserved for the platoon sergeants responsible for supervising the trainees. Officer candidates and student officers were provided partitions between every two beds, which afforded some privacy, but hindered ventilation (Figure 57). "Permanently assigned officers lived in two-story buildings that had private rooms or permanent partitions. Lieutenant colonels and majors had single rooms; captains and lieutenants had to double

---

[106] Ibid.

up."[107] Additionally, each building was outfitted with makeshift kitchen, reception room, and dayroom, as well as having individual showers and at least one bathtub for every 75 women.

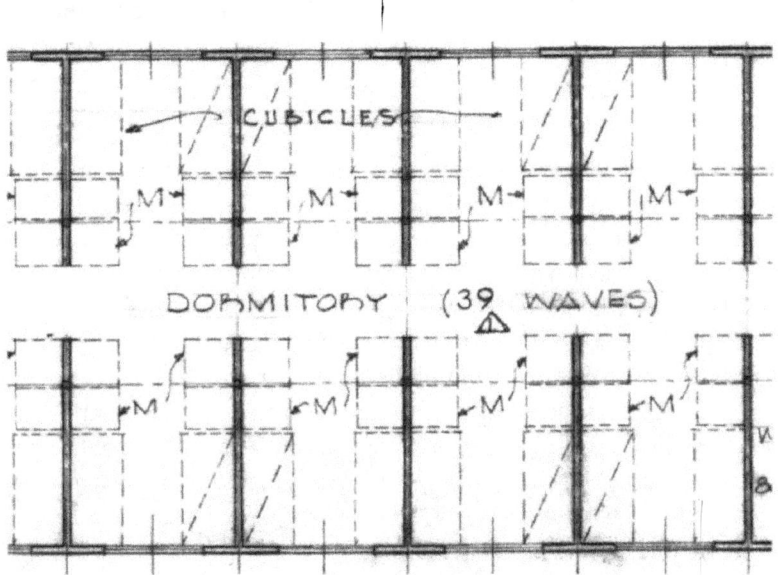

Figure 57. Barracks layout showing rudimentary partitions between bunks, 1952 (NARA).

Even though new construction was not needed, the housing of servicewomen still posed a problem in some places. This was primarily because as women were demobilized following the war and prior to the Integration Act, the barracks and facilities they used either fell dormant and into disrepair, or were taken over by the men. At Parris Island, for example, the Director of the Women Marines found that although the facilities required little renovation, they needed to be cleaned out and re-outfitted with bunks, locker boxes, linens, and other supplies before they could be occupied.[108] Conversely, because the barracks provided to the WAVES were in good condition and far more attractive with their cubicles versus an open bay layout, the Navy found that male chiefs as well as lower grade petty officers were moving into these barracks.[109] The result was that when the

---

[107] Morden, *Women's Army Corps*, 76.

[108] Stremlow, *History of the Women Marines*, 28-30.

[109] Hancock, *Lady in the Navy*, 260.

services once again began enlisting women, they had far fewer available spaces than anticipated. Further complicating the numbers was that "at some locations the services of women could not be utilized in sufficient numbers to fill available housing; at others, the women exceeded the housing facilities."[110]

Training

In addition to housing, the services also had to accommodate women in terms of permanent training facilities. Aside from the Air Force, all services continued the practice of segregated training for its basic recruits, and in a change from World War II, instituted segregated officer training. The Air Force's Officer Candidate School at Lackland Training Center in San Antonio, Texas, on the other hand, became the first, and only, service to have a major coed officer-commissioning program. "Men and women met the same scholastic requirements and received the same instruction except for physical training and field exercises. While the men participated in field exercises, the women studied the administration of enlisted women—a job to which most of them were expected to be assigned at some point in their careers."[111] Of course, women were housed separately from the men.

For basic recruits, the Marine Corps simply reopened the women's area at Parris Island, although this time around women would share some of the recreation, athletic, and classroom facilities on base with the men. For officers, the Marine Corps established a training facility at Quantico, Virginia, where Women Officer Candidates were sent during the summer months.[112] From 1948 to 1973, Marine officer training at Quantico was conducted separately for men and women, and the women lived and trained in a nearly self-contained area located in the southeast corner of the base containing barracks, mess hall, a small dispensary, drill field, and

---

[110] Ibid.

[111] Holm, *Women in the Military*, 134-35; see also Benjamin Goldman, Rex M. Naylor, and G.W. Hueners (compilers), *History of the Tactical Air Command, 1 July through 30 November 1950*, Vol. I– Narrative) (Tactical Air Command, 1951), USAF Collection, K417.01 Jul 1 – Nov 1950 V.I, IRIS No. 502588, Air Force Historical Research Agency, Maxwell AFB, Montgomery, AL, 3.

[112] United States Marine Corps, *Marine Corps Recruit Depot Yearbook, Platoon 4B, Parris Island, South Carolina*, (n.p., 1967), Collection no. 4167, Women in Military Service for America Memorial Foundation, Inc. Archives, Washington, DC.

classroom.[113] Following the Integration Act, training for women in the Navy began in October 1948 at the Naval Recruit Training Center, Great Lakes, Illinois, while new officers trained in the Officer Indoctrination Unit (W) at the Navel Base, Newport, Rhode Island. "As during World War II, women officers' training remained segregated from men's, although the male Officer Candidate School was also at Newport. Another similarity to wartime training was the continued emphasis on ladylike conduct."[114]

As stated above, the Army opened its first WAC Training Center at Camp Lee in October 1948. Camp Lee was all-inclusive for WAC training: it conducted basic training, common specialist and cadre training, as well as an officer candidate school. It also served as a reception and processing center for recruits and re-enlistees, as well as a reserve training center.[115] It was one-third the size of any facility established for women during World War II, but still carried out all of the functions performed at the prior centers, except for overseas training. Its mission was "to prepare the woman soldier for the job she will be assigned in the Army; to indoctrinate her into the elements of military life and customs; and to imbue her with the high moral and ethical standards which the Army demands."[116]

---

[113] Stremlow, *History of the Women Marines*, 125-26.

[114] Godson, *Serving Proudly*, 173.

[115] U.S. Women's Army Corps School, *Role of the WAC*, 17 and Morden, *Women's Army Corps*, 82.

[116] Morden, *Women's Army Corps*, 82.

4 The Korean War and the 1950s: Recruitment and Retention

The Korean War (1950-1953) was the first major United States engagement of the Cold War. As such, it reinforced and validated the newly adopted military paradigm. It "awakened the nation" to the need for a properly maintained permanent military "ready to meet, if need be, armed aggression anywhere in the world at an instant's notice."[117] On June 25, 1950, communist North Korean troops crossed the 38th parallel into South Korea. This drew the United States, on behalf of the United Nations, into a troop-centric land-based war (somewhat unexpected in a nuclear age). The war served as a field test of the post-World War II military structure, including the women's programs that had been established during the integration period. Among the lessons learned from the Korean War was that, once again, women had a vital role to serve in the military. Another lesson learned was that the military would have to make an effort to recruit and retain a high-quality corps of women. Men could be drafted into the military to meet recruitment goals, but for women, service was voluntary. Further, the military faced competition from the private sector that was also employing women to do similar work. Complicating things was the persistence of negative social connotations associated with women in the military.

This lesson was driven home by the fact that all of the women's programs had trouble meeting recruitment goals during the war. The American public, still weary from World War II, continued to strongly question the appropriateness of women in the military, and unlike the prior war, the Korean War did not create enough societal upheaval to overcome these reservations. Additionally, conflicting reports out of Southeast Asia gave the misleading impression by 1952 that the war was ramping down, and with it the need for an expanded military. This created another barrier to recruiting women. The military's inability to recruit and retain enough women for the Korean War affected the women's programs for the remainder of the decade. The most immediate ramification was that it

---

[117] U.S. Women's Army Corps School, *Role of the WAC*, 19.

"raised serious doubts about the value of women's programs to the peacetime defense forces."[118] As a result, in the years following the Korean War, the women's programs became "small token force[s] of young women with low career potential but with the mental and educational capacity for making a contribution out of proportion to their numbers, provided they were properly trained, motivated, and employed."[119]

Policy and Utilization Studies

It was the training, motivating, and employing of women that would become the focus of numerous studies and committees throughout the 1950s. Once again military leaders were faced with the challenge of finding a compromise between opposing thoughts on the issue of what role women would have in the military. For example, in the Marine Corps, while the Korean War brought permanent changes to the women's programs, "the most obvious being the return of WMs to major posts and stations," following the war, the Marine Corps, along with all the services, struggled with finding a balance between the desire to "cut the strength of women forces," and define the nature of the role that the remaining women would play.[120] On the one hand, societal attitudes on gender norms and the traditional male military mindset preferred that women not have any role; while on the other hand, historical experience indicated a definite need for women in order to maintain an effective military. Historical experience also had shown that there were some military jobs that women simply did better than men.

To address the issue of women's role in the military, the Office of the Secretary of Defense commissioned a study in 1951 on the maximum utilization of military women. The study compiled a list of what it felt were the problems preventing the maximum utilization of women. Included among these problems were: a) women were physically different from men, with "childbearing" as their "primary social function," and therefore any policies established for them "must take into consideration differences in physique and social responsibility;" b) while women were capable of doing any type of work, the problem was in establishing under what conditions

---

[118] See Holm, *Women in the Military*, 158, see also pages 148-157 for a discussion on this topic.
[119] Holm, *Women in the Military*, 157.
[120] Stremlow, *History of the Women Marines*, 62.

would the services of women "be of maximum value to the military service;" c) specific provisions, such as "sanitary facilities and housing, protection of privacy and person," were considered essential, and as such the "feasibility of providing these requirements enter into the decision concerning the utilization of womanpower"; and d) stereotypes regarding the proper or appropriate use of women were "a block to the maximum utilization of womanpower" and had to be realistically dealt with in order to achieve recruitment goals and maximum utilization."[121] In the Air Force, a similar Staff Study on WAF administration and command found that the restrictions on the use of women were "imposed by law, by women's physical limitations and by social custom."[122]

These were the obstacles facing the women's programs in the 1950s in their efforts to not only recruit, but also retain quality women (Figure 58). To overcome or work around these obstacles, military leaders developed policies, regulations, and practices intended to create a more attractive environment for women. For the Army, in particular, "the years during and following the end of the Korean War saw the Women's Army Corps reach maturity as a branch of the US Army. Numerous studies brought improvements in job opportunities, housing, new uniforms, and changes in personnel policies which placed women on equal footing with men in the Army."[123] The notion of equal footing, of course, was subjective and did not mean identical. The Air Force's Staff Study acknowledged that because of the restrictions placed on the use of women, as discussed above, and due also to the fact that women were required to "live apart from the male squadron members," usually in a separate dormitory and sometimes in a completely separate area, that the "complete integration of the WAF into a predominantly male organization" could not be accomplished.[124] The best

---

[121] Office of the Secretary of Defense, Personnel Policy Board, "Study on Maximum Utilization of Military Womanpower," October 12, 1950, Report is located at Tab B of "Commissioned Women Personnel in the Services, A Study," August 1951, USAF Collection, K141.33-8 1951, IRIS No. 469735, Air Force Historical Research Agency, Maxwell AFB, Montgomery, AL, 1-2.

[122] Lt.Col. Martha L. Cross (Deputy Director, WAF), "Staff Study—WAF Administration and Command Control," April 6, 1956, USAF Collection, K141.35-9 6 Apr 1956, IRIS No. 469736, Air Force Historical Research Agency, Maxwell AFB, Montgomery, AL, 2; see also *Women in the Air Force, Enlisted Personnel*, Air Force Manual 39-5 (Washington, DC: Department of the Air Force, July 12, 1957), J. Sewell Papers,168.7172-2 1907 – Jul 1957, IRIS No. 1041204, Air Force Historical Research Agency, Maxwell AFB, Montgomery, AL, 8.

[123] U.S. Women's Army Corps School, *Role of the WAC*, 22.

[124] Cross, "Staff Study," 2.

that could be hoped for was equal, but separate, footing. Still, while this was true for all of the services, military leaders strove to create the best environment they could, while accommodating societal attitudes on gender norms.

Figure 58. WAVES recruits arriving for training, U.S. Naval Training Center, Bainbridge, MD, 1956. From yearbook "The Portal" for Company 15 (WIMSA, Document File, Collection of Doris Brown #4642).

Thus, the compromise reached between public opinion and military need and reflected in official policy often used broad terms that left room for changing interpretations. This was particularly true in the language used to define the mission for the women's program of each service. In the Air Force, for example, the primary objective was "to make available to the Air Force an additional source of enlisted personnel of above average intelligence and education, to provide a mobilization pattern for any required expansion, and to provide up-to-date information on the utilization of women's skills in Air Force jobs, other than in the Nurse Corps or the

Medical Specialists Corps."[125] The objective of the WAF program was also to support the Air Force mission by providing "a component of servicewomen qualified to perform efficiently in authorized assignments," accomplished by having WAF personnel "participate in technical training and fill authorized military manning spaces on the same general basis as Air Force male personnel."[126] Simply, the specifics for implementing official policy were often intentionally vague and thus left up to the Major Air Commanders. It was their responsibility to judge the appropriateness of their procedures and policies against prevailing social customs and the double standard they imposed on women.

Social custom, in turn, made the physical accommodation of servicewomen of paramount importance in the assignment and utilization of women. That is, the goal of creating the best environment possible for women often translated into a focus on improving and/or expanding not just job opportunities, but better housing. Additionally, physically accommodating women also continued to be one of the biggest obstacles to the full utilization of women. This was foremost because the prior policy requiring that women be stationed in groups of 50 or more was still in place. Regulations further dictated that women could train only at centers prepared to accommodate them and likewise be stationed only at installations that provided adequate housing and protection.[127] Standing policy also required women to have separate and segregated housing from men, and instituted minimum standards for female housing slightly higher than those for men, thus prohibiting the interchangeability of barracks space. Therefore, because women required slightly different barracks, and not every military installation had these barracks, the stationing, and in turn, utilization of women required forethought and careful planning.

At the same time, the military was learning that simply providing adequate housing and protection for servicewomen was not enough. If the military hoped to compete with the private sector and combat the negative association of female military service in its efforts to recruit and retain a group of high-quality women, it would have to provide attractive living conditions. As one 1958 study found, adequate housing was "one of the most impor-

---

[125] Ibid., 1.

[126] *Women in the Air Force, Enlisted Personnel*, 1 and 8.

[127] Office of the Secretary of Defense, "Study on Maximum Utilization of Military Womanpower," 4 and 6.

tant factors in the retention of women in the Army and in the maintenance of high morale," especially given that 92 percent of enlisted women were unmarried and lived in barracks.[128] In the Air Force, a 1957 study showed that nearly 88 percent of enlisted WAFs lived in government quarters and of them, only 63 percent rated them as good or excellent. The two major complaints for those WAF who considered their quarters inadequate were the lack of privacy and overcrowding.[129] Women Marines likewise reported poor living conditions as the number one criticism they had about their service life.[130]

Housing Standards

Housing was thus regarded by military leaders as a primary target for improvement. Of course, these housing improvements were limited by policy and available funding. The Navy, for example, initiated a program allowing most first-class personnel and chiefs to live in their own apartments instead of barracks, while pushing for new or remodeled barracks.[131] The Air Force, recognizing that the lack of privacy in barracks was a difficult adjustment for young servicewomen, allowed enlisted women to "express their individuality to a degree" such as with pictures, window curtains or area rugs, while working to improve conditions for privacy.[132] As for the Army, the Women's Army Corps felt "strongly about the importance of good housing," and had the "ultimate aim" of providing living conditions that paralleled those of "working women in a comparable civilian position," including such amenities as "privacy, cooking and laundry facilities, sufficient storage space, recreational areas, and areas for entertaining guests."[133]

---

[128] Women's Army Corps, "Housing for Enlisted Women," May 29, 1958, Ft. Lee 228-01, WHC-377, Folder—Housing, Enlisted/Officer (General) (1957-63), WAC Museum Archives, Ft. Lee, VA; see also DACOWITS, "Review of Ad-Hoc Housing Committee," April 7, 1959, Ft. Lee 228-01, WHC-377, Folder—Housing, Enlisted/Officer (General) (1957-63), WAC Museum Archives, Ft. Lee, VA, for a similar report.

[129] Directorate of Statistical Services, Personnel Statistics Division, "U.S. Air Force Military Personnel Surveys: Air Force Female Military Personnel," Series ASC-4B, No. 2, Source of Information: RCS: AF-P3, (Washington, DC: Headquarters, U.S. Air Force, 1957), J. Sewell Papers, 168.7172-2, IRIS No. 1041204, Air Force Historical Research Agency, Maxwell AFB, Montgomery, AL, 3.

[130] Lyons, "The Women Marines: 11th Anniversary," 24; the second highest criticism was the food.

[131] Godson, *Serving Proudly*, 192-93.

[132] *Women in the Air Force, Enlisted Personnel*, 12.

[133] U.S. Women's Army Corps School, *Role of the WAC*, 34.

Housing conditions for female officers also began to receive attention. Prior to the 1950s, female officers generally received the same housing conditions as those provided to male officers. However, in 1955, the Surgeon General of the Army informed the Army Chief of Staff that akin to enlisted women, recruiting and retaining female officers was seriously hampered by inadequate housing. The Surgeon General found that "the most privacy an officer could hope for was a private bedroom," as women shared living rooms, baths, and messing facilities, and that "these conditions were particularly onerous for female officers."[134] In response to this situation, the Defense Advisory Council on Women in the Services (DACOWITS) conducted its own study and in 1955 issued its own recommendations. Foremost, DACOWITS declared "a need for a completely new concept in regard to housing for bachelor officers," especially in light of the fact that the military was "in competition with the civilian world for the services of intelligent and well-trained women."[135] Its study found that although WAC housing had improved in recent years, and while housing for WAVES and WM was considered "good," WAF housing was still considered less than satisfactory.

The 1957 survey conducted by the Air Force of its female officers supported the findings of both the Army Surgeon General and DACOWITS studies. The survey revealed that approximately 60 percent of female officers lived in Bachelor Officers' Quarters (BOQs), and even though 90 percent of the women occupied private rooms, less than one-third of the rooms had private bathrooms, and not every officer had the same amenities available to them: 10 percent lacked living rooms, 18 percent had no kitchen facilities, and 26 percent had no laundry facilities. As a result, only 39 percent of the officers felt that their BOQs were adequate, with "the greater the number sharing a room, or other facilities, the lesser the feeling of satisfaction." The vast majority of female officers desired improve-

---

[134] *Report of ASD(M) Task Force on Bachelor Accommodations, Troop Housing, Bachelor Officer Quarters* (Washington, DC: Department of Defense, May 1966), Ft. Lee 228-01, WHC-375, Folder—Housing DOD Report (1966), WAC Museum Archives, Ft. Lee, VA, 62.

[135] DACOWITS, "Report of the Ad Hoc Housing Committee," May 1955, Ft. Lee 228-01, WHC-377, Folder—Housing, Enlisted/Officer (General) (1957-63), WAC Museum Archives, Ft. Lee, VA, 2-3; see also DACOWITS, "Review of DACOWITS Ad-Hoc Housing Studies," 1959, Ft. Lee 228-01, WHC-377, Folder—Housing, Enlisted/Officer (General) (1957-63), WAC Museum Archives, Ft. Lee, VA, 1.

ments in housing or facilities with 55 percent wanting more privacy and space, as well as better furnishings.[136]

Recognizing that housing conditions were an important factor in retaining qualified military women, DACOWITS argued that minimum housing standards needed to be established. To this end, they recommended that new construction "should provide for a combination of private apartments and suites to accommodate both field grade (senior) and company grade (junior) officers."[137] The recommendation was for individual apartments (separate entrance, bedroom, living room, bath, cooking facilities, and sufficient closet space) or suites (combination living room-bedroom, semi-private bath and community recreation and kitchen facilities).

The poor conditions revealed by these studies resonated with several high-ranking military officials. In one instance, the 1958 resignation letter from Army Captain Virginia Schneider recalled the findings of the DACOWITS study and spurred commentary from Major General George E. Martin. In Captain Schneider's resignation letter, she cited poor housing conditions, particularly a "lack of private bathroom facilities and having to share a small kitchen with anywhere from ten to sixteen people" as the reason for her desire to leave the service.[138] Maj. Gen. Martin responded that Captain Schneider had identified a problem of concern to all bachelor officers, male and female. Namely, although the bachelor officer was usually satisfied with "relatively modest arrangements for quarters" during the first few years of commissioned service, after a few years of active duty, the young officer would develop new ideas as to what constituted adequate living conditions. As such, Maj. Gen. Martin argued that "there should be some scales of standards that would allow the career bachelor to phase into improved living conditions as the years pass." He also noted that fe-

---

[136] Directorate of Statistical Services, "U.S. Air Force Military Personnel Surveys," 2.

[137] DACOWITS, "Report of the Ad Hoc Housing Committee," 2-3; see also Idem. "Review of DACOWITS Ad-Hoc Housing Studies," 1.

[138] Capt. Virginia M. Schneider (WAC) to Headquarters, Department of the Army, "Resignation," May 3, 1958, and follow-up response by Maj. Gen. George E. Martin, Headquarters, U.S. Army Europe, May 29, 1958, Ft. Lee 228-01, WHC-377, Folder—Housing, Enlisted/Officer (General) (1957-63), WAC Museum Archives, Ft. Lee, VA.

male officers would want to have part-time access to facilities "that are of interest to women," such as cooking and sewing.[139]

Indeed, as exemplified by Maj. General Martin, there was ever increasing recognition of the negative impact that poor housing conditions were having on recruitment and retention. It was because of the challenge posed by housing as well as to help combat the persistent negative social connotations associated with female military service that the Secretary of Defense established DACOWITS in the first place.[140] DACOWITS was established in October 1951 with the following objectives: "1) to inform the public of the need for women in the Services; 2) to emphasize to parents the responsibilities assumed by the Military Departments to provide for welfare of women in the Services; and 3) to accelerate the recruitment of women, stressing both quality and quantity."[141] The committee was further charged with recommending standards for the housing, health, training, recreation, and general welfare of women, as well as on ways to ensure the effective utilization of women's capabilities.[142] The 1955 study on housing generated by DACOWITS (discussed above), was one of the Council's first major initiatives and resulted in Department of Defense authorization for the services to build pilot projects that incorporated the study's recommended standards.[143] The Air Force was the only service to accept and build its bachelor officer housing pilot project at its base in Abilene, Texas. The building, completed in 1958 at a cost of $9,077 per person (plus a 2½ percent contingency), was a motel-type structure, the plans for which evolved out of the DACOWITS recommendations.[144]

---

[139] Schneider, "Resignation."

[140] Sandra Lee Katzman, "DACOWITS Looks at Women in the Military," *Family* (October 1978), Mabel M. Gilliam Collection, 168.7342-35 1 Jan – 31 Dec 1978, IRIS No. 1126948, Air Force Historical Research Agency, Maxwell AFB, Montgomery, AL, 26, and "DACOWITS—a DOD Advisory Council," *On Guard* XIX, no. 6 (March 1990): 13, Box 131-7, General Files; Folder: Woman in the Corps of Engineers, U.S. Army Corps of Engineers History Office Archives, Alexandria, VA, 13.

[141] Mae Sue Talley, *Highlights of the Defense Advisory Committee on Women in the Services: 25 Years of Service to the Department of Defense*, (Washington, DC: Department of Defense, 1976), Box 4, BUPERS 00W, Folder: History 1975-1976, Washington Navy Yards, Naval Historical Center Archives, Washington, DC, 2.

[142] "DACOWITS," *Women's Army Corps Journal* 3, no. 2 (April -June 1972): 10-13, WAC Museum Archives, Ft. Lee, VA, 3.

[143] Talley, *Highlights of the Defense Advisory Committee on Women in the Services*, 5.

[144] DACOWITS, "Review of DACOWITS Ad-Hoc Housing Studies," 3 and Talley, *Highlights of the Defense Advisory Committee on Women in the Services*, 6.

Establishing housing standards was no small matter for DACOWITS or the military, and finding a happy medium between both entities was equally challenging. That is, DACOWITS, as a civilian committee, tended to aim high in its standards while the military was hampered by construction budgets and cost restrictions established by Congress. Still, because at the time there was "a wide divergence in the standards from installation to installation and among the services," the object was not only to establish but also to assure minimum standards were implemented across the services.[145] Nonetheless, in establishing the minimum housing standards for servicewomen, both the military and DACOWITS put forth many elements that had been envisioned during the design and planning phase of the late 1940s—those designs that were drafted and approved but never built.

Housing Design

The first policy change regarding housing standards occurred in 1950, when the Munitions Board Committee mandated a basic space allowance of 125 square feet per enlisted man, and authorized an additional 15 square feet be added to this figure per enlisted women for a total of 140 square feet. The additional square footage was to accommodate additional space requirements deemed necessary for women, such as reception areas, increased laundry and latrine facilities, and minor cooking facilities (Figure 59 and Figure 60).[146] That is, men and women received the same amount of actual living space, but because women's barracks were to provide additional amenities not extended to the men, the space allowance per individual had to be increased. From this starting point, DACOWITS recommended, and the services concurred, that building plans include cubicle arrangements for increased privacy in the sleeping area. The Army authorized the installation of partitions between every two sleeping areas in women's barracks in 1953. The Army further added clothing wardrobes and electrical outlets to each sleeping area, as well as cooking facilities to the common areas. Still, even though these improvements were author-

---

[145] Office of the Director, WAC, "Background on Enlisted Housing," 3; see also U.S. Women's Army Corps School, *Role of the WAC*, 34.

[146] Office of the Director, WAC, "Background on Enlisted Housing," 3.

ized, they "emerged slowly" as commanders could only implement them when they had funds available to do so.[147]

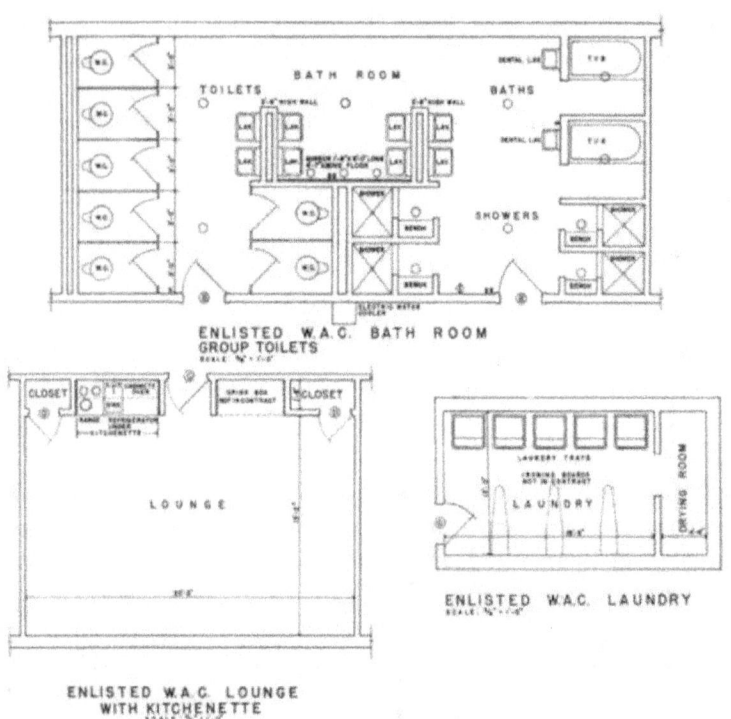

Figure 59. Additional barracks facilities provided for women, including privacy considerations in bathrooms, 1954 (USACEHQ).

---

[147] Morden, *Women's Army Corps*, 198. See also "Present Authorizations for Army Enlisted Women for Permanent Housing," 29 May 1958, Ft. Lee 228-01, WHC-377, Folder—Housing, Enlisted/Officer (General) (1957-63), WAC Museum Archives, Ft. Lee, VA for details on space authorizations and configurations.

Figure 60. WAC barrack kitchenette, Ft. McClellan, 1954
(WAC Museum, Vertical Files, File: Inspections of Construction VI-A-13).

The Army's brand new WAC Training Center, opened in 1954 at Fort McClellan, Alabama, however, incorporated all of the new standards (Figure 61). Basic recruits were housed in barracks that had 3 stories and a basement (Figure 62). The recruits lived on the second and third floors in open, unpartitioned squad bays, with each bay containing 45 to 50 cots, footlockers, wall lockers, and steel clothes closets (Figure 63). Each floor also had several cadre rooms, a large bathroom, and a laundry room equipped with ironing boards and automatic washers and dryers. Located on the first floor of the building were offices for the company commander and staff, a kitchen, reception area, dayroom, and bathroom with private toilets, individual showers, and two bathtubs. Offices and storage rooms for the unit supply officer, luggage rooms, and a mailroom were contained in the basement.[148] Enlisted students, student officers, and officer candidates attending the WAC School were housed in barracks similar in design to those for basic recruits, except that partitions were provided between every two cots in the squad bays.

---

[148] Morden, *Women's Army Corps*, 149-50; see also *Women's Army Corps* (Recruitment Brochure), circa 1955, Women in Military Service for America Memorial Foundation, Inc. Archives, Washington, DC, 1-2 for description of WAC Center barracks facilities.

Figure 61. WAC Training Center at Fort McClellan, AL, mid-1950s
(WAC Museum, Vertical Files, File: Activation VI-A-1).

Figure 62. Typical Enlisted Women's barracks under construction at WAC Training Center,
Fort McClellan, 1953 (WAC Museum, Vertical Files, File: Construction VI-A-13).

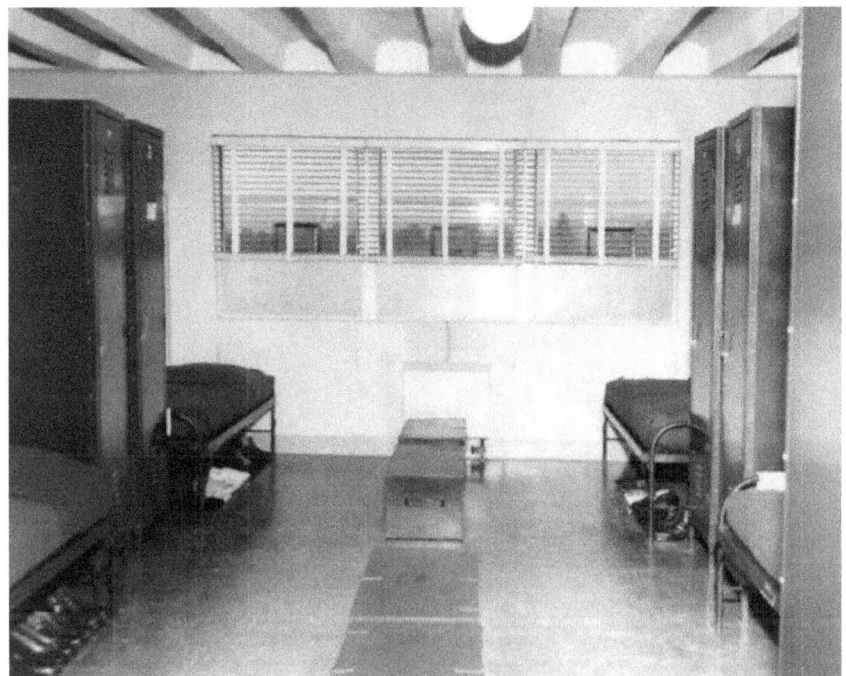

Figure 63. Basic trainee barracks interior, WAC Center, Fort McClellan, 1955 (WAC Museum, Vertical Files, File: UA WAC School – Facilities/Buildings/Grounds VI-A-17).

WAC officers, on the other hand, lived in BOQs in the WAC area. "Lieutenants and captains shared a suite, which consisted of two bedrooms separated by a bathroom [Figure 64]. Majors and above had individual suites-living room, bedroom, and bath [Figure 65]. The few small cottages available were assigned to the officers who occupied key positions, e.g., the WAC Center commander/School commandant, assistant commandant, battalion commander" [Figure 66].[149]

---

[149] Morden, *Women's Army Corps*, 149-50.

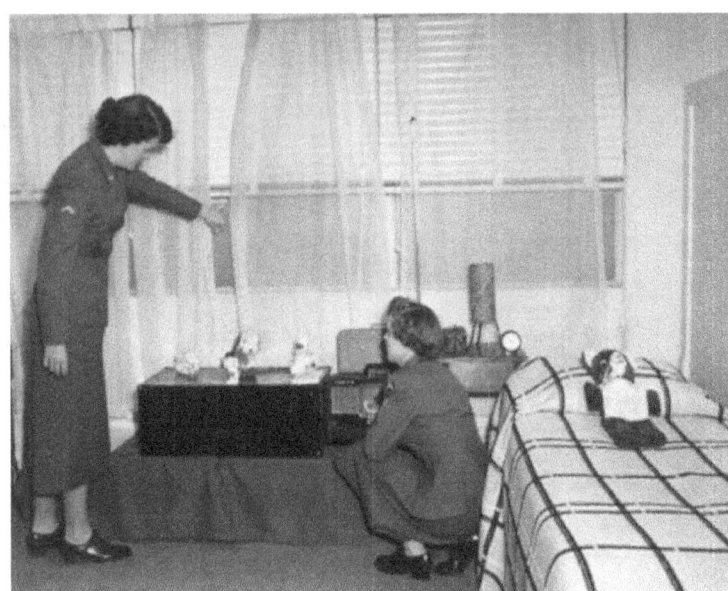

Figure 64. Two-person officer suite, WAC Center, Fort McClellan, 1955 (WAC Museum, Vertical Files: File: UA WAC School – Facilities/Buildings/Grounds VI-A-17).

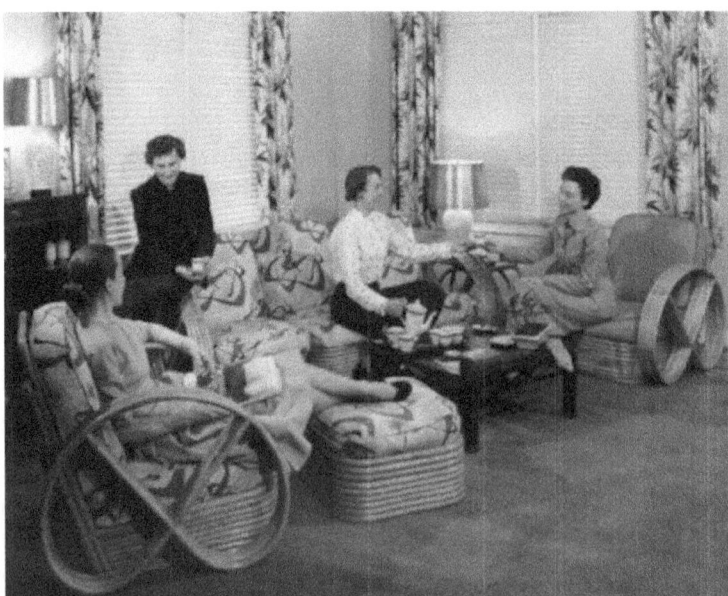

Figure 65. WAC Center Commander's living room, Fort McClellan (WAC Museum, Vertical Files, File: UA WAC School – Facilities/Buildings/Grounds VI-A-17).

Figure 66. Senior officers quarters at WAC Center, Fort McClellan (WAC Museum, Vertical Files, File: UA WAC School – Facilities/Buildings/Grounds VI-A-17).

Physical accommodations for women were similar in the other services, particularly for basic recruits. Each service promised that the women would reside in "dormitory-style" barracks, that were comfortable, well-lighted and heated, and often included "laundry rooms; kitchenettes; lounges for reading, writing, or just relaxing," as well as game rooms.[150] For enlisted servicewomen stationed to regular duty, housing standards called for partitioned cubicles, to allow for increased privacy.

For bachelor officer housing, there were significant discrepancies both among and within the services regarding what was accepted as suitable or

---

[150] *Share a Proud Tradition, The United States Marine Corps* (Recruitment Brochure), Lithographed by McCandlish Lithograph Corporation, 1958, Women in Military Service for America Memorial Foundation, Inc. Archives, Washington, DC, 9; *Women's Army Corps* (Recruitment Brochure), 1-2; *It's the Vogue* (Recruit Brochure), circa 1950s, Reference File—Women Marines: (2 of 2) Brochures/Publications, Washington Navy Yards, Marine Corps Historical Center Archives, Washington, DC; and William O. Grossman (USAF Recruiting Office), *Your Daughter in the U.S. Air Force* (Stockton, CA: USAF Recruiting Office, 1966), Collection no. 171964AIC (Sidney Dungey Keen), Women in Military Service for America Memorial Foundation, Inc. Archives, Washington, DC, 7.

unsuitable.[151] In 1954, standards were set that provided 450 square feet for male officers and 460 square feet for female officers, with the additional 10 square feet allowed for laundry and minor cooking facilities. Aside from the 10 additional square feet for women, BOQ standards were similar for men and women, with the minimum gross living area set at 65 percent of the gross floor area, and semi-private bathrooms (one for every two rooms—Figure 67).

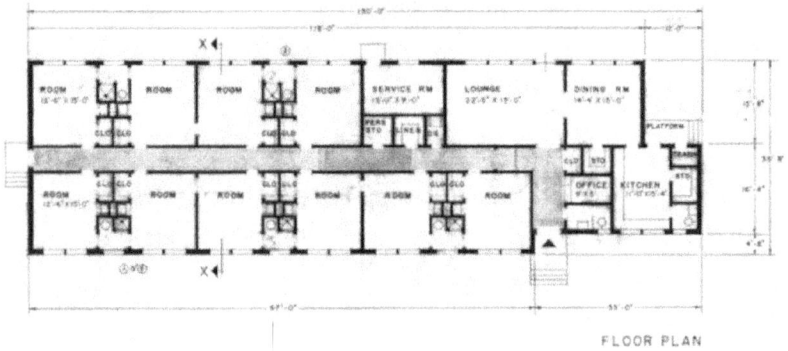

Figure 67. Plan for Navy BOQ with bath for every two rooms, 1953 (NARA).

However, "the Services experienced extreme difficulty in attempting to build suitable BOQ's under these standards and within the $5,000 Congressional cost limitation."[152] The Army, in particular, found that these types of facilities fared poorly in comparison to apartments provided to civilians in comparable occupations receiving comparable pay, insofar as officers received only minimum privacy. "The most privacy an officer could hope for was a private bedroom. Baths, living rooms, and messing facilities were all shared."[153]

In response, in 1958 and incorporating recommendations put forth by DACOWITS, the services developed what was known as the Fort Knox design for BOQs. The Fort Knox design allowed 500 square feet per officer in a garden style apartment. Junior officers were to have two-person suites (private bedrooms, shared living room, kitchens and bath), while field

---

[151] DACOWITS, "Report of the Ad Hoc Housing Committee," 1.

[152] *Report of ASD(M) Task Force on Bachelor Accommodations*, 62.

[153] Ibid., 62.

grade officers received private suites (bedroom, living room, and bath) with a shared kitchen for every two suites (Figure 68). While the Fort Knox design was not intended to differentiate between male and female housing (allowing for interchangeable spaces), it was mostly built for female BOQs (sometimes referred to as WOQs, Women's Officers Quarters) and Nurses.

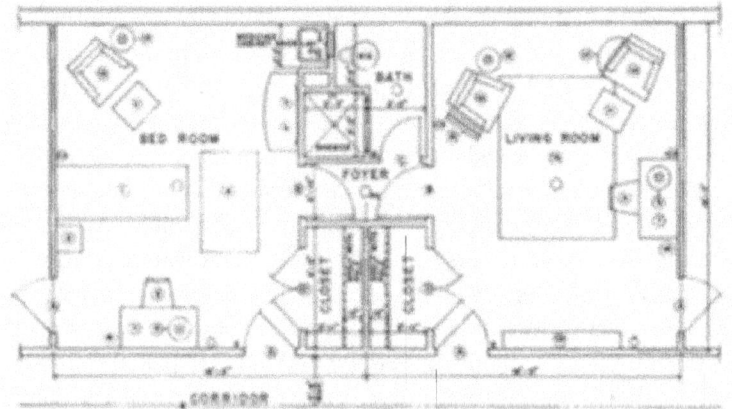

Figure 68. Two-person junior officer BOQ suite with bedrooms flanking a shared living room and bath (second bedroom not shown), similar to the Fort Knox design, 1954 (NARA).

Color Schemes

In addition to higher housing standards, during the 1950s women were also granted other amenities and special considerations with regard to their built environment. Most interesting among them was the use of pastel colored paint for barrack interiors. Traditionally, the services proscribed specific paint colors for various interiors, usually of grey, green, or tan shades. Women, however, were allowed (or found ways around the regulations) to use alternative colors, usually in a pastel shade. The Navy, for example, devised optimum paint color applications based on function, as determined by a comprehensive case history study.[154] According to the guidelines, the color peach was "best for spaces having little or no sun and for spaces occupied largely by women," whereas the men's walls were painted light green. Light green walls with medium green trim was deemed "suitable for ships' service stores, men's rooms, such as barber

---

[154] Faber Birren and Company, *The Application of Color to Shore Establishments* (Washington, DC: U.S. Navy Department, 1948).

shops, heads, and wash, locker and recreation rooms," but peach walls with terra cotta dado (molding) and trim were "adapted to women's rooms, such as wash, locker, and rest rooms," and toilet stalls could either have matching trim or be painted in light ivory."[155]

The other services were not always so specific in the pastel color shades that could be applied to the interior spaces occupied by women (Figure 69). In one instance, an Army barracks had been "brightened considerably" by the use of pastel pink paint applied to bulletin boards, scrub brushes, wash buckets, tin cans for cigarette ashes, and in the latrine, which was reportedly decked out with pink mirror frames, pink shelves over the sinks, pink toilet doors, and "pink elephants bounding across the drab pine walls."[156] In the highly traditional and regimented Marine Corps, where pastel colored paint was considered "a very radical innovation in the 1950s," many squad rooms were painted in soft shades of green with cream colored Venetian blinds, and "a persuasive commanding officer could often talk the battalion commander and S-4 into pastel colored paint."[157] Such was the case at the new Marine Corps barracks at Kaneohe Bay, Hawaii, referred to as "The Waldorf" because of its amenities, increased privacy, modern facilities, and the use of pastel colored paint.[158]

---

[155] Faber Birren and Company, *The Application of Color*, 30 and 36.

[156] Mildred K. and Milton Lehman, "The Lady Privates of Company D," *Cosmopolitan* (October 1951), Collection no. 4348 (Frances D. Ames), Women in Military Service for America Memorial Foundation, Inc. Archives, Washington, DC, 69.

[157] Stremlow, *History of the Women Marines*, 142; see also "Marine Women's Barracks," circa 1950s, Reference File—Women Marines: Press Releases, Washington Navy Yards, Marine Corps Historical Center Archives, Washington, DC, 2.

[158] Stremlow, *History of the Women Marines*, 53.

Figure 69. WAC barracks with pastel painting, White Sands, 1965 (WAC Museum, Vertical Files, File: Housing Enlisted Survey of 1964-65).

Support Facilities

Other amenities that began appearing on the installation landscape during this time period often included Service Clubs for women, or at minimum, modifications to existing Service Clubs to incorporate female-oriented activities, such as "ceramics, costume jewelry making, dress design and sewing, painting and sculpture, music, dramatics, folk and ballroom dancing, photography and group singing" (Figure 70 and Figure 71).[159] Also, female restrooms and "powder rooms"—provided for women only—were also added to Service Clubs, Reception Centers, Officers' Clubs and other similar facilities (Figure 72 and Figure 73).

---

[159] (AFP 34-7-1, The Air Force Service Club Program), cited in *Women in the Air Force, Enlisted Personnel*, 39-5, 9.

Figure 70. Dance at WAC Service Club #1, Fort McClellan. Club had TV room, music room, reading room, game room, snack bar, craft and hobby shop (WAC Museum, Vertical Files, File: Facilities/Buildings/Grounds VI-A-17).

Figure 71. Hobby shop with yarn and loom at Fort Lee, VA (WAC Museum, Vertical Files, File: Crafts V-b-17).

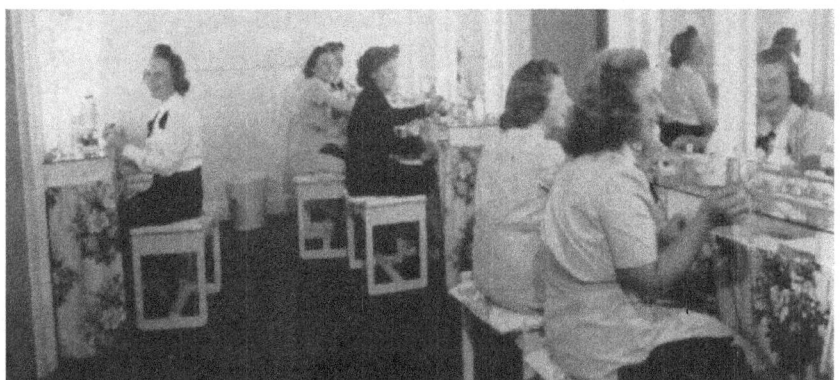

Figure 72. WAVES Town Club powder room, Naval Air Training Base, Pensacola, FL, WWII (WIMSA, Document File, Collection of Blanche Schultz #3464, in *The Naval Air Training Bases, Pensacola, Florida Thru World War II*, 1945).

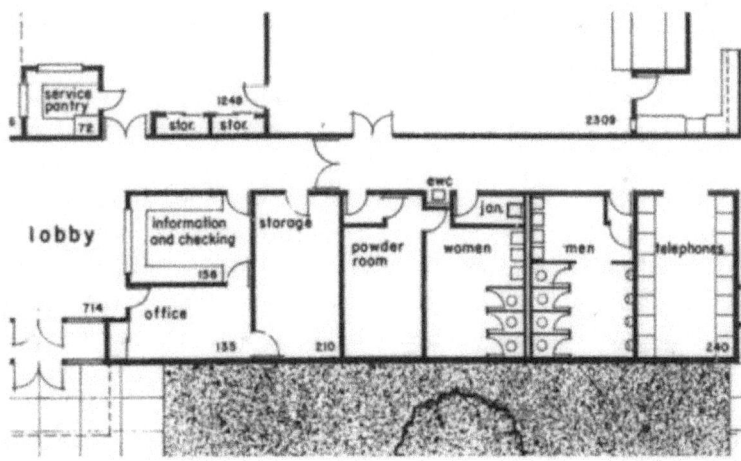

Figure 73. Plan showing powder room in service club/post exchange building, 1966 (USACEHQ).

Training

Official policy regarding training changed very little during the 1950s. Women continued to receive essentially the same basic training as the men, except for combat training and the addition of female-specific courses, such as make-up and hygiene (Figure 74).

Figure 74. Class in restaurant etiquette for "Individual Standards & Social Concepts" course, Fort Lee, VA (WAC Museum, Vertical Files, File: Enlisted Permanent Party Training V-a-27).

In some service schools, women began attending classes with men in a coeducational environment, which was deemed acceptable because it mirrored emerging civilian trends.[160] The training centers established by the Marine Corps, Navy, and Air Force were still in operation and still maintained their segregated women's area. The Army, however, as mentioned above, moved its WAC Center and School from Fort Lee, Virginia, to Fort McClellan, Alabama. Fort McClellan was chosen for the new WAC Center in 1951, construction began in 1952, and it was opened in 1954. The WAC area was situated on approximately 249 acres of land, and was divided into two major sections—the WAC School and the WAC Center.[161] The headquarters building of the WAC Center contained offices, twenty-five classrooms, a bookstore, library, a small auditorium/gymnasium, message center and printing shop (Figure 75 and Figure 76). The battalion complex also included a mess hall capable of seating 400 at a time, and a building for "fitting and issuing WAC uniforms, and parade grounds."[162] Other fa-

---

[160] Department of the Army, *Troop Topics: Leave It To the WAC*, Department of the Army Pamphlet No. 20, (Washington, DC: Department of the Army, 1951), Collection no. 3547, Women in Military Service for America Memorial Foundation, Inc. Archives, Washington, DC, 8.

[161] Morden, *Women's Army Corps*, 148; and see also U.S. Women's Army Corps School, *Role of the WAC*, 22, 27, 30, and 37.

[162] Morden, *Women's Army Corps*, 148, 149-50.

cilities provided for the Center and School included service clubs and a beauty shop.

Figure 75. Headquarters of the U.S. Women's Army Corps Center, Fort McClellan, AL, 1971 (WIMSA, Document File, Collection of Christine Henry #4780).

Figure 76. WAC Classroom, Fort McClellan (WAC Museum, Vertical files, File: UA WAC School – Facilities/Buildings/Grounds VI-A-17).

Figure 77. WACS march past barracks, Fort McClellan, 1654 (WAC Museum, Vertical Files, File: UA WAC School – Facilities/Buildings/Grounds VI-A-17).

5 Vietnam and the 1960s: Typewriter Soldiers

In historical terms, as well as in our collective memory, the "1960s," more than just merely a decade reference, has become a phrase that stands for social change. It encapsulated a time of radical change in American culture and society caused by the generational clash between emerging liberal modernism and conservative traditionalism. Referencing the "1960s" conjures images of such things as race riots and the Civil Rights Movement, political assassinations, violent demonstrations, free love, hippies, Woodstock, drugs, bra burning and the rise of feminism, and, of course, the anti-government and anti-war movement. "During this period, the country became immersed in computers, the space program, the problems of the poor and the minorities, the resistance to the draft, drug usage, the generation gap, the mini, the midi, and the maxi. The impact of the technological, sociological, and economic changes in society challenged the Army and indeed all organizations and institutions in America to modernize and humanize their approach to people problems."[163]

This sea change in culture and society affected the military, especially the role of women in the military. The women's movement and the growth of feminism resulted not only in the proposal (but not ratification) of the Equal Rights Amendment, but "presented society with more liberal ideas regarding women's work, dress, and legal status," and "with them, changes in long-standing social customs, relationships, and moral standards."[164] While society accepted these changes over the course of the 1960s, the military establishment spent the 1960s resisting these changes. As America prepared for war in Vietnam, Jack Anderson of the *Washington Post* charged that the military had produced servicewomen who were 'typewriter soldiers,' "more concerned with the arts of makeup than the arts of war [Figure 78]." Indeed, in ignoring the fledgling feminist movement of

---

[163] U.S. Women's Army Corps School, *Role of the WAC*, 41.

[164] Morden, *Women's Army Corps*, 233.

the 1960s, "the women's programs remained wedded to the dead-ended, outmoded philosophies of women's roles devised in the fifties."[165]

Figure 78. WAC "typewriter soldiers" alongside men, Fort Custer, MI, WWII (WIMSA, Vertical Photo File, Collection of Ann Zimmerman).

For the traditional and conservative minded military leaders, including the leaders of the women's programs, incorporating the changes pushed by the women's movement would have meant a decline in both the standards and status of military women. One of the many improvements for women in the military to have developed in the 1950s was the significant decline in the negative connotations associated with female military service. This resulted largely from a dedicated effort to ensure that servicewomen not only were perceived as, but actually were, elite in terms of education, decorum, and appearance. Having won this hard-fought battle, military leaders were reluctant to accept that the majority of society had let go of its narrow definitions of appropriate gender role behavior. In the early 1960s, two general themes characterized the women's programs, the "continued commitment to the concept of 'elitism,' manifested by double standards in recruitment, assignments, and other policies," and "an almost obsessive emphasis on preserving femininity and projecting a 'ladylike image'."[166]

---

[165] Holm, *Women in the Military*, 175.

[166] Ibid., 179.

Despite the military's initial rejection of the women's movement, the pressure of necessity and growing public interest in and sympathy for the movement eventually forced the military to consider change. The growing anti-establishment and anti-war movements, in conjunction with other social movements of the 1960s, caused manpower shortages for the military. Furthermore, the acceptance of the women's movement by American society directly correlated to expanding opportunities in the labor force for women. These combined trends directly challenged the military's ability to meet strength quotas, especially in its women's programs as American women were choosing the more liberal and progressive opportunities offered in the private sector over the restrictive and limited opportunities offered by the military. As a result, the advent of the Vietnam War (1965-1975) forced military leaders to make changes that fell more in line with mainstream America.

Quality of Life and Housing Studies

For the bulk of the 1960s, especially in the early days of the war when the government believed that it would prevail in the Far East, the military was more about conducting studies on what type of changes were needed and how to implement them than it was about implementing actual change. It was not until the very end of the decade and the beginning of the 1970s, when the war bogged down and public opinion at home began to turn against the conflict, that the military began enacting change.

One such study, conducted in 1962 by the Army's Enlisted Personnel Directorate in the Office of Personnel Operations, sought explanations for the declining enlistment rate of women and offered recommendations on ways to reverse the trend. What this study, as well as the numerous others conducted across all service branches, revealed was that the limited career and promotional opportunities available to women in the military was not competitive with what women could obtain in the private sector. Further, the study found that the "restrictive" and "unappealing" living conditions were also driving women away.[167] As a result, throughout the 1960s, the military focused increasing attention on quality-of-life issues, particularly housing conditions. This was manifested in study after study, many of which included personnel surveys, the formation of committees whose sole

---

[167] Report cited in Morden, *Women's Army Corps*, 192-93.

purpose was to devise new housing recommendations and building designs, and, eventually, the implementation of these new designs. More than ever before, the military realized how important housing and living conditions were in the recruitment and retention of quality personnel, something that became of paramount importance by the end of the decade.

In large part, the emphasis on housing conditions as a factor of morale and quality of life was carried over from experience and conclusions obtained during the 1950s. In 1959, a DACOWITS report on recommended standards for enlisted women argued that adequate housing was "one of the most important factors in the retention of women in the services and in the maintenance of high morale."[168] The Army reenlistment study mentioned above delved further into the connection between housing and the career decisions of servicewomen, revealing that privacy mattered much more to women than such things as modern or air-conditioned buildings. "Men and women expressed different concerns regarding housing. Enlisted men seldom asked for privacy or considered their barracks a home. Women, on the other hand, wanted a secure, private place to call home, with kitchens, reception rooms, and laundry facilities. For building security some post commanders provided only signs that read, 'off limits to male personnel.' Some provided locked doors that opened from the inside with a crash bar. When commanders could not provide adequate security, some units bought their own locks or kept a night watch in their own barracks; most improvised kitchens, reception rooms, and laundry rooms."[169]

Privacy was also important to female officers. Memos circulating at the highest levels of the military acknowledged the impact of inadequate BOQs on the military's ability to attract and retain women with a high career potential.[170] The biggest mark against the current standards of BOQs was shared bathrooms, kitchens, and community areas. Studies found the lack

---

[168] DACOWITS, "Review of Ad-Hoc Housing Committee," 3.

[169] Morden, *Women's Army Corps*, 196.

[170] Lt. Gen. J.L. Richardson (Deputy Chief of Staff for Personnel) to Chief of Staff, U.S. Army, "Policies and Objectives to Improve Living Conditions for Officers Without Dependents," June 1963, and Gen. Barksdale Hamlett (Acting Chief of Staff, U.S. Army) to Lt. Gen. Leonard D. Heaton, June 28, 1963, Ft. Lee 228-01, WHC-373, Folder—Housing, WAC Museum Archives, Ft. Lee, VA, 1.

of privacy in BOQs frequently caused officers to live off post at their own expense in order to achieve "a reasonable degree of freedom and privacy," which in turn caused "a substantial curtailment of income and subsequent dissatisfaction with service life."[171] It was also argued that the lack of private bathrooms in BOQs made it impossible to house both male and female officers in the same building, which could improve housing efficiency. In response to the findings of these initial studies, housing moved to the forefront of domestic military concerns, particularly after President Johnson announced his intent to improve morale and review housing standards. In a speech to the National War College at Fort McNair in August 1964, President Johnson stated, "I very much want our uniformed citizens to be first-class citizens in every respect... I am in this regard directing...review of such matters as housing...so that we can at the earliest possible moment take whatever steps both human equity and national defense may require to enhance the standing and the morale of those who defend us."[172]

By the end of 1964, three major housing studies had been completed and submitted to the Secretary of Defense, who appointed a new study group to evaluate these reports and present recommendations based on them. One of the reports, prepared by DACOWITS, presented a "formal study of bachelor officer and enlisted housing including a summary of past DACOWITS recommendations, an assessment of current housing, the effect of the present housing situation on morale and on retention of trained and skilled personnel, factors affecting construction of bachelor officer quarters, and a comparison between standards presently applied nationally to civilian and to military housing."[173] The Army also submitted a report based on extensive surveys and studies it had completed within the

---

[171] Lt. Col. Carol M. Williams (Executive Officer) to Lt. Col. Kathryn J. Royster (Executive Secretary to DACOWITS), "Comments Pertaining to BOQ Housing Plans," May 14, 1963, Ft. Lee 228-01, WHC-373, Folder—Housing, WAC Museum Archives, Ft. Lee, VA, 2.

[172] Office of the Deputy Chief of Staff for Logistics (Department of the Army), "Bachelor Officer Housing," October 16, 1964, Ft. Lee 228-01, WHC-373, Folder—Housing, WAC Museum Archives, Ft. Lee, VA, foreword.

[173] Talley, *Highlights of the Defense Advisory Committee on Women in the Services*, 10.

past several years.[174] The final report submitted was referred to as the Tri-Service Study. The Tri-Service Study originated in the Department of Defense, which distributed a draft of revised housing standards to the Army, Navy, and Air Force for comments. At the suggestion of the Air Force, a tri-service committee was formed to study the habitability of current housing and develop standards for both officers and enlisted personnel, which would then be submitted as the official position of all three services.[175] The Tri-Service Study found "startling deficiencies" that had military personnel, in many instances, living in BOQs and barracks that were "wholly inadequate and inconsistent with current standards of living throughout the United States."[176]

The Marine Corps, although its construction and design services were provided by the Navy's Bureau of Yards and Docks and used Navy housing standards, conducted its own study in 1964 on the issue of poor recruitment and retention of Women Marines. Colonel Bishop, Director of Women Marines, commissioned Women Marines Study No. 1-64, which recommended the improvement of living conditions. On this "she was emphatic. It was not just that the women needed more privacy, she argued, but they spend more time in the barracks than men; the women staff NCOs who remain in the service are more likely to be single than male Marines who marry and live in their family homes; the majority of career women Marines would never share in the large expenditures made on married quarters and in the support of dependents' programs; and because the women took such good care of their barracks, inspecting officers

---

[174] In 1964, the Army DWAC conducted extensive housing surveys of conditions and facilities available for women at Army installations across the country, see "Completed WAC Housing Questionnaires from all CONUS WAC Detachments in response to call for information from the Office of the Director, U.S. Women's Army Corps," 1964, Ft. Lee 228-01, WHC-376, Folder—Housing, Enlisted Survey of (1964-65), WAC Museum Archives, Ft. Lee, VA. It also produced several reports on housing, see Deputy Chief of Staff for Personnel, Director—WAC, *Department of Defense Instruction: Standards and Criteria for Construction—Permanent Barracks and Bachelor Officer Quarters* (Washington, DC: Department of Defense, August 1964), Ft. Lee 228-01, WHC-374, Folder—Housing Doctrine & Policy (1963-65), WAC Museum Archives, Ft. Lee, VA; Office of the Director, WAC, "Background on Enlisted Housing;" Office of the Deputy Chief of Staff for Logistics, "Bachelor Officer Housing."

[175] See Office of the Director, WAC, "Background on Enlisted Housing," 4.

[176] Robert G. McClintic, "BOQ/Barracks Plan Expected to Get Green Light," *Journal of the Armed Forces* 103, no. 37 (May 14, 1966), Ft. Lee 228-01, WHC-378, Folder—Housing, Misc Reports (1965-67), WAC Museum Archives, Ft. Lee, VA; Tri-Service Committee, "Tri-Service Recommended Changes to Proposed Department of Defense Instruction," (*Standards and Criteria for Construction—Permanent Housing for Bachelor Officer and Bachelor Enlisted Personnel*), 1964, Ft. Lee 228-01, WHC-377, Folder—Housing, Enlisted/Officer (General) (1957-63), WAC Museum Archives, Ft. Lee, VA.

were duly impressed by the cleanliness and attempts to create a homelike atmosphere."[177] As such, Colonel Bishop recommended the construction of new barracks designed with the particular needs of women in mind, or at least the complete rehabilitation of existing buildings.

Because this report "precipitated so much opposition," the Marine Corps Commandant established the Pepper Board, a study group charged with proposing "a program to render the peacetime service of Women Marines of optimum benefit to the Marine Corps."[178] The Pepper Board made several recommendations that were enacted, including adding new duty stations for Women Marines, and making it possible to be assigned to any post or station, by allowing women to live off post in the absence of space availability in designated female barracks. Essentially, this by-passed the prior regulation prohibiting the assignment of women in groups of fewer than 50.[179] When it came to housing conditions, however, the Pepper Board deferred the issue to the Department of Defense task force organized by the Assistant Secretary of Defense (Manpower). In the meantime, though, the Marine Corps did reevaluate barracks and furnishings and installed lockers and dressers in recruit housing in order to reduce the austerity of the barracks (Figure 79).[180]

---

[177] Stremlow, *History of the Women Marines*, 71.

[178] Ibid. The "Woman Marine Program Study Group," was named the Pepper Board after its chairman, Lieutenant General Robert H. Pepper.

[179] Ibid., 72.

[180] A new clothing layout inspection requiring certain items to be displayed hanging in a locker hastened the addition of lockers to recruit barracks. See Stremlow, *History of the Women Marines*, 72.

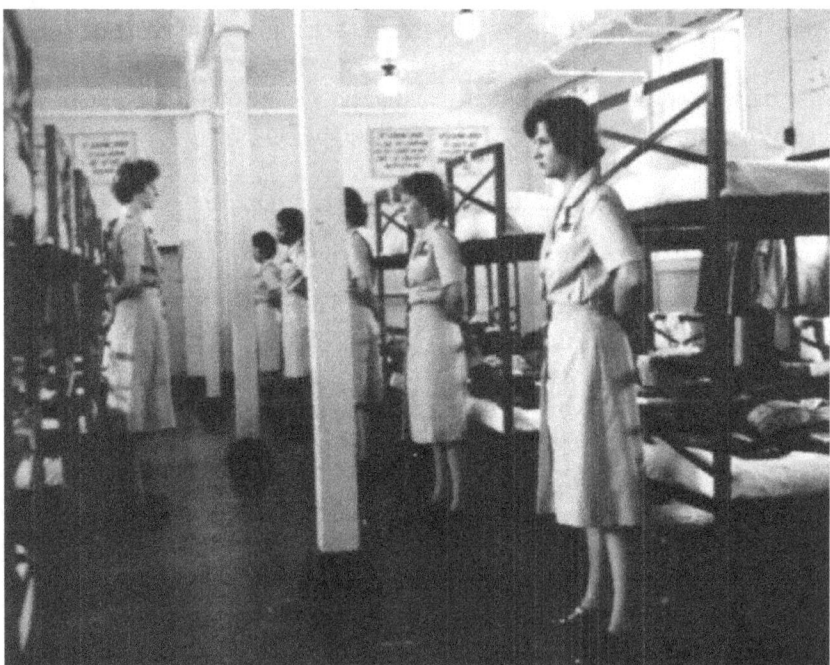

Figure 79. Austere WM recruit barracks at Parris Island, SC, 1967. In *Marine Corps Recruit Depot Yearbook, Platoon 4B* (WIMSA, Document File, Collection of Ellie Lopez #4167).

The task force issued its report in May 1966, entitled *Report of ASD(M) Task Force on Bachelor Accommodations, Troop Housing, Bachelor Officer Quarters.* The task force relied not only on the three studies submitted in 1964, but also conducted its own housing surveys in 1965. These surveys revealed that installation commanders and military personnel alike "indicated a direct relationship between quarters satisfaction, mission effectiveness, and career intentions."[181] Both male and female personnel considered living conditions provided by barracks as a major factor in their career conditions. Specifically, when presented with a list of 20 items, and asked to choose from this list the most important reason for leaving the service (whether or not they actually intended to leave), male personnel ranked barracks housing conditions as one of the top three reasons. Asked the same question, female personnel of all ranks rated barracks housing conditions as the major reason for leaving the service. Furthermore, when asked to choose from the same list, fewer than 1 percent of the respon-

---

[181] *Report of ASD(M) Task Force on Bachelor Accommodations*, 122.

dents selected barracks housing conditions as a major reason for staying in the service, instead ranking this factor, usually, as number 15 out of 20. As such, the report found it evident that present barracks housing conditions did almost nothing "to influence them to remain in the service," and indeed caused people to leave the service.[182]

Housing Design

Hand in hand with all of these housing studies came numerous recommendations for policy changes and proposed new building plans. Until the mid to late 1960s, the only change made to housing policy since the mid 1950s was the approval of the Fort Knox design for BOQs in 1959, which increased the gross maximum floor area to 500 square feet per officer, with a gross minimum living area of 330 square feet per unit. This policy revision permitted a private bath for each officer as well as "a kitchenette where messing facilities were not an integral part of the structure," but more significantly removed the distinction between male and female officer housing standards.[183] By 1962, interchangeable spaces for BOQs was initiated (implemented in 1963) so long as the BOQs provided private baths and bedrooms for each officer. In accordance, BOQ design plans were developed that provided for coed facilities with buildings for 16 or fewer officers in the residential style, 16 to 100 officers in the motel-type style, and more than 100 officers in the high-rise style of construction (Figure 80).[184]

Of course, simply because plans were in place did not mean they were implemented—construction budgets often prevented their full implementation and thus much of the 1960s was spent haggling over standards, space

---

[182] Ibid.

[183] DACOWITS, "Review of DACOWITS Ad-Hoc Housing Studies," 4 and *Report of ASD(M) Task Force on Bachelor Accommodations*, 64; kitchens were still perceived as being primarily for women as "Civilian and army social customs prescribe that, in meeting social obligations, women entertain in their homes." Col. Emily C. Gorman (Director, Women's Army Corps) to Deputy Chief of Staff for Personnel, "Furnishings for Female Officers' Quarters," with FY58 "Housing" addendum attached, January 18, 1963, Ft. Lee 228-01, WHC-373, Folder—Housing, WAC Museum Archives, Ft. Lee, VA, see addendum.

[184] Randall Shoemaker, "Better BOQs Seen In Latest DA Plan," *Army Times* (August 7, 1963), Ft. Lee 228-01, WHC-377, Folder—Housing, Enlisted/Officer (General) (1957-63), WAC Museum Archives, Ft. Lee, VA.

requirements and cost limitations.[185] DACOWITS and the women's program directors continuously argued with engineers over not sacrificing bath, kitchen, and closet facilities for cost-per-square-foot limitations. Private kitchen space, in particular, was often controversial and viewed as unnecessary. This was encapsulated by a conversation between Lt. Colonel Hyatt and WAC representative Colonel Harper. Colonel Hyatt "had some idea the reason women wanted single kitchens was they couldn't get along sharing kitchens," but Colonel Harper "disabused him of this idea," stating the "objective was that BOQ's could be occupied by both sexes," and afford accommodations more in line with that available in civilian life. Simply, if only certain rooms had kitchens, then this limited the interchangeability of spaces between men and women. It was not that women could not share kitchens with each other but that regulations prohibited them from sharing with men. In addition, Colonel Harper argued against cutting the size

---

[185] See Talley, *Highlights of the Defense Advisory Committee on Women in the Services*; Emily C. Gorman, Col. (Director, Women's Army Corps) to Post Engineer, Fort Myer, Virginia, "Enlisted Women's Barracks, Fort Myer, Virginia," November 24, 1964, Ft. Lee 228-01, WHC-378, Folder—Housing, Misc Reports (1965-67), WAC Museum Archives, Ft. Lee, VA; J.L. Richardson, Lt. Gen. (Deputy Chief of Staff for Personnel, U.S. Army) to Deputy Chief of Staff for Logistics, "Enlisted Women's Barracks, Fort Myer, Virginia," December 8, 1964, Ft. Lee 228-01, WHC-378, Folder—Housing, Misc Reports (1965-67), WAC Museum Archives, Ft. Lee, VA; L.J. Lincoln, Lt. Gen. (Deputy Chief of Staff for Logistics, U.S. Army) to Deputy Chief of Staff for Personnel, "Enlisted Women's Barracks, Fort Myer, Virginia," December 18, 1964, Ft. Lee 228-01, WHC-378, Folder—Housing, Misc Reports (1965-67), WAC Museum Archives, Ft. Lee, VA; and see also a series of memos dealing with space criteria in EW barracks, all contained in Ft. Lee 228-01, WHC-377, Folder—Housing, Enlisted/Officer (General) (1957-63); for example, Maj. Marie Kehrer, wrote two Memorandum for Record titled, "Exclusion of Company Storage Space from 140 Square Feet Per EW Gross Barracks," dated April 2, 1958 and August 3, 1960; see also, Floyd S. Bryant to Secretary of the Army, "Request for Waiver in Provisions of Department of Defense Instruction NO. 4270.4," August 12, 1957; Col. E.C. Paules, (Acting Chief, Construction Division) to Director of Women's Army Corps, "Request for Waiver of DOD Instruction 4270.4," September 5, 1957; Col. E.C. Paules, (Acting Chief, Construction Division) to Chief of Engineers, "Standard Plans for Enlisted Women's Barracks," September 5, 1957; Brig. Gen. E.A. Brown, Jr., (Assistant Chief of Engineers for Military Construction), to Assistant Secretary of the Army, CMA, "Request for Waiver in Provisions of Department of Defense Instruction 4270.4, June 16, 1954," June 19. 1957; and Dewey Short (Assistant Secretary of the Army, Civil-Military Affairs) to Assistant Secretary of Defense (Properties and Installations), "Request for Waiver in Provisions of Department of Defense Instruction 4270.4, June 16, 1954," n.d., Ft. Lee 228-01, WHC-377, Folder—Housing, Enlisted/Officer (General) (1957-63), WAC Museum Archives, Ft. Lee, VA; see also series of memos dealing with the impact of cost limitations on square footage and amenities, all contained in Ft. Lee 228-01, WHC-377, Folder—Housing, Enlisted/Officer (General) (1957-63); for example, Maj. Gen. J.B. Lampert (Director of Military Construction) to Deputy Chief of Staff for Logistics, "EW Barracks," June 6, 1962; Col. Emily C. Gorman (Director, Women's Army Corps) to Deputy Chief of Staff for Personnel, "EW Barracks," August 16, 1962; and Lt. Col. H. Foster, Memorandum for Record, "Meeting on WAC Enlisted Barracks," September 18, 1962, Ft. Lee 228-01, WHC-377, Folder—Housing, Enlisted/Officer (General) (1957-63), WAC Museum Archives, Ft. Lee, VA.

of the kitchen as proposed designs that did so left "barely room for one person."[186]

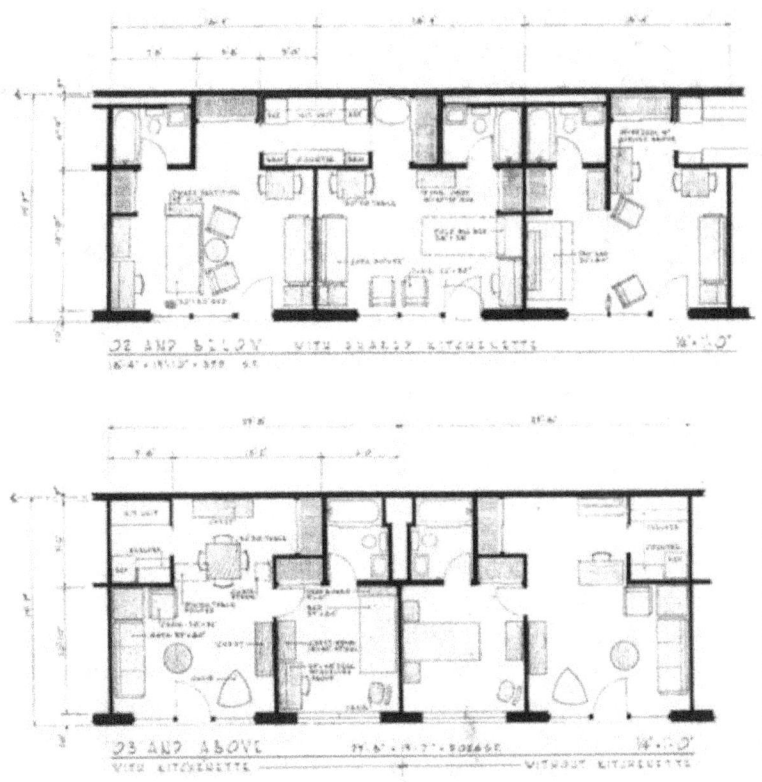

Figure 80. Gender-neutral motel type BOQ concept sketch, 1967 (NARA).

---

[186] Deputy Chief of Staff for Logistics (U.S. Army) to Chief of Engineers (U.S. Army), "Design of Bachelor Officer Quarters," 1963, Ft. Lee 228-01, WHC-373, Folder—Housing, WAC Museum Archives, Ft. Lee, VA.

Tri-Service Design

As for enlisted personnel housing, even though DACOWITS was encouraged by the Department of Defense's special task force on housing and the reports coming out of that committee, they continued pressuring the Secretary of Defense to implement the standards they recommended in 1964.[187] In particular, DACOWITS set their sights on design and construction plans for the new barracks complex to be built at Fort Myer, Virginia. Congress authorized $2.3 million in 1965 (and an additional $278,000 in 1966) to build the Tri-Service Enlisted Women's Barracks capable of housing 700 women from the Army, Navy, and Air Force at Fort Myer.[188] Ground-breaking for the barracks occurred in May 1966 and women began occupying the building in March 1968. Each service was assigned a section of the building and the women "followed the regulations and policies of their parent service regarding personnel management, wearing of the uniform, military courtesy, and other procedures."[189]

Similar to the ongoing arguments regarding space allocations and amenities in BOQ designs, the WAC Director and her representatives also clashed with engineers over the building design in terms of the size of bedrooms, closets, shower rooms, laundry rooms, company offices, and visitor reception areas. Although the Director demanded the "greatest possible space for privacy, storage, and convenience," she was overruled by the engineers with regard to room and closet size and the placement of offices and storage rooms. Despite these shortcomings, kitchenettes were installed on each floor and central bathrooms and laundry rooms were included in each wing and every floor of the H-shaped building (Figure 81). The building was also equipped with air-conditioning, telephone system, lounge, game rooms, recreation areas, and private mail boxes for each woman (Figure 82).[190] Still, "when four women were assigned to one room, beds were double-decked to make room for chairs, TV stands, lockers, and desks," although non-commissioned officers (NCOs) were eventually authorized to live off post in order to make more room in the barracks and

---

[187] Talley, *Highlights of the Defense Advisory Committee on Women in the Services*, 12.

[188] See Morden, *Women's Army Corps*, 200; Women Marines in the area continued to live at Marine Corps headquarters, in the Henderson Hall barracks.

[189] Morden, *Women's Army Corps*, 201.

[190] Ibid., 200.

undeck the beds. At the heart of the issue was the belief on behalf of WAC representatives that decision-makers failed to "understand that singles want the same amount of space and comforts that married people do," and that decision-makers assumed "single people spend their time at the clubs or sitting around in dayrooms watching TV."[191] In direct rebuttal to this, members of DACOWITS and the women's programs began arguing against the "theory that barracks should only be used for sleeping accommodations," in favor of designs that were more in line with "real living accommodations," that enabled residents to "pursue hobbies and play games in their quarters."[192]

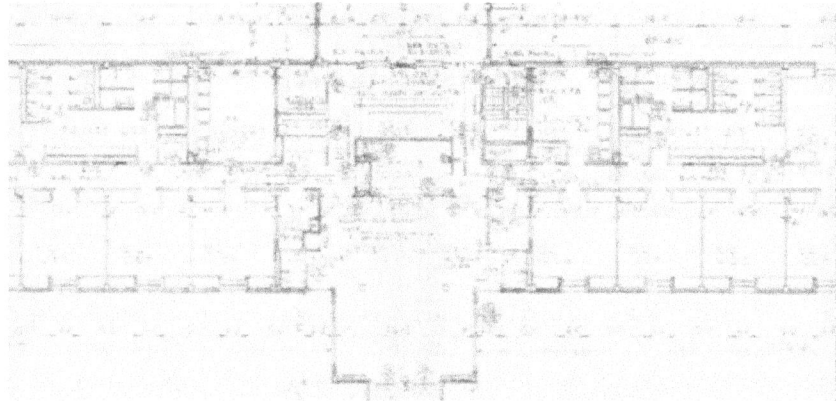

Figure 81. Bathrooms, kitchens, and lounges, Tri-Service Enlisted Women's Barracks, 1955 (Fort Myer).

---

[191] Ibid., 201.

[192] Robert G. McClintic, "Life in Bachelor Quarters May Undergo Face-Lifting," *Journal of the Armed Forces* 103, no. 37 (May 14, 1966), Ft. Lee 228-01, WHC-378, Folder—Housing, Misc Reports (1965-67), WAC Museum Archives, Ft. Lee, VA.

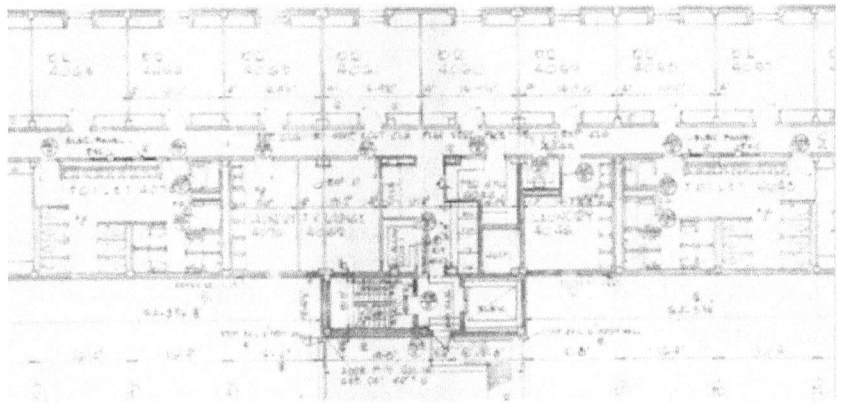

Figure 82. Recreation and visitor facilities Tri-Service Enlisted Women's Barracks, 1955 (Fort Myer).

DoD Minimum Housing Standards

Although too late for the Tri-Service design, this argument was reflected in Department of Defense Directive No. 4165.47 of April 6, 1967, issued by Secretary of Defense McNamara, establishing DoD-wide minimum housing standards.[193] The directives called for center hall motel-type barracks and three-person rooms with 166 square feet per enlisted woman (Figure 83).[194] Laundry, kitchen, and bathroom facilities, although still shared, became part of the standard design. The directives marked an increase in the amount of living space, up from 140 square feet per woman, in new construction which acknowledged the difficulty designers faced prior to 1964 (when the 140 square feet figure was first challenged) in trying to incorporate adequate standards within this limit, especially given cost restrictions.[195]

---

[193] Talley, *Highlights of the Defense Advisory Committee on Women in the Services*, 13.

[194] Beginning in 1968, enlisted men also received improved housing accommodations: E-1 men were housed in open bays with privacy partitions; E-2 through E-9 were housed in fully enclosed 1-, 2-, or 3-men rooms with shared latrines.

[195] Office of the Director, WAC, "Background on Enlisted Housing," 4.

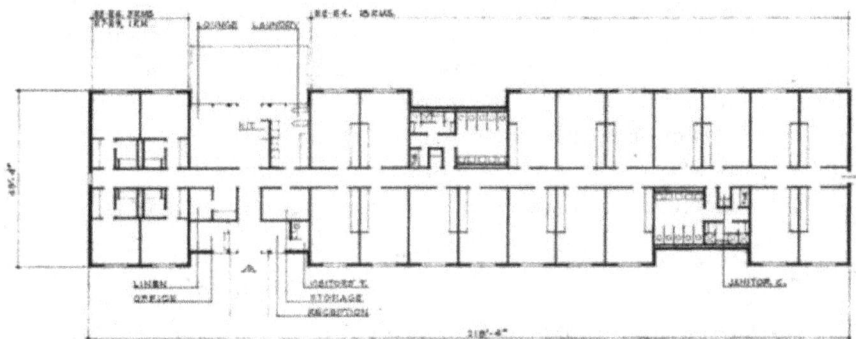

Figure 83. Enlisted Women's center-hall type barracks concept sketch, 1967 (USACEHQ).

In November, the Department of Defense Construction Criteria Manual was published, which outlined minimum housing standards.[196] The established standards allowed the following living area accommodations by rank: E-1 (Recruits) were to be housed in large rooms with a central toilet that accommodated between 30 to 60 people at 72 square feet per person; E-2 through E-4 received 310-square-foot rooms with 3 people per room and a central toilet for every 18 to 30 people; E-5 through E-6 received a 310-square-foot suite with a private bathroom shared by two people; and E-7 through E-9 personnel received private 310-square-foot suites with private bathrooms. New minimum standards dictated that women's toilets and showers be "enclosed in separate compartments." Men, while gaining enclosed toilets still had gang showers. Women also received a higher ratio of "water closets" and "lavatories" per person than men. This was true for all bathroom facilities in all buildings—usually at a ratio of one water closet for every 10 women in any facility where food was served or prepared, and 1 for every 15 in most other facilities (1 for every 25 in educational facilities).[197]

The new regulations also authorized enlisted personnel graded E-7 and above, as well as all officers, to receive a quarters allowance and live off post if not provided with adequate accommodations under the new stan-

---

[196] Department of Defense, Assistant Secretary of Defense (Installation and Logistics, "Department of Defense Instruction: Department of Defense Construction Criteria Manual," (Washington, DC: Department of Defense, 17 November 1967) (hereafter cited as DOD Construction Criteria Manual).

[197] Ibid., 3-3, 8-46, 8-54.

dards: "E-7 through E-9: A private sleeping room. Captains and up: An unshared bedroom, living room, and bathroom; access to a kitchen. Lieutenants and warrant officers: An unshared combination living and bedroom and a bathroom."[198] The last modification made to housing policy in the 1960s was in 1968 with the cancellation of the policy requiring that male and WAC barracks be separated. This allowed more flexibility in installation land use in terms of constructing and modifying barracks.

Training

Concerning training, the policies established in the 1950s still held sway throughout most of the 1960s. Recruit training was segregated, while advanced training and officer schools typically offered coeducational classes. Still, in the early part of the 1960s, physical training for women was "viewed as a means to keep the ladies 'fit and trim' and to improve posture, instead of as a method to build endurance, strength, or coordination or to prepare women to live in the field."[199] As the women's movement gained momentum, however, the changes it forced in the traditional military mindset eventually extended to training as well. By the late 1960s, as a direct reflection of larger social cultural changes, "training methods were revised to stress the relevance of training to the individual," and even hemlines were conservatively raised.[200]

---

[198] Morden, *Women's Army Corps*, 199.
[199] Holm, *Women in the Military*, 182-83.
[200] U.S. Women's Army Corps School, *Role of the WAC*, 41.

6 All Volunteer Force and the 1970s: Typewriter Soldiers No More

"The difficulty lies not in new ideas, but in escaping from old ones." Major General Jeanne Holm (USAF Ret.) used the above quote by Economist John Maynard Keyes to describe the nature of the conflict that began in the early 1970s between progressive social movements and the traditionally conservative military.[201] If the 1960s were a time of resistance to change, the 1970s were a time of both evolutionary and revolutionary change, especially for servicewomen.[202] President Richard Nixon's decision to end the draft, effective 30 June 1973, and institute an All-Volunteer Force (AVF) had a significant and dramatic impact on the United States military. The largest impact, it can be argued, was in how the military was forced to recruit women in greater numbers than ever before in order to compensate for the projected shortfall of eligible males. The ramifications of this impact were felt throughout the services, marking a watershed moment for the role of servicewomen. Like never before, the floodgates of opportunity and advancement for women were opened. Indeed, during the first half of the 1970s there was a veritable whirlwind of change with respect to policies oriented toward the increased utilization of women.

All-Volunteer Force

Stemming from the social movements of the 1960s, and particularly the growing anti-establishment/anti-war movement, was a strong visceral reaction against the draft. Always a divisive and controversial issue since its inception during World War II,[203] the draft came to epitomize, for the liberal generation of the 1960s, a corrupt and tyrannical government. In turn, the American public as a whole, reacting to televised images of the rising body count in Vietnam, was becoming increasingly opposed to military involvement in Southeast Asia. Richard Nixon not only capitalized on this

---

[201] Holm, *Women in the Military*, 261.

[202] M.C. Devilbiss, *Women and Military Service: A History, Analysis, and Overview of Key Issues* (Montgomery, AL: Air University Press, 1990), 18.

[203] The first time the draft law came up for extension in 1941, it passed by only a single vote; James A. Henretta, W. Elliot Brownlee, David Brody, and Susan Ware, *America's History* (Chicago: The Dorsey Press, 1987), 807.

prevailing sentiment in his presidential campaign by promising to end the war, but, in a politically savvy move, initiated a process shortly after taking office in 1969 intended to end the draft and institute an all-volunteer military. Nixon organized the Gates Commission, headed by former Secretary of Defense Thomas S. Gates, to study the feasibility of ending the draft. Based on the findings and recommendations of the Gates Commission, President Nixon informed Congress in April 1970 that "From now on, the objective of this Administration is to reduce draft calls to zero, subject to the overriding considerations of national security."[204] Despite the ongoing war in Vietnam, draft calls were reduced until in June 1973 they were completely eliminated signaling the beginning of the AVF.

Although politically beneficial to the President, the AVF presented several challenges for America's military, the most serious of which was filling manpower quotas. The social revolution of the 1960s fostered an anti-establishment and anti-military mentality amongst the majority of America's youth, which meant that in the absence of a draft, eligible men were slow to volunteer for the service. Further, the coalescence of several social factors in the late 1950s and early 1960s, namely the growing trend of women working outside the household, the push for equal rights and women's liberation, and the introduction of the birth control pill all resulted in a sharp drop in the United States birth rate during the 1960s. Demographic trends indicated that the number of 18-year-old males would peak in 1979 at 2.1 million, fall to 2 million in 1983, and hit its projected bottom of 1.7 million in 1988.[205] Conversely, projected manpower requirements for the AVF called for roughly 2 million able bodies in 1979 and 2.1 million in both 1983 and 1988. This created a significant gap between the number of men needed and the number available within the population to serve. A plan compensating for this shortfall thus became imperative before the AVF could be approved and implemented.

---

[204] *Public Papers of Presidents of the United States, Richard Nixon, 1970* (Washington: National Archives and Records Service, 1971): 394-99; see also Morden, *Women's Army Corps*, 229, and Judith Hicks Stiehm, "The Generations of U.S. Enlisted Women," *Signs: Journal of Women in Culture and Society* 11, no. 11 (1985): 155-175, Reference File—Women Marines: General (2 of 2), Washington Navy Yards, Marine Corps Historical Center Archives, Washington, DC, 166.

[205] "Women May Yet Save the Army," *Time* (October 30, 1978), Reference File—Women Marines: Combat Training, Washington Navy Yards, Marine Corps Historical Center Archives, Washington, DC, 42. See also Katzman, "DACOWITS Looks at Women in the Military," 27 for discussion of birthrate decline.

In response, several committees were formed and plans proposed for overcoming the projected shortfall in manpower.[206] The proposed plans focused on how to reduce the need for male uniformed personnel either through the increased use of civilians or servicewomen. Military planners, having learned from prior experience, realized that there was a limit to how much civilian labor could be utilized without jeopardizing professional standards.[207] Thus, in order to "close the military manpower gap," officials once again were forced to rely on women with the final proposal being to expand the women's corps.[208] The proposed solution, as well as its ensuing implementation, had pundits pondering whether or not, as Colorado Democrat Patricia Schroeder, a member of the House Armed Services Committee, stated, "women may yet save the Army," as well as the Navy, Air Force, and Marines.[209]

Women's Roles and Expansion

Expanding the women's corps, however, was not a simple matter. Obstacles included existing federal legislation that dictated structural organization, career restrictions, and strength limitations for women. Additionally, just like men, women were not exactly clamoring at the military's gates to sign up. Women in particular, especially following the sexual and social revolution of the 1960s, tended to view the career limitations and inequalities built into the organizational structure of the women's corps as outdated and unattractive. And, the fact was, they *were* outdated, having

---

[206] For example, the Army formed the PROVIDE Committee (Project Volunteer in Defense of the Nation) led by Lt. Col. Jack R. Butler from ODCSPER Studies and Research Directorate; the Gates Committee, discussed previously, also offered proposals.

[207] During World War II, the Army initially tried to hire women into the civilian-based Women'sArmy Auxiliary Corps (WAAC) to compensate for the manpower shortage only to find that it caused more trouble than it alleviated. The WAAC was administered under separate regulations and lacked any legal contracts, which meant that its members could leave anytime they wanted. Army command quickly learned that it was difficult to run a professional organization when a significant percentage of their force was not directly under their control, and could leave if they felt unfairly treated. As a result, the Army created the Women's Army Corps (WAC) and began recruiting women into the regular Army. See Holm, *Women in the Military*, Chapter 3, for a discussion of the WAAC and its subsequent conversion to the WAC.

[208] In 1972, Secretary of the Army Richard F. Froehlke ordered military leaders to close the military manpower gap. See Morden, *Women's Army Corps*, 264.

[209] Marine Corps Headquarters, trans., "Off to the Battle," originally published in German Magazine, *Stern* (December 1, 1978), Reference File—Women Marines: Liberation Articles, Washington Navy Yards, Marine Corps Historical Center Archives, Washington, DC, 3 and "Women May Yet Save the Army," 42.

been, for the most part and with little modification, established as part of the Women's Armed Services Integration Act of 1948 (P.L. 625, 80th Congress). Furthermore, with societal attitudes regarding gender roles still in flux from the events of the 1960s, the advent of the AVF "rekindled debates about the role of women in the military."[210]

Just as in the past, the expanding role of women in the military was "so closely allied with social and legal changes occurring in society at large," that "in a very potent sense, the will of the People," affected the course of female military careers.[211] But the "will of the People" was in conflict, despite the proposal of the Equal Rights Amendment by Congress in 1972. A Brookings Institute report described the situation as two powerful social forces in collision, "the push for women's equal rights…in conflict with deeply rooted traditions that question the propriety of women under arms."[212] Similarly, Bernard Weinraub of the *New York Times* argued that "women's role in the armed forces will ultimately depend on the extent to which national institutions—social, political, judicial and military—are willing to break with their past, a past reflecting a persistent pattern of male dominance."[213] Although the social environment of the 1960s proved fertile for the growth, awareness, and support of the women's movement, and the public interest it generated began to change attitudes and social customs by the 1970s, these changes were slow to permeate the military.[214] The Marine Corps perhaps presented the most resistance to change, arguing that "America, not necessarily the Marine Corps," was not yet "ready to see women in roles that have historically been male dominated."[215]

---

[210] Tracy Timmons, "'We're Looking for a Few Good Men': The Impact of Gender Stereotypes on Women in the Military." *Minerva* 10, no. 2 (Summer 1992): 24.

[211] Patricia J. Thomas, *Role of Women in the Military: Australia, Canada, the United Kingdom, and the United States* (San Diego, CA: Navy Personnel Research and Development Center, May 1978), Reference File—Women Marines: Australia, Canada, United Kingdom, Washington Navy Yards, Marine Corps Historical Center Archives, Washington, DC, 25.

[212] Bernard Weinraub, "Pentagon Criticized on Jobs for Women," *New York Times* (July 25, 1977), Reference File—Women Marines: Combat Training, Washington Navy Yards, Marine Corps Historical Center Archives, Washington, DC, 9; Martin Binkin and Shirley J. Bach, *Women and the Military* (Washington, DC: Brookings Institute, 1977).

[213] Weinraub, "Pentagon Criticized on Jobs for Women," 9.

[214] Morden, *Women's Army Corps*, 232.

[215] LCpl. Marla J. Schuh, "Women find Success, Recognition during Women's History Month," *Henderson Hall News* 13, no. 13 (March 26, 1999), Reference File—Women Marines: History, Washington Navy Yards, Marine Corps Historical Center Archives, Washington, DC.

Despite growing support in American society for women's rights, this empathy did not easily translate into tangible results. As stated by Captain Kathryn Gordon of the Marine Corps, while "tradition has usually granted women the prerogative to change their minds, society has been extremely reluctant to allow them to change their roles."[216] As reluctant as society was for the role of women in the military to change, the extremely traditional mindset of the military itself was even more reluctant and unprepared to fully integrate women into the AVF. As one study concluded, "overall, the most troublesome difficulties are attitudinal, having little to do with what women can actually accomplish and much to do with what others think they can or should accomplish."[217] As the Air Force acknowledged, culturally determined sex role stereotypes dictated what "acceptable behavior" was for men and women.[218] Thus, for example, until 1971, married women were not accepted into the military because it was socially expected that married women did not work outside the home; likewise, illegitimate pregnancies were socially unacceptable and therefore made a woman unsuitable for service under the strict and elite standards set by the women's corps.[219]

In short, expanding the role of women in the military was barred by three sources: "the attitudes of women and men both in and out of the military, the laws of the land, and the regulations of the individual services."[220] Removing these socially endorsed legal barriers was the purview of Congress, which followed the will of public majority. The services, in turn, would revise regulations only if compelled either by social attitude or court ruling that existing regulations were discriminatory. In response, the women's

---

[216] Capt. Kathryn A. Gordon, "A Larger Role for Women Marines," *Marine Corps Gazette* (November 1977): 19-20, Reference File—Women Marines: Combat Training, Washington Navy Yards, Marine Corps Historical Center Archives, Washington, DC, 19.

[217] Virginia Adams, "Jane Crow in the Army: Obstacles to Sexual Integration," *Psychology Today* (October 1980): 50-65, Box 3, Women in Aviation: General Info, Folder 3, Washington Navy Yards, Naval Aviation Office Archives, Washington, DC, 50.

[218] *Enlisted Personnel: Guide for the Administration and Management of Enlisted Women in the Air Force*, Air Force Pamphlet 39-3 (Washington, DC: Department of the Air Force, April 30, 1975), (hereafter referred to as "Enlisted Personnel"), contained in Staff of the Directorate, Women in the Air Force, *History of the Women in the Air Force: 1 January 1975 – 30 June 1975*, (Washington, DC: Headquarters, United States Air Force, Director, Women in the Air Force, 1975), Director, Women in the Air Force Collection, K141.33 75/01/01-75/06/30 Dir of WAF, IRIS No. 1007190, Air Force Historical Research Agency, Maxwell AFB, Montgomery, AL, A-2.

[219] Morden, *Women's Army Corps*, ix-x.

[220] Thomas, *Role of Women in the Military*, 51.

liberation movement proved instrumental in forcing change, by building overwhelming sympathy, both public and by extension Congressional, for women's rights. The movement's leaders specifically targeted the military urging that women be given the same benefits, opportunities, and treatment as men.[221]

This external pressure began to cause internal change. For example, the Army's expansion plan for the WAC called for a change in Army policy that reflected a "willingness to increase the use of women," in order to compensate for male personnel shortages and as a means of achieving enlistment goals.[222] One of the factors driving this recommendation was *increasing pressures from outside Army.*"[223] Naval historians also observed how "advancement in the Navy generally mirrored the situation of women in American society; the avenues that opened for all women soon had parallels in the Navy."[224]

Still, the women's liberation movement was not solely responsible for the changes enacted as part of the AVF. The actual catalyst to change was the absolute need for women to compensate for personnel shortages. According to Brigadier General Mildred C. Bailey, then Director of the WAC, the increased utilization of women was "an important part of the overall plan to achieve a volunteer force of high-quality soldiers," and expanding the corps was "based upon a need to exploit the personnel resources represented by women in order to meet numerical goals…consistent with the needs of the national defense."[225] As the saying goes, "needs must when the devil drives," and in implementing the AVF, the "devil" was the military's dire need for women to fill manpower quotas. In fact, officials readily ad-

---

[221] Morden, *Women's Army Corps*, 257.

[222] Bernard Rogers (Deputy Chief of Staff for Personnel), "Plans for Expansion of the Women's Army Corps (Study)," U.S. Department of the Army (DAPL-PBP), October 6, 1973, Collection no. 2096 (Shirley Minge), Women in Military Service for America Memorial Foundation, Inc. Archives, Washington, DC.

[223] Ibid., 1, [emphasis added].

[224] Godson, *Serving Proudly*, 290.

[225] Brig. Gen. Mildred C. Bailey, (Director, Women's Army Corps), "Women in the Army," *Commanders Digest* 18, no. 2 (July 10, 1975), Reference File—Women Marines: General (1 of 2), Washington Navy Yards, Marine Corps Historical Center Archives, Washington, DC, 4.

mitted to recruiting large numbers of women as a means of making the all-volunteer force work.[226]

As a result, the needs of this "devil" allowed women to, in a sense, dictate the terms of their service, and in doing so, the women drew guidance from the liberation movement. This resulted in a period of rapid change in the policies, doctrine, lifestyle, standards, and operating procedures, the likes of which the military had not experienced since World War II when it first admitted women for active duty. In a nutshell, the convergence of the national drive for women's legal and economic equality, the transition to an all-volunteer force, and the declining birthrate "combined to make military careers for women more widely acceptable."[227]

Policy

The first significant policy change actually occurred in 1967 when the 2 percent ceiling cap on female enlistment, along with promotion restrictions were eliminated. This policy change, although in advance of the AVF, was in response to the growing manpower shortage, and to reduce "the number of men who must be involuntarily called to duty."[228] As the Marshall Commission, which recommended the modification, observed: "Particularly at a time when manpower demands are great—such as the present—there is a disturbing paradox in this circumstance: Women willing to volunteer for military duty exist in far greater numbers than the services will accommodate; but at the same time there are undoubtedly military tasks suitable for women which are being filled by men who have to be involuntarily inducted."[229] Yet, even though the enlistment ceiling was lifted in 1967, it was not until the start of the AVF, and the other policy changes

---

[226] Joseph E. Revell, "WACs in Combat: If the Army Expects Its Women to Fight, Why Aren't They Trained Like the Men?" *The Times Magazine* (February 9, 1976), Reference File—Women Marines: Combat Training, Washington Navy Yards, Marine Corps Historical Center Archives, Washington, DC, 11.

[227] Joyce Walker-Tyson, "Serve Country, Not Coffee: Women Marine Recruits Typical of Our Changing Military," *Detroit Free Press (MI)* (October 28, 1977), Reference File—Women Marines: Combat Training, Washington Navy Yards, Marine Corps Historical Center Archives, Washington, DC, D-1.

[228] Language used by the Marshall Commission, a National Advisory Commission on Selective Service appointed by President Johnson in 1967, and chaired by Burke Marshall. The Commission's task was to study the Selective Service System and its alternatives. See Holm, *Women in the Military*, Chapter 15 (186-204) for a discussion of this committee along with the process of removing the ceiling and promotion restrictions.

[229] Holm, *Women in the Military*, 191.

enacted as part of the AVF, that the volume of servicewomen would begin increasing exponentially. With the AVF, the military engaged in a major drive to attract and recruit significant numbers of women, and to do so, it was forced to enact policy changes and eliminate antiquated restrictions. This removed many of the traditional barriers to women regarding career opportunities, job assignments, benefits, and educational opportunities and the result was that more women were willing to make a career out of the military.

In preparation for the AVF, the Department of Defense instructed the Army, Navy, and Air Force to prepare plans for doubling the size of their women's programs by 1977 (the Marine Corps planned a 40 percent increase).[230] These initial plans proved shortsighted, however, as the number of women willing to volunteer surpassed expectation, both in terms of enlistment and reenlistment rates. In the Army for example, because "the draft was gone and the addition of 41,000 women was tantamount to receiving three divisions, a gift any army welcomed," plans were initiated for further increases in the number of women.[231] As Rear Admiral George P. Koch, Commandant of the Washington Naval District declared, womanpower meant "Navypower," and given budgetary restrictions and reductions in force, "but no reduction in mission," the Navy needed to "use every person to the maximum of his or her talents."[232] As a result, rather than merely doubling the size of the women's programs, by 1976, they were tripled, and almost quintupled by 1980. Most interesting regarding the increase in women was the fact that women were no longer simply replacing men to fight on the front lines, as they did during World War II and the Korean War, but rather, "if thought of as replacements at all, they must be seen as replacements for men who preferred to remain civilians."[233]

---

[230] Stiehm, "Generations of U.S. Enlisted Women," 166.

[231] Morden, *Women's Army Corps*, 266 and 403; see also Charles Hillinger, "Women Equal: In the Military, War of Sexes Is All But Won," *Los Angeles Times* (December 18, 1978), Box 4, BUPERS 00W, Folder: History 1978, Washington Navy Yards, Naval Historical Center Archives, Washington, DC, 19.

[232] D.E.L. Tuttle, "WomanPower means NavyPower," *Direction* (October 1970), Reference File—Women Marines: Liberation Articles, Washington Navy Yards, Marine Corps Historical Center Archives, Washington, DC, 5.

[233] Stiehm, "Generations of U.S. Enlisted Women," 160 and 166.

For the women's programs, whose numbers, except in times of conflict, had remained relatively stable prior to the AVF, the dramatic and exponential increase in womanpower seemingly occurred overnight in the first half of the 1970s. Although the rate of expansion began leveling off by the late 1970s and recruitment goals for women were reduced in the 1980s, the number of women in the military still continued to increase.[234] Whereas in 1972 only one in every thirty new recruits was female, by 1976, this statistic increased to one in every thirteen.[235] By the end of the 1970s, America not only had more women serving in its armed forces than any other country, but American servicewomen had more major military responsibilities than in any other country.[236] Women not only took over men's recruitment slots, they took over their jobs as well.

Military Occupation Specialties

Perhaps the most causal relationship between increased female recruitment and policy change was the opening up of Military Occupational Specialties (MOS). Prior to lifting the 2 percent ceiling on female enlistment, servicewomen (except during crucial wartime manpower shortages) were primarily restricted to the traditionally female occupations of clerical and administrative support in order to replace men from those jobs for combat duty. Even though women did serve in nontraditional jobs during times of war, their actions were sanctioned by the government and they served in predominantly female units. With the lifting of MOS restrictions in the 1970s, however, women who worked in nontraditional occupations began serving in units that were predominantly male. "Even more than the WACs and WAVES before them, this new breed of amazons invaded men's territory."[237] The days of women serving as "typewriter soldiers"—as women soldiers were commonly dubbed—were drawing to a close.

In preparation for the AVF, policy was changed allowing women access to all fields except those that were a) "beyond the physical capabilities of most women," b) "still considered socially undesirable" and c) "closed be-

---

[234] Devilbiss, *Women and Military Service*, 22-24.

[235] Stiehm, "Generations of U.S. Enlisted Women," 167; see also Marine Corps Headquarters, "Off to the Battle," 3.

[236] "Women May Yet Save the Army," 39.

[237] Timmons, "'We're Looking For A Few Good Men'," 24.

cause of combat restrictions."[238] This meant that, for example in the Army, women could serve in all but 48 of the 482 MOS.[239] By 1976, this figure had dropped to all but 35 of the 419 MOS, with the only restrictions being that women could not serve in any combat, or combat-support positions.[240] In broader terms, the Air Force's position was that there were three primary objectives to the increased utilization of women, namely "(1) to support the achievement of an all volunteer force, (2) to provide greater opportunities for women to serve their country, and (3) to fully utilize the talents of our nation's resource of women."[241] Of course, the opening of previously male-only jobs to women during the 1970s was also in response to the Congressional passage of the Equal Rights Amendment and the military's stated commitment to promoting equal opportunity.[242] As part of this commitment, quotas were established to "force a more balanced representation of women" in all of the available MOS (women still tended to concentrate in traditional job areas), which proved somewhat effective as the percentage of enlisted women in traditional occupations dropped from 90 percent in 1972 to 54 percent by 1980.[243]

Equal Treatment

The military's endeavor to provide equal opportunity for, and greater utilization of, women also brought about other significant policy changes. In particular, targeted for change were those policies, regulations, and practices that were either unique to women or specifically exempted women, and which "inevitably led to differential treatment by male personnel and by the organizations to which they belonged."[244] Air Force Regulation 35-30, for example, stated that all policies and procedures for men and women were to be the same unless there was a "legal or rational reason" for the difference, and that military personnel were to be utilized "based

---

[238] Holm, *Women in the Military*, 274.

[239] Jan Dickerson, "WAC Expansion—Getting It All Together," *Women's Army Corps Journal* 4, no. 2 (April-June 1973), WAC Museum Archives, Ft. Lee, VA, 7.

[240] Celia Hoke (American Forces Press Service), *Women in the Armed Forces* (Washington, DC: Office of Information for the Armed Forces, Assistant Secretary of Defense (Public Affairs), 1976), Reference File—Women Marines: (1 of 2) Brochures/Publications, Washington Navy Yards, Marine Corps Historical Center Archives, Washington, DC.

[241] *Enlisted Personnel*, 1-1.

[242] Revell, "WACs in Combat," 11-12.

[243] Holm, *Women in the Military*, 275.

[244] Thomas, *Role of Women in the Military*," 57.

on their grade and professional qualifications without regard to sex."[245] Most interesting, this regulation specifically listed conditions no longer considered valid for excluding qualified women from any positions, among them: exposure to weather, unpleasant and unfavorable living or working conditions, working with teams of units of opposite sex, marital status, or being the parent of minor child(ren). The Air Force even went one step further by stating in Air Force Pamphlet 39-3 that the Air Force's philosophy was to treat men and women equally, and that there should be no perception that a conflict existed "between being feminine and military," that servicewomen would not be "treated or viewed as defective men," and that they should not be "overprotected, patronized," or "exempted from jobs, duties, and responsibilities" for which they were qualified and capable of doing.[246]

The Marine Corps, the most conservative of the services regarding the role of women, also adopted a similar philosophy. By 1975, the Marine Corps began a review of its regulations in order to revise or eliminate any that allowed for differential treatment of men and women unless there was a "valid rational justification" for said difference.[247] By 1978, the Commandant of the Marine Corps issued a letter stating that "in view of our changing outlook," it was "imperative that commanders now reassess local policies and practices relative to the assignment, training, utilization and welfare of their women members," and that regulations that differentiated "without valid and rational purpose between men and women should be reviewed for possible revision or elimination."[248] Similar changes occurred in the Army and Navy."[249]

The effort to remove policies and regulations that differentiated between men and women meant doing away with the 1948 Integration Act, includ-

---

[245] *Enlisted Personnel*, 1.

[246] Ibid., 2-1.

[247] Col. Margaret A. Brewer, (Director of Women Marines), "Women in the Marine Corps," *Commanders Digest* 18, no. 2 (July 10, 1975), Reference File—Women Marines: General (1 of 2), Washington Navy Yards, Marine Corps Historical Center Archives, Washington, DC, 18-19.

[248] Louis H. Wilson (Commandant of the Marine Corps) to All General Officers, All Commanding Officers, All Officers in Charge, "Women Marines," White Letter No. 5-76, June 23, 1976, Reference File—Report on Progress of Women in the Marine Corps (1988), Washington Navy Yards, Marine Corps Historical Center Archives, Washington, DC, 1.

[249] See Morden, *Women's Army Corps*, 269.

ing the dual standards for enlistment between men and women. Beginning in World War II, women were held to higher educational, mental, and physical standards than men before being allowed to join the military, as well as being subjected to further processing including "an investigation of the records of local police, mental hospitals, schools, former employers, and personal references to detect 'personality problems' or an inability of the applicant to deal with people or 'conform to the requirements of community living'."[250] Although these standards were still adhered to at the beginning of the AVF (largely at the urging of the Directors of the women's programs), by the late 1970s, they were replaced with the same standards used for recruiting men. Additionally, the military was legally forced to modify many of its other policies deemed prejudicial and unfair to women. In 1973, a Supreme Court decision in *Frontiero v. Richardson* mandated that servicewomen were entitled to the same dependent's benefits as men, and in 1975, reading the writing on the wall, the Department of Defense made discharge for pregnancy voluntary, policy that would be legally mandated in 1976 as a result of a U.S. Court of Appeals ruling in *Crawford v. Cushman*.[251]

Also over the course of the 1970s, women became eligible to join Reserve Officer Training Corps (ROTC) programs, experienced equalizing changes to their training programs, both physical and in the classroom (discussed below), and in 1976, were admitted for the first time in history to the service academies.[252] The biggest change for women, however, came with the dissolution of the individual women's corps. The Navy discontinued the WAVES as early as 1973 (although they officially stopped using the name

---

[250] Holm, *Women in the Military*, 54-155.

[251] Stiehm, "Generations of U.S. Enlisted Women," 166-67; see also Women's Research and Education Institute, *Chronology of Significant Legal & Policy Changes*. Also, as a side note to this policy change, at the time, there was a phone conversation between Lt.Col. Brewer and Mary Ann Kuhn of Washington Daily News regarding the rationale for regulations separating Women Marines who are pregnant or have minor children residing in household. Lt.Col. Brewer stated that the rationale dated back to their entrance in WWII "At that time there was no intent that the Marine Corps would be a career for women. It was believed that a mother's concern for her child and the duty of a Woman Marine to the Marine Corps should not be placed in conflict. This was an attitude which reflected society's generally accepted attitude about motherhood." Mary Ann Kuhn (*Washington Daily News*), telephone conversation with Lt. Col. Brewer, October 1, 1970, Reference File—Women Marines: Liberation Articles, Washington Navy Yards, Marine Corps Historical Center Archives, Washington, DC.

[252] Heike Hasenauer, "From WAAC to Regular Army," *Soldiers* (May 1992), Vertical Files: Women in the Military, 1940-1949, Washington Navy Yards, Naval Historical Foundation Library, Washington, DC, 32; see also Holm, *Women in the Military*, 260.

in 1972); Air Force dissolved the WAF Directorate in 1976; the Marine Corps disbanded the WMs in 1977; and by Act of Congress, the WACs were dissolved in 1978. With the end of the WACs, a *Los Angeles Times* article of the time proclaimed: "Today, women are soldiers, not WACs; sailors, not WAVES; airmen, not WAFs; marines, not WMs."[253] Eliminating the separate organizations also eliminated separate command structures for women, separate regulations, and most importantly, allowed for the full integration of training, housing and unit formations.[254] As the Congressional Committee that dissolved the WACs argued, "having a separate corps is a vestige of the time when women were not treated equally and that such a corps is inconsistent with the insistence on equal treatment."[255]

Housing Policy

The concept of equal treatment did not fully extend to housing however. Biologically and socially, men and women were undeniably different, which more than anywhere else in the military, was expressed in facility accommodation. (For example, men still needed urinals and women still required privacy.) As a result of the numerous housing studies conducted in the 1960s and with the recruitment demands of the AVF, there was no way that the military could impose equal treatment to enlisted housing. Official policy provided much higher standards for women in terms of privacy and amenities. Thus, to enforce equal treatment the military would either have to elevate the men's standards—which it could not afford financially, or lower the women's standards—which it could not afford in terms of enlistment and retention. This stalemate resulted in severe housing shortages as a result of the rapid influx of women associated with the AVF (Figure 84).[256] These shortages were predicted though. As early as 1967, studies found that, based on current housing policy, a lack of adequate housing for female personnel would seriously inhibit their ability to

---

[253] Hillinger, "Women Equal: In the Military."

[254] See Women's Army Corps Veteran's Association, *History of the Women's Army Corps* (http://www.armywomen.org/frames.html, 2003), and Marine Corps Headquarters, "Women in the Marine Corps (draft)," February 1979, Reference File—Women Marines: General (1 of 2), Washington Navy Yards, Marine Corps Historical Center Archives, Washington, DC.

[255] Quoted in Morden, *Women's Army Corps*, 318.

[256] Severe supply shortages were felt across the board from uniforms to training facilities to housing.

Figure 84. Chesney cartoon (WIMSA).

expand their programs.[257] Unless more facilities were provided, the studies warned that the services would have difficulty meeting the housing demands of the rapidly expanding women's programs, and might (and in fact did) result in the services having to restrict enlistment based on the availability of funds to provide and/or improve housing and facilities.[258]

The Army's solution to the problem, typical of all the services, was twofold: program new construction and modify policy to facilitate maximum use of existing housing. The Army estimated that $15 million was needed for new construction at the WAC Center and WAC School, and an addi-

---

[257] See, for example, *Utilization of Women in the Air Force: Report of Ad Hoc Study Group* (Washington, DC: Department of the Air Force, October 1967), USAF Collection, K141.04-21 Oct 1967, IRIS No. 645048, Air Force Historical Research Agency, Maxwell AFB, Montgomery, AL, for the Air Force's study. Also, see Devilbiss, *Women and Military Service*, 25-26.

[258] Rogers, "Plans for Expansion of the Women's Army Corps (Study)"; U.S. Women's Army Corps School, *Role of the WAC*, 41; Dickerson, "WAC Expansion," 3; Morden, *Women's Army Corps*, 279-80.

tional $1.5 million required to modify male barracks for women at installations world-wide. Additionally, large numbers of existing structures for servicewomen were renovated to meet established criteria for women's housing across all Army installations where women were stationed or received training. Long-range construction plans were also modified to allow for continued increasing demand for female housing.[259] To meet immediate needs, post commanders were directed to double-deck beds in female barracks or lease civilian facilities until rehabilitation and/or construction projects were completed.

Still, the expanding women's corps rapidly outpaced all efforts to provide appropriate housing under existing policy. So, in 1973, General Bailey, Director of the WACs, issued new housing guidelines that afforded commanders several options for providing female enlisted housing.[260] One option encouraged implementing only minimum standards for converting male barracks for female occupancy (separate sleeping quarters, separate latrines with partitioned showers and partitioned toilets, and sufficient laundry facilities). Other options allowed Commanders to lease civilian facilities for housing women, or authorized funds for off-post living for women in grades E-4 through E-6.[261] Another, more dramatic option allowed commanders to house men and women in the same building as long as women were located on a separate floor or wing and provided with separate entrances and exits (although these were not mandatory). The policy restricting the assignment of women to only those stations with established female units was also changed, and in the case of overcrowding, women could be assigned to male units for housing, feeding, and administration, as long as privacy and a female supervisor were provided.[262]

---

[259] Morden, *Women's Army Corps*, 263, 275-76.

[260] Ibid., 404.

[261] Rogers, "Plans for Expansion of the Women's Army Corps (Study)," 4.

[262] Morden, *Women's Army Corps*, 275-276. See also Pat Pond, "Coed Share and Share Alike," *Women's Army Corps Journal* 5, no. 5 (October-December 1974), WAC Museum Archives, Ft. Lee, VA, 25; United States Women's Army Corps, *WAC Basic Training Battalion Training Brigade, Ft. McClellan, Alabama Yearbook* (Fort McClellan, AL: U.S. Women's Army Corps, 1977), Collection no. 4674 (unknown), Women in Military Service for America Memorial Foundation, Inc. Archives, Washington, DC; Bailey, "Women in the Army," 7; and Col. Ann Fisher (WAC Staff Adviser), "U.S. Army Training and Doctrine Command WAC Utilization/Integration Symposium, 25-26 June 1974, After-Action Report," Headquarters, U.S. Army Training and Doctrine Command, August 20, 1974, Ft. Lee 228-01, WHC-846, Folder—TRADOC Symposium on Women (1974), WAC Museum Archives, Ft. Lee, VA, Message Extract, for changes in housing policy.

This last policy change had a significant impact as it resulted in the deactivation of several female companies and detachments that were merged with male units. In the Army, as well as Marine Corps and Navy, "commanders eagerly grasped the opportunity to merge enlisted units, for they could now provide more housing for women, obtain maximum use of barracks facilities, and reduce the number of cadre needed to operate units."[263] Although military leaders welcomed the integration of administrative units as being more efficient, housing was still problematic. Women often continued to be housed in separate facilities as it was the only means of ensuring privacy, particularly of restroom and sleeping facilities.[264] This was due in part to a continued sense of propriety, but perhaps more so to the lack of funds needed to convert buildings for female occupancy. Rather than rehabilitate existing structures, the military channeled its limited funds into new construction, building barracks that would eventually provide for integrated housing.

Providing integrated housing, of course, not only helped to alleviate the housing shortage, but adhered to the new philosophy of equal treatment. Integrated housing, however, required an integrated housing policy that did not differentiate based on gender. Thus, in 1977, a new housing policy was instituted by the Army mandating that space and adequacy criteria of barracks designs be based on the grade, not the sex, of the occupant, thereby truly allowing for interchangeable spaces between men and women. This policy still mandated that joint-use housing provide secure sleeping and latrine facilities, and assure privacy and security for enlisted personnel, only now the policy applied to men as well.[265] The main intent of this policy was to remove housing as a constraint to assignment, allowing for male and female barracks spaces to be interchangeable.

The direct result was not only an overall improvement in housing, especially for men, but once barracks designs incorporated interchangeable spaces, it was a short step from a design standpoint to coed barracks. If joint-use facilities were suitable for either men or women, the only re-

---

[263] Morden, *Women's Army Corps*, 275-76.

[264] Women's Army Corps Veteran's Association, *History of the Women's Army Corps*.

[265] United States Army, *Personnel Utilizations: Female Military Personnel*, Pamphlet No. 616-1 (Washington, DC: Department of the Army, May 18, 1977), Collection no. 4582 (Becky Miller), Women in Military Service for America Memorial Foundation, Inc. Archives, Washington, DC, 1.

maining obstacle preventing joint-use facilities from becoming coed—with men and women freely sharing the same building, although living on separate floors—was social and military custom and propriety. But, this obstacle was quickly receding. The Army, in fact, had experimented with coed barracks beginning in 1974, and based on the success of the experiment, the 1977 policy formalized and encouraged the concept. Coed barracks provided some relief for the expansion-related housing shortage, but more importantly, they fostered increased unit cohesion by allowing integrated units to be housed *and* administered together. As Captain Linda Phillips, commander of the Aberdeen Proving Ground WAC Detachment (one of the units to live in a coed barracks in 1974) stated, "I think it means a lot from the standpoint of the 'One Army' concept and what the Army's trying to do for its women."[266]

The Air Force instituted a similar policy for joint-use facilities, "provided the two areas can be isolated; i.e., separate entrances and exits," but still considered separate facilities for men and women as the most desirable situation; in the absence of separate facilities, having "an entire floor or wing of a facility with separate entrances, exits, and latrine facilities," for the women was the next most desirable solution.[267] The reasoning for this policy was that although most Air Force dormitories were capable of housing either men or women "the physical structure of existing buildings precludes fully integrated, coeducational billeting." It was further felt that until facilities could be constructed that guaranteed personnel an "atmosphere of privacy and relaxation in their day-to-day lifestyle," segregated facilities were the best solution.[268]

In 1976, the Marine Corps began their own pilot program for integrated units and coed housing. Forty-two women were integrated into the command structure of a non-combat rear echelon unit in the Fleet Marine Force, which included sharing a motel-like barracks with the men to promote unit integrity. The unit's commanding officer reported that although

---

[266] Pond, "Coed Share and Share Alike," 24.

[267] *Fact Sheet: Women in the Air Force*, revised 1975, contained in Staff of the Directorate, Women in the Air Force, *History of the Women in the Air Force: 1 January 1975 – 30 June 1975*, (Washington, DC: Headquarters, United States Air Force, Director, Women in the Air Force, 1975), Director, Women in the Air Force Collection, K141.33 75/01/01-75/06/30 Dir of WAF, IRIS No. 1007190, Air Force Historical Research Agency, Maxwell AFB, Montgomery, AL.

[268] *Enlisted Personnel*, 4-1.

"obvious problems" such as restroom facilities were "nettlesome," the anticipated problems arising from coed barracks did not occur. Rather, the women "tended to keep their quarters better policed," expressed a greater sense of urgency than the men over equipment failure, such as for laundry, and seemed more concerned with appearance, and the presence of women seemed to cause the men to improve their manners and language with little resentment.[269] Based on the success of this pilot program, other Woman Marine Companies were absorbed into the male units they served with, and as new motel-like barracks became available, were also housed together. At the Base Material Battalion at Camp Lejeune, for example, "the battalion occupied a new motel-like barracks in which all rooms had outside entrances," and both men and women shared the lounges, laundries, and other common areas (Figure 85).[270]

Figure 85. Motel type housing with exterior room doors (USACEHQ).

Housing Design

Even with integrated housing, though, all was not entirely equal. Some historical aspects of women's design standards remained, as "American views on privacy in living accommodations," for women continued to influence military design.[271] Women still wanted, and received, a few amenities

---

[269] Stremlow, *History of the Women Marines*, 98.

[270] Ibid., 138.

[271] "Now Military is Putting Women into 'Men Only' Jobs," *U.S. News & World Report* (December 10, 1973), Series III, Box 30, Box Post 1946 Command File (1066), Washington Navy Yards, Naval Historical Center Archives, Washington, DC, 83-84.

above and beyond those provided to men, partly in response to the concerns of women, and justified by the fact that women continued to spend more time in their barracks than men.[272] For example, according to the Air Force, the dormitory was "the center of off-duty life for most young, single women," having "a decided impact on their attitude toward Air Force life in general," and that young women particularly desired "a cheerful living environment."[273] Such amenities included snack kitchens, expanded laundry facilities, sewing rooms, and lounges for male guests, also known as date rooms, inclusive of a guest bathroom. (No such reciprocal facilities for women were provided in male barracks.) Even as late as 1975, Air Force doctrine adhered to the tradition which dictated that men called on women in their homes "when escorting her to social functions."[274] Thus, women's enlisted barracks required date rooms, equipped with male lavatories where the men could visit.

By the late 1970s, integrated housing had become the norm. Both men and women seemed to like the arrangement, particularly the level of privacy afforded while still forming one cohesive unit. As one WAC sergeant put it, integrated housing was "just doing away with the philosophy that servicewomen must live cloistered in a corner of a military post, like members of a religious order."[275]

The housing shortage was not the only problematic issue the military dealt with in implementing the AVF. Recruiting and, perhaps more importantly, retaining quality personnel also posed a significant challenge, especially in a time where service was voluntary but socially undesirable. Beginning in the 1960s, but brought to a head with the AVF, was a growing acknowledgement in the military that morale and quality-of-life issues were strong determinants in the retention of service members, a significant concern for maintaining military professionalism. Thus, raising the living standards for soldiers (both male and female) became imperative when relying on volunteers to fill the ranks. Military life had to be attractive to potential recruits, and quality of life aspects played a significant role. In 1973, the

---

[272] See Baldwin, William C. "A History of Army Peacetime Housing To the End of the Cold War." *Occasional Papers 4*. Society for History in the Federal Government, 2004, 18.

[273] *Enlisted Personnel*, 4-1.

[274] *Ibid.*, 4-2.

[275] "Now Military is Putting Women into 'Men Only' Jobs," 83-84.

DACOWITS Committee noted that if the military hoped to retain personnel, it would have to compete with the private sector and provide housing standards commensurate with the "living conditions available to civilians of comparable status." Moreover, the Committee pointed out those civilian institutions having a housing responsibility were "rapidly re-evaluating and upgrading their housing standards."[276]

The military responded by enacting "personnel-oriented" construction programs aimed at improving housing satisfaction and living conditions for all of its members, with a particular emphasis on recruitment satisfaction and soldier retention. The Army, for example, from 1972 through 1976, "rehabilitated or built more than 200,000 barracks spaces in the largest unaccompanied enlisted personnel housing program since the 1920s," which uncoincidentally was the last time America had an all-volunteer force.[277] A 1975 Corps of Engineers report on the construction program informed that, "The Army's program to support the volunteer Army revolves around the effort to improve Army life—we want to benefit the soldier where he lives, where he works, where he plays, and where we treat him when he is sick. As a matter of fact, over 72% of the FY 74 Army military construction budget request is in so called soldier oriented projects."[278] It further reported that the troop housing program had quadrupled since Fiscal Year (FY) 1970 to a FY 1974 total of $368M. These personnel-oriented projects for the women included improving privacy, and continuing to provide and/or update cooking, laundry, and latrine facilities, increase storage space and electrical outlets, provide recreation areas, as well as areas for entertaining guests.[279] For the men, these projects included such things as "quick fix" privacy partitions in sleeping quarters, and modernizing barracks to include better traffic flow conditions, install-

---

[276] DACOWITS, *DACOWITS History of Recommendations: Fall Conference 1973* (Washington, DC: DACOWITS), available online at
http://www.dtic.mil/dacowits/tablerecommendation_subpage.html; See also Baldwin, "History of Army Peacetime Housing," 24 who discusses the issue of how the military has to compete with the civilian market in housing.

[277] Baldwin, "History of Army Peacetime Housing," 18.

[278] U.S. Army Corps of Engineers, "Suggested text for the Military Construction Area: Military Construction, 1974-75," Box XV-1, Military: Domestic Military Construction 1945-; Folder: Construction—Articles & Memos, Updates, U.S. Army Corps of Engineers History Office Archives, Alexandria, VA.

[279] See U.S. Women's Army Corps School, *Role of the WAC*, 34; see also U.S. Army Corps of Engineers, "Suggested text for the Military Construction Area."

ing air-conditioning units and new lighting, and improving/upgrading recreational areas.[280]

New Barracks Designs

The most important thing the services did to improve living conditions, however, was to approve new barracks designs based on new and updated housing standards for new construction. New barracks designs were crafted in the beginning of the decade in order to facilitate the needs of the AVF. Building largely on the studies done and trends established during the 1960s, particularly related to the tri-service definitive designs for officer housing, these new building designs were organized into three categories: the residential style (DEF 25-06-75 & 73), the motel-type (DEF 25-06-72), and the high-rise (DEF 25-06-74) design (Figure 86 and Figure 87).

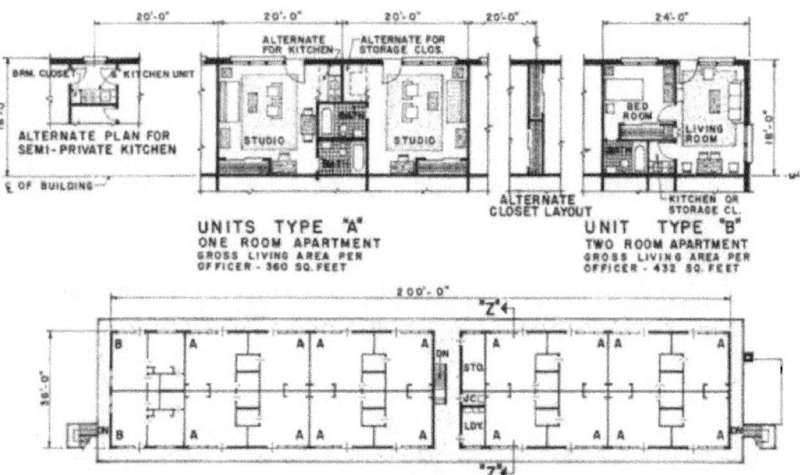

Figure 86. Tri-Service design for motel type Officer's quarters, 1962 (USACEHQ).

---

[280] See U.S. Army Corps of Engineers, "Suggested text for the Military Construction Area."

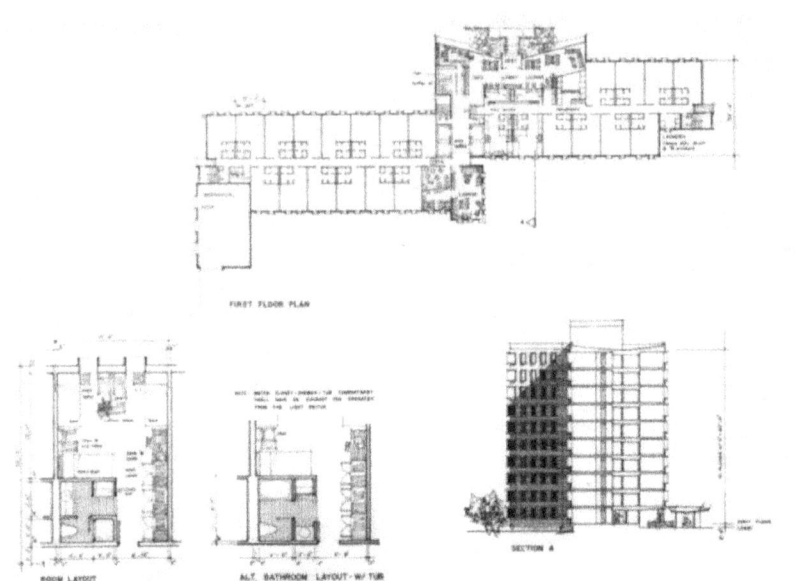

Figure 87. Navy high-rise enlisted quarters influenced by 1962 Tri-Service designs, 1975 (NARA)

Based on the recommendations of DACOWITS, these designs emphasized privacy, for both men and women. In 1972, DACOWITS made the following recommendations: "(1) that all permanent party enlisted personnel be billeted not more than two to a room, (2) that all officers and senior noncommissioned officers (grades E-6 and above) be given the option of living off post and (3) that all open bay quarters and other quarters which do not meet recommended standards for enlisted permanent party personnel be phased out and/or modified as soon as possible."[281]

In 1973, the Department of Defense published new regulations calling for more space and privacy in barracks. In response, the Army generated a standard three-person room modular design that replaced the open squad-bays that typically housed 20 troops (Figure 88 and Figure 89).[282]

---

[281] "DACOWITS," 7; See also Talley, *Highlights of the Defense Advisory Committee on Women in the Services*, 18.

[282] See Sharon M. Odle, "Army Leaders Set Standard Design Goals," *Engineer Update, USACE* (May 1986), Box 10, General Files; Folder 10-1-3: Army Leaders Set Standard Design Goals-May 1986, U.S. Army Corps of Engineers History Office Archives, Alexandria, VA.

Figure 88. Interior of barracks showing old-style open squad bay (note irons under bunks), 1973 (WAC Museum, Vertical Files, File: US WAC Center Barracks/Dayrooms VI-A-17).

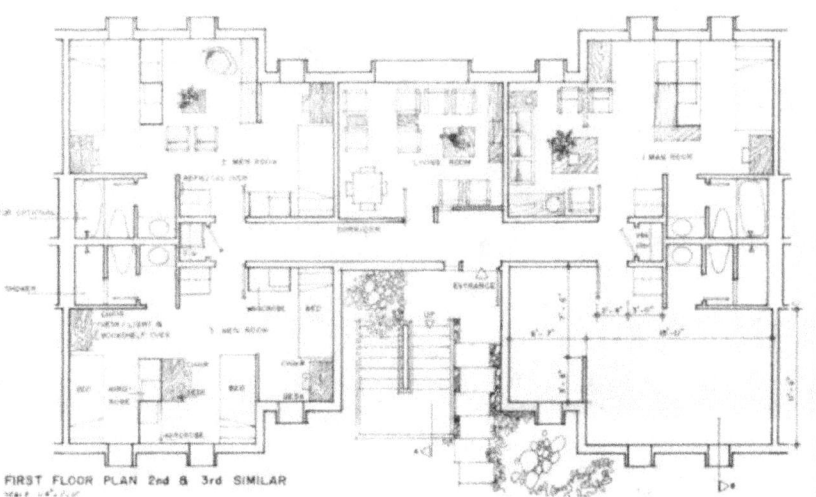

Figure 89. Navy/Marine version of three-man rooms with bath, 1975 (NARA).

The design featured "clusters of four, one-to-three-man rooms arrayed around a small lounge," with each room having its own bathroom and each soldier being provided with "a separate cubicle containing a window, desk and chair, wardrobe and bed," that could be closed off for privacy.²⁸³ Separate service modules would be constructed for every 165 men containing a control desk, mail boxes, phones, vending machines, toilets, lobby, a large dayroom, laundry facilities, and space for dry cleaning storage. The design required a 10 percent increase in space, and associated costs, but according to Brigadier General Richard McConnell, the increase was acceptable as he sincerely felt "the lack of personal privacy and the insufficiency of security of personal belongings," were "significant irritants" to soldiers that must be eliminated.²⁸⁴

Male and female Marines, perhaps, benefited most from the new regulations. Prior to 1973, men were housed in open squad rooms with double metal bunks, lockers, and locker boxes, and the women did not always receive much better (Figure 90). In fact, female recruits were housed in very similar conditions, except that they would receive amenities, such as laundry, latrine, lounge and cooking facilities not extended to the men (Figure 91).

Figure 90. Metal bunks and lockers at Parris Island, 1967. In *Marine Corps Recruit Depot Yearbook, Platoon 4B* (WIMSA, Document File, Collection of Ellie Lopez #4167).

---

²⁸³ Gene Famiglietti, "New Barracks to be 'Home Style' Complete with Lounge," *Army Times* (June 21, 1972), Ft. Lee 228-01, WHC-378, Folder—Housing, Misc Reports (1965-67), WAC Museum Archives, Ft. Lee, VA, 1, and Baldwin, "History of Army Peacetime Housing," 18.

²⁸⁴ Famiglietti, "New Barracks to be 'Home Style' Complete with Lounge," 1.

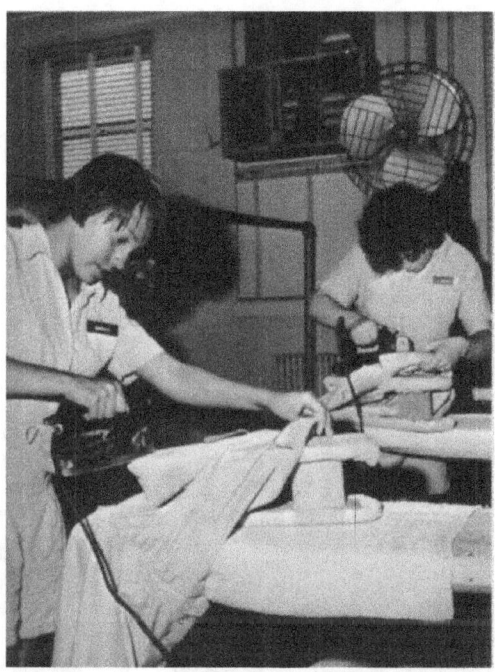

Figure 91. Women Marines doing laundry, Parris Island, 1967. In *Marine Corps Recruit Depot Yearbook, Platoon 4B* (WIMSA, Document File, Collection of Ellie Lopez #4167).

These new regulations were incorporated into the new WM complex constructed at Parris Island in the early 1970s. Original suggestions had been to merely rehabilitate and air condition the existing World War II barracks, but because the cost exceeded more than 50 percent of the replacement value of the buildings, new construction for the WMs was approved, and it was completed in 1975. The new, completely self-contained complex was organized around a central courtyard area and housed WMs stationed there, as well as recruits. It included a "fully equipped gymnasium, headquarters areas for the battalion and recruit company, a dining facility, storage areas, a conference room, four classrooms, a Laundromat, clothing issue area, sickbay, tennis courts, volleyball court, and television and telephones on each level of the three-story barracks."[285] While recruits still lived in "austere, albeit more modern and comfortable" open squad-bays,

---

[285] Stremlow, *History of the Women Marines*, 123-24. The old barracks were retained to house the increased number of recruits that enlisted as part of the AVF, and plans for an addition to the new complex were underway before it was finished.

permanent women lived in one- to three-person rooms with "new, motel-like furnishings," and a patio with fountain. "Beds replaced metal bunks, closets replaced lockers, and the women were allowed to decorate their rooms with colorful bed spreads, rugs, flowers, photographs, and other personal touches" (Figure 92).[286]

Figure 92. WAC double room showing personal touches, White Sands Missile Range, 1965 (WAC Museum, Vertical Files, File: Housing Enlisted Survey of 1964-65).

The Navy and the Air Force, always at the forefront in providing quality housing to its bachelors, also adhered to the new space and privacy regulations. However, unlike the Army, both services had already provided their men with higher standards of privacy prior to the 1970s. The Navy had already instituted four-person cubicles as a basic requirement in new construction for men (a standard already extended to the women), and upgraded the women to permanent partitions.[287] Still, both services approved the new designs for motel-type and high-rise barracks for new construction. In doing so, the services facilitated the gradual integration of housing for men and women. These designs, in eliminating common hallways, gang latrines, and shared facilities, "made it easier to accommodate a mixed population with the necessary privacy and protection."[288]

---

[286] Ibid.
[287] Hancock, *Lady in the Navy*, 173-4.
[288] Holm, *Women in the Military*, 279.

Detention Facilities

The trend toward providing equal opportunity, integration, and placing servicewomen on an even footing with servicemen also called for a rethinking of standing policy regarding the use of brigs and detention facilities. In 1974, the Army Training and Doctrine Command (TRADOC) hosted a symposium on the utilization and integration of the WAC, at which the issue of detention facilities was examined. Standing policy enacted during World War II prohibited the detention of female personnel in any military facility other than specially designated rooms in female barracks. This policy was based largely on societal expectations at the time of gender norms in which women were not typically known to be aggressive, dangerous, or engage in behaviors so heinous or unacceptable as to warrant serious confinement. Prior to the 1970s, if a servicewoman should engage in an act requiring more serious detainment than the barracks facility, she was to be discharged from the military and turned over to the civilian authorities. However, the turbulent events of the 1960s and 1970s, especially the Civil Rights Movement, demonstrated that women were just as capable and just as likely as men of engaging in activities warranting confinement and detention.

Because of this, the panel members determined that current policy was not capable of addressing female offenders who manifested aggressive behavior, and recommended that "confinement facilities for men be modified to provide like service, custody and treatment for females."[289] In response, the Army modified its policy, and its detention facilities, thus enabling female soldiers to be confined in detention cells "under the same circumstances as other soldiers," except that they were to be placed in a cell apart from male detainees and under the continuous observation of a female MP. Further, detention was not to exceed a "reasonable period of time," and those women requiring "extended confinement due to court-martial convictions" were to be transferred to the facility located at Fort Riley, Kansas.[290] Also at issue was the fact that the new integrated barracks facilities did not provide detention rooms for women. This posed a problem for the Marine Corps, which did not modify its policy to allow for the con-

---

[289] Fisher, "U.S. Army Training and Doctrine Command WAC Utilization," Work Shop No. 1 Report, 2-3.

[290] United States Army, *Personnel Utilizations*, 2.

finement of women in the male detention centers, but rather allowed for a "more liberal use of civilian jails."[291]

Equipment

Physically accommodating women in an increasingly integrated and equal opportunity military also required the services to make other physical changes in addition to those related to buildings and structures. Particularly, as women moved into occupations formerly open to men only, equipment sometimes needed to be modified, redesigned, or adjusted to accommodate the different female physiology. For example, the Air Force introduced dollies for use by female mechanics to roll heavy tool boxes around hangars, and provided special oxygen masks for female pilots to fit their thinner facial structure.[292] A Department of Defense study also found that there were no physiological reasons why women could not perform in any position, even though service leaders raised lack of strength as the most common problem for women.[293] The study pointed out, however, that "many of the problems arising in using women in nontraditional positions were also faced when adapting American equipment and procedures to the use of male Oriental allied troops who were also generally smaller than American men."[294] Assistant Secretary of Defense for Manpower, John White, reiterated this point when he stated: "We've made the accommodations before, and we see no insurmountable problems."[295]

Training

On par with the changes made to the physical accommodation of servicewomen during the 1970s were the changes to training standards, doctrine and practices instituted as part of the AVF. As stated earlier, the first change came in 1972 when all ROTC programs were opened to women.[296]

---

[291] Stremlow, *History of the Women Marines*, 144.

[292] "Women May Yet Save the Army," 43.

[293] Vernon A. Guldry, Jr., "Pentagon SOS: Women, Sign Up," *Washington Star* (June 26, 1977), Reference File—Women Marines: Combat Training, Washington Navy Yards, Marine Corps Historical Center Archives, Washington, DC.

[294] Ibid.

[295] "Women May Yet Save the Army," 43.

[296] The Air Force ROTC program was opened to women in 1969. The Army and Navy were opened in 1972.

As the decade progressed, Officer Candidate Schools, and advanced training schools were integrated, women were required to receive defensive weapons training, and women were allowed to enroll at the service academies. Then, in the late 1970s, with the dissolution of separate corps for women, the Army, Navy, and Air Force consolidated basic training; the Marine Corps was the only service to continuously maintain segregated basic recruit training for men and women. Along with the dissolution of the separate corps came the closing of the WAC and WAVES separate training centers at Fort McClellan, Alabama, and the Recruit Training Command (Women) at Bainbridge, Maryland. The Marine Corps continued to train women only at its Parris Island facility, and the Air Force continued training women at Lackland Air Force Base in Texas.

Integrated training, at all levels (recruit, advanced, officer) proved somewhat of a culture shock for both men and women, as prior to the 1970s, women had received their training and had served in units that were significantly, if not entirely, comprised of women.[297] "Male commanders and NCOs in the 1970s had not yet become accustomed to volunteers instead of draftees when women entered in large numbers, an event for which they had little warning and no preparation."[298] These male leaders found that their old techniques for managing men did not work with the women, who required "more information, privacy, and counseling than men;" they also discovered that, unlike most men, "women complained about harassment, discrimination, and poor housing; women got pregnant, needed child-care facilities, and, without training, could not lift heavy objects or make a six-mile run," all of which required an adjustment on the part of both men and women.[299]

Adjustments were also required on the part of the women of the Army, Navy, and Air Force as with integration they not only conducted their basic training alongside their male counterparts, but received nearly identical

---

[297] See Timmons, "'We're Looking For A Few Good Men'," 24; and Larry Reibstein, "Women No Longer Separate at Ft. Dix; Are They Equal?" *Philadelphia Bulletin* (October 18, 1978), Reference File—Women Marines: Recruit Posters, Washington Navy Yards, Marine Corps Historical Center Archives, Washington, DC, 6C.

[298] Morden, *Women's Army Corps*, 405.

[299] Ibid.

basic recruit training programs.[300] Women began "firing machine guns, bazookas and M-16 rifles and hurling hand grenades, crawling through the woods at night, moving forward from bunker to bunker and practicing war games on week-long bivouac, side by side with men" (Figure 93)[301] Yet, not everything about basic recruit training was identical between the sexes. Female recruits underwent different medical examinations, attended separate and gender-tailored hygiene classes, as well as classes on birth control, hair care, skin care, weight control, make-up application, and were subjected to different physical fitness test standards (Figure 94).[302]

Figure 93. Gender-integrated basic combat training, Fort Jackson, SC (Courtesy of Fort Jackson, U.S. Army).

---

[300] See Reibstein, "Women No Longer Separate at Ft. Dix," 6C, and U.S. Government Accounting Office, *Gender Integration in Basic Training: The Services Are Using A Variety of Approaches*, GAO/T-NSIAD-97-174 (Washington, DC: GAO, 1997), 2; Davida Matthews, "Orlando Recruit Training...It's Coed," *All Hands* (May 1976), Box 20, BUPERS 00W, Folder: Clippings 1971-1978, Washington Navy Yards, Naval Historical Center Archives, Washington, DC, 1.

[301] Hillinger, "In the Military"; See also Revell, "WACs in Combat," 11.

[302] Reibstein, "Women No Longer Separate at Ft. Dix," 6C, and U.S. Government Accounting Office, *Gender Integration in Basic Training*; Revell, "WACs in Combat," 16.

Figure 94. WACs receive training in hair care and cosmetics, U.S. Army Training Center, Fort Jackson, 1977. In Company book for *Women's Army Corps (WAC) Company A, 18th Battalion, 5th Brigade* (WIMSA, Document File, Collection of William Polcsa #4637).

Physical standards were modified to accommodate physiological differences between men and women, who on average, were "shorter, lighter and slower," and could not maintain a 30-inch regulation stride, without causing severe hip pain.[303] Thus, standards were changed so that at some places, "women do flexed arm hangs instead of chin-ups, take karate instead of boxing, and shoulder 8-pound M-16 rifles instead of 11-pound M-14s," and at others, "women do only eighteen, not 35, push-ups in two minutes, and need not qualify on the rifle range," depending on what the training standards were at individual centers.[304]

At the Marine Corps Recruit Training Depot at Parris Island, women were trained by women, housed in completely segregated facilities, and they did not train or eat with the male recruits, run an obstacle course, or fire weapons.[305] However, by 1977, the Marine Corps did consolidate officer and advanced training with men and women receiving essentially the same

---

[303] Melinda Beck, "Women in the Armed Forces," *Newsweek* (February 18, 1981), Reference File—Women Marines: Combat Training, Washington Navy Yards, Marine Corps Historical Center Archives, Washington, DC, 36, and DACOWITS, "Notes and minutes from the Fall Meeting, 21-25 October 1979 in Columbia, South Carolina," DACOWITS Meetings Series, Women in Military Service for America Memorial Foundation, Inc. Archives, Washington, DC, H-7, 6.

[304] Beck, "Women in the Armed Forces," 36.

[305] Hillinger, "Women Equal."

coeducational training except for certain classes such as those related to personal hygiene and grooming. To integrate the women, the Marine Corps, rather than lower the standards established for men, raised them for women. This meant that the women's courses, which were generally "slightly shorter in duration, and did not go into as much depth in physical fitness, marksmanship or infantry tactics training," were modified to equal the men's.[306] However, some adjustments were made to account for the physiological differences between men and women. For example, although men and women performed on the same agility course, performance requirements were adjusted in the obstacle course, conditioning hikes, and endurance runs to account for women's smaller size and stride length, as well as strength.[307] In some training exercises, the women were not required to run the same distance as men (1½ miles for women as compared to 3 miles for men), and rather than doing pull-ups, women would substitute more physiologically appropriate exercises, such as the flexed-arm hang.[308]

In all of the services, doctrine for field training was modified to account for the perceived special needs of women. At first, women in the field were subject to special rules in place to "protect" them, such as having to pitch their tents in the center of the company encampment, visit the latrine in pairs, and being barred from serving sentry duty.[309] Eventually, these restrictions were lifted, and replaced with more practical policies. By 1977, for example, Army doctrine provided guidance which stated: "(a) There must be at least two women in the field to remain overnight. Units will not assign joint sleeping facilities to male and female soldiers during field exercises. (b) A separate latrine will be established with an opaque parti-

---

[306] Marine Corps Headquarters, "Women in the Marine Corps (draft)," 4.

[307] Ibid., 5; *Women Marines in the 1980s*, (Washington, DC: Headquarters, U.S. Marine Corps, Division of Public Affairs (CODE PAM), 1986 rev.), Reference File—Women Marines: General (1 of 2), Washington Navy Yards, Marine Corps Historical Center Archives, Washington, DC, 2.

[308] See Caryle Murphy, "Female Marines Get 'In-the-Mud' Field Training," *The Washington Post* (February 14, 1977), Reference File—Women Marines: Combat Training, Washington Navy Yards, Marine Corps Historical Center Archives, Washington, DC; *Women Marines in the 1980s*, 2; and "A Little Slower, But…Women Marines Sample Combat," *Herald-Examiner, Los Angeles* (March 25, 1977): 1, Reference File—Women Marines: Combat Training, Washington Navy Yards, Marine Corps Historical Center Archives, Washington, DC.

[309] Phil Stanford, "Should Women Be Combat Soldiers?" *DivInfo Daily Press Clips* (June 27, 1977), Reference File—Women Marines: Combat Training, Washington Navy Yards, Marine Corps Historical Center Archives, Washington, DC.

tion...(d) Hot water should be provided for female personnel that remain in the field over 24 hours. This is provided for female hygiene purposes and to minimize the risk of internal infection to which women are vulnerable due to body structure."[310]

Integrated training also marked a shift in the military's attitude toward gender roles. If the military was to be serious about fully integrating women and allowing them almost-full access to occupations and opportunities, it would have to acknowledge that it was "impossible for women to behave like 'ideal' women and 'ideal' soldiers" at the same time.[311] With the advent of the AVF, and its reliance on women, "the military officially removed most femininity requirements from women's performance. Women's training 'lacked the 1960s emphasis on 'ladylike' appearance and behavior: women were now expected to perform most of their activities with, and like, men'."[312] A clear indication of this new outlook on women and training was the switch in training uniforms. Amazingly enough, it was not until the 1970s, with the increased emphasis on physical, field, and weapons training that women were issued heavy-duty fatigues, with helmet liners and combat boots, rather than "exercise suits" (Figure 95).[313]

Indeed just as the 1960s marked a social revolution for a generation of Americans, the 1970s marked a sea change in the role of women in the military, reflecting the social and political movements of both the 1960s and 1970s. At no other point in our country's military history had so much change occurred in such a short period of time. At the beginning of the decade, most military commanders did not "allow enlisted women to wear blue jeans or slacks outside the unit area unless the women were en route to the softball field or bowling alley," and servicewomen in uniform were not allowed to enter liquor stores or bars, "smoke while walking, or chew gum in public." By the end of the decade, however, "the strict morality and social proprieties of earlier years faded from existence," and society accepted such things as unwed mothers, unmarried couples living together, and vastly different standards for dress codes, and gender behavior.[314] This

---

[310] United States Army, *Personnel Utilizations*, 2.

[311] Timmons, "'We're Looking For A Few Good Men'," 20.

[312] Ibid., 24.

[313] Morden, *Women's Army Corps*, 363.

[314] Ibid., ix, x.

translated into radical changes for women in the military as well. As compared to the beginning of the 1970s, by the end of the decade women were living in integrated barracks, conducting integrated training, and serving in integrated units alongside their male counterparts. Aside from being barred from combat or occupying a position that involved combat, and from serving on ships, in submarines, or on combat aircraft, the role of women in the military had become almost entirely the same as that for men.

Figure 95. WACs on obstacle course, Fort McClellan, AL, 1977. In yearbook from *WAC Basic Training Battalion Training Brigade*, 1977 (WIMSA, Document File, donor unknown #4674).

7 Police Actions and the 1980s: All But Combat

A 1980 psychology study cited gender integration as the major challenge facing the armed forces of the United States, as where only a generation beforehand, racial integration had been the major issue.[315] The widespread changes of the 1970s resulted in a military where women had access to essentially the same opportunities, responsibilities, and experiences as men. The integration of training, working, and housing environments created a different landscape for servicemen in the 1980s than had ever been experienced before. As the former Chairman of the Joint Chiefs of Staff, General John W. Vessey, Jr., stated in 1984: "We have wonderful servicewomen doing extraordinary things and doing very well, but we have taken a male institution in a very short period of time and turned it into a coed institution, and it has been a traumatic exercise for us."[316] General Vessey further stated that the influx of women brought greater change to the military than the introduction of nuclear weapons.

Over the course of the 1980s, as the Cold War came to a close, the military adjusted to (some might say recovered from) the significant changes that had been instituted during the 1970s with regard to the role of servicewomen. Complicating this adjustment was a shift in foreign policy concerning the involvement of American troops overseas, brought on by the U.S. involvement in Southeast Asia during the Vietnam War. Fearing public backlash and military failure, government officials became hesitant to commit large numbers of troops to fight communism in foreign countries. Rather than declaring war and mobilizing the country's armed forces, America instead participated in police actions—strategic, smaller-scale operations against specific persons or in response to clearly defined events—or, what would come to be officially known as Military Operations Other Than War (MOOTW). Hence the 1980s witnessed American involvement

---

[315] Adams, "Jane Crow in the Army," 50.

[316] Molly Moore, "Open Doors Don't Yield Equality: Combat Ban Symbolizes Limits to Female Advancement in Services," *The Washington Post* (September 24, 1989), Box 1, Women in Aviation: Women in the Military, Washington Navy Yards, Naval Aviation Office Archives, Washington, DC; also quoted in Holm, *Women in the Military*, 381.

in Grenada, Libya, Panama, and the ramping up for the first Persian Gulf War.

Refining Women's Roles

This shift facilitated the expansion of women's roles in the military, as well as supporting the need for their increased recruitment. Not only were high-quality women less expensive to recruit than lower-quality males,[317] but demographic statistics showed that the number of eligible males available would continue to drop over the decade by as much as 25 percent by 1992.[318] In order to maintain a professional force, within budget restrictions, women continued to be the means by which peacetime quotas were met. Despite a pause in recruitment in 1981, dubbed "womenpause," called for by the Reagan administration to assess recruitment goals, estimates projected that the number of women in the military would reach a level of 12 percent of the total force by 1985.[319] Indeed, as the Secretary of Defense stated in 1982, qualified women were "essential to obtaining the numbers of quality people required to maintain the readiness of our forces."[320]

As women joined the services in record numbers throughout the decade, the military continued to remove barriers to advancement and opportunity for women, especially in terms of the MOS that women could occupy. Policies enacted in the late 1970s and early 1980s allowed women to occupy non-traditional jobs, including serving on non-combat ships and flying non-combat aircraft. In 1988, when the DoD Risk Rule was promulgated, establishing a single standard for determining which positions and units were closed to women, an additional 30,000 positions were opened to women, including the ability to serve in missile launch control centers.[321] Allowing women access to these positions called for further policy modifications that provided guidance on how to treat women in these circumstances. For example, official Marine policy dictated that women were subject to the same policies as men at every level of command, with the standard disclaimer for legal or physical differences mandating separate

---

[317] "Women May Yet Save the Army," 42.
[318] Beck, "Women in the Armed Forces," 35.
[319] Morden, *Women's Army Corps*, 405 and Beck, "Women in the Armed Forces," 35.
[320] Quoted in Devilbiss, *Women and Military Service*, 26.
[321] Women's Research and Education Institute, *Chronology of Significant Legal & Policy Changes*.

treatment. Still, regulations stated that in order for female Marines to serve or be transported on non-combat ships, they had to be berthed in suitable accommodations in terms of security and privacy approved by the Fleet Commander.[322]

This was also the case for women in the Navy. In order to accommodate women on board ships, the Navy modified its berthing arrangements to provide semi-private areas, as well as modifying the latrine facilities.[323] Design modifications were also called for in aircraft in order to accommodate the needs of women. The initial lack of adequate latrine facilities on aircraft was particularly troublesome; until better, more adequate facilities were provided, women used devices designed for men, which tended to cause certain gynecological problems.[324] The significant variance in body dimensions between men and women caused further issues in aircraft design: aircrew systems were built to accommodate the average male physique. Female aviators, as a result, encountered issues that included, "precise alignment of the aircrew member eyes for maximum field of view, accessibility of cockpit controls during all phases of flight and proper seat fit to ensure proper function of ejection and crashworthy seat systems."[325]

As the decade progressed, however, increasing advances in, and reliance on, technology began to favor the female body type. The technology adopted by the military often favored a more compact body type, particularly in terms of space-limited vehicles such as ships, tanks, aircraft, and

---

[322] *Women Marines in the 1980s*, 1, and Lt. Gen. E. J. Bronars (USMC Deputy Chief of Staff for Manpower) to Assistant Secretary of the Navy (Manpower, Reserve Affairs & Logistics), "Assignment of Women Marines," January 9, 1980, Reference File—Women Marines: Distribution & Location, Washington Navy Yards, Marine Corps Historical Center Archives, Washington, DC, 2-3; see also Molly Moore, "In Close Quarters, Obstacles Are Many," *The Washington Post* (September 25, 1989): A-9, Box 1, Women in Aviation: Women in the Military, Washington Navy Yards, Naval Aviation Office Archives, Washington, DC.

[323] See Dorothy Lilly, "USS Lexington: Women at Sea," *Campus* IX, no. 12 (December 12, 1980), Box 3, Women in Aviation: General Info, Folder 2, Washington Navy Yards, Naval Aviation Office Archives, Washington, DC, and Godson, *Serving Proudly*, 259-60.

[324] LCDR P. Stratton, to the Surgeon General of the Navy, Chief of Naval Operations, via the Commander of the National Naval Medical Center, Bethesda, MD, "Toilet Facilities In Navy Aircraft," April 26, 1989, Box 4, Women in Aviation: General Info, Folder 3, Washington Navy Yards, Naval Aviation Office Archives, Washington, DC.

[325] Brent M. Bennitt (Director, Air Warfare), "Draft Mission Need Statement for Accommodation of Women Aircrew in Aviation, Potential ACAT IV," (Washington, DC.: Department of the Navy, Office of the Chief of Naval Operations, May 12, 1994), Box 1, Women in Aviation: Employment & Utilization of Women in the Navy, Washington Navy Yards, Naval Aviation Office Archives, Washington, DC.

submarines.[326] Rather than brute strength, the military required individuals skilled with multi-tasking and agile dexterity. This continued to open more doors of opportunity for women as technological change greatly reduced "the fraction of military jobs requiring physical strength standards that women would be less likely to meet."[327]

But, as women moved into new occupational territories, especially territory involving confined spaces, societal norms regarding gender still played a role in dictating the terms of their service. There was "no sharper issue raised by the integration of women into the nation's military than the delicate matter of men and women living and working together—in tents, on ships and in small spaces."[328] This statement, of course, encompassed the social and fraternization issues of an integrated force, but also the issue of physical accommodation. In 1988, for example, the Air Force finally allowed women to serve on missile launch teams, but only after years of intense debate. At issue was the fact that missile launch teams consisted of 2 to 4 crew members who served 24 hour shifts in isolated one-room control centers containing one bed and one toilet among the computer banks of equipment. Thus, the issue was both physical and social. The concern was that mixed teams would threaten both the operational and family environment, as well as require extensive and/or expensive modifications to the control room. Ultimately, accommodating women in this environment entailed erecting a privacy barrier around the bed and toilet, and scheduling meetings between Base Commanders, spouses, and female crew members to discuss and address concerns. As one of the first women assigned to a mixed crew reported, after the meeting, the wives "realized we weren't terrible people who were going to come in and take their husbands away."[329]

Although most acute in the tight confines of the missile launch center, the social issues of men and women living (and working) together remained a significant consideration in the physical accommodation of servicewomen

---

[326] Jean W. Fletcher, Joyce S. McMahon and Aline O. Quester, "Tradition, Technology, and the Changing Roles of Women in the Navy," *Minerva* 11, nos. 3&4 (Fall/Winter 1993), 67; see also Holm, *Women in the Military*, 386.

[327] Fletcher et al., "Tradition, Technology, and the Changing Roles of Women in the Navy," 65.

[328] Moore, "In Close Quarters, Obstacles Are Many."

[329] Ibid.

throughout the 1980s. This concern had to be balanced against the need to establish equal treatment and unit integrity through integration, especially with regard to housing. By the 1980s, integrated hotel/motel style barracks had become the standard for new construction. Not only did integrated housing allow for greater unit integrity by enabling the entire unit to be housed and administered jointly, but it also dispelled the perception that men or women were receiving better facilities at any particular command and reinforced the policy of equal treatment for all.[330]

Housing and Facility Design

This policy was reaffirmed in 1983 when the Secretary of Defense, by Congressional directive, revised the housing standards for new construction for all enlisted personnel. Both male and female enlisted personnel were to receive semi-private accommodations based on the "2 plus 2" room module—two rooms each with two persons, sharing a bathroom—derived from Army design criteria (Figure 96).[331] Soldiers ranked E-7 and above received a private bath. This 1983 revision finally brought the men's housing standards on par with the women for the first time in military history. Men finally received the same amenities and housing considerations that women had been receiving for decades.

All was not entirely equal, though, in terms of physically accommodating servicewomen. Detainment and brig facilities were still gender-segregated, although the services began providing such facilities for women outside of the barracks during the 1980s.[332] Also, locker rooms at post gym facilities exhibited gender-based design differences. Men's locker rooms still provided gang showers, while the women's provided shower stalls, but sometimes without an attached dressing cubicle; the family locker rooms, a new addition in the modernized military, provided partitioned showers with attached dressing cubicles (Figure 97).[333]

---

[330] Wilson, "Women Marines," 6-19.

[331] Odle, "Army Leaders Set Standard Design Goals"; see also Baldwin, "History of Army Peacetime Housing," 22-23.

[332] See Bulletin Board, "Marines Establish New Female Brig," *Minerva* 4, no. 2 (Summer 1986), 59-60.

[333] U.S. Department of Defense, *Military Handbook: Indoor Fitness/Recreational Facilities,* MIL-HDBK-1037/8 (Washington, DC: Department of Defense, August 1996), 47-48, 53.

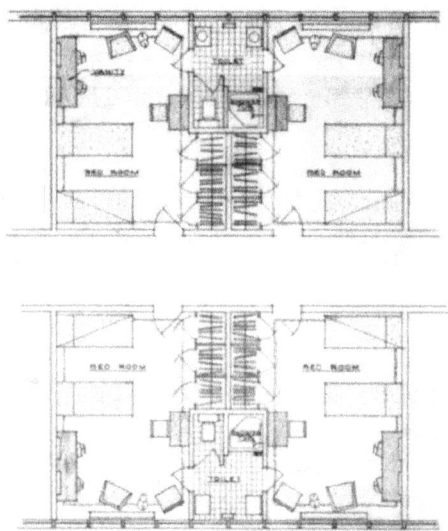

Figure 96. Two double-room/shared bath design (NARA).

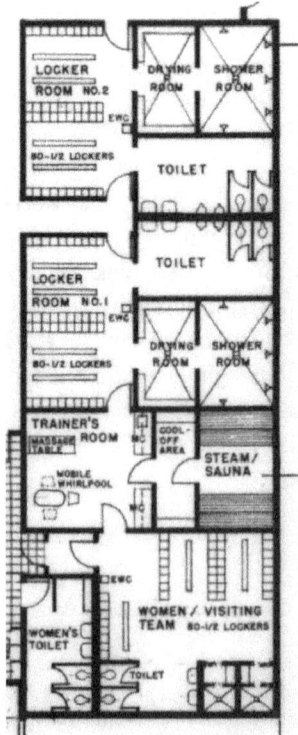

Figure 97. Gymnasium plan from 1969 showing gender differences in bathroom facilities (NARA).

Training

In direct opposition to housing, which followed a fairly straight trajectory toward full integration, training policy went through a state of flux in the 1980s. The Army, which had integrated training in 1978, reverted to segregated training in 1983. Although women continued to receive similar training to men, the Army felt gender-integrated basic training was not successful and that, due to their physiological differences, women were holding men back (Figure 98).[334]

Figure 98. 15 S&T Battalion gender-segregated training, Fort Hood, TX, 1983 (1st CAV Museum, Fort Hood).

Similarly, training for female Marines was integrated from 1978 until 1980 (except for boot camp, which has always been segregated), including both offensive and defensive tactics training for women. From 1980 to 1988, however, the Marine Corps again restricted women from training in offensive tactics.[335] The reason for this was attributed to the recognition of

---

[334] Maj. Gen. Mary E. Clark (Ret.), "Women Could Make Things Happen (Excerpts from an Address Presented by Maj. Gen. Mary E. Clark, USA (Ret.) for Fort Bragg's Federal Woman's Week Activities, August 25, 1983," *Minerva* 1, no. 4 (Winter 1983), 108.

[335] "TBS Expands Training for Women," 1988, Reference File—Women Marines: Combat Training, Washington Navy Yards, Marine Corps Historical Center Archives, Washington, DC.

physical differences between men and women, and that offensive tactics were deemed necessary only for combat Marines, a role from which women were barred. Women still received some training in marksmanship and weapons familiarization, as well as field training, which were considered essential for their role in combat support.[336] Basic Warrior Training was once again added to the training regime for female Marines in 1988.[337]

---

[336] Sgt. Scott Jenkins, "Women Marine Training Expanded," (USMC, Division of Public Affairs, Headquarters, Press Release, No. SJ-229-80, November 26, 1980), Reference File—Women Marines: Combat Training, Washington Navy Yards, Marine Corps Historical Center Archives, Washington, DC; 1st Lt. Mike La Bonne, "Distaff Warriors," *The Leatherneck* (November 1980), Reference File—Women Marines: Combat Training, Washington Navy Yards, Marine Corps Historical Center Archives, Washington, DC, 44; C.E. McLaurin, "Marines to Train Women in Marksmanship," *Savannah Morning News* (February 19, 1981): 1-B, Reference File—Women Marines: Combat Training, Washington Navy Yards, Marine Corps Historical Center Archives, Washington, DC.

[337] Jane Goldman, "A Few Good Women," *Savvy Woman Magazine* (January 1989), Reference File—Women Marines: Women Marines in the 1980s Press Releases/Publications, Washington Navy Yards, Marine Corps Historical Center Archives, Washington, DC, 63.

8 Conclusion: This Man's Army No More

By the end of the Cold War, approximately one in every ten members of the armed forces was female, reflecting an increase of almost six and a half times over the number of women serving in the early 1970s. Furthermore, more women served in the military in the United States than in any other country in the world.[338] According to government reports, in 1972, men comprised 98.1 percent and women only 1.9 percent of the military, but by 1990, men comprised 89.0 percent and women 11.0 percent.[339] Also by the end of the Cold War, the role of women in the military had been completely revolutionized from its original intentions established during World War II. As Alice Bradley Davey, WAAC 3rd Officer, stated in 1942, "We are performing a man's work in a man's Army—and that's what the Women's Army Auxiliary Corps was organized for in the first place."[340]

By the 1990s, "this man's Army" was an anachronism, and women were no longer considered to be doing "men's work," but simply doing their job. The only similarity between the role of women in the military during World War II and at the end of the Cold War was that in both cases the women were absolutely essential for maintaining a successful military. Neither the force of yesteryear nor the force of today could function without the contributions of women. As such, in many ways the history of women in the military during the Cold War was a story of the gradual, and perhaps sometimes painful, progress made by the military to accept and accommodate women. Brigadier General Evelyn Foote, former WAC Director, once stated that women "had come into an institution that was totally unprepared to support them—with uniforms, billeting or training facilities—at first," but how before long women "went all over the world to support the U.S. mission."[341] Not only were women supported with adequate uniforms, billeting, and training facilities by 1989, but they were

---

[338] Moore, "Open Doors Don't Yield Equality."

[339] U.S. Government Accounting Office, *Military Personnel: Composition of the Active Duty Forces by Race or National Origin Identification and be Gender*, GAO/NSIAD-91-134FS (Washington, DC: GAO, 1991), 1.

[340] Alice Bradley Davey, "I am a WAAC," *Mademoiselle* (June 1943), Mabel M. Gilliam Collection, 168.7342-1, IRIS No. 1126914, Air Force Historical Research Agency, Maxwell AFB, Montgomery, AL.

[341] Hasenauer, "From WAAC to Regular Army," 30.

also provided with substantially the same opportunities offered to men, as well as placed on equal footing in terms of housing standards, promotion potential, career opportunities, and training (Figure 99).

Figure 99. U.S. Army servicewomen, King Fahd International Airport, Saudi Arabia, January 1991 (WIMSA, Vertical File, Collection of Lorraine Souza).

Moreover, the momentum built up during the Cold War for advancing opportunities carried over beyond 1989. In the early 1990s, additional changes in legislation and policy occurred, allowing women to be assigned to "all positions for which they are qualified, except for those positions below the brigade level whose primary mission is to engage in direct combat on the ground."[342] These changes specifically eliminated the restrictions on women for flying combat aircraft or serving on combat ships. More pertinently, they reflected a gradual shift in philosophy concerning women's role in the military. As more women began occupying more MOS, officials began to recognize that the traditional explanations for why women were restricted from certain occupations no longer resonated with society or with the shape of the armed forces. By the 1980s, it was noted that as

---

[342] U.S. Government Accounting Office, *Gender Issues: Analysis of Methodologies in Reports to the Secretaries of Defense and the Army*, GAO/NSIAD-98-125 (Washington, DC: GAO, 1998), 3.

weaponry and warfare became more sophisticated, intellect was more important than brawn, with fewer than 10 percent of military jobs requiring actual infantry duty. This prompted Rep. Patricia Schroeder, a member of the House Armed Services Committee to ask: "How much muscle does it take to launch an ICBM?"[343]

Still, old habits and notions die hard. While many issues related to training and occupations were resolved in the 1990s, military leaders, and the country for that matter, still struggle with traditional concepts regarding gender and issues of privacy and protection. It is this notion that is at the center of the swirling debate surrounding whether or not women should be allowed into combat. It also influences continuing debates regarding whether or not it should be legal to draft women. And, even though gender-integrated housing and equalized housing standards have been the established norm since the early 1980s, government officials still revisit the issue. A 1998 article in the *Washington Times* discussing the role of women in the military summarized the issue thusly: "What we are really seeing is the two sides of an age-old feminist dilemma. Should the military treat men and women alike and ignore the problems, or take special care to protect women and ignore the resulting inequality?"[344]

In terms of housing, the National Defense Authorization Act for Fiscal Year 1999 required that the services provide "separate and secure housing for male and female recruits with separate entrances and with sleeping and latrine areas separated by permanent walls."[345] The Act further mandated that if installations could not meet this requirement by October 1, 2001, than they must house men and women in separate facilities. Of course, this was in basic terms a reiteration of policy that had been established in 1972 when the military first contended with means to alleviate the housing shortage brought on by the increased number of women enlisting in the AVF. As where in 1972, there was real concern whether or not privacy and security would be maintained for servicewomen under

---

[343] Beck, "Women in the Armed Forces," 36.

[344] Brian Mitchell, "Do we need women in the military?" *The Washington Times* (April 2, 1998), Vertical Files: Women in the Military, Washington Navy Yards, Naval Historical Foundation Library, Washington, DC.

[345] U.S. Government Accounting Office, *Military Housing: Cost of Separate Barracks for Male and Female Recruits in Basic Training*, GAO/NSIAD-99-75 (Washington, DC: GAO, 1999), 1.

these standards, in 1999, the consensus was that "current recruit housing practices provide separate and secure housing for male and females and that little, if any, additional security would be achieved if males and females were housed in separate buildings."[346] More importantly, perhaps, were the feelings on the part of servicewomen; in the words of one Army Major, "One does not join the military to lead a sheltered and protected life."[347]

While privacy and protection for women in housing were still issues in the wake of the Cold War, by the late 1990s, they were practically absent from training concerns. Although the Marine Corps continued its practice of segregated recruit training, all other service branches conducted integrated training (the Army reintegrated training in 1993). Further, by the late 1990s, training programs were nearly identical for men and women, except that men and women were housed separately, had different medical examinations and hygiene classes, and in some instances, met different physical fitness test standards.[348] The Marine Corps, however, decided in 1996 that women would be held to the same physical fitness standards as men, except for the pull-up event. For health reasons based on the physiological differences between men and women, female Marines performed the flexed-arm hang from a bar, rather than pull-ups, and were judged on how long they could hold their chin above the bar. Still, they were required to run the same 3 mile course as the men, attended every class the men did, and took "every step" the men did.[349] When it came to training, both physical and job-related, the military finally seemed to recognize that, as Major Rhonda Cornum, a Prisoner of War during Operation Desert Storm, stated, "The qualities that are most important in all military jobs—things like integrity, moral courage, and determination—have nothing to do with gender."

Finally, regardless of the status of women in the military today, there can be no doubt that much of what women have gained in equal opportunities

---

[346] Ibid., 12-13.

[347] Quoted in Holm, *Women in the Military*, 405.

[348] U.S. Government Accounting Office, *Gender Integration in Basic Training*, 2.

[349] J.B. Walker, "Equal to the Task: Fourth Recruit Training Battalion Prepares Women for Success," *The Leatherneck* (February 2001): 16-18, Reference File—Women Marines: Combat Training, Washington Navy Yards, Marine Corps Historical Center Archives, Washington, DC, 17.

in the military is owed to the work and efforts of Cold War Era servicewomen. In fact, both military men and women of today's force owe a debt of gratitude to the servicewomen of the Cold War, especially with regard to the standards of living and quality of life that they enjoy. If not for the need to physically accommodate women to the standard which society dictated, it is unlikely that military personnel today would enjoy the semi-private rooms, increased space allowances, or added amenities of kitchens and expanded laundry facilities they currently do. Indeed, Cold War Era servicewomen have left a significant heritage evident in the built environment of our country's military installations.

Aside from their influence on current design standards that can be witnessed at any military installation, the potential for legacy buildings incorporating outdated design standards specifically intended for women is great. Female restrooms that come with attached "powder rooms," which can be found in most every building more than 30 years old, are a legacy architectural feature leftover from the 1950s and 1960s. Stairs, rather than ladders for fire escapes, or mess halls with individual chairs rather than attached benches, are design features attributable to women. TV lounges, guest bathrooms, kitchens, and laundry facilities in barracks are also attributed to women. Increased space per individual, bathtubs, shower stalls, and increased privacy both in latrine and living space is yet another design feature attributable to women. As such, barracks complexes more than 30 years old at installations that accommodated female units hold great potential for historic value in terms of their design features.

In September 1942, an editorial in *Life* magazine, responding to the rapidly changing role of women for wartime necessity, made the following plea: "For it is profoundly true that the responsibilities that men acknowledge are always in the custody of their womenfolk. Men may create ideals, but women must maintain them. The standard that the women set for America today will determine the stature of our victory. Set that standard high, women of America, make it tough, so that we may win something of which we can be proud."[350] Although the editor was speaking to all women, including those serving in private industry, public philanthropy, or the military, the message is particularly appropriate to military women. The

---

[350] "What Women Can Do: Think War, Buy Little, Maintain Our Ideals," *Life* (September 28, 1942): 32.

high standard that military women have always aimed for, whether set by themselves or military leaders, resulted in a rich and proud tradition of service. It also contributed to a unique and culturally significant landscape contained within our nation's military installations.

Bibliography

"A Little Slower, But…Women Marines Sample Combat." *Herald-Examiner, Los Angeles* (March 25, 1977): 1. Reference File—Women Marines: Combat Training. Washington Navy Yards, Marine Corps Historical Center Archives, Washington, DC.

Adams, Virginia. "Jane Crow in the Army: Obstacles to Sexual Integration." *Psychology Today* (October 1980): 50-65. Box 3, Women in Aviation: General Info, Folder 3. Washington Navy Yards, Naval Aviation Office Archives, Washington, DC.

Akers, Regina T. "Negro WACS and WAVES, 1942-1945: Some Notable Differences (Draft)." November 16, 1990. Vertical Files: WWII African American Women. Washington Navy Yards, Naval Historical Foundation Library, Washington, DC.

Akers, Regina T. comp. "Select Bibliography on Blacks and Women in the United States Military During the Twentieth Century." Reference File—Women Marines: (2 of 2) Brochures/Publications. Washington Navy Yards, Marine Corps Historical Center Archives, Washington, DC.

American Military History. Army Historical Series, Center of Military History. Washington, DC: Center of Military History, United States Army, 1989. [online version: http://www.army.mil/cmh/books/AMH/amh-toc.htm; updated April 25, 2001].

"American Women: Draft Them? Too Bad We Can't Draft Their Grandmothers." *Life* (January 29, 1945): 28.

"Analyses of Building and Fixtures for 700 EW Barracks, Fort Myer." circa 1960s. Ft. Lee 228-01, WHC-378, Folder—Housing, Misc Reports (1965-67). WAC Museum Archives, Ft. Lee, VA.

Bailey, Brig. Gen. Mildred C. "Women in the Army." *Commanders Digest* 18, no. 2 (July 10, 1975). Reference File—Women Marines: General (1 of 2). Washington Navy Yards, Marine Corps Historical Center Archives, Washington, DC.

Baldwin, William C. "A History of Army Peacetime Housing To the End of the Cold War." *Occasional Papers 4*. Society for History in the Federal Government, 2004.

Beck, Melinda. "Women in the Armed Forces." *Newsweek* (February 18, 1981). Reference File—Women Marines: Combat Training. Washington Navy Yards, Marine Corps Historical Center Archives, Washington, DC.

Bellafaire, Judith A. *The Army Nurse Corps in World War II*. Washington, DC: Center for Military History, 1993.

Bennitt, Brent M. "Draft Mission Need Statement for Accommodation of Women Aircrew in Aviation, Potential ACAT IV." Washington, DC: Department of the Navy, Office of the Chief of Naval Operations, May 12, 1994. Box 1, Women in Aviation: Employment & Utilization of Women in the Navy. Washington Navy Yards, Naval Aviation Office Archives, Washington, DC.

Binkin, Martin and Shirley J. Bach. *Women and the Military*. Washington, DC: Brookings Institute, 1977.

Brewer, Col. Margaret A. "Women in the Marine Corps." *Commanders Digest* 18, no. 2 (July 10, 1975). Reference File—Women Marines: General (1 of 2). Washington Navy Yards, Marine Corps Historical Center Archives, Washington, DC.

Bronars, Lt. Gen. E. J. "Assignment of Women Marines." Memo to Assistant Secretary of the Navy (Manpower, Reserve Affairs & Logistics) dated January 9, 1980. Reference File—Women Marines: Distribution & Location. Washington Navy Yards, Marine Corps Historical Center Archives, Washington, DC.

Brown, Brig. Gen. E.A., Jr. "Request for Waiver in Provisions of Department of Defense Instruction 4270.4, June 16, 1954." Memo to Assistant Secretary of the Army, CMA dated June 19. 1957. Ft. Lee 228-01, WHC-377, Folder—Housing, Enlisted/Officer (General) (1957-63). WAC Museum Archives, Ft. Lee, VA.

Bryant, Floyd S. "Request for Waiver in Provisions of Department of Defense Instruction No. 4270.4." Memo to Secretary of the Army dated August 12, 1957. Ft. Lee 228-01, WHC-377, Folder—Housing, Enlisted/Officer (General) (1957-63). WAC Museum Archives, Ft. Lee, VA.

Building the Navy's Bases in World War II: History of the Bureau of Yards and Docks and the Civil Engineers Corps, 1940-1946. Vol. 1. Washington: GPO, 1947.

Bulletin Board. "Marines Establish New Female Brig." *Minerva* 4, no. 2 (Summer 1986), 59-60.

"Camp Facilities for Females." Memo dated 21 August 1944. Box X-115-19 "Military Theaters of Operations SWPA, General Operations—Women-Camp Facilities for Females." U.S. Army Corps of Engineers History Office Archives. Alexandria, VA.

Clark, Maj. Gen. Mary E. "Women Could Make Things Happen (Excerpts from an Address Presented by Maj. Gen. Mary E. Clark, USA (Ret.) for Fort Bragg's Federal Woman's Week Activities, August 25, 1983." *Minerva* 1, no. 4 (Winter 1983):101-108.

Commandant, U.S. Marine Corps. "Marine Corps Women's Reserve General Policies, pertaining to." Memo dated November 25, 1943. Reference File—Women Marines: WWII Regulations. Washington Navy Yards, Marine Corps Historical Center Archives, Washington, DC.

———. "Marine Corps Women's Reserve, matters affecting." Memo dated May 19, 1944. Reference File—Women Marines: WWII Regulations. Washington Navy Yards, Marine Corps Historical Center Archives, Washington, DC.

"Completed WAC Housing Questionnaires from all CONUS WAC Detachments in response to call for information from the Office of the Director, U.S. Women's Army Corps." 1964. Ft. Lee 228-01, WHC-376, Folder—Housing, Enlisted Survey of (1964-65). WAC Museum Archives, Ft. Lee, VA.

Cross, Lt.Col. Martha L. "Staff Study—WAF Administration and Command Control." April 6, 1956. USAF Collection, K141.35-9 6 Apr 1956, IRIS No. 469736. Air Force Historical Research Agency, Maxwell AFB, Montgomery, AL.

"DACOWITS." *Women's Army Corps Journal* 3, no. 2 (April -June 1972): 10-13. WAC Museum Archives, Ft. Lee, VA.

"DACOWITS—a DOD Advisory Council." *On Guard* XIX, no. 6 (March 1990): 13. Box 131-7, General Files; Folder: Woman in the Corps of Engineers. U.S. Army Corps of Engineers History Office Archives, Alexandria, VA.

DACOWITS. *DACOWITS History of Recommendations: Fall Conference 1973.* Washington, DC: DACOWITS. [http://www.dtic.mil/dacowits/tablerecommendation_subpage.html].

———. "Notes and minutes from the Fall Meeting, 21-25 October 1979 in Columbia, South Carolina." DACOWITS Meetings Series. Women in Military Service for America Memorial Foundation, Inc. Archives, Washington, DC.

———. "Report of the Ad Hoc Housing Committee." May 1955. Ft. Lee 228-01, WHC-377, Folder—Housing, Enlisted/Officer (General) (1957-63). WAC Museum Archives, Ft. Lee, VA.

———. "Review of Ad-Hoc Housing Committee." April 7, 1959. Ft. Lee 228-01, WHC-377, Folder—Housing, Enlisted/Officer (General) (1957-63). WAC Museum Archives, Ft. Lee, VA.

———. "Review of DACOWITS Ad-Hoc Housing Studies." 1959. Ft. Lee 228-01, WHC-377, Folder—Housing, Enlisted/Officer (General) (1957-63). WAC Museum Archives, Ft. Lee, VA.

Davey, Alice B. "I am a WAAC." *Mademoiselle* (June 1943). Mabel M. Gilliam collection, 168.7342-1, IRIS No. 1126914. Air Force Historical Research Agency, Maxwell AFB, Montgomery, AL.

Department of Defense, Assistant Secretary of Defense (Installation and Logistics. "Department of Defense Instruction: Department of Defense Construction Criteria Manual." .Washington, DC: Department of Defense, 17 November 1967.

Department of the Army. *Troop Topics: Leave It To the WAC.* Department of the Army Pamphlet No. 20. Washington, DC: Department of the Army, 1951. Collection no. 3547. Women in Military Service for America Memorial Foundation, Inc. Archives, Washington, DC.

Department of the Navy, Naval Historical Center. "World War II Era WAVES—Quarters & Meals." Online Library of Selected Images: People-Topics—Women & The U.S. Navy. [http://www.history.navy.mil/photos/prs-tpic/females/wvw2-qf.htm]. Last updated February 18, 2001.

Deputy Chief of Staff for Logistics, U.S. Army. "Design of Bachelor Officer Quarters." Memo to Chief of Engineers, U.S. Army, 1963. Ft. Lee 228-01, WHC-373, Folder—Housing. WAC Museum Archives, Ft. Lee, VA.

Deputy Chief of Staff for Personnel, Director—WAC. *Department of Defense Instruction: Standards and Criteria for Construction—Permanent Barracks and Bachelor Officer Quarters.* Washington, DC: Department of Defense, August 1964. Ft. Lee 228-01, WHC-374, Folder—Housing Doctrine & Policy (1963-65). WAC Museum Archives, Ft. Lee, VA.

Devilbiss, M.C. *Women and Military Service: A History, Analysis, and Overview of Key Issues.* Montgomery, AL: Air University Press, 1990.

Dickerson, Jan. "WAC Expansion—Getting It All Together." *Women's Army Corps Journal* 4, no. 2 (April-June 1973). WAC Museum Archives, Ft. Lee, VA.

Directorate of Statistical Services, Personnel Statistics Division. "U.S. Air Force Military Personnel Surveys: Air Force Female Military Personnel." Series ASC-4B, No. 2. Source of Information: RCS: AF-P3. Washington, DC: Headquarters, U.S. Air Force, 1957. J. Sewell Papers, 168.7172-2, IRIS No. 1041204. Air Force Historical Research Agency, Maxwell AFB, Montgomery, AL.

Enlisted Personnel: Guide for the Administration and Management of Enlisted Women in the Air Force. Air Force Pamphlet 39-3. Washington, DC: Department of the Air Force, April 30, 1975. In Staff of the Directorate, Women in the Air Force. *History of the Women in the Air Force: 1 January 1975 – 30 June 1975.* Washington, DC: Headquarters, United States Air Force, Director, Women in the Air Force, 1975. Director, Women in the Air Force Collection, K141.33 75/01/01-75/06/30 Dir of WAF, IRIS No. 1007190. Air Force Historical Research Agency, Maxwell AFB, Montgomery, AL.

Faber Birren and Company. *The Application of Color to Shore Establishments.* Washington, DC: U.S. Navy Department, 1948.

Fact Sheet: Women in the Air Force. Revised 1975. In Staff of the Directorate, Women in the Air Force. *History of the Women in the Air Force: 1 January 1975 – 30 June 1975.* Washington, DC: Headquarters, United States Air Force, Director, Women in the Air Force, 1975. Director, Women in the Air Force Collection, K141.33 75/01/01-75/06/30 Dir of WAF, IRIS No. 1007190. Air Force Historical Research Agency, Maxwell AFB, Montgomery, AL.

Famiglietti, Gene. "New Barracks to be 'Home Style' Complete with Lounge." *Army Times* (June 21, 1972). Ft. Lee 228-01, WHC-378, Folder—Housing, Misc Reports (1965-67). WAC Museum Archives, Ft. Lee, VA.

Fisher, Col. Ann. "U.S. Army Training and Doctrine Command WAC Utilization/Integration Symposium, 25-26 June 1974, After-Action Report." Headquarters, U.S. Army Training and Doctrine Command, August 20, 1974. Ft. Lee 228-01, WHC-846, Folder—TRADOC Symposium on Women (1974). WAC Museum Archives, Ft. Lee, VA.

Fletcher, Jean W., Joyce S. McMahon and Aline O. Quester. "Tradition, Technology, and the Changing Roles of Women in the Navy." *Minerva* 11, nos. 3&4 (Fall/Winter 1993): 57-85.

Foster, Lt. Col. H. "Meeting on WAC Enlisted Barracks." Memo dated September 18, 1962. Ft. Lee 228-01, WHC-377, Folder—Housing, Enlisted/Officer (General) (1957-63). WAC Museum Archives, Ft. Lee, VA.

Godson, Susan H. "Capt. Joy Bright Hancock: Builder of the Co-Ed Navy." *The Retired Officer* (December 1982): 15-17. Box 2, RG Women in Aviation: WAVES folder. Washington Navy Yards, Naval Aviation Office Archives, Washington, DC.

———. *Serving Proudly: A History Of Women in the U.S. Navy*. Annapolis, MD: Naval Institute Press, 2001.

Goldman, Benjamin, Rex M. Naylor, and G.W. Hueners (compilers). *History of the Tactical Air Command, 1 July through 30 November 1950*. Vol. I—Narrative. (Tactical Air Command, 1951). USAF Collection, K417.01 Jul 1 – Nov 1950 V.I, IRIS No. 502588. Air Force Historical Research Agency, Maxwell AFB, Montgomery, AL.

Goldman, Jane. "A Few Good Women." *Savvy Woman Magazine* (January 1989). Reference File—Women Marines: Women Marines in the 1980s Press Releases/Publications. Washington Navy Yards, Marine Corps Historical Center Archives, Washington, DC.

Gordon, Capt. Kathryn A. "A Larger Role for Women Marines." *Marine Corps Gazette* (November 1977): 19-20. Reference File—Women Marines: Combat Training. Washington Navy Yards, Marine Corps Historical Center Archives, Washington, DC.

Gorman, Col. Emily C. "Enlisted Women's Barracks, Fort Myer, Virginia." Memo to Post Engineer, Fort Myer, Virginia, November 24, 1964. Ft. Lee 228-01, WHC-378, Folder—Housing, Misc Reports (1965-67). WAC Museum Archives, Ft. Lee, VA.

———. "EW Barracks." Memo to Deputy Chief of Staff for Personnel dated August 16, 1962. Ft. Lee 228-01, WHC-377, Folder—Housing, Enlisted/Officer (General) (1957-63). WAC Museum Archives, Ft. Lee, VA.

———. "Furnishings for Female Officers' Quarters." Memo to Deputy Chief of Staff for Personnel. Also has FY58 "Housing" addendum attached. January 18, 1963. Ft. Lee 228-01, WHC-373, Folder—Housing. WAC Museum Archives, Ft. Lee, VA.

Grossman, William O. *Your Daughter in the U.S. Air Force*. Stockton, CA: USAF Recruiting Office, 1966. Collection no. 171964AIC (Sidney Dungey Keen). Women in Military Service for America Memorial Foundation, Inc. Archives, Washington, DC.

Guldry, Vernon A., Jr., "Pentagon SOS: Women, Sign Up." *Washington Star* (June 26, 1977). Reference File—Women Marines: Combat Training. Washington Navy Yards, Marine Corps Historical Center Archives, Washington, DC.

Hancock, Joy Bright. "Conference with Mr. Random of the Eberstadt Committee." Memo dated September 14, 1948. Box 2, WAVES, Folder: (I-21) Eberstadt Committee (1948). Washington Navy Yards, Naval Historical Center Archives, Washington, DC.

———. *Lady in the Navy: A Personal Reminiscence*. Annapolis MD: Naval Institute Press, 1972.

———. "Material on the Women's Reserve Section for inclusion in the Secretary of the Navy's Annual Report and the Annual Reports of the Bureaus and Offices for the Fiscal Year 1943." August 12, 1943. WNY, RG Women in Aviation: WAVES Folder. Washington Navy Yards, Naval Aviation Office Archives, Washington, DC.

Hasenauer, Heike. "From WAAC to Regular Army." *Soldiers* (May 1992). Vertical Files: Women in the Military, 1940-1949. Washington Navy Yards, Naval Historical Foundation Library, Washington, DC.

Henretta, James A., W. Elliot Brownlee, David Brody, and Susan Ware. *America's History*. Chicago: The Dorsey Press, 1987.

Hillinger, Charles. "Women Equal: In the Military, War of Sexes Is All But Won." *Los Angeles Times* (December 18, 1978). Box 4, BUPERS 00W, Folder: History 1978. Washington Navy Yards, Naval Historical Center Archives, Washington, DC.

Hoke, Celia. *Women in the Armed Forces*. Washington, DC: Office of Information for the Armed Forces, Assistant Secretary of Defense (Public Affairs), 1976. Reference File—Women Marines: (1 of 2) Brochures/Publications. Washington Navy Yards, Marine Corps Historical Center Archives, Washington, DC.

Holm, Maj. Gen. Jeanne, USAF (Ret.). *Women in the Military: An Unfinished Revolution*. Novato, CA: Presido Press, 1982.

Howard, Grendel. "Carrying Forth A Tradition." *Soldiers* 40, no. 2 (February 1985). Collection no. 3547. Women in Military Service for America Memorial Foundation, Inc. Archives, Washington, DC.

It's the Vogue (Recruit Brochure). Circa 1950s. Reference File—Women Marines: (2 of 2) Brochures/Publications. Washington Navy Yards, Marine Corps Historical Center Archives, Washington, DC.

Jacobs, Randall. "General Policies Pertaining to the Women's Reserve." Women's Reserve Circular Letter No. 1-43, April 30, 1943. Box 3, WAVES, Folder: (I-31) Historical—Women's Reserve Circular Letters (1943-1946). Washington Navy Yards, Naval Historical Center Archives, Washington, DC.

Jenkins, Sgt. Scott. "Women Marine Training Expanded." USMC, Division of Public Affairs, Headquarters. Press Release, No. SJ-229-80 dated November 26, 1980. Reference File—Women Marines: Combat Training. Washington Navy Yards, Marine Corps Historical Center Archives, Washington, DC.

Katzman, Sandra Lee. "DACOWITS Looks at Women in the Military." *Family* (October 1978). Mabel M. Gilliam Collection, 168.7342-35 1 Jan – 31 Dec 1978, IRIS No. 1126948. Air Force Historical Research Agency, Maxwell AFB, Montgomery, AL.

Kehrer, Maj. Marie. "Exclusion of Company Storage Space from 140 Square Feet Per EW Gross Barracks." Two memos of same title dated April 2, 1958 and August 3, 1960. Ft. Lee 228-01, WHC-377, Folder—Housing, Enlisted/Officer (General) (1957-63). WAC Museum Archives, Ft. Lee, VA.

Kuhn, Mary Ann. Telephone conversation with Lt. Col. Brewer, October 1, 1970. Reference File—Women Marines: Liberation Articles. Washington Navy Yards, Marine Corps Historical Center Archives, Washington, DC.

La Bonne, 1st Lt. Mike. "Distaff Warriors." *The Leatherneck* (November 1980). Reference File—Women Marines: Combat Training. Washington Navy Yards, Marine Corps Historical Center Archives, Washington, DC.

Lampert, Maj. Gen. J.B. "EW Barracks." Memo to Deputy Chief of Staff for Logistics dated June 6, 1962. Ft. Lee 228-01, WHC-377, Folder—Housing, Enlisted/Officer (General) (1957-63). WAC Museum Archives, Ft. Lee, VA.

Lehman, Mildred K. and Milton Lehman. "The Lady Privates of Company D." *Cosmopolitan* (October 1951). Collection no. 4348 (Frances D. Ames). Women in Military Service for America Memorial Foundation, Inc. Archives, Washington, DC.

Lilly, Dorothy. "USS Lexington: Women at Sea." *Campus* IX, no. 12 (December 12, 1980). Box 3, Women in Aviation: General Info, Folder 2. Washington Navy Yards, Naval Aviation Office Archives, Washington, DC.

Lyons, R.D. and Steven Marcus. "The Women Marines: 11th Anniversary." *Leatherneck* 37, no. 2 (February 1954): 14-30. Collection no. 1704 (Margaret Stinson). Women in Military Service for America Memorial Foundation, Inc. Archives, Washington, DC.

"Manpower: An Army of 7,500,000 Men With Draft of 18-Year-Olds is First Step in Solution." *Life* (October 26, 1942): 29-37.

Marine Corps Headquarters, trans. "Off to the Battle." *Stern* (December 1, 1978). Reference File—Women Marines: Liberation Articles. Washington Navy Yards, Marine Corps Historical Center Archives, Washington, DC.

Marine Corps Headquarters. "Women in the Marine Corps (draft)." February 1979. Reference File—Women Marines: General (1 of 2). Washington Navy Yards, Marine Corps Historical Center Archives, Washington, DC.

"Marine Women's Barracks." circa 1950s. Reference File—Women Marines: Press Releases. Washington Navy Yards, Marine Corps Historical Center Archives, Washington, DC.

Marshall, G.C. *Women's Army Corps Regulations*. Circular No. 289. Washington, DC: Government Printing Office, 1943. USAF Collection, 247.911, 1 Nov 1943 – 10 Feb 1944, IRIS No. 5228512. Air Force Historical Research Agency, Maxwell AFB, Montgomery, AL.

Matthews, Davida. "Orlando Recruit Training...It's Coed." *All Hands* (May 1976). Box 20, BUPERS 00W, Folder: Clippings 1971-1978. Washington Navy Yards, Naval Historical Center Archives, Washington, DC.

McClintic, Robert G. "BOQ/Barracks Plan Expected to Get Green Light." *Journal of the Armed Forces* 103, no. 37 (May 14, 1966). Ft. Lee 228-01, WHC-378, Folder—Housing, Misc Reports (1965-67). WAC Museum Archives, Ft. Lee, VA.

———. "Life in Bachelor Quarters May Undergo Face-Lifting." *Journal of the Armed Forces* 103, no. 37 (May 14, 1966). Ft. Lee 228-01, WHC-378, Folder—Housing, Misc Reports (1965-67). WAC Museum Archives, Ft. Lee, VA.

McLaurin, C.E. "Marines to Train Women in Marksmanship." *Savannah Morning News* (February 19, 1981): 1-B. Reference File—Women Marines: Combat Training. Washington Navy Yards, Marine Corps Historical Center Archives, Washington, DC.

Military Personnel: Assignment and Administration of WAF Personnel. AFR 35-44. Washington, DC: Department of the Air Force, 1949. USAF Collection, 168.12035-44, October 25, 1949, Air Force Historical Research Agency, Maxwell AFB, Montgomery, AL.

Mitchell, Brian. "Do we need women in the military?" *The Washington Times* (April 2, 1998). Vertical Files: Women in the Military. Washington Navy Yards, Naval Historical Foundation Library, Washington, DC.

Moore, Molly. "In Close Quarters, Obstacles Are Many." *The Washington Post* (September 25, 1989): A-9. Box 1, Women in Aviation: Women in the Military. Washington Navy Yards, Naval Aviation Office Archives, Washington, DC.

———. "Open Doors Don't Yield Equality: Combat Ban Symbolizes Limits to Female Advancement in Services." *The Washington Post* (September 24, 1989). Box 1, Women in Aviation: Women in the Military. Washington Navy Yards, Naval Aviation Office Archives, Washington, DC.

Morden, Bettie J. *The Women's Army Corps, 1945-1978*. 2d ed. Washington, DC: Center of Military History, U.S. Army, 2000.

Murphy, Caryle. "Female Marines Get 'In-the-Mud' Field Training." *The Washington Post* (February 14, 1977). Reference File—Women Marines: Combat Training. Washington Navy Yards, Marine Corps Historical Center Archives, Washington, DC.

Newman, Debra L. "The Propaganda and the Truth: Black Women and World War II." *Minerva* 4, no. 4 (Winter 1986): 72-92.

"Now Military is Putting Women into 'Men Only' Jobs." *U.S. News & World Report* (December 10, 1973). Series III, Box 30, Box Post 1946 Command File (1066). Washington Navy Yards, Naval Historical Center Archives, Washington, DC.

Odle, Sharon M. "Army Leaders Set Standard Design Goals." *Engineer Update, USACE* (May 1986). Box 10, General Files; Folder 10-1-3: Army Leaders Set Standard Design Goals-May 1986. U.S. Army Corps of Engineers History Office Archives, Alexandria, VA.

Office of the Deputy Chief of Staff for Logistics (Department of the Army). "Bachelor Officer Housing." October 16, 1964. Ft. Lee 228-01, WHC-373, Folder—Housing. WAC Museum Archives, Ft. Lee, VA.

Office of the Director, WAC. "Background on Enlisted Housing." Document prepared for WSA Conference, November 1964. Ft. Lee 228-01, WHC-377, Folder—Housing, Enlisted/Officer (General) (1957-63). WAC Museum Archives, Ft. Lee, VA.

Office of the Secretary of Defense, Personnel Policy Board. "Study on Maximum Utilization of Military Womanpower." October 12, 1950. [Located at Tab B of "Commissioned Women Personnel in the Services, A Study," August 1951.] USAF Collection, K141.33-8 1951, IRIS No. 469735. Air Force Historical Research Agency, Maxwell AFB, Montgomery, AL.

Paules, Col. E.C. "Request for Waiver of DOD Instruction 4270.4." Memo to Director of Women's Army Corps dated September 5, 1957. Ft. Lee 228-01, WHC-377, Folder—Housing, Enlisted/Officer (General) (1957-63). WAC Museum Archives, Ft. Lee, VA.

———. "Standard Plans for Enlisted Women's Barracks." Memo to Chief of Engineers dated September 5, 1957. Ft. Lee 228-01, WHC-377, Folder—Housing, Enlisted/Officer (General) (1957-63). WAC Museum Archives, Ft. Lee, VA.

Pomper, Mindy (producer/director). *Free a Man to Fight! Women Soldiers of World War II*. Falls Church, VA: Landmark Media, Inc., 1999. [Video recording].

Pond, Pat. "Coed Share and Share Alike." *Women's Army Corps Journal* 5, no. 5 (October-December 1974). WAC Museum Archives, Ft. Lee, VA.

"Present Authorizations for Army Enlisted Women for Permanent Housing." 29 May 1958. Ft. Lee 228-01, WHC-377, Folder—Housing, Enlisted/Officer (General) (1957-63). WAC Museum Archives, Ft. Lee, VA.

"Presentation of Merits of Four Plans for Inclusion of Women, Other than those of the Medical Department in the Postwar Military Establishment." January 1946. Ft. Lee 228-01, WHC-310, Folder—Four Plans for a Women's Corps (1946). WAC Museum Archives, Ft. Lee, VA.

Public Papers of Presidents of the United States, Richard Nixon, 1970. Washington: National Archives and Records Service, 1971.

Radom, Matthew. "Points discussed at Mayflower Hotel with heads of Women's Services." September 10, 1948. Box 2, WAVES, Folder: (I-21) Eberstadt Committee (1948). Washington Navy Yards, Naval Historical Center Archives, Washington, DC.

Reibstein, Larry. "Women No Longer Separate at Ft. Dix; Are They Equal?" *Philadelphia Bulletin* (October 18, 1978). Reference File—Women Marines: Recruit Posters. Washington Navy Yards, Marine Corps Historical Center Archives, Washington, DC.

Revell, Joseph E. "WACs in Combat: If the Army Expects Its Women to Fight, Why Aren't They Trained Like the Men?" *The Times Magazine* (February 9, 1976). Reference File—Women Marines: Combat Training. Washington Navy Yards, Marine Corps Historical Center Archives, Washington, DC.

Richardson, Lt. Gen. J.L. "Enlisted Women's Barracks, Fort Myer, Virginia." Memo to Deputy Chief of Staff for Logistics dated December 8, 1964. Also, Memo to Deputy Chief of Staff for Personnel dated December 18, 1964. Ft. Lee 228-01, WHC-378, Folder—Housing, Misc Reports (1965-67). WAC Museum Archives, Ft. Lee, VA.

———. "Policies and Objectives to Improve Living Conditions for Officers Without Dependents." Memo to Chief of Staff, U.S. Army, dated June 1963. Also includes Gen. Barksdale Hamlett Memo to Lt. Gen. Leonard D. Heaton, June 28, 1963. Ft. Lee 228-01, WHC-373, Folder—Housing. WAC Museum Archives, Ft. Lee, VA.

Report of ASD(M) Task Force on Bachelor Accommodations, Troop Housing, Bachelor Officer Quarters. Washington, DC: Department of Defense, May 1966. Ft. Lee 228-01, WHC-375, Folder—Housing DOD Report (1966). WAC Museum Archives, Ft. Lee, VA.

Rogers, Bernard. "Plans for Expansion of the Women's Army Corps (Study)." U.S. Department of the Army (DAPL-PBP). October 6, 1973. Collection no. 2096 (Shirley Minge). Women in Military Service for America Memorial Foundation, Inc. Archives, Washington, DC.

Schneider, Capt. Virginia M. "Resignation," Memo to Headquarters, Department of the Army dated May 3, 1958. Includes attached follow-up response by Maj. Gen. George E. Martin, Headquarters, U.S. Army Europe dated May 29, 1958. Ft. Lee 228-01, WHC-377, Folder—Housing, Enlisted/Officer (General) (1957-63). WAC Museum Archives, Ft. Lee, VA.

Schuh, LCpl. Marla J. "Women find Success, Recognition during Women's History Month." *Henderson Hall News* 13, no. 13 (March 26, 1999). Reference File—Women Marines: History. Washington Navy Yards, Marine Corps Historical Center Archives, Washington, DC.

Schultz, Edna Hill. "Free a Marine to Fight." *Naval History* 17, no. 1 (February 2003): 46-49. Reference File—Women Marines: Newspaper Clippings—WWII. Washington Navy Yards, Marine Corps Historical Center Archives, Washington, DC.

Secretary of War. *Circular No. 307, Amendments.* Washington, DC.: War Department, July 19, 1944. WAC Museum Archives, Ft. Lee, VA.

———. *Circular No. 325, Amendments.* Washington, DC: War Department, December 14, 1943. WAC Museum Archives, Ft. Lee, VA.

Share a Proud Tradition, The United States Marine Corps (Recruitment Brochure). Lithographed by McCandlish Lithograph Corporation, 1958. Women in Military Service for America Memorial Foundation, Inc. Archives, Washington, DC.

Shields, Elizabeth A., ed. *Highlights of the History of the Army Nurse Corps.* Washington, DC: U.S. Army Center of Military History, 1981.

Shoemaker, Randall. "Better BOQs Seen In Latest DA Plan." Army Times (August 7, 1963). Ft. Lee 228-01, WHC-377, Folder—Housing, Enlisted/Officer (General) (1957-63). WAC Museum Archives, Ft. Lee, VA.

Short, Dewey. "Request for Waiver in Provisions of Department of Defense Instruction 4270.4, June 16, 1954." Memo to Assistant Secretary of Defense (Properties and Installations). Ft. Lee 228-01, WHC-377, Folder—Housing, Enlisted/Officer (General) (1957-63). WAC Museum Archives, Ft. Lee, VA.

"Significant Events in the History of Women Marines." *Marines* (June 1988). Reference File—Report on Progress of Women in the Marine Corps (1988). Washington Navy Yards, Marine Corps Historical Center Archives, Washington, DC.

Staff of the Directorate, Women in the Air Force. *History of the Women in the Air Force: 1 January 1975 – 30 June 1975*. Washington, DC: Headquarters, United States Air Force, Director, Women in the Air Force, 1975. Director, Women in the Air Force Collection, K141.33 75/01/01-75/06/30 Dir of WAF, IRIS No. 1007190. Air Force Historical Research Agency, Maxwell AFB, Montgomery, AL.

Stanford, Phil. "Should Women Be Combat Soldiers?" *DivInfo Daily Press Clips* (June 27, 1977). Reference File—Women Marines: Combat Training. Washington Navy Yards, Marine Corps Historical Center Archives, Washington, DC.

Stewart, Lt. Louise USMCR. "Women in Uniform." *Sea Power* 3, no. 11 (November 1943). Vertical Files: Women in the Military, 1940-1949. Washington Navy Yards, Naval Historical Foundation Library, Washington, DC.

Stiehm, Judith Hicks. "The Generations of U.S. Enlisted Women." *Signs: Journal of Women in Culture and Society* 11, no. 11 (1985): 155-175. Reference File—Women Marines: General (2 of 2). Washington Navy Yards, Marine Corps Historical Center Archives, Washington, DC.

Stoddard, Eleanor. "The Education of Margaret Jackson: Member of the Women's Army Corps, September 1943 – March 1946." *Minerva* 9, no. 4 (Winter 1991): 56-77.

———. "One Woman's War: The Story of Joan Campbell, Member of the Women's Army Corps, World War II, April 1943 – September 1945." *Minerva* 4, no. 1 (Spring 1986): 122-156.

Stratton, LCDR, P. "Toilet Facilities In Navy Aircraft." Memo to the Surgeon General of the Navy, Chief of Naval Operations, via the Commander of the National Naval Medical Center, Bethesda, MD, dated April 26, 1989. Box 4, Women in Aviation: General Info, Folder 3. Washington Navy Yards, Naval Aviation Office Archives, Washington, DC.

Stremlow, Col. Mary V. *Free a Marine to Fight: Women in World War II*. World War II Commemorative Series Pamphlet. Washington, DC: Marine Corps Historical Center, 1994.

———. *A History of the Women Marines, 1946-1977*. Washington, DC: History and Museums Division, Headquarters, U.S. Marine Corps, 1986.

Talley, Mae Sue. *Highlights of the Defense Advisory Committee on Women in the Services: 25 Years of Service to the Department of Defense*. Washington, DC: Department of Defense, 1976. Box 4, BUPERS 00W, Folder: History 1975-1976. Washington Navy Yards, Naval Historical Center Archives, Washington, DC.

"TBS Expands Training for Women." 1988. Reference File—Women Marines: Combat Training. Washington Navy Yards, Marine Corps Historical Center Archives, Washington, DC.

Techteler, W.M. "Women's Reserve Policies; clarification of." Memo dated May 25, 1945. Box 3, WAVES, Folder: (I-23) Future Planning (1943-1947). Washington Navy Yards, Naval Historical Center Archives, Washington, DC.

The Naval Air Training Bases, Pensacola, Florida Thru World War II. Pensacola, FL: Office of Public Information, Naval Air Training Bases, 1945.

Thomas, Patricia J. *Role of Women in the Military: Australia, Canada, the United Kingdom, and the United States.* San Diego, CA: Navy Personnel Research and Development Center, May 1978. Reference File—Women Marines: Australia, Canada, United Kingdom. Washington Navy Yards, Marine Corps Historical Center Archives, Washington, DC.

Timmons, Tracy. "'We're Looking for a Few Good Men': The Impact of Gender Stereotypes on Women in the Military." *Minerva* 10, no. 2 (Summer 1992): 20-33.

Treadwell, Mattie E. *The Women's Army Corps.* U.S. Army in World War II, Special Studies. Washington, DC: Department of the Army, Office of the Chief of Military History, 1954.

Tri-Service Committee. "Tri-Service Recommended Changes to Proposed Department of Defense Instruction." 1964. Ft. Lee 228-01, WHC-377, Folder—Housing, Enlisted/Officer (General) (1957-63). WAC Museum Archives, Ft. Lee, VA.

Tuttle, D.E.L. "WomanPower means NavyPower." *Direction* (October 1970). Reference File—Women Marines: Liberation Articles. Washington Navy Yards, Marine Corps Historical Center Archives, Washington, DC.

United States Army. *Environmental Protection and Enhancement.* DA PAM 200-1. Washington, DC: Department of the Army, 1998.

United States Army. *Personnel Utilizations: Female Military Personnel.* Pamphlet No. 616-1. Washington, DC: Department of the Army, May 18, 1977. Collection no. 4582 (Becky Miller). Women in Military Service for America Memorial Foundation, Inc. Archives, Washington, DC.

U.S. Army Corps of Engineers. "Suggested text for the Military Construction Area: Military Construction, 1974-75." Box XV-1, Military: Domestic Military Construction 1945-; Folder: Construction—Articles & Memos, Updates. U.S. Army Corps of Engineers History Office Archives, Alexandria, VA.

U.S. Department of Defense. *Military Handbook: Indoor Fitness/Recreational Facilities.* MIL-HDBK-1037/8. Washington, DC: Department of Defense, August 1996.

U.S. Government Accounting Office. *Gender Integration in Basic Training: The Services Are Using A Variety of Approaches.* GAO/T-NSIAD-97-174. Washington, DC: GAO, 1997.

———. *Gender Issues: Analysis of Methodologies in Reports to the Secretaries of Defense and the Army.* GAO/NSIAD-98-125. Washington, DC: GAO, 1998.

———. *Military Housing: Cost of Separate Barracks for Male and Female Recruits in Basic Training.* GAO/NSIAD-99-75. Washington, DC: GAO, 1999.

———. *Military Personnel: Composition of the Active Duty Forces by Race or National Origin Identification and be Gender.* GAO/NSIAD-91-134FS. Washington, DC: GAO, 1991.

United States Marine Corps, *Marine Corps Recruit Depot Yearbook, Platoon 4B, Parris Island, South Carolina*. (n.p., 1967). Collection no. 4167. Women in Military Service for America Memorial Foundation, Inc. Archives, Washington, DC.

United States Women's Army Corps. *WAC Basic Training Battalion Training Brigade, Ft. McClellan, Alabama Yearbook*. Fort McClellan, AL: U.S. Women's Army Corps, 1977. Collection no. 4674 (unknown). Women in Military Service for America Memorial Foundation, Inc. Archives, Washington, DC.

U.S. Women's Army Corps School. *Role of the WAC: History, Organization, and Function of the U.S. Women's Army Corps*. Special Text 35-150. Fort McClellan, AL: Office of Doctrine, Literature, Plans and Programs, 1972. Collection no. 4814 (Wendy Wadinger). Women in Military Service for America Memorial Foundation, Inc. Archives, Washington, DC.

Utilization of Women in the Air Force: Report of Ad Hoc Study Group. Washington, DC: Department of the Air Force, October 1967. USAF Collection, K141.04-21 Oct 1967, IRIS No. 645048. Air Force Historical Research Agency, Maxwell AFB, Montgomery, AL.

"WAACS: First Women Soldiers Join Army." *Life* (September 7, 1942): 74-81.

Walker, J.B. "Equal to the Task: Fourth Recruit Training Battalion Prepares Women for Success." *The Leatherneck* (February 2001): 16 18. Reference File—Women Marines: Combat Training. Washington Navy Yards, Marine Corps Historical Center Archives, Washington, DC.

Walker-Tyson, Joyce. "Serve Country, Not Coffee: Women Marine Recruits Typical of Our Changing Military." *Detroit Free Press (MI)* (October 28, 1977). Reference File—Women Marines: Combat Training. Washington Navy Yards, Marine Corps Historical Center Archives, Washington, DC.

Wallace, Tiffany. "Corps Woman is WWII Veteran." *Engineer Update, USACE* 16, no. 8 (August 1992). Box 131, General Files. Folder 130-2-1: Corps Woman is WWII Veteran. U.S. Army Corps of Engineers History Office Archives. Alexandria, VA.

Wasch, Diane S., Perry Bush, Keith Landreth, and James Glass. *World War II and the U.S. Army Mobilization Program: A History of 700 and 800 Series Cantonment Construction*. Edited by Arlene R. Kriv. Washington, DC: U.S. Department of Defense, Legacy Resource Management Program and U.S. Department of the Interior, National Park Service, 1988.

Weinraub, Bernard. "Pentagon Criticized on Jobs for Women." *New York Times* (July 25, 1977). Reference File—Women Marines: Combat Training. Washington Navy Yards, Marine Corps Historical Center Archives, Washington, DC.

"What Women Can Do: Think War, Buy Little, Maintain Our Ideals." *Life* (September 28, 1942): 32.

Williams, Lt. Col. Carol M. "Comments Pertaining to BOQ Housing Plans." Memo to Lt. Col. Kathryn J. Royster, May 14, 1963. Ft. Lee 228-01, WHC-373, Folder—Housing. WAC Museum Archives, Ft. Lee, VA.

Willis, Ellen R. "Segregation in the WAC." Student Paper (May 21, 1963). WAC School and Center, Fort McClellan, AL. Student Study Files (1003-12 Permanent), WAC Museum Archives, Ft. Lee, VA.

Wilson, Louis H. "Women Marines." White Letter No. 5-76 to All General Officers, All Commanding Officers, All Officers in Charge dated June 23, 1976. Reference File—Report on Progress of Women in the Marine Corps (1988). Washington Navy Yards, Marine Corps Historical Center Archives, Washington, DC.

Women in the Air Force, Enlisted Personnel. Air Force Manual 39-5. Washington, DC: Department of the Air Force, July 12, 1957. J. Sewell Papers, 168.7172-2 1907 – Jul 1957, IRIS No. 1041204. Air Force Historical Research Agency, Maxwell AFB, Montgomery, AL.

Women in Military Service for America Memorial Foundation, Inc. "Education Webpage." [http://womensmemorial.org].

Women Marines in the 1980s. Washington, DC: Headquarters, U.S. Marine Corps, Division of Public Affairs (CODE PAM), 1986 rev. Reference File—Women Marines: General (1 of 2). Washington Navy Yards, Marine Corps Historical Center Archives, Washington, DC.

"Women May Yet Save the Army." *Time* (October 30, 1978). Reference File—Women Marines: Combat Training. Washington Navy Yards, Marine Corps Historical Center Archives, Washington, DC.

Women's Army Corps (Recruitment Brochure). circa 1955. Women in Military Service for America Memorial Foundation, Inc. Archives, Washington, DC.

"The Women's Army Corps: Fact Sheet." December 1, 1945. J. Sewell Papers, 168.7172-2 1907 – Jul 1957, IRIS No. 1041204. Air Force Historical Research Agency, Maxwell AFB, Montgomery, AL.

Women's Army Corps. "Housing for Enlisted Women." May 29, 1958. Ft. Lee 228-01, WHC-377, Folder—Housing, Enlisted/Officer (General) (1957-63). WAC Museum Archives, Ft. Lee, VA.

Women's Army Corps Veteran's Association. *History of the Women's Army Corps*. [http://www.armywomen.org/frames.html, 2003].

Women's Research and Education Institute. *Chronology of Significant Legal & Policy Changes Affecting Women in the Military: 1947-2003*. Washington DC: Women's Research and Education Institute, 2003. [available online at http://www.wrei.org/projects/wiu/index.htm.]

Appendix A: List of Plans and Drawings

As part of the research effort for this project, the authors compiled a database of approximately 440 architectural/engineering/design drawings. The lists and brief descriptions of drawings provided in this appendix are divided to focus on particular attributes for reader research. Each section presents different information about the same set of drawings. Drawing numbers and repositories are provided for use in retrieving the actual drawing for further research. Blank fields indicate information for that feature of the building was not contained in the respective drawing.

This appendix includes the following four sections:

- Administrative Data, page 180
- Building Data, page 197
- Housing/Sleeping Data, page 216
- Restroom Facilities Data, page 249

Administrative Data

Building Type	Drawing Number	Date	Service Branch	Drawing Type (Standard, Schematic, Geo-Specific)	Drawing Source	Digital Copy of Drawing Available
See legend or list type of building of not included in legend	Identifying number	date of drawing	What branch of military is drawing intended for	Standard, schematic, proposed, designed for specific installation, etc.	Where was drawing plan obtained: NARA, USACE HQ, other	Is a digital copy of the drawing available for inclusion on the CD
Typical Landscape Planting for Company Officers' and Double NCO Quarters	630-100	12/14/1933	Army	Schematic	USACEHQ	Yes
Typical Landscape Planting for HQ Admin. Bldg, BOQs, Barracks Bldgs	630-101	12/18/1933	Army	Schematic	USACEHQ	Yes
Marine Barracks	129241	11/24/1939	Navy Yard-Marine Corps	Specific Installation	NARA	yes
Marine Barracks	129247	11/24/1939	Navy Yard-Marine Corps	Specific Installation (Restroom Details)	NARA	yes
EMB	137497 - 137498	7/13/1940	Navy	Definitive	NARA	yes
Mobilization Buildings Hospital (Nurses) Quarters	800-1422 (2)	5/29/1941	Army	Standard Type NQM 14 & 16 Elevations & Sections	USACEHQ	Yes
Mobilization Buildings Hospital (Nurses) Quarters	800-1421	6/6/1941	Army	Standard Type NQM 13-15 Foundation, Framing, Floor Plans	USACEHQ	Yes
Mobilization Buildings Hospital (Nurses) Quarters	800-1422	6/6/1941	Army	Standard Type NQM 13 & 15 Elevations & Sections	USACEHQ	Yes
Mobilization Buildings Hospital (Nurses) Quarters	800-1423	6/9/1941	Army	Standard Type NQM 13 & 15 Heating, Plumbing, Electrical	USACEHQ	Yes
Mobilization Buildings Nurses (Hospital) Quarters	800-1435	6/14/1941	Army	Standard Type NQM 34 First Floor, Framing & Foundation Plans	USACEHQ	Yes
Mobilization Buildings Nurses (Hospital) Quarters	800-1436	6/14/1941	Army	Standard Type NQM 34 Second Floor, Framing & Foundation Plans	USACEHQ	Yes
Mobilization Buildings Hospital (Nurses) Quarters	800-1423.1	7/31/1941	Army	Standard Type NQM 13 - 15 Heating	USACEHQ	Yes
EMB	188167	12/2/1941	Navy	Specific Installation	NARA	yes
EMB	184324 - 184325	12/27/1941	Navy	Standard	NARA	yes
Typical Layout Diagram for Camouflage Demonstration - Practice Area	614-1602	3/5/1942	Army	Schematic	USACEHQ	Yes
Typical Layout Diagrams for WAAC Replacement Training Center	614-703	4/4/1942	Army	Schematic	USACEHQ	Yes
Mobilization Buildings WAAC Exchange - Type - WPX - A-M	700-3516	5/20/1942	Army	Standard Foundation and Framing Plans and Details	USACEHQ	Yes
Mobilization Buildings WAAC Exchange - Type - WPX - A-M	700-3517	5/20/1942	Army	Standard Floor plan, elevations, sections, & schedules	USACEHQ	Yes
Mobilization Buildings	700-3518	5/20/1942	Army	Standard Details and	USACEHQ	Yes

Building Type	Drawing Number	Date	Service Branch	Drawing Type (Standard, Schematic, Geo-Specific)	Drawing Source	Digital Copy of Drawing Available
See legend or list type of building of not included in legend	Identifying number	date of drawing	What branch of military is drawing intended for	Standard, schematic, proposed, designed for specific installation, etc.	Where was drawing plan obtained: NARA, USACE HQ, other	Is a digital copy of the drawing available for inclusion on the CD
WAAC Exchange - Type - WPX - A-M				Roofing Plan		
Mobilization Buildings WAAC Exchange - Type - WPX - A-M	700-3519	5/20/1942	Army	Standard Elevations and Details	USACEHQ	Yes
Mobilization Buildings WAAC Exchange - Type - WPX - A-M	700-3520	5/20/1942	Army	Standard Electrical Plan	USACEHQ	Yes
Mobilization Buildings WAAC Exchange - Type - WPX - A-M	700-3521	5/20/1942	Army	Standard Plumbing Plan	USACEHQ	Yes
Mobilization Buildings WAAC Exchange - Type - WPX - A-M	700-3522	5/20/1942	Army	Standard HVAC Plan	USACEHQ	Yes
Mobilization Buildings WAC Barracks	800-425	5/20/1942	Army	Standard Type WBKS-50 Foundation & Framing Plans	USACEHQ	Yes
Mobilization Buildings WAC Barracks	800-426	5/20/1942	Army	Standard Type WBKS-50 Floor Plans & Elevations	USACEHQ	Yes
Mobilization Buildings WAC Barracks	800-427	5/20/1942	Army	Standard Type WBKS-50 Details	USACEHQ	Yes
Mobilization Buildings WAC Barracks	800-428	5/20/1942	Army	Standard Type WBKS-50 Alternate Elevations & Details	USACEHQ	Yes
Mobilization Buildings WAC Barracks	800-429	5/20/1942	Army	Standard Type WBKS-50 Electrical	USACEHQ	Yes
Mobilization Buildings WAC Barracks	800-430	5/20/1942	Army	Standard Type WBKS-50 Plumbing	USACEHQ	Yes
Mobilization Buildings WAC Barracks	800-431	5/20/1942	Army	Standard Type WBKS-50 Heating	USACEHQ	Yes
Mobilization Buildings WAC Exchange	800-1124	5/20/1942	Army	Standard Type E-4 Foundation and Framing Plans	USACEHQ	Yes
Mobilization Buildings WAC Exchange	800-1125	5/20/1942	Army	Standard Type E-4 Floor plans, elevations, sections, schedules	USACEHQ	Yes
Mobilization Buildings WAC Exchange	800-1126	5/20/1942	Army	Standard Type E-4 Roof framing plan & Details	USACEHQ	Yes
Mobilization Buildings WAC Exchange	800-1127	5/20/1942	Army	Standard Type E-4 Alternate Elevations & Door Details	USACEHQ	Yes
Mobilization Buildings WAC Exchange	800-1128	5/20/1942	Army	Standard Type E-4 Electrical	USACEHQ	Yes
Mobilization Buildings WAC Exchange	800-1129	5/20/1942	Army	Standard Type E-4 Plumbing	USACEHQ	Yes
Mobilization Buildings WAC Exchange	800-1130	5/20/1942	Army	Standard Type E-4 Heating	USACEHQ	Yes
Barracks for 150 Women WAC Training Center Fort Des Moines, Iowa	193A-49	6/10/1942	Army	Specific Installation Plans for Bldg 81, 83	NARA	Yes
Laundry & Toilet Bldg Addition for Barracks Training Center Fort Des Moines, Iowa	193A-22	6/10/1942	Army	Specific Installation Plans, Elevation, & Section for Bldg 18B (20B, 21B, 23B, 24B,	NARA	Yes

Building Type	Drawing Number	Date	Service Branch	Drawing Type (Standard, Schematic, Geo-Specific)	Drawing Source	Digital Copy of Drawing Available
See legend or list type of building of not included in legend	Identifying number	date of drawing	What branch of military is drawing intended for	Standard, schematic, proposed, designed for specific installation, etc.	Where was drawing plan obtained: NARA, USACE HQ, other	Is a digital copy of the drawing available for inclusion on the CD
				26B, 28B, 29B, 31B are similar)		
Recreation Buildings in connection with Barracks Training Center Fort Des Moines, Iowa	193A-25	6/10/1942	Army	Specific Installation Floor Plans (Additions to existing Barracks Buildings)	NARA	Yes
WAC Barracks Training Center Fort Des Moines, Iowa	193A-19	6/10/1942	Army	Specific Installation Plans, Elevation, & Section for Bldg # 68, 70, 71, 73, 76, 78, 80	NARA	Yes (difficult to read)
Co. Unit Layout Diagrams for WAAC	614-702	6/28/1942	Army	Schematic	USACEHQ	Yes
Training Center Fort Des Moines, Iowa	193A-16	7/3/1942	Army	Specific Installation South Cantonment Plan	NARA	Yes
Mobilization Buildings WAAC Barracks	700-3525	7/7/1942	Army	Standard Plans and Elevations	USACEHQ	Yes
Mobilization Buildings WAAC Barracks (Alt. for sloping site)	700-3526	7/7/1942	Army	Standard Plans and Elevations	USACEHQ	Yes
Mobilization Buildings WAAC Barracks	700-3527	7/7/1942	Army	Standard HVAC Plan	USACEHQ	Yes
Mobilization Buildings WAAC Barracks	700-3528	7/7/1942	Army	Standard Plumbing Plan	USACEHQ	Yes
Mobilization Buildings WAAC Barracks	700-3529	7/7/1942	Army	Standard Electrical Plan	USACEHQ	Yes
WAC Latrine (Temporary Structure) Training Center Fort Des Moines, Iowa	193A-31	7/8/1942	Army	Specific Installation Plans, Elevations, Sections	NARA	Yes
Mobilization Buildings WAC Recreation, Supply, Co. Admin., & Quarters	700-3540	7/9/1942	Army	Standard Type REC-D-M Foundation and Framing Plan & Schedule	USACEHQ	Yes
Mobilization Buildings WAC Recreation, Supply, Co. Admin., & Quarters	700-3541	7/9/1942	Army	Standard Type REC-D-M Floor Plan	USACEHQ	Yes
Mobilization Buildings WAC Recreation, Supply, Co. Admin., & Quarters	700-3542	7/9/1942	Army	Standard Type REC-D-M Elevations & Sections	USACEHQ	Yes
Mobilization Buildings WAC Recreation, Supply, Co. Admin., & Quarters	700-3543	7/9/1942	Army	Standard Type REC-D-M Heating Plan	USACEHQ	Yes
Mobilization Buildings WAC Recreation, Supply, Co. Admin., & Quarters	700-3544	7/9/1942	Army	Standard Type REC-D-M Plumbing Plan	USACEHQ	Yes
Mobilization Buildings WAC Recreation, Supply, Co. Admin., & Quarters	700-3545	7/9/1942	Army	Standard Type REC-D-M Electrical Plan	USACEHQ	Yes
Mobilization Buildings WAC Recreation,	700-3546	7/11/1942	Army	Standard Type REC-E-M Foundation & Floor	USACEHQ	Yes

Building Type	Drawing Number	Date	Service Branch	Drawing Type (Standard, Schematic, Geo-Specific)	Drawing Source	Digital Copy of Drawing Available
See legend or list type of building of not included in legend	Identifying number	date of drawing	What branch of military is drawing intended for	Standard, schematic, proposed, designed for specific installation, etc.	Where was drawing plan obtained: NARA, USACE HQ, other	Is a digital copy of the drawing available for inclusion on the CD
Supply, Co. Admin., & Quarters				Framing Plan		
Mobilization Buildings WAC Recreation, Supply, Co. Admin., & Quarters	700-3547	7/11/1942	Army	Standard Type REC-E-M Floor Plan	USACEHQ	Yes
Mobilization Buildings WAC Recreation, Supply, Co. Admin., & Quarters	700-3548	7/11/1942	Army	Standard Type REC-E-M Elevations & Sections	USACEHQ	Yes
Mobilization Buildings WAC Recreation, Supply, Co. Admin., & Quarters	700-3549	7/11/1942	Army	Standard Type REC-E-M Heating	USACEHQ	Yes
Mobilization Buildings WAC Recreation, Supply, Co. Admin., & Quarters	700-3550	7/11/1942	Army	Standard Type REC-E-M Plumbing	USACEHQ	Yes
Mobilization Buildings WAC Recreation, Supply, Co. Admin., & Quarters	700-3551	7/11/1942	Army	Standard Type REC-E-M Electrical	USACEHQ	Yes
Barracks (30 Men) WAC Training Center Fort Des Moines, Iowa	193A-46	7/16/1942	Army	Specific Installation Plans, Elevations, Sections	NARA	Yes
Mobilization Buildings WAAC Officers' Quarters	700-3532	7/17/1942	Army	Standard Type WOQ-A-M Plans and Elevations	USACEHQ	Yes
Mobilization Buildings WAAC Officers' Quarters	700-3533	7/17/1942	Army	Standard Type WOQ-A-M Heating, Plumbing, Electrical	USACEHQ	Yes
Office Building of Engineer (Additions & Remodelling) WAC Training Center Fort Des Moines, Iowa	193A-33	7/30/1942	Army	Specific Installation Plans, Elevations, Sections	NARA	Yes
EMB	188660	8/10/1942	Navy	Standard	NARA	yes
Post Hospital and Drill Hall WAC Training Center Fort Des Moines, Iowa	193A-39	10/1/1942	Army	Specific Installation Plans, Elevations, Sections	NARA	Yes
Nurses' Quarters	1100-361	10/19/1942	Army	Standard Type NQ-A-TH Heating, Plumbing, Electrical	USACEHQ	Yes
Typical Layout Diagrams for WAAC Battalion Organization	614-701	10/29/1942	Army	Schematic	USACEHQ	Yes
Mobilization General Hospital Nurses Quarters Officers Quarters	1100-2136	10/31/1942	Army	Standard Type A, NQ-A to C-H, OQ-E to G-H, Elevations & Sections	USACEHQ	Yes
Mobilization General Hospital Nurses Quarters Officers Quarters	1100-2137	10/31/1942	Army	Standard Type A, NQ-A to C-H, OQ-E to G-H, Foundation & Framing Plans	USACEHQ	Yes

Building Type	Drawing Number	Date	Service Branch	Drawing Type (Standard, Schematic, Geo-Specific)	Drawing Source	Digital Copy of Drawing Available
See legend or list type of building of not included in legend	Identifying number	date of drawing	What branch of military is drawing intended for	Standard, schematic, proposed, designed for specific installation, etc.	Where was drawing plan obtained: NARA, USACE HQ, other	Is a digital copy of the drawing available for inclusion on the CD
Mobilization General Hospital Nurses Quarters Officers Quarters	1100-2138	10/31/1942	Army	Standard Type A, NQ-A to C-H, OQ-E to G-H, Electrical Plans	USACEHQ	Yes
Mobilization General Hospital Nurses Quarters Officers Quarters	1100-2139	10/31/1942	Army	Standard Type A, NQ-A to C-H, OQ-E to G-H, Plumbing Plans	USACEHQ	Yes
Mobilization General Hospital Nurses QuartersOfficers Quarters	1100-2140	10/31/1942	Army	Standard Type A, NQ-A to C-H, OQ-E to G-H, Heating Plans	USACEHQ	Yes
Option 1: Mobilization General Hospital Nurses Quarters	1100-2135	10/31/1942	Army	Standard Type A, NQ-A to C-H, 1st & 2nd floor plans	USACEHQ	Yes
Option 2: Mobilization General Hospital Officers Quarters	1100-2135 (Same dwg as above, different occupant)	10/31/1942	Army	Standard Type A, OQ-E to G-H, 1st & 2nd floor plans	USACEHQ	Yes
Mobilization Buildings WAC Barracks	700-3560	11/3/1942	Army	Standard Type WBKS-B-M Plans & Elevations	USACEHQ	Yes
Mobilization Buildings WAC Barracks	700-3561	11/3/1942	Army	Standard Type WBKS-B-M Heating Plan	USACEHQ	Yes
Mobilization Buildings WAC Barracks	700-3562	11/3/1942	Army	Standard Type WBKS-B-M Plumbing Plan	USACEHQ	Yes
Mobilization Buildings WAC Barracks	700-3563	11/3/1942	Army	Standard Type WBKS-B-M Electrical Plan	USACEHQ	Yes
Nurses' Quarters	1100-360	11/13/1942	Army	Standard Type NQ-A-TH Plan & Elevations	USACEHQ	Yes
W	188697	11/16/1942	Navy	Standard	NARA	yes
W	188699	11/16/1942	Navy	Standard	NARA	yes
W	188702	11/17/1942	Navy	Standard	NARA	yes
Mobilization Buildings Conversion of Existing 74 Man Barracks for WAC	700-3570	11/24/1942	Army	Standard Conversion of EMB to EWB Plans	USACEHQ	Yes
Mobilization Buildings Conversion of Existing 74 Man Barracks for WAC	700-3571	11/24/1942	Army	Standard Conversion of EMB to EWB Plumbing & Electrical	USACEHQ	Yes
Mobilization Buildings WAC BOQ	700-3565	11/24/1942	Army	Standard Type WOQ-B-M Plans & Elevation	USACEHQ	Yes
Mobilization Buildings WAC BOQ	700-3566	11/24/1942	Army	Standard Type WOQ-B-M Heating Plan	USACEHQ	Yes
Mobilization Buildings WAC BOQ	700-3567	11/24/1942	Army	Standard Type WOQ-B-M Plumbing Plan	USACEHQ	Yes
Mobilization Buildings WAC BOQ	700-3568	11/24/1942	Army	Standard Type WOQ-B-M Electrical Plan	USACEHQ	Yes
Typical Layout Diagram for Camouflage Demonstration - Practice Area	614-1601	11/30/1942	Army	Schematic	USACEHQ	Yes
W	312559	00/00/1943	Navy	Conversion	NARA	yes
W	312559-2	00/00/1943	Navy	Conversion	NARA	yes
W	188767	3/24/1943	Navy	Schematic	NARA	yes

Building Type	Drawing Number	Date	Service Branch	Drawing Type (Standard, Schematic, Geo-Specific)	Drawing Source	Digital Copy of Drawing Available
See legend or list type of building of not included in legend	Identifying number	date of drawing	What branch of military is drawing intended for	Standard, schematic, proposed, designed for specific installation, etc.	Where was drawing plan obtained: NARA, USACE HQ, other	Is a digital copy of the drawing available for inclusion on the CD
Symbols for Camouflage - General Plan	614-1603	4/5/1943	Army	Schematic	USACEHQ	Yes
Typical Layout Diagrams for one company of WAC	614-t.o.738	4/15/1943	Army	Schematic	USACEHQ	Yes
Nurses & WAVE Officers	317319	4/21/1943	Navy	Specific Installation	NARA	yes
MW	256516	5/17/1943	Navy Yard-Marine Corps	Specific Installation	NARA	yes
MW	256517	5/17/1943	Navy Yard-Marine Corps	Specific Installation	NARA	
EWB	271541	6/9/1943	Navy	Specific Installation	NARA	yes
SP (Women's Club)	291251	6/22/1943	Navy	Specific Installation (10th floor plan)	NARA	yes
SP (Women's Club)	291252	6/22/1943	Navy	Specific Installation (11th floor plan)	NARA	yes
SP (Women's Club)	291254	6/22/1943	Navy	Specific Installation (Ground & 1st floor plans	NARA	yes
BOQ	256638	7/18/1943	Navy	Standard	NARA	yes
Mobilization Buildings WAC Barracks	700-3560.1	7/22/1943	Army	Standard Type WBKS-B-M Alternate Plans for 79 WAC	USACEHQ	Yes
Mobilization Buildings Conversion of Existing Detachment Barracks for WAC	700-3585	8/2/1943	Army	Standard Conversion Type BKS-D-H; Dwgs: Architectural (Floor plan) & Heating	USACEHQ	Yes
Mobilization Buildings Conversion of Existing Detachment Barracks for WAC	700-3586	8/2/1943	Army	Standard Conversion Type BKS-D-H; Dwgs: Plumbing & Electrical	USACEHQ	Yes
W	288273	8/3/1943	Navy	Standard	NARA	yes
Mobilization Buildings Conversion of Hospital Barracks for WAC	700-3580	8/5/1943	Army	Standard Conversion; Dwgs: Architectural (Floor plan) & Heating	USACEHQ	Yes
Mobilization Buildings Conversion of Hospital Barracks for WAC	700-3581	8/5/1943	Army	Standard Conversion; Dwgs: Electrical and Plumbing	USACEHQ	Yes
W	264793	8/18/1943	Navy	Specific Installation	NARA	yes
WB	288273	9/3/1943	Navy	Standard	NARA	yes
W	288280	9/11/1943	Navy	Standard	NARA	yes
W	288282	9/11/1943	Navy	Standard (Details for above plan)	NARA	yes
W	288283	9/11/1943	Navy	Standard (Details for above plan)	NARA	yes
W	320100	10/8/1943	Navy	Standard	NARA	yes
W	304236	10/21/1943	Navy	Specific Installation (1st Floor)	NARA	yes
W	304237	10/21/1943	Navy	Specific Installation (2nd Floor)	NARA	yes
W	257696	11/6/1943	Navy	Standard	NARA	yes
WB	257055	11/23/1943	Navy	Standard Lockers	NARA	yes
SP (Swimming Pool)	304510 - 304511	11/25/1943	Navy	Standard	NARA	yes
W	257698	12/16/1943	Navy	Standard	NARA	yes

Building Type	Drawing Number	Date	Service Branch	Drawing Type (Standard, Schematic, Geo-Specific)	Drawing Source	Digital Copy of Drawing Available
See legend or list type of building of not included in legend	Identifying number	date of drawing	What branch of military is drawing intended for	Standard, schematic, proposed, designed for specific installation, etc.	Where was drawing plan obtained: NARA, USACE HQ, other	Is a digital copy of the drawing available for inclusion on the CD
W	257701	12/16/1943	Navy	Standard	NARA	yes
W	257669	12/23/1943	Navy	Standard	NARA	yes
EW & EM	326815	2/18/1944	Navy	Standard	NARA	yes
W	326814	2/18/1944	Navy	Standard	NARA	yes
W	257734	3/14/1944	Navy	Standard	NARA	yes
MW	290949	3/14/1944	Navy Yard-Marine Corps	Standard	NARA	yes
SP (Office, Lunch, Locker)	364804	4/22/1944	Navy	Specific Installation	NARA	yes
WAC Training Center Fort Des Moines, Iowa	194A-12	5/1/1944	Army	Specific Installation General Plan (Site Plan) Group 'A' Buildings	NARA	Yes
W	342059	5/4/1944	Navy	Proposed	NARA	yes
W	328676	5/4/1944	Navy	Standard	NARA	yes
WAVE Mess Hall	328687	5/4/1944	Navy	Specific Installation	NARA	yes
W	328678	5/10/1944	Navy	Standard (Details for above plan)	NARA	yes
WAVE Clinic	328711	5/10/1944	Navy	Specific Installation	NARA	yes
EWB	329667 - 329668	5/18/1944	Navy	Specific Installation	NARA	yes
W	309299	6/5/1944	Navy	Specific Installation	NARA	yes
EWB	347315	8/4/1944	Navy	Specific Installation	NARA	yes
SP (Lunch, Locker)	309610	9/26/1944	Navy	Specific Installation	NARA	yes
SP Auditorium	360741	10/11/1944	Navy	Specific Installation	NARA	yes
SP (Dispensary)	370691	10/12/1944	Navy	Specific Installation (Addition)	NARA	yes
SP (Admin.)	342622	10/28/1944	Navy	Specific Installation (Addition)	NARA	yes
Study for Typical Landscape Development Plan	614-1117	11/9/1944	Army	Schematic	USACEHQ	Yes
BOQ	360765	12/11/1944	Navy	Specific Installation	NARA	yes
SP (Ships Service Bldg)	360764	12/11/1944	Navy	Specific Installation	NARA	yes
SP (Subsistence Building)	360777	12/11/1944	Navy	Specific Installation	NARA	yes
SP Auditorium & Gym	361229	12/18/1944	Navy	Specific Installation	NARA	yes
EWB	339687 - 339688	12/30/1944	Navy	Specific Installation	NARA	yes
SP (Dispensary)	373477	1/27/1945	Navy	Specific Installation	NARA	yes
W	373486	1/31/1945	Navy	Specific Installation	NARA	yes
WAVES Dispensary	409987	2/19/1945	Navy	Specific Installation	NARA	yes
BOQ	306882	5/1/1945	Navy	Specific Installation	NARA	yes
BOQ	306883	5/1/1945	Navy	Specific Installation	NARA	yes
SP (Base Site Plan)	401885	8/25/1945	Navy	Specific Installation	NARA	yes
SP Dispensary	401836	8/28/1945	Navy	Specific Installation	NARA	yes
Barrack - WAC - Apartment Type	SK210109	12/18/1946	Army	Schematic Floor Plans	USACEHQ	Yes
Barrack - WAC - Hotel Type	SK210108	12/18/1946	Army	Schematic Floor Plans	USACEHQ	Yes
WM	450230	12/20/1948	Navy Yard-Marine Corps	Specific Installation	NARA	yes
Emergency Type Construction, EW	DEFE210201-1	11/29/1949	Army	Definitive Drawings Floor Plans	USACEHQ	Yes

Building Type	Drawing Number	Date	Service Branch	Drawing Type (Standard, Schematic, Geo-Specific)	Drawing Source	Digital Copy of Drawing Available
See legend or list type of building of not included in legend	Identifying number	date of drawing	What branch of military is drawing intended for	Standard, schematic, proposed, designed for specific installation, etc.	Where was drawing plan obtained: NARA, USACE HQ, other	Is a digital copy of the drawing available for inclusion on the CD
Barracks Emergency Type Construction, EW Barracks	DEFE210201-2	11/29/1949	Army	Definitive Drawings Elevations	USACEHQ	Yes
Emergency Type Construction, EW Barracks	DEFE250704-1	11/29/1949	Army	Definitive Drawings Type Q-5 Plans & Elevations	USACEHQ	Yes
MW	472352	2/28/1950	Navy Yard-Marine Corps	Specific Installation	NARA	yes
MW	472353	2/28/1950	Navy Yard-Marine Corps	Specific Installation (2nd flr of above plan)	NARA	yes
MW	472354	2/28/1950	Navy Yard-Marine Corps	Specific Installation	NARA	yes
MW	472355	2/28/1950	Navy Yard-Marine Corps	Specific Installation (2nd flr of above plan)	NARA	yes
MW	472366	3/23/1950	Navy Yard-Marine Corps	Specific Installation	NARA	yes
MW	472367	3/23/1950	Navy Yard-Marine Corps	Specific Installation (2nd flr of above plan)	NARA	yes
MW	472519	11/1/1950	Navy Yard-Marine Corps	Specific Installation (2nd flr of above plan)	NARA	yes
MW	472518	11/2/1950	Navy Yard-Marine Corps	Specific Installation	NARA	yes
BOQ	500363	12/12/1950	Navy	Schematic	NARA	yes
EMB	500359	12/12/1950	Navy	Schematic	NARA	
EMB	500360	12/12/1950	Navy	Schematic	NARA	
EWB	500361	12/12/1950	Navy		NARA	yes
EWB	500362	12/12/1950	Navy		NARA	yes
BOQ	496842	2/8/1951	Navy	Standard (Temporary)	NARA	yes
EWB	496812	2/8/1951	Navy		NARA	yes
EWB	496830	2/8/1951	Navy		NARA	yes
Nurses' or WAF Officers' Quarters	DEF250706-1	2/15/1951	Air Force	Schematic Floor Plans	USACEHQ	Yes
Nurses' or WAF Officers' Quarters	DEF250706-2	2/15/1951	Air Force	Schematic Elevations, Sections, Schematic Plans (3 alternatives)	USACEHQ	Yes
Airmens Dormitory	210171-2	9/17/1951	Air Force	Standard 2-Story above grade +20 degree zone 1st & 2nd Floor Plan	USACEHQ	Yes
Airmens Dormitory	210171-3	9/17/1951	Air Force	Standard 2-Story above grade +20 degree zone Elevations & Details	USACEHQ	Yes
Airmens Dormitory	210171-7	9/17/1951	Air Force	Standard 2-Story above grade +20 degree zone Toilet Room & Door Details	USACEHQ	Yes
Airmens Dormitory	210171-8	9/17/1951	Air Force	Standard 2-Story above grade +20 degree zone Sleeping Room Closet Units & Misc. Details	USACEHQ	Yes
Airmens Dormitory	210171-9	9/17/1951	Air Force	Standard 2-Story above grade +20 degree zone Stair Details	USACEHQ	Yes
Airmens Dormitory	210171-1	9/17/1951	Army	Standard 2-Story above grade +20 degree zone	USACEHQ	Yes

Building Type	Drawing Number	Date	Service Branch	Drawing Type (Standard, Schematic, Geo-Specific)	Drawing Source	Digital Copy of Drawing Available
See legend or list type of building of not included in legend	Identifying number	date of drawing	What branch of military is drawing intended for	Standard, schematic, proposed, designed for specific installation, etc.	Where was drawing plan obtained: NARA, USACE HQ, other	Is a digital copy of the drawing available for inclusion on the CD
				Title Sheet		
Airmens Dormitory Modified for Women	210189-1	9/28/1951	Air Force	Standard 2-Story above grade +20 degree zone Title Sheet	USACEHQ	Yes
Airmens Dormitory Modified for Women	210189-2	9/28/1951	Air Force	Standard 2-Story above grade +20 degree zone 1st & 2nd Floor Plan	USACEHQ	Yes
Airmens Dormitory Modified for Women	210189-3	9/28/1951	Air Force	Standard 2-Story above grade +20 degree zone Elevations & Details	USACEHQ	Yes
Airmens Dormitory Modified for Women	210189-3	9/28/1951	Air Force	Standard 2-Story above grade +20 degree zone Elevations & Details	USACEHQ	Yes
Airmens Dormitory Modified for Women	210189-4	9/28/1951	Air Force	Standard 2-Story above grade +20 degree zone Elevations & Details	USACEHQ	Yes
Airmens Dormitory Modified for Women	210189-5	9/28/1951	Air Force	Standard 2-Story above grade +20 degree zone Wall Sections	USACEHQ	Yes
Airmens Dormitory Modified for Women	210189-6	9/28/1951	Air Force	Standard 2-Story above grade +20 degree zone Wall Sections	USACEHQ	Yes
Airmens Dormitory Modified for Women	210189-7	9/28/1951	Air Force	Standard 2-Story above grade +20 degree zone Toilet Room & Door Details	USACEHQ	Yes
Airmens Dormitory Modified for Women	210189-8	9/28/1951	Air Force	Standard 2-Story above grade +20 degree zone Sleeping Room Closet Units & Misc. Details	USACEHQ	Yes
Airmens Dormitory Modified for Women	210189-9	9/28/1951	Air Force	Standard 2-Story above grade +20 degree zone Stair Details	USACEHQ	Yes
Airmens Dormitory Modified for Women	210189-10	9/28/1951	Air Force	Standard 2-Story above grade +20 degree zone Foundation Plan & Details	USACEHQ	Yes
Airmens Dormitory Modified for Women	210189-11	9/28/1951	Air Force	Standard 2-Story above grade +20 degree zone Framing Plans & Details	USACEHQ	Yes
Airmens Dormitory Modified for Women	210189-12	9/28/1951	Air Force	Standard 2-Story above grade +20 degree zone Alternate: Utility Room on First Floor	USACEHQ	Yes
Airmens Dormitory Modified for Women	210189-13	9/28/1951	Air Force	Standard 2-Story above grade +20 degree zone Alternate: Boiler Room in Basement - Coal	USACEHQ	Yes
Airmens Dormitory Modified for Women	210189-14	9/28/1951	Air Force	Standard 2-Story above grade +20 degree zone Alternate: Boiler Room in Basement - Oil or Gas	USACEHQ	Yes
Airmens Dormitory Modified for Women	210189-15	9/28/1951	Air Force	Standard 2-Story above grade +20 degree zone Alternate: Boiler Room	USACEHQ	Yes

Building Type	Drawing Number	Date	Service Branch	Drawing Type (Standard, Schematic, Geo-Specific)	Drawing Source	Digital Copy of Drawing Available
See legend or list type of building of not included in legend	Identifying number	date of drawing	What branch of military is drawing intended for	Standard, schematic, proposed, designed for specific installation, etc.	Where was drawing plan obtained: NARA, USACE HQ, other	Is a digital copy of the drawing available for inclusion on the CD
				on 1st Floor - Coal		
Airmens Dormitory Modified for Women	210189-16	9/28/1951	Air Force	Standard 2-Story above grade +20 degree zone Alternate: Boiler Room on 1st Floor - Oil or Gas	USACEHQ	Yes
Airmens Dormitory Modified for Women	210189-17	9/28/1951	Air Force	Standard 2-Story above grade +20 degree zone Alternate: Forced Warm Air System	USACEHQ	Yes
Airmens Dormitory Modified for Women	210189-18	9/28/1951	Air Force	Standard 2-Story above grade +20 degree zone Heating Layout - Hot Water	USACEHQ	Yes
Airmens Dormitory Modified for Women	210189-19	9/28/1951	Air Force	Standard 2-Story above grade +20 degree zone Electrical, Plumbing, Heating - Alt. Boiler Room in Basement	USACEHQ	Yes
Airmens Dormitory Modified for Women	210189-20	9/28/1951	Air Force	Standard 2-Story above grade +20 degree zone Electrical, Plumbing, Heating - Alt. Boiler Room 1st Floor	USACEHQ	Yes
Airmens Dormitory Modified for Women	210189-21	9/28/1951	Air Force	Standard 2-Story above grade +20 degree zone Electrical Layout - Hot Water System	USACEHQ	Yes
Airmens Dormitory Modified for Women	210189-22	9/28/1951	Air Force	Standard 2-Story above grade +20 degree zone Plumbing Layout - Hot Water System	USACEHQ	Yes
Airmens Dormitory Modified for Women	210189-23	9/28/1951	Air Force	Standard 2-Story above grade +20 degree zone Plumbing Details	USACEHQ	Yes
Airmens Dormitory Modified for Women	210189-24	9/28/1951	Air Force	Standard 2-Story above grade +20 degree zone Heating Layout - Forced Warm Air System	USACEHQ	Yes
Airmens Dormitory Modified for Women	210189-25	9/28/1951	Air Force	Standard 2-Story above grade +20 degree zone Electrical Layout - Forced Warm Air System	USACEHQ	Yes
Airmens Dormitory Modified for Women	210189-26	9/28/1951	Air Force	Standard 2-Story above grade +20 degree zone Plumbing Layout - Forced Warm Air System	USACEHQ	Yes
Airmens Dormitory Modified for Women	210189-27	9/28/1951	Air Force	Standard 2-Story Special Construction +20 degree zone Plans & Elevations	USACEHQ	Yes
Airmens Dormitory Modified for Women	210189-28	9/28/1951	Air Force	Standard 2-Story Special Construction +20 degree zone Alternate Heating Sys-	USACEHQ	Yes

Building Type	Drawing Number	Date	Service Branch	Drawing Type (Standard, Schematic, Geo-Specific)	Drawing Source	Digital Copy of Drawing Available
See legend or list type of building of not included in legend	Identifying number	date of drawing	What branch of military is drawing intended for	Standard, schematic, proposed, designed for specific installation, etc.	Where was drawing plan obtained: NARA, USACE HQ, other	Is a digital copy of the drawing available for inclusion on the CD
				tem Schemes		
Airmens Dormitory Modified for Women	210190-1	9/28/1951	Air Force	Standard 2-Story above grade 0 degree zone Title Sheet	USACEHQ	Yes
Airmens Dormitory Modified for Women	210190-2	9/28/1951	Air Force	Standard 2-Story above grade 0 degree zone 1st & 2nd Floor Plans	USACEHQ	Yes
Airmens Dormitory Modified for Women	210190-3	9/28/1951	Air Force	Standard 2-Story above grade 0 degree zone Elevations & Details	USACEHQ	Yes
Airmens Dormitory Modified for Women	210190-4	9/28/1951	Air Force	Standard 2-Story above grade 0 degree zone Elevations & Details	USACEHQ	Yes
Airmens Dormitory Modified for Women	210190-5	9/28/1951	Air Force	Standard 2-Story above grade 0 degree zone Wall Sections	USACEHQ	Yes
Airmens Dormitory Modified for Women	210190-6	9/28/1951	Air Force	Standard 2-Story above grade 0 degree zone Wall Sections	USACEHQ	Yes
Airmens Dormitory Modified for Women	210190-7	9/28/1951	Air Force	Standard 2-Story above grade 0 degree zone Toilet Room & Door Details	USACEHQ	Yes
Airmens Dormitory Modified for Women	210190-8	9/28/1951	Air Force	Standard 2-Story above grade 0 degree zone Sleeping Room Closet Units & Misc. Details	USACEHQ	Yes
Airmens Dormitory Modified for Women	210190-9	9/28/1951	Air Force	Standard 2-Story above grade 0 degree zone Stair Details	USACEHQ	Yes
Airmens Dormitory Modified for Women	210190-10	9/28/1951	Air Force	Standard 2-Story above grade 0 degree zone Foundation Plan & Details	USACEHQ	Yes
Airmens Dormitory Modified for Women	210190-11	9/28/1951	Air Force	Standard 2-Story above grade 0 degree zone Framing Plans & Details	USACEHQ	Yes
Airmens Dormitory Modified for Women	210190-12	9/28/1951	Air Force	Standard 2-Story above grade 0 degree zone Alternate: Utility Room on First Floor	USACEHQ	Yes
Airmens Dormitory Modified for Women	210190-13	9/28/1951	Air Force	Standard 2-Story above grade 0 degree zone Alternate: Boiler Room in Basement - Coal	USACEHQ	Yes
Airmens Dormitory Modified for Women	210190-14	9/28/1951	Air Force	Standard 2-Story above grade 0 degree zone Alternate: Boiler Room in Basement - Oil or Gas	USACEHQ	Yes
Airmens Dormitory Modified for Women	210190-15	9/28/1951	Air Force	Standard 2-Story above grade 0 degree zone Alternate: Boiler Room on 1st Floor - Coal	USACEHQ	Yes
Airmens Dormitory Modified for Women	210190-16	9/28/1951	Air Force	Standard 2-Story above grade 0 degree zone	USACEHQ	Yes

Building Type	Drawing Number	Date	Service Branch	Drawing Type (Standard, Schematic, Geo-Specific)	Drawing Source	Digital Copy of Drawing Available
See legend or list type of building of not included in legend	Identifying number	date of drawing	What branch of military is drawing intended for	Standard, schematic, proposed, designed for specific installation, etc.	Where was drawing plan obtained: NARA, USACE HQ, other	Is a digital copy of the drawing available for inclusion on the CD
				Alternate: Boiler Room on 1st Floor - Oil or Gas		
Airmens Dormitory Modified for Women	210190-17	9/28/1951	Air Force	Standard 2-Story above grade 0 degree zone Alternate: Forced Warm Air System	USACEHQ	Yes
Airmens Dormitory Modified for Women	210190-18	9/28/1951	Air Force	Standard 2-Story above grade 0 degree zone Heating Layout - Hot Water	USACEHQ	Yes
Airmens Dormitory Modified for Women	210190-19	9/28/1951	Air Force	Standard 2-Story above grade 0 degree zone Electrical, Plumbing, Heating - Alt. Boiler Room in Basement	USACEHQ	Yes
Airmens Dormitory Modified for Women	210190-20	9/28/1951	Air Force	Standard 2-Story above grade 0 degree zone Electrical, Plumbing, Heating - Alt. Boiler Room 1st Floor	USACEHQ	Yes
Airmens Dormitory Modified for Women	210190-21	9/28/1951	Air Force	Standard 2-Story above grade 0 degree zone Electrical Layout - Hot Water System	USACEHQ	Yes
Airmens Dormitory Modified for Women	210190-22	9/28/1951	Air Force	Standard 2-Story above grade 0 degree zone Plumbing Layout - Hot Water System	USACEHQ	Yes
Airmens Dormitory Modified for Women	210190-23	9/28/1951	Air Force	Standard 2-Story above grade 0 degree zone Plumbing Details	USACEHQ	Yes
Airmens Dormitory Modified for Women	210190-24	9/28/1951	Air Force	Standard 2-Story above grade 0 degree zone Heating Layout - Forced Warm Air System	USACEHQ	Yes
Airmens Dormitory Modified for Women	210190-25	9/28/1951	Air Force	Standard 2-Story above grade 0 degree zone Electrical Layout - Forced Warm Air System	USACEHQ	Yes
Airmens Dormitory Modified for Women	210190-26	9/28/1951	Air Force	Standard 2-Story above grade 0 degree zone Plumbing Layout - Forced Warm Air System	USACEHQ	Yes
Airmens Dormitory Modified for Women	210190-27	9/28/1951	Air Force	Standard 2-Story Special Construction 0 degree zone Plans & Elevations	USACEHQ	Yes
Airmens Dormitory Modified for Women	210190-28	9/28/1951	Air Force	Standard 2-Story Special Construction 0 degree zone Alternate Heating System Schemes	USACEHQ	Yes
Airmens Dormitory Modified for Women	210193-1	9/28/1951	Air Force	Standard 3-Story Concrete Frame 0 degree	USACEHQ	Yes

Building Type	Drawing Number	Date	Service Branch	Drawing Type (Standard, Schematic, Geo-Specific)	Drawing Source	Digital Copy of Drawing Available
See legend or list type of building of not included in legend	Identifying number	date of drawing	What branch of military is drawing intended for	Standard, schematic, proposed, designed for specific installation, etc.	Where was drawing plan obtained: NARA, USACE HQ, other	Is a digital copy of the drawing available for inclusion on the CD
				zone Title Sheet		
Airmens Dormitory Modified for Women	210193-2	9/28/1951	Air Force	Standard 3-Story Concrete Frame 0 degree zone Basement & 1st Floor Plans	USACEHQ	Yes
Airmens Dormitory Modified for Women	210193-3	9/28/1951	Air Force	Standard 3-Story Concrete Frame 0 degree zone 2nd & 3rd Floor Plans	USACEHQ	Yes
Airmens Dormitory Modified for Women	210193-4	9/28/1951	Air Force	Standard 3-Story Concrete Frame 0 degree zone Elevations & Details	USACEHQ	Yes
Airmens Dormitory Modified for Women	210193-6	9/28/1951	Air Force	Standard 3-Story Concrete Frame 0 degree zone Wall Sections	USACEHQ	Yes
Airmens Dormitory Modified for Women	210193-7	9/28/1951	Air Force	Standard 3-Story Concrete Frame 0 degree zone Bedroom Closet & Toilet Room Details	USACEHQ	Yes
Airmens Dormitory Modified for Women	210193-8	9/28/1951	Air Force	Standard 3-Story Concrete Frame 0 degree zone Stair & Fire Escape Details	USACEHQ	Yes
Airmens Dormitory Modified for Women	210193-13	9/28/1951	Air Force	Standard 3-Story Concrete Frame 0 degree zone Alternate: Utility Room on 1st Floor	USACEHQ	Yes
Airmens Dormitory Modified for Women	210193-21	9/28/1951	Air Force	Standard 3-Story Concrete Frame 0 degree zone Electrical Layout Hot Water Heating System	USACEHQ	Yes
Airmens Dormitory Modified for Women	210193-22	9/28/1951	Air Force	Standard 3-Story Concrete Frame 0 degree zone Plumbing Layout Hot Water Heating System	USACEHQ	Yes
Airmens Dormitory Modified for Women	210193-23	9/28/1951	Air Force	Standard 3-Story Concrete Frame 0 degree zone Plumbing Details	USACEHQ	Yes
Airmens Dormitory Modified for Women	210193-27	9/28/1951	Air Force	Standard 3-Story Special Construction 0 degree zone Plans & Elevations	USACEHQ	Yes
Nurses or WAF Officers Quarters	SK250706-1	2/5/1952	Air Force	Schematic Floor Plans	USACEHQ	Yes
Nurses or WAF Officers Quarters	SK250706-2	2/5/1952	Air Force	Schematic Elevations & Alt. Plans	USACEHQ	Yes

Building Type	Drawing Number	Date	Service Branch	Drawing Type (Standard, Schematic, Geo-Specific)	Drawing Source	Digital Copy of Drawing Available
See legend or list type of building of not included in legend	Identifying number	date of drawing	What branch of military is drawing intended for	Standard, schematic, proposed, designed for specific installation, etc.	Where was drawing plan obtained: NARA, USACE HQ, other	Is a digital copy of the drawing available for inclusion on the CD
Nurses or WAF Officers Quarters	SK250709-1	2/5/1952	Air Force	Schematic Plans, Elevations, Sections	USACEHQ	Yes
Nurses or WAF Officers Quarters	SK250708-1	2/8/1952	Air Force	Schematic Plans, Elevations, Sections	USACEHQ	Yes
EMB	556010	4/21/1952	Navy	Standard	NARA	yes
EMB	556012	4/21/1952	Navy		NARA	yes
Air Force Dormitory for Enlisted Women	2101107-1	8/8/1952	Air Force	Standard 3-Story Masonry Design Utility Room in Basement Floor Plans	USACEHQ	Yes
Air Force Dormitory for Enlisted Women	2101107-2	8/8/1952	Air Force	Standard 3-Story Masonry Design Utility Room in Basement Elevations & Sections	USACEHQ	Yes
Air Force Dormitory for Enlisted Women	2101109-1	8/8/1952	Air Force	Standard 2-Story Wood Design Utility Room in Basement Floor Plans	USACEHQ	Yes
Air Force Dormitory for Enlisted Women	2101109-2	8/8/1952	Air Force	Standard 2-Story Wood Design Utility Room in Basement Floor Plans	USACEHQ	Yes
EWB	621844	10/12/1953	Navy		NARA	yes
EMB	621843	10/12/1953	Navy & Marines		NARA	
Women's BOQ	un-numbered	11/2/1953	Navy	Schematic	NARA	yes
BOQ	un-numbered	11/2/1953	Navy	Schematic	NARA	yes
EWB	un-numbered	11/2/1953	Navy	Schematic	NARA	yes
EMB	un-numbered	11/2/1953	Navy	Schematic	NARA	yes
CPO Quarters	un-numbered	11/2/1953	Navy	Schematic	NARA	Yes
BOQ	539042	11/2/1953	Navy	Schematic	NARA	yes
EMB	539037	11/2/1953	Navy	Schematic	NARA	yes
EMB	539038	11/2/1953	Navy	Schematic	NARA	yes
EWB	539039	11/2/1953	Navy	Schematic	NARA	yes
EWB	539040	11/2/1953	Navy	Schematic	NARA	yes
BOQ	621837	12/11/1953	Navy	Definitive	NARA	yes
BOQ	621838	12/11/1953	Navy	Definitive	NARA	yes
Standard Components Layout	400140-1	6/28/1954	Army	Standard Preface & Index	USACEHQ	Yes
Standard Components Layout	400140-2	6/28/1954	Army	Standard BOQ (Male or Female)	USACEHQ	Yes
Standard Components Layout	400140-3	6/28/1954	Army	Standard Enlisted WAC Facilities	USACEHQ	Yes
EMB	658441	6/29/1954	Navy	Standard	NARA	yes
EWB	658440	6/29/1954	Navy	Standard	NARA	yes
Air Force Dormitory for Enlisted Women	210204-1	10/27/1954	Air Force	Standard 2-Story Wood Frame Warm and Cold Climate Plans & Details	USACEHQ	Yes
Air Force Dormitory for Enlisted Women	210204-2	10/27/1954	Air Force	Standard 2-Story Wood Frame Warm and Cold Climate Elevations & Sections	USACEHQ	Yes
Air Force Dormitory for Enlisted Women	210205-1	10/27/1954	Air Force	Standard 3-Story Concrete Frame Warm and	USACEHQ	Yes

Building Type	Drawing Number	Date	Service Branch	Drawing Type (Standard, Schematic, Geo-Specific)	Drawing Source	Digital Copy of Drawing Available
See legend or list type of building of not included in legend	Identifying number	date of drawing	What branch of military is drawing intended for	Standard, schematic, proposed, designed for specific installation, etc.	Where was drawing plan obtained: NARA, USACE HQ, other	Is a digital copy of the drawing available for inclusion on the CD
				Cold Climate Floor Plans		
Air Force Dormitory for Enlisted Women	210205-2	10/27/1954	Air Force	Standard 3-Story Concrete Frame Warm and Cold Climate Elevations & Sections	USACEHQ	Yes
EMB	665169	4/21/1955	Navy	Scheme A	NARA	yes
EMB	665171	4/21/1955	Navy	Scheme B	NARA	yes
EMB	665192	8/3/1955	Navy	Scheme D	NARA	yes
EMB	665209	8/3/1955	Navy	Scheme	NARA	yes
BOQ	723357	10/6/1955	Navy	Standard (Tropical Design)	NARA	yes
EMB	723347	10/6/1955	Navy	Standard	NARA	yes
EMB	720647	9/17/1956	Navy	Proposed	NARA	yes
Battalion Admin. & Classroom Building	Sheet 4	12/17/1956	Army	Schematic Plan & Elevation	USACEHQ	Yes
BOQ	756740	2/5/1957	Navy	Definitive	NARA	yes
EMB	788341	8/20/1957	Navy	Proposed	NARA	yes
EMB	795610	8/27/1957	Navy	Definitive	NARA	yes
EMB	795611	8/27/1957	Navy	Definitive	NARA	yes
EMB	795614	8/27/1957	Navy	Definitive	NARA	yes
EMB	795615	8/27/1957	Navy	Definitive	NARA	yes
EMB	795616	8/27/1957	Navy	Definitive	NARA	yes
EWB	795612	8/27/1957	Navy	Definitive	NARA	yes
EMB	795613	9/27/1957	Navy	Definitive	NARA	yes
EWB	808316	12/31/1957	Navy	Standard (Mobilization Type)	NARA	yes
EMB	817037	3/11/1958	Navy	Definitive	NARA	yes
EMB	817038	3/11/1958	Navy	Definitive	NARA	yes
EMB	817039	3/11/1958	Navy	Definitive	NARA	yes
EMB	817040	3/11/1958	Navy	Definitive	NARA	yes
EMB	817041	3/11/1958	Navy	Definitive	NARA	yes
SP	817043	4/8/1958	Navy	Definitive	NARA	yes
EWB	817046	4/11/1958	Navy	Definitive	NARA	yes
SP	817185	4/14/1958	Navy	Definitive	NARA	yes
EWB	745932	12/8/1958	Navy	Standard (Mobilization Type)	NARA	yes
EWB	745933	12/8/1958	Navy	Standard (Mobilization Type)	NARA	yes
EWB	808224	12/8/1958	Navy	Standard (Mobilization Type)	NARA	yes
EWB	808326	12/8/1958	Navy	Standard (Mobilization Type)	NARA	yes
EWB	808234	12/8/1958	Navy	Standard (Mobilization Type)	NARA	yes
EWB	836726	12/8/1958	Navy	Standard (Mobilization Type)	NARA	yes
EWB	836734	12/8/1958	Navy	Standard (Mobilization Type)	NARA	yes
SP	745934	12/8/1958	Navy	Standard (Mobilization Type)	NARA	yes
SP	808243	12/8/1958	Navy	Standard (Mobilization Type)	NARA	yes
SP	808335	12/8/1958	Navy	Standard (Mobilization Type)	NARA	yes

Building Type	Drawing Number	Date	Service Branch	Drawing Type (Standard, Schematic, Geo-Specific)	Drawing Source	Digital Copy of Drawing Available
See legend or list type of building of not included in legend	Identifying number	date of drawing	What branch of military is drawing intended for	Standard, schematic, proposed, designed for specific installation, etc.	Where was drawing plan obtained: NARA, USACE HQ, other	Is a digital copy of the drawing available for inclusion on the CD
EMB	745930	12/9/1958	Navy	Standard (Mobilization Type)	NARA	yes
EMB	745931	12/9/1958	Navy	Standard (Mobilization Type)	NARA	yes
BOQ Motel Type	AD250672-1	2/23/1962	Air Force	Schematic Tri-Service Definitive Drawing Plans, Elevations, Sections	USACEHQ	Yes
BOQ Motel Type	AD250672-2	2/23/1962	Air Force	Schematic Tri-Service Definitive Drawing Plans, Elevations, Sections	USACEHQ	Yes
EMB	895054	6/27/1963	Navy	Definitive	NARA	yes
SP	1038068	12/13/1965	Navy	Specific Installation	NARA	yes
BEQ	1038070	2/10/1966	Navy	Definitive (Typ. Room Arrangements)	NARA	yes
BEQ	1038071	2/10/1966	Navy	Definitive (Typ. Room Arrangements)	NARA	yes
BEQ	1038076	5/20/1966	Navy	Definitive	NARA	yes
Processing Building	380905-3	11/8/1966	Army	Schematic Reception Station Complex	USACEHQ	Yes
Barracks Reception Station Complex	SK2101153-6	11/18/1966	Army	Schematic Plans	USACEHQ	Yes
Dining Hall	3605118-4	11/18/1966	Army	Standard Reception Station Complex Floor/Site Plan	USACEHQ	Yes
Enlisted Barracks Reception Station Complex	2101153-6	11/18/1966	Army	Standard Floor Plans	USACEHQ	Yes
Reception Station Complex	1606328-2	11/18/1966	Army	Standard Site Plan	USACEHQ	Yes
Service Club/ Post Exchange	311847-5	11/18/1966	Army	Schematic Reception Station Complex	USACEHQ	Yes
Service Club/ Post Exchange Reception Station Complex	SK311847-5	11/18/1966	Army	Schematic Plan	USACEHQ	Yes
EMB	1038075	1/25/1967	Navy	Definitive	NARA	yes
EWB (Center Hall & Motel Type)	4	9/5/1967	Army	Concept Sketches	USACEHQ	Yes
Officer Personnel Typical Living Units - Center Hall Type	6	9/5/1967	Army	Concept Sketches	USACEHQ	Yes
Officer Personnel Typical Living Units - Motel	5	9/5/1967	Army	Concept Sketches	USACEHQ	Yes
SP (Gym)	1294389 (NAVFAC)	5/29/1968	Navy	Definitive	NARA	yes
BOQ	1297661 - 1297662 (FEC)	4/24/1969	Navy	Specific Installation	NARA	yes
SP (Gym)	1294390	6/1/1969	Navy	Definitive	NARA	yes

Building Type	Drawing Number	Date	Service Branch	Drawing Type (Standard, Schematic, Geo-Specific)	Drawing Source	Digital Copy of Drawing Available
See legend or list type of building of not included in legend	Identifying number	date of drawing	What branch of military is drawing intended for	Standard, schematic, proposed, designed for specific installation, etc.	Where was drawing plan obtained: NARA, USACE HQ, other	Is a digital copy of the drawing available for inclusion on the CD
BEQ	1403100 (NAVFAC)	4/17/1974	Navy	Definitive	NARA	yes
BEQ	1403797 (NAVFAC)	5/12/1975	Navy	Definitive	NARA	yes
BEQ	1403798 (NAVFAC)	5/12/1975	Navy	Definitive	NARA	yes
BOQ	1403795 (NAVFAC)	5/14/1975	Navy	Definitive	NARA	yes
BOQ	1403796 (NAVFAC)	5/14/1975	Navy	Definitive	NARA	yes
BOQ (Men)	306887 - 306888	Illegible	Navy	Specific Installation	NARA	yes
EWB	306869	Illegible	Navy	Specific Installation	NARA	yes
EWB	306870	Illegible	Navy	Specific Installation (Elevations for above plans)	NARA	yes
Alterations to Bldg # 268 Training Center Fort Des Moines, Iowa	193A-28	N/A	Army	Specific Installation Plans & Details	NARA	Yes
Alterations to Building # 81 Training Center Fort Des Moines, Iowa	193A-27	N/A	Army	Specific Installation Plans & Details	NARA	Yes
EWB	21-02-06	N/A	Army	Standard	UIUC Library	yes
Improved Bachelor Officer Quarters - Women	Sheet 303	N/A	Army	Schematic Plan & Elevation	USACEHQ	Yes
Perspective Sketch Drawing	sketch_ reception	N/A	Army	sketch	USACEHQ	Yes
BEQ	1341195 (NAVFAC)	N/A	Navy	Standard (Motel Type)	NARA	yes
EB	731427	N/A	Navy	Definitive	NARA	yes
EB	731428	N/A	Navy	Definitive	NARA	yes
EB	756735	N/A	Navy	Definitive	NARA	yes
EB	756736	N/A	Navy	Standard	NARA	yes
EMB	171065	N/A	Navy	Standard	NARA	yes
SP (Chapel)	367912	N/A	Navy	Specific Installation (Scheme A)	NARA	yes
SP (Chapel)	367912	N/A	Navy	Specific Installation (Scheme B)	NARA	yes
W	318064	N/A	Navy	Proposed	NARA	yes
WB	318064	N/A	Navy	Specific Installation	NARA	yes

Building Data

Building Type	Drawing Number	Total Floor Area (sq. ft.)	Number of Stories	Building Components (other than barracks and restroom)
See legend or list type of building of not included in legend	Identifying number	total square footage of the floor area for the entire building	how many stories in the building; if basement included, then states so: e.g., 2 + basement	What room types are included in building other than barracks and restrooms?
Typical Landscape Planting for Company Officers' and Double NCO Quarters	630-100			
Typical Landscape Planting for HQ Admin. Bldg, BOQs, Barracks Bldgs	630-101			
Marine Barracks	129241	17,800	2	Stair Hall; Store Room; Heater Room
Marine Barracks	129247			
EMB	137497 - 137498	8,736	2	Recreation Room; Canteen; Cobbler; Barber; Tailor; Office; Clothing Issue Room; Living Room; Dispensary Room; Storage Room; Straddle Room; Sick Bay; Brig; Instruction Room; Day Room; Scrub Room
Mobilization Buildings Hospital (Nurses) Quarters	800-1422 (2)			
Mobilization Buildings Hospital (Nurses) Quarters	800-1421	4,720	1	Living Room, Dining Room, Kitchen, Pantry, Office, Boiler Room
Mobilization Buildings Hospital (Nurses) Quarters	800-1422			
Mobilization Buildings Hospital (Nurses) Quarters	800-1423			
Mobilization Buildings Nurses (Hospital) Quarters	800-1435	9,345	2	Living Room, Dining Room, Kitchen, Storeroom, Office, Trunk Room, Boiler Room (all on 1st floor)
Mobilization Buildings Nurses (Hospital) Quarters	800-1436	See above	See above	See above
Mobilization Buildings Hospital (Nurses) Quarters	800-1423.1			
EMB	188167	75,000	1	Supply Office; Tailor; Barber; Issue Room; Clothing Storage; Ships Storage; Sick Bay; Lab; Dr. Office; Exam Room; Mess Hall; Galley; Dry Storage; Scullery; Office; Spud Locker; Bread Storage; Veg. Prep; Butcher
EMB	184324 - 184325	N/A	2	Lobby; Living Room; Mess Hall; Galley; Officer's Living & Dining Rooms; Reading Room
Typical Layout Diagram for Camouflage Demonstration - Practice Area	614-1602			
Typical Layout Diagrams for WAAC Replacement Training Center	614-703			

Building Type	Drawing Number	Total Floor Area (sq. ft.)	Number of Stories	Building Components (other than barracks and restroom)
See legend or list type of building of not included in legend	Identifying number	total square footage of the floor area for the entire building	how many stories in the building; if basement included, then states so: e.g., 2 + basement	What room types are included in building other than barracks and restrooms?
Mobilization Buildings WAAC Exchange - Type - WPX - A-M	700-3516			
Mobilization Buildings WAAC Exchange - Type - WPX - A-M	700-3517	8,000	1	Heater Room, scullery, stores, store room, exchange, office, facial room, supply closet, manicure, beauty shop, tailor shop, screened porch
Mobilization Buildings WAAC Exchange - Type - WPX - A-M	700-3518			
Mobilization Buildings WAAC Exchange - Type - WPX - A-M	700-3519			
Mobilization Buildings WAAC Exchange - Type - WPX - A-M	700-3520			
Mobilization Buildings WAAC Exchange - Type - WPX - A-M	700-3521			
Mobilization Buildings WAAC Exchange - Type - WPX - A-M	700-3522			
Mobilization Buildings WAC Barracks	800-425			
Mobilization Buildings WAC Barracks	800-426	5,310	2 + partital basement	Laundry, boiler room
Mobilization Buildings WAC Barracks	800-427			
Mobilization Buildings WAC Barracks	800-428			
Mobilization Buildings WAC Barracks	800-429			
Mobilization Buildings WAC Barracks	800-430			
Mobilization Buildings WAC Barracks	800-431			
Mobilization Buildings WAC Exchange	800-1124			
Mobilization Buildings WAC Exchange	800-1125	8,000	1	Heater Room, scullery, stores, store room, exchange, office, facial room, supply closet, manicure, beauty shop, tailor shop, screened porch
Mobilization Buildings WAC Exchange	800-1126			
Mobilization Buildings WAC Exchange	800-1127			
Mobilization Buildings WAC Exchange	800-1128			
Mobilization Buildings WAC Exchange	800-1129			
Mobilization Buildings WAC Exchange	800-1130			
Barracks for 150 Women WAC Training Center Fort Des Moines, Iowa	193A-49	Indeterminate	1	Boiler room additions
Laundry & Toilet Bldg Addition for Barracks Training Center Fort Des Moines, Iowa	193A-22	3,516	1 + basement	Laundry room

Building Type	Drawing Number	Total Floor Area (sq. ft.)	Number of Stories	Building Components (other than barracks and restroom)
See legend or list type of building of not included in legend	Identifying number	total square footage of the floor area for the entire building	how many stories in the building; if basement included, then states so: e.g., 2 + basement	What room types are included in building other than barracks and restrooms?
Recreation Buildings in connection with Barracks Training Center Fort Des Moines, Iowa	193A-25	Bldg # 19B: 2445 22B: 2441 25B: 1580 27B: 1732 30B: 1207	1	Recreation Room
WAC Barracks Training Center Fort Des Moines, Iowa	193A-19	Indeterminate	1	none
Co. Unit Layout Diagrams for WAAC	614-702			
Training Center Fort Des Moines, Iowa	193A-16			
Mobilization Buildings WAAC Barracks	700-3525	5,310	2	Laundry, Boiler Room
Mobilization Buildings WAAC Barracks (Alt. for sloping site)	700-3526	5,310	2	Laundry, Boiler Room
Mobilization Buildings WAAC Barracks	700-3527			
Mobilization Buildings WAAC Barracks	700-3528			
Mobilization Buildings WAAC Barracks	700-3529			
WAC Latrine (Temporary Structure) Training Center Fort Des Moines, Iowa	193A-31	193	1	none
Mobilization Buildings WAC Recreation, Supply, Co. Admin., & Quarters	700-3540			
Mobilization Buildings WAC Recreation, Supply, Co. Admin., & Quarters	700-3541	3,614	1	Recreation Room, Living Room, CO Office, Orderly, Beauty Shop, Supply Room, Heater Room
Mobilization Buildings WAC Recreation, Supply, Co. Admin., & Quarters	700-3542			
Mobilization Buildings WAC Recreation, Supply, Co. Admin., & Quarters	700-3543			
Mobilization Buildings WAC Recreation, Supply, Co. Admin., & Quarters	700-3544			
Mobilization Buildings WAC Recreation, Supply, Co. Admin., & Quarters	700-3545			
Mobilization Buildings WAC Recreation, Supply, Co. Admin., & Quarters	700-3546			
Mobilization Buildings WAC Recreation, Supply, Co. Admin., & Quarters	700-3547	6,087	1	Living Rooms, Supply Rooms, Orderly, CO Offices, Beauty Shop, Canteen, Recreation Room, Game Room, Library

Building Type	Drawing Number	Total Floor Area (sq. ft.)	Number of Stories	Building Components (other than barracks and restroom)
See legend or list type of building of not included in legend	Identifying number	total square footage of the floor area for the entire building	how many stories in the building; if basement included, then states so: e.g., 2 + basement	What room types are included in building other than barracks and restrooms?
Mobilization Buildings WAC Recreation, Supply, Co. Admin., & Quarters	700-3548			
Mobilization Buildings WAC Recreation, Supply, Co. Admin., & Quarters	700-3549			
Mobilization Buildings WAC Recreation, Supply, Co. Admin., & Quarters	700-3550			
Mobilization Buildings WAC Recreation, Supply, Co. Admin., & Quarters	700-3551			
Barracks (30 Men) WAC Training Center Fort Des Moines, Iowa	193A-46	2,033	1	none
Mobilization Buildings WAAC Officers' Quarters	700-3532	2,390	1	Living Room, Laundry Room
Mobilization Buildings WAAC Officers' Quarters	700-3533			
Office Building of Engineer (Additions & Remodelling) WAC Training Center Fort Des Moines, Iowa	193A-33	Indeterminate	1	Administration office, engineer office, control room, general offices
EMB	188660	N/A	2	Entry hall; heater room; storage room
Post Hospital and Drill Hall WAC Training Center Fort Des Moines, Iowa	193A-39	Indeterminate	3 + basement	Record storage, library & conference, physiotherapy, boiler room, storage, reception, adjutant, admin. Office, general offices, x-ray room, sew room, dark room, waiting room, emergency room, operating room, nurse workroom, dressing room, locker room, prep ward, recovery ward, ward room, communicable disease room
Nurses' Quarters	1100-361			
Typical Layout Diagrams for WAAC Battalion Organization	614-701			
Mobilization General Hospital Nurses Quarters Officers Quarters	1100-2136			
Mobilization General Hospital Nurses Quarters Officers Quarters	1100-2137			
Mobilization General Hospital Nurses Quarters Officers Quarters	1100-2138			

Building Type	Drawing Number	Total Floor Area (sq. ft.)	Number of Stories	Building Components (other than barracks and restroom)
See legend or list type of building of not included in legend	Identifying number	total square footage of the floor area for the entire building	how many stories in the building; if basement included, then states so: e.g., 2 + basement	What room types are included in building other than barracks and restrooms?
Mobilization General Hospital Nurses Quarters Officers Quarters	1100-2139			
Mobilization General Hospital Nurses QuartersOfficers Quarters	1100-2140			
Option 1: Mobilization General Hospital Nurses Quarters	1100-2135	12,000	2	Laundry, office, trunk room, Living Room (1 on each flr)
Option 2: Mobilization General Hospital Officers Quarters	1100-2135 (Same dwg as above, different occupant)	12,000	2	Office, trunk room, Living Room (1 on each flr); Laundry is substituted with additional bedroom
Mobilization Buildings WAC Barracks	700-3560	5,310	2	Laundry, Heater Room
Mobilization Buildings WAC Barracks	700-3561			
Mobilization Buildings WAC Barracks	700-3562			
Mobilization Buildings WAC Barracks	700-3563			
Nurses' Quarters	1100-360	2,000	1	Living Rooms, 1 for every 2 bedrooms (separate entry for each 4 woman unit)
W	188697	7,814	2	Lobby; Recreation Room; Linen Room; Heater Room
W	188699	7,814	2	Lobby; Recreation Room; Linen Room; Heater Room
W	188702	15,553	2	Lobby; Recreation Room; Storage Room; Laundry Room
Mobilization Buildings Conversion of Existing 74 Man Barracks for WAC	700-3570		2	Laundry, heater room
Mobilization Buildings Conversion of Existing 74 Man Barracks for WAC	700-3571			
Mobilization Buildings WAC BOQ	700-3565	3,540	1	Living Room, Linen closet, Laundry (Alternate plan), heating room (Alt. plan)
Mobilization Buildings WAC BOQ	700-3566			
Mobilization Buildings WAC BOQ	700-3567			
Mobilization Buildings WAC BOQ	700-3568			
Typical Layout Diagram for Camouflage Demonstration - Practice Area	614-1601			
W	312559	N/A	1	Recreation Room; Bag Room; Heater Room; Laundry Room; Office
W	312559-2	N/A	1	Recreation Room; Office; Laundry Room
W	188767	6,300	2	Recreation Room; Storage Room; Laundry Room; Heater Room; Utility Room

Building Type	Drawing Number	Total Floor Area (sq. ft.)	Number of Stories	Building Components (other than barracks and restroom)
See legend or list type of building of not included in legend	Identifying number	total square footage of the floor area for the entire building	how many stories in the building; if basement included, then states so: e.g., 2 + basement	What room types are included in building other than barracks and restrooms?
Symbols for Camouflage - General Plan	614-1603			
Typical Layout Diagrams for one company of WAC	614-t.o.738			
Nurses & WAVE Officers	317319	N/A	2	Living room; trunk storage; linen room; enclosed porch
MW	256516	30,770	2	Lounge; Storage Room; Laundry Room
MW	256517	30,770	2	Lounge; Storage Room; Laundry Room
EWB	271541	16,202	2	Stair Hall; Lobby; Lounge; Office; Bag Storage; Heater Room; Laundry Room
SP (Women's Club)	291251	N/A	N/A	Vestibule; elevator lobby; library; recreation room; mess hall; cafeteria; galley
SP (Women's Club)	291252	N/A	N/A	Elevator lobby; vegetable preparation room
SP (Women's Club)	291254	N/A	N/A	Elevator lobby; office; recruiting; cleaner; cobbler; tailor; treatment room; waiting room; locker room; laundry room; hydrotherapy room
BOQ	256638	11,602	2	Lobby; Recreation Room; Laundry Room; Storage; Kitchen
Mobilization Buildings WAC Barracks	700-3560.1	5,900	2	Laundry, heater room on 1st floor
Mobilization Buildings Conversion of Existing Detachment Barracks for WAC	700-3585		1	Laundry, Separate shower room
Mobilization Buildings Conversion of Existing Detachment Barracks for WAC	700-3586			
W	288273	5,460	1	Lobby; Office; Lounge; Linen Room; Bag Storage; Uniform Storage; Scrub Room; Laundry Room
Mobilization Buildings Conversion of Hospital Barracks for WAC	700-3580		1	Laundry
Mobilization Buildings Conversion of Hospital Barracks for WAC	700-3581			
W	264793	7,480	1	Entry; Lounge; Storage; Galley; Linen Room; Heater Room; Washroom
WB	288273	5,460	1	Lobby; Lounge; Office; Uniform Storage; Bag Storage; Linen Room; Laundry Room; Scrub Room
W	288280	10,920	2	Lobby; Office; Lounge; Uniform Storage; Hall; Bag Storage; Linen Room; Scrub Room; Laundry Room
W	288282			
W	288283			

Building Type	Drawing Number	Total Floor Area (sq. ft.)	Number of Stories	Building Components (other than barracks and restroom)
See legend or list type of building of not included in legend	Identifying number	total square footage of the floor area for the entire building	how many stories in the building; if basement included, then states so: e.g., 2 + basement	What room types are included in building other than barracks and restrooms?
W	320100	13,824	2	Lounge; Office; Linen Room; Blues & Bag Room; Laundry Room; Heater Room; Recreation Room; Storage Room
W	304236	N/A	2	Vestibule; Coat Room; Officer in Charge; Clerk; Mail Room; Counselor; Formal Rest Room; Ward Room; Briefing Room; Linen Room; Laundry Room; Rest Room
W	304237	N/A	2	Rest Room; Laundry Room (Domestic); Linen Room
W	257696	12,132	2	Lounge; Laundry Room; Storage Room; Linen Room; Office
WB	257055			
SP (Swimming Pool)	304510 - 304511	N/A	1	Enlisted Men's Locker Room; WAVES locker room; equipment room; office; chlorination room; swimming pool
W	257698	10,962	2	Lobby; Office; Linen Storage; Trunk Storage; Uniform Storage; Utility Room; Laundry Room; Recreation Room
W	257701	10,962	2	Lobby; Office; Linen Storage; Trunk Storage; Uniform Storage; Utility Room; Laundry Room; Recreation Room
W	257669	N/A	2	Lobby; Office; Linen storage; Blues; Laundry Room; Heater Room; Recreation Room; Bag Storage
EW & EM	326815	N/A	2	Recreation Room; Dry Room; Scrub Room; Bag Storage; Uniform Storage; Linen Room
W	326814	N/A	2	Recreation Room; Dry Room; Scrub Room; Bag Storage; Uniform Storage; Linen Room
W	257734	N/A	2	Lobby; Office; Linen Room; Heater Room; Laundry Room; Bag Room; Blues
MW	290949	20,620	2	Recreation Room; Lounge; Linen Room; Storage Room; Office; Telephone booths
SP (Office, Lunch, Locker)	364804	N/A	1	Lobby; Office; First Aid; Lunch Room; Storage; Kitchen; Dish Washing Room; Colored Men's Locker Room; White Men's Locker Room; Colored Women's Locker Rooms; White Women's Locker Room
WAC Training Center Fort Des Moines, Iowa	194A-12			
W	342059	12,020	1	Vestibule; Entry Hall; Office; Gear Room; Mail Room; Suitcase & Bag storage; Uniform storage; Linen Room; Recreation Room; Laundry Room; Sewing Room

Building Type	Drawing Number	Total Floor Area (sq. ft.)	Number of Stories	Building Components (other than barracks and restroom)
See legend or list type of building of not included in legend	Identifying number	total square footage of the floor area for the entire building	how many stories in the building; if basement included, then states so: e.g., 2 + basement	What room types are included in building other than barracks and restrooms?
W	328676	11,288	2	Lobby; Office; Lounge; Uniform Storage; Hall; Bag Storage; Linen Room; Scrub Room; Laundry Room
WAVE Mess Hall	328687	13,260	1	Mess Hall; cafeteria; scullery; galley
W	328678			
WAVE Clinic	328711	1,560	1	Vestibule; Doctor's office; Isolation room; kitchen; exam room; nurse's room; supply room; ward
EWB	329667 - 329668	25,256	2 + basement	Entry; Stair Hall; Living Room; Lounge; Porch; Laundry Room; Ironing Room; Trunk Room; Linen Room
W	309299	23,944	1	Entrance hall; Recreation room; Office; Sewing room; Linen room; Mail room; Gear room; Suitcase & Bag room; screened porch
EWB	347315	21,587	2	Lobby; Office; Lounge; Trunk Storage; Utility; Linen Storage; Washing/Drying/Ironing Rooms; Recreation Room; Reading Room
SP (Lunch, Locker)	309610	N/A	1	Lobby; Office; Storage; Women's Locker Room; Men's Locker Room; Dining Room; Kitchen; Bake Shop; Butcher Shop; Storage
SP Auditorium	360741	21,561	2	Lobby; Auditorium; Office; Locker Room; Control Room; Chair Storage; Dressing Room; Stage; Mechanical Room; Gallery; Projection Room
SP (Dispensary)	370691	10,212	1	Waiting Room; Doctor's Office; Exam Room; Pharmacy Lab; Diet Kitchen; Nurses' Station; Utility Room; Solarium; Patient Rooms; Nurses' rooms
SP (Admin.)	342622	2,712	2	Lobby; Post Office; OD Office; Quarter Master; Mail File Room; Mess. Service Room; CO office; Exec. Office; Dup. Room
Study for Typical Landscape Development Plan	614-1117			
BOQ	360765	N/A	2	Entry Hall; Recreation Room; Writing Room; Laundry Room; Drying Room; Linen Storage; Ironing Room; Heater Room
SP (Ships Service Bldg)	360764	6,664	1	Lobby; Post Office; Beauty Salon; Financial Section; Laundry & Cleaner; Storage; Store & Soda Fountain
SP (Subsistence Building)	360777	N/A	1	Mess Hall; Officers' Mess; Scullery; Galley; Cafeteria; Bake Shop; Storage Rooms; Issue Room; Office; Mech. Room; Dry Storage

Building Type	Drawing Number	Total Floor Area (sq. ft.)	Number of Stories	Building Components (other than barracks and restroom)
See legend or list type of building of not included in legend	Identifying number	total square footage of the floor area for the entire building	how many stories in the building; if basement included, then states so: e.g., 2 + basement	What room types are included in building other than barracks and restrooms?
SP Auditorium & Gym	361229	21,561	2	Lobby; Auditorium; Office; Locker Room; Control Room; Chair Storage; Dressing Room; Stage; Mechanical Room; Gallery; Projection Room
EWB	339687 - 339688	24,990	2	Lobby; Office; Supplies; Bag Storage; Linen Storage; Lounge; Study; Laundry Room; Drying Room; Scrub Room; Quiet Room; Sewing Room
SP (Dispensary)	373477	2,976	1	Porch; Officers Ward; Womens Ward; Mens Ward; Utility Room; Diet Kitchen; Women's Sick Bay; Men's Sick Bay; Medical Store; Pharmacy; Doctor's Office; Record Office; Waiting Room
W	373486	11,935	2	Entry hall; lounge; office; linen room; luggage room; scrub room; dry room; ironing room; boiler room
WAVES Dispensary	409987	N/A	2	Diet Kitchen; Scullery; Bag Storage; Lab; Office; Gear Room; Physiotherapy room; waiting room; treatment room; overflow ward; night duty room; instruction and assembly room; linen room
BOQ	306882	8,822	2	Lobby; Recreation room; heater room; drying room; ironing room
BOQ	306883	8,822	2	Lobby; Recreation room; heater room; drying room; ironing room
SP (Base Site Plan)	401885			
SP Dispensary	401836	N/A	2	Lobby; Lecture Room; Medical Records Storage; Medical Office; Exam Rooms; Dental; Dressing Room; Legal; Education; Red Cross; Admin. Office; Pool; Reassemby; Interview Booths; Chaplain; Records; Machine Room
Barrack - WAC - Apartment Type	SK210109	19,386	3	Vestibule, stair hall, living room and kitchen (each apartment)
Barrack - WAC - Hotel Type	SK210108	1-story: 11,216 2-story: 19,532 3-story: 27,848	1 to 3 (depends on need of individual bases)	Lobby, date room, day room, lounges, kitchen, laundry, office, luggage room
WM	450230	N/A	2	Public Lounge; Private Lounge; Offices; Assembly Room; Classroom; Storage Room; Waiting Room; Laundry Room; Kitchen; Dispensary; Exam Room; Lab
Emergency Type Construction, EW Barracks	DEFE210201-1	6940 sf	1	Dayroom, dateroom, laundry, storage
Emergency Type Construction, EW Barracks	DEFE210201-2			
Emergency Type Construction, EW Barracks	DEFE250704-1	6,992	1	2 dayrooms, laundry room, heater room

Building Type	Drawing Number	Total Floor Area (sq. ft.)	Number of Stories	Building Components (other than barracks and restroom)
See legend or list type of building of not included in legend	Identifying number	total square footage of the floor area for the entire building	how many stories in the building; if basement included, then states so: e.g., 2 + basement	What room types are included in building other than barracks and restrooms?
MW	472352	8,544	2	Recreation Room; Date Room; Linen Room; Laundry Room; Trunk room
MW	472353	8,544	2	Recreation Room; Beauty Room; Sewing Room; Laundry Room
MW	472354	20,783	2	Recreation Room; Date Room; Linen Room; Laundry Room; Trunk room; Uniform room
MW	472355	20,783	2	Recreation Room; Beauty Room; Sewing Room; Laundry Room; Baggage Storage
MW	472366	20,783	2	Recreation Room; Date Room; Linen Room; Trunk Room; Laundry Room
MW	472367	20,783	2	Recreation Room; Beauty Room; Laundry Room; Baggage Storage
MW	472519	14,343	2	Recreation Room; Beauty Room; Laundry Room; Baggage Storage
MW	472518	14,343	2	Recreation Room; Linen Room; Trunk Storage; Laundry Room; Office
BOQ	500363	8,998	2	Lounge; Reading Room; Linen Room; Boiler Room; SO lounge
EMB	500359	8,400	2	Writing/Reading Room; Scrub Room; Bag Storage/linen closet; M.A.A. Room
EMB	500360	4,200	1	Scrub Room; Bag Storage/linen closet; M.A.A. Room
EWB	500361	8,960	2	Date Room; Scrub Room; Pressing & Drying Room; Linen Room, Trunk Room
EWB	500362	4,480	1	Date Room; Scrub Room; Pressing & Drying Room; Linen Room, Trunk Room
BOQ	496842	9,280	2	Entrance hall; Lounge; Reading room; linen room; SO lounge
EWB	496812	8,960	2	Date Room; Scrub Room; Pressing & Drying Room; Linen Room, Trunk Room
EWB	496830	4,640	1	Date Room; Scrub Room; Pressing & Drying Room; Linen Room, Trunk Room
Nurses' or WAF Officers' Quarters	DEF250706-1	24,000	2 + basement	Vestibule, lounge (1 on each floor), guest waiting room, laundry, storage, linen closet, office, boiler room, fuel room
Nurses' or WAF Officers' Quarters	DEF250706-2	Unit A: 24000 sf Unit B: 21360 sf Unit C: 18720 sf	2 + basement	
Airmens Dormitory	210171-2	15,790	2 + basement	Entry hall, laundry room, cleaning gear storage, utility room, lounge (1 on each floor)
Airmens Dormitory	210171-3		2 + basement	
Airmens Dormitory	210171-7			

Building Type	Drawing Number	Total Floor Area (sq. ft.)	Number of Stories	Building Components (other than barracks and restroom)
See legend or list type of building of not included in legend	Identifying number	total square footage of the floor area for the entire building	how many stories in the building; if basement included, then states so: e.g., 2 + basement	What room types are included in building other than barracks and restrooms?
Airmens Dormitory	210171-8			
Airmens Dormitory	210171-9			
Airmens Dormitory	210171-1			
Airmens Dormitory Modified for Women	210189-1			
Airmens Dormitory Modified for Women	210189-2	15,790	2 + basement	Entry hall, laundry room, cleaning gear storage, utility room, lounge (1 on each floor, 2nd flr lounge has kitchenette)
Airmens Dormitory Modified for Women	210189-3			
Airmens Dormitory Modified for Women	210189-3			
Airmens Dormitory Modified for Women	210189-4			
Airmens Dormitory Modified for Women	210189-5			
Airmens Dormitory Modified for Women	210189-6			
Airmens Dormitory Modified for Women	210189-7			
Airmens Dormitory Modified for Women	210189-8			
Airmens Dormitory Modified for Women	210189-9			
Airmens Dormitory Modified for Women	210189-10			
Airmens Dormitory Modified for Women	210189-11			
Airmens Dormitory Modified for Women	210189-12	15,790	2	Entry hall, laundry room, cleaning gear storage, utility room, lounge (1 on each floor, 2nd flr lounge has kitchenette)
Airmens Dormitory Modified for Women	210189-13	15,790	2 + basement	Entry hall, laundry room, cleaning gear storage, boiler room, coal storage, lounge (1 on each floor, 2nd flr lounge has kitchenette)
Airmens Dormitory Modified for Women	210189-14	15,790	2 + basement	Entry hall, laundry room, cleaning gear storage, boiler room, lounge (1 on each floor, 2nd flr lounge has kitchenette)
Airmens Dormitory Modified for Women	210189-15	16,512	2 + basement (lower boiler room and coal storage)	Entry hall, laundry room, cleaning gear storage, boiler room, coal storage, lounge (1 on each floor, 2nd flr lounge has kitchenette)
Airmens Dormitory Modified for Women	210189-16	15,978	2 + basement (lower boiler room)	Entry hall, laundry room, cleaning gear storage, boiler room, lounge (1 on each floor, 2nd flr lounge has kitchenette)
Airmens Dormitory Modified for Women	210189-17	15,907	2 + basement (lower heater room)	Entry hall, laundry room, cleaning gear storage, heater room (1st & 2nd floor), lounge (1 on each floor, 2nd flr lounge has kitchenette)
Airmens Dormitory Modified for Women	210189-18			
Airmens Dormitory Modified for Women	210189-19			

Building Type	Drawing Number	Total Floor Area (sq. ft.)	Number of Stories	Building Components (other than barracks and restroom)
See legend or list type of building of not included in legend	Identifying number	total square footage of the floor area for the entire building	how many stories in the building; if basement included, then states so: e.g., 2 + basement	What room types are included in building other than barracks and restrooms?
Airmens Dormitory Modified for Women	210189-20			
Airmens Dormitory Modified for Women	210189-21			
Airmens Dormitory Modified for Women	210189-22			
Airmens Dormitory Modified for Women	210189-23			
Airmens Dormitory Modified for Women	210189-24			
Airmens Dormitory Modified for Women	210189-25			
Airmens Dormitory Modified for Women	210189-26			
Airmens Dormitory Modified for Women	210189-27	15,790	2 + basement	Entry hall, laundry room, cleaning gear storage, utility room, lounge (1 on each floor, 2nd flr lounge has kitchenette)
Airmens Dormitory Modified for Women	210189-28			
Airmens Dormitory Modified for Women	210190-1			
Airmens Dormitory Modified for Women	210190-2	15,790	2 + basement	Entry hall, laundry room, cleaning gear storage, utility room, lounge (1 on each floor, 2nd flr lounge has kitchenette)
Airmens Dormitory Modified for Women	210190-3			
Airmens Dormitory Modified for Women	210190-4			
Airmens Dormitory Modified for Women	210190-5			
Airmens Dormitory Modified for Women	210190-6			
Airmens Dormitory Modified for Women	210190-7			
Airmens Dormitory Modified for Women	210190-8			
Airmens Dormitory Modified for Women	210190-9			
Airmens Dormitory Modified for Women	210190-10			
Airmens Dormitory Modified for Women	210190-11			
Airmens Dormitory Modified for Women	210190-12	15,790	2	Entry hall, laundry room, cleaning gear storage, utility room, lounge (1 on each floor, 2nd flr lounge has kitchenette)
Airmens Dormitory Modified for Women	210190-13	15,790	2 + basement	Entry hall, laundry room, cleaning gear storage, boiler room, coal storage, lounge (1 on each floor, 2nd flr lounge has kitchenette)
Airmens Dormitory Modified for Women	210190-14	15,790	2 + basement	Entry hall, laundry room, cleaning gear storage, boiler room, lounge (1 on each floor, 2nd flr lounge has kitchenette)
Airmens Dormitory Modified for Women	210190-15	16,512	2 + basement (lower boiler room and coal storage)	Entry hall, laundry room, cleaning gear storage, boiler room, coal storage, lounge (1 on each floor, 2nd flr lounge has kitchenette)

Building Type	Drawing Number	Total Floor Area (sq. ft.)	Number of Stories	Building Components (other than barracks and restroom)
See legend or list type of building of not included in legend	Identifying number	total square footage of the floor area for the entire building	how many stories in the building; if basement included, then states so: e.g., 2 + basement	What room types are included in building other than barracks and restrooms?
Airmens Dormitory Modified for Women	210190-16	15,978	2 + basement (lower boiler room)	Entry hall, laundry room, cleaning gear storage, boiler room, lounge (1 on each floor, 2nd flr lounge has kitchenette)
Airmens Dormitory Modified for Women	210190-17	15,907	2 + basement (lower heater room)	Entry hall, laundry room, cleaning gear storage, heater room (1st & 2nd floor), lounge (1 on each floor, 2nd flr lounge has kitchenette)
Airmens Dormitory Modified for Women	210190-18			
Airmens Dormitory Modified for Women	210190-19			
Airmens Dormitory Modified for Women	210190-20			
Airmens Dormitory Modified for Women	210190-21			
Airmens Dormitory Modified for Women	210190-22			
Airmens Dormitory Modified for Women	210190-23			
Airmens Dormitory Modified for Women	210190-24			
Airmens Dormitory Modified for Women	210190-25			
Airmens Dormitory Modified for Women	210190-26			
Airmens Dormitory Modified for Women	210190-27	15,790	2 + basement	Entry hall, laundry room, cleaning gear storage, utility room, lounge (1 on each floor, 2nd flr lounge has kitchenette)
Airmens Dormitory Modified for Women	210190-28			
Airmens Dormitory Modified for Women	210193-1			
Airmens Dormitory Modified for Women	210193-2	25,182	3 + basement	Lounge (1 on each floor), laundry (1st, 2nd floor), utility room, cleaning gear room, entry hall
Airmens Dormitory Modified for Women	210193-3	25,182	3 + basement	Lounge (1 on each floor), laundry (1st, 2nd floor), utility room, cleaning gear room, entry hall
Airmens Dormitory Modified for Women	210193-4			
Airmens Dormitory Modified for Women	210193-6			
Airmens Dormitory Modified for Women	210193-7			
Airmens Dormitory Modified for Women	210193-8			
Airmens Dormitory Modified for Women	210193-13	24,903	3	Lounge (1 on each floor), laundry (1st, 2nd floor), utility room, cleaning gear room, entry hall
Airmens Dormitory Modified for Women	210193-21			
Airmens Dormitory Modified for Women	210193-22			
Airmens Dormitory Modified for Women	210193-23			

Building Type	Drawing Number	Total Floor Area (sq. ft.)	Number of Stories	Building Components (other than barracks and restroom)
See legend or list type of building of not included in legend	Identifying number	total square footage of the floor area for the entire building	how many stories in the building; if basement included, then states so: e.g., 2 + basement	What room types are included in building other than barracks and restrooms?
Airmens Dormitory Modified for Women	210193-27	25,182	3 + basement	Lounge (1 on each floor), laundry (1st, 2nd floor), utility room, cleaning gear room, entry hall
Nurses or WAF Officers Quarters	SK250706-1	23,990	2	Lobby, laundry, storage, waiting room, lounge (1 on each floor), boiler room
Nurses or WAF Officers Quarters	SK250706-2	Unit A: 23,990 Unit B: 21,350 Unit C: 18,710	2	Lobby, laundry, storage, waiting room, lounge (1 on each floor), boiler room
Nurses or WAF Officers Quarters	SK250709-1	Unit F: 6,570 Unit G: 5,250	1 + basement	Lobby, laundry, storage, guest waiting room, office, lounge, boiler room
Nurses or WAF Officers Quarters	SK250708-1	Unit D: 13,560 Unit E: 10,920	2 + basement	Lobby, laundry, storage, guest waiting room, office, lounge (1 on each floor), boiler room
EMB	556010	19,800	3 +basement	Day Room; Lounge; Scrub Room; M.A. Office; Bag Storage/linen closet
EMB	556012	19,890	3 +basement	Day Room; Scrub Room; M.A. Office; Gear Cleaning Room; Bag Storage/linen closet
Air Force Dormitory for Enlisted Women	2101107-1	25,304	3 + basement	Lounges (2 per floor), laundry (1st floor), entry, utility room
Air Force Dormitory for Enlisted Women	2101107-2			
Air Force Dormitory for Enlisted Women	2101109-1	15,024	2 + basement	Lounges (2 per floor), laundry (1st floor), entry, utility room
Air Force Dormitory for Enlisted Women	2101109-2			
EWB	621844	21,405	3	Reception Room; Kitchenette; Writing Room; Lounge; Storage Room; Laundry Room; Luggage Room; Linen Room
EMB	621843	19,680	3	Day Room; Scrub Room; Bag Storage/linen closet
Women's BOQ	un-numbered	10,100	2	Entrance Hall; Lounge; Reading room; Laundry Room; Linen Room; Boiler Room
BOQ	un-numbered	9,860	2	Entrance Hall; Lounge; Reading room; Laundry Room; Linen Room; Boiler Room
EWB	un-numbered	9,435	2	Entrance Hall; Office; Linen Room; Date Room; Trunk Storage; Laundry Room; Boiler Room; Writing & Reading Room
EMB	un-numbered	9,278	2	Entrance Hall; Bag Storage; Scrub Room; Linen Room; Writing & Reading Room
CPO Quarters	un-numbered	8,719	2	Entrance Hall; Day Room; Linen Room; Boiler Room; Bag Storage;
BOQ	539042	9,860	2	Entrance hall; Lounge; Reading room; linen room; SO lounge
EMB	539037	4,400	1	Scrub Room; Bag Storage/linen closet
EMB	539038	9,278	2	Scrub Room; Bag Storage/linen closet; Writing & Reading Room
EWB	539039	4,690	1	Date Room; Scrub Room; Pressing & Drying Room; Linen Room, Trunk Room, Writing Room

Building Type	Drawing Number	Total Floor Area (sq. ft.)	Number of Stories	Building Components (other than barracks and restroom)
See legend or list type of building of not included in legend	Identifying number	total square footage of the floor area for the entire building	how many stories in the building; if basement included, then states so: e.g., 2 + basement	What room types are included in building other than barracks and restrooms?
EWB	539040	9,435	2	Date Room; Kitchenette; Pressing & Drying area; Scrub Room; Storage Room; Trunk Room; Writing Room
BOQ	621837	8,452	2	Vestibule; Lounge; Snack Bar; Dining Room; Kitchen; Storage; Linen Room; Office
BOQ	621838	19,901	2	Lobby; Office; Lounge; Dining Room; Kitchen; Storage; Cleaning Gear; Linen Room; Snack Bar; Coat Room; Service Room
Standard Components Layout	400140-1			
Standard Components Layout	400140-2			Living Rooms
Standard Components Layout	400140-3			Typical Laundry, Lounge w/ Kitchenette, Barbershop, & Classroom
EMB	658441	960	1	none
EWB	658440	960	1	Workroom
Air Force Dormitory for Enlisted Women	210204-1	16,827	2 + basement	Entry, office, reception, lounge (1 on each floor), laundry, heater room, storage
Air Force Dormitory for Enlisted Women	210204-2			
Air Force Dormitory for Enlisted Women	210205-1	25,200	3 + basement	Entry, office, lounge (1 on each floor), laundry, heater room, storage
Air Force Dormitory for Enlisted Women	210205-2			
EMB	665169	25,050	3 + basement	Scrub Room; Bag Room; Office; Day Room; Writing Room; Laundry Room
EMB	665171	25,050	3 + basement	Scrub Room; Bag Room; Office; Day Room; Writing Room; Laundry Room
EMB	665192	25,050	3+ basement	Scrub Room; Bag Room; Office; Day Room; Writing Room; Laundry Room
EMB	665209	25,050	3+ basement	Scrub Room; Bag Room; Office; Day Room; Writing Room; Laundry Room
BOQ	723357	2,880	2	Lounge; Office; Snack; Storage; Linen Room
EMB	723347	11,750	2	Scrub Room; Day Room; Treatment Room; Sick Bay; Storage
EMB	720647	17,275	2 + basement	Day Room; TV Room; Reading Room; Bag Room; Laundry Room; PO Day Room
Battalion Admin. & Classroom Building	Sheet 4	6,348	1	Lobby, offices, clerical, classrooms, storage
BOQ	756740	2,416	1	Studio; Snacks; Kitchenette; Heater Room; Storage Room
EMB	788341	12,960	2	Storage Room
EMB	795610	12,400	2	Lounge; Storage Room; Equipment Room; Office; Laundry Room
EMB	795611	14,292	2	Lounge (with phone booths); Lobby, Equipment Room, Laundry Room; CO Storage Room

Building Type	Drawing Number	Total Floor Area (sq. ft.)	Number of Stories	Building Components (other than barracks and restroom)
See legend or list type of building of not included in legend	Identifying number	total square footage of the floor area for the entire building	how many stories in the building; if basement included, then states so: e.g., 2 + basement	What room types are included in building other than barracks and restrooms?
EMB	795614	20,625	2	Lounge; Equipment Room; Bag Storage; Laundry Room; Reading Room; PO Lounge; Telephone booths
EMB	795615	22,320	3	Lounge; Telephone booths; Bag Storage; Equipment Room; Office; Laundry Room
EMB	795616	31,374	3	Lounge; Equipment Room; Bag Storage; Laundry Room; Reading Room; PO Lounge; Telephone booths; office
EWB	795612	16,526	2	Reception Room; Kitchen; Laundry Room; Bag Storage; Office; Heater room; Lounge; Sewing Room
EMB	795613	18,890	3	Lounge; CO Storage Room; Laundry Room;
EWB	808316	12,670	2	Lounge; Bag storage; Laundry room; linen room
EMB	817037	14,508	2	Lobby; Lounge; CO Storage Room; Laundry Room; Equipment Room
EMB	817038	19,296	3	Lobby; Lounge; CO Storage Room; Laundry Room; Equipment Room
EMB	817039	20,625	2	Lounge; Laundry Room; Equipment Room; Bag Storage; Office; Reading Room; PO Lounge
EMB	817040	22,476	3	Lounge; Telephone Booths; Laundry Room; Equipment Room; Bag Room; Office; Storage Room
EMB	817041	31,475	3	Lounge; Telephone Booths; Laundry Room; Equipment Room; Bag Room; Office; Storage Room; Reading Room; PO Lounge
SP	817043	92,200	3	Assembly & Briefing Area; Gear Storage; Administration; Heater Room
EWB	817046	17,084	2	Reception Room; Bag Storage; Office; Laundry Room; Linen Room; Heater Room; Lounge; Sewing Room
SP	817185	6,500	1	Lobby; Office; Lounge; Coat Room; Cocktail Lounge; Dining Room; Kitchen
EWB	745932	13,050	2	Lounge; Office; Storage Room; Laundry Room; Linen Room; Day Room
EWB	745933	6,525	1	Lounge; Office; Storage Room; Laundry Room; Linen Room; Day Room
EWB	808224	12,960	2	Lounge; Laundry Room; Linen Room; Storage Room
EWB	808326	6,335	1	Reception Room; Office; Storage Room; Laundry Room; Linen Room; Day Room

Building Type	Drawing Number	Total Floor Area (sq. ft.)	Number of Stories	Building Components (other than barracks and restroom)
See legend or list type of building of not included in legend	Identifying number	total square footage of the floor area for the entire building	how many stories in the building; if basement included, then states so: e.g., 2 + basement	What room types are included in building other than barracks and restrooms?
EWB	808234	6,335	1	Reception Room; Office; Storage Room; Laundry Room; Linen Room; Day Room
EWB	836726	13,050	2	Lounge; Office; Storage Room; Laundry Room; Linen Room; Day Room
EWB	836734	6,525	1	Reception Room; Office; Storage Room; Laundry Room; Linen Room; Day Room
SP	745934	13,050	2	Dayroom; Storage Room; Mechanical Room
SP	808243	12,672	2	Dayroom; Storage Room; Mechanical Room
SP	808335	12,672	2	Dayroom; Storage Room; Mechanical Room
EMB	745930	13,050	2	Bag/Linen Storage; Mech. Equipment Room
EMB	745931	6,525	1	Bag/Linen Storage; Mech. Equipment Room
BOQ Motel Type	AD250672-1	1-story: ~7200 2-story: ~14400	1 or 2	Laundry, storage, units include kitchenette, Unit Type B have living rooms; Alternate plan has lounge, lobby, & office on 1st floor
BOQ Motel Type	AD250672-2	17,536	2 + basement	Laundry, storage, units include kitchenette, Unit Type B have living rooms; Alternate plan has lounge, lobby, & office on 1st floor
EMB	895054	30,635	3	Lounge; Telephone Booths; Laundry Room; Equipment Room; Bag Room; Office; Storage Room; Reading Room; PO Lounge
SP	1038068	67,891	2	Concession; MAA; Mechnaical Room; Office; D1 classroom
BEQ	1038070	N/A	N/A	N/A
BEQ	1038071	N/A	N/A	Living Room; Kitchen
BEQ	1038076	32,890	2	Lobby; Lounge; Laundry Room; Concessions; Storage; TV room; PO lounge
Processing Building	380905-3	~ 138000	1	Lobby, lounges/waiting rooms, assembly rooms, chapel, issue rooms, medical clinic, administration, records, classrooms, personal affairs, classification, kitchen, mail room, conference, etc
Barracks Reception Station Complex	SK2101153-6	34,804	3	Dayrooms (2 on 1st floor), supply room, storage, laundry
Dining Hall	3605118-4	27,577	1	Coat room, dishwashing, dining hall, kitchen, storage, office, locker room, mechanical
Enlisted Barracks Reception Station Complex	2101153-6	40,652	3	Dayrooms (2 on 1st floor), supply room, storage, laundry
Reception Station Complex	1606328-2			

Building Type	Drawing Number	Total Floor Area (sq. ft.)	Number of Stories	Building Components (other than barracks and restroom)
See legend or list type of building of not included in legend	Identifying number	total square footage of the floor area for the entire building	how many stories in the building; if basement included, then states so: e.g., 2 + basement	What room types are included in building other than barracks and restrooms?
Service Club/ Post Exchange	311847-5	15,900	1	Lobby, Information & checking, game room, ballroom, cards & tv room, service pantry, storage, kitchen, telephone room, mechanical, post exchange, post office
Service Club/ Post Exchange Reception Station Complex	SK311847-5	15,900	1	Lobby, game room, ballroom, cards & tv room, snack bar, kitchen, office, storage, post office, post exchange, mechanical
EMB	1038075	31,475	3	Lobby; Lounge; TV Room; Telephone Booths; Laundry Room; Equipment Room; Bag Room; Office; Storage Room; Reading Room; PO Lounge
EWB (Center Hall & Motel Type)	4	Center Hall: 10,157 Motel Type: 10,144	1 story for each type	Reception; Office; Lounge; Kitchen; Laundry; Linen Closet
Officer Personnel Typical Living Units - Center Hall Type	6	O2 & below: 359 sf/unit O3 & above: 502.6 sf/unit; Cadet 2 man room: 359 sf/unit; Cadet 4 man suite; 718 sf/unit		Private/semi-private kitchenette, living rooms
Officer Personnel Typical Living Units - Motel	5	O2 & below: 359 sf/unit O3 & above: 502.6 sf/unit		02 & below: Private rooms with living/bedroom, bath, shared kitchenette O3 & above: Private rooms with living room, bedroom, bath, kitchenette
SP (Gym)	1294389 (NAVFAC)	11,000	1	Lobby; Office; Storage Room; Laundry Room; Locker Room; Visiting/Women's Locker Room; Trainer's Room; Sauna; Exercise Room; Gymnasium
BOQ	1297661 - 1297662 (FEC)	45,558	5	Lobby; Lounge; MAA Office; Telephone Room; Storage Room; Laundry Room
SP (Gym)	1294390 (NAVFAC)	23,142	1	Lobby; Office; Laundry; Storage; Gymnasium; Locker Room; Visiting/Women's Lockers; Trainer Room; Sauna; Handball Court; Squash Court; Exercise Room
BEQ	1403100 (NAVFAC)	1845/ module	3	Core Building: Lobby; Lounge; Laundry Room; Bag Storage; Office; Linen Storage
BEQ	1403797 (NAVFAC)	22,326	3	Core Building: Lounge; Office; Linen Room; Laundry Room; Concessions; Telephone booths, information desk
BEQ	1403798 (NAVFAC)	132,480	10	Lobby; Lounge; TV room; Laundry Room; Telephone booths; Office; Linen Room; Mech. Room; Bag Storage
BOQ	1403795 (NAVFAC)	varies	3	Central Lounge; Dining Room; Kitchen; Laundry; Office; Linen Room; Storage

Building Type	Drawing Number	Total Floor Area (sq. ft.)	Number of Stories	Building Components (other than barracks and restroom)
See legend or list type of building of not included in legend	Identifying number	total square footage of the floor area for the entire building	how many stories in the building; if basement included, then states so: e.g., 2 + basement	What room types are included in building other than barracks and restrooms?
BOQ	1403796 (NAVFAC)	varies	3	Central Lounge; Dining Room; Kitchen; Laundry; Office; Linen Room; Storage
BOQ (Men)	306887 - 306888	N/A	2	Lobby; Linen Storage; Uniform Storage; Bag Storage; Laundry Room; Lounge
EWB	306869	N/A	2	Lobby; Office; Linen Storage; Trunk Storage; Uniform Storage; Utility Room; Laundry Room
EWB	306870			
Alterations to Bldg # 268 Training Center Fort Des Moines, Iowa	193A-28	N/A	N/A	Clothes changing booths, other spaces not labeled
Alterations to Building # 81 Training Center Fort Des Moines, Iowa	193A-27	N/A	N/A	Clothes changing booths, other spaces not labeled
EWB	21-02-06	8,987	2	Vestibule; Mail Room; Reception Room; Administration area; Office; Unit Storage; Day Room; Laundry Room
Improved Bachelor Officer Quarters - Women	Sheet 303	9,440	2	Vestibule, lobby, laundry, living room (in each separate unit), boiler room
Perspective Sketch Drawing	sketch_ reception			
BEQ	1341195 (NAVFAC)	30,282	3	Lobby; Office; Storage; Vending; Mechanical Room; Laundry; Lounge; Bag Storage
EB	731427	27,500	3	Lounge; Snack; Laundry room; Office; Storage Room; TV room; MA room; Reading Room
EB	731428	varies	3	N/A
EB	756735	25,420	3	Lounge; Snack; Laundry room; Office; Storage Room; TV room; Reading Room
EB	756736	20,500	3	Lounge; Storage Room; Laundry Room
EMB	171065	N/A	1	Recreation & Dining; Kitchen; Storage Room
SP (Chapel)	367912	N/A	1	Catholic Chapel; Narthex; Sanctuary; Waiting Room; Confessional; Protestant Chapel
SP (Chapel)	367912	N/A	1	Chapel; Confessionals; Clergy Room
W	318064	N/A	1	Recreation Room; Uniform Storage; Bag Storage; Office; Linen Room; Heater Room
WB	318064	N/A	1	Reception Room; Laundry Room; Linen Room; Storage Room; Office; Heater Room

Housing/Sleeping Data

Building Type	Drawing Number	Number of Persons Accommodated	Sq. Ft./Person	Floor Plan/Privacy Configuration	Room Configuration	Number of Beds/Bunks	Multi-Rank Capability	Multi-Rank Capability Configuration
See legend or list type of building of not included in legend	Identifying number	How many people is the barrack building designed to accommodate?	How much square footage per person does the design provide for?	How is the barracks sleeping area laid out: open bay, cubicle/partitioned, semi-private, private?	How is the sleeping area configured: what type of beds, how are they arranged, any elements used to define private space, etc.?	How many beds are included in the design?	Does the barracks provide separate area for people of different rank, e.g., Petty Officer in an enlisted barrack?	How is the area for different rank configured?
Typical Landscape Planting for Company Officers' and Double NCO Quarters	630-100							
Typical Landscape Planting for HQ Admin. Bldg, BOQs, Barracks Bldgs	630-101							
Marine Barracks	129241	236	75.4	Open Squad Rooms	No arrangement indicated	236	Officer	4 private rooms w/ attached bath
Marine Barracks	129247							
EMB	137497 - 137498	114	76.6	Open plan	Beds arranged perpendicular to exterior walls in 2 rows with center aisle	56 double bunks	Petty Officers	3 Petty Officers in shared bedroom; Chief Petty Officer has private room w/ attached bath
Mobilization Buildings Hospital (Nurses) Quarters	800-1422 (2)							
Mobilization Buildings Hospital (Nurses) Quarters	800-1421	16	180	16 Private Rooms	1 single bed and 1 wardrobe per room	16	Nurses, dietician, servants, cook	4 Servant Rooms, 1 Dietician, 10 Nurses Rooms, 1 Cook's Room
Mobilization Buildings Hospital (Nurses) Quarters	800-1422							
Mobilization Buildings Hospital (Nurses) Quarters	800-1423							
Mobilization Buildings Nurses (Hospital) Quarters	800-1435	12 (35 for both floors)	120	Private Rooms	1 single bed and 1 wardrobe per room	12 singles	Nurses, servants, cook	7 nurses rooms, 4 servants rooms, 1 cook's room
Mobilization Buildings Nurses (Hospital) Quarters	800-1436	23 (35 for both floors)	120	Private Rooms	1 single bed and 1 wardrobe per room	12 singles	Nurses	23 nurses rooms
Mobilization Buildings Hospital (Nurses) Quarters	800-1423.1							
EMB	188167	900	83.3	Open Squad Rooms	2 large squad rooms w/ 12 rows of double bunks; aisles between every 2 rows; lockers between bunks	450 double bunks	MAA	Private room w/ attached bath

Building Type	Drawing Number	Number of Persons Accommodated	Sq. Ft./ Person	Floor Plan/Privacy Configuration	Room Configuration	Number of Beds/Bunks	Multi-Rank Capability	Multi-Rank Capability Configuration
See legend or list type of building of not included in legend	Identifying number	How many people is the barrack building designed to accommodate?	How much square footage per person does the design provide for?	How is the barracks sleeping area laid out: open bay, cubicle/ partitioned, semi-private, private?	How is the sleeping area configured: what type of beds, how are they arranged, any elements used to define private space, etc.?	How many beds are included in the design?	Does the barracks provide separate area for people of different rank, e.g., Petty Officer in an enlisted barrack?	How is the area for different rank configured?
EMB	184324 - 184325	100	N/A	Open Squad Rooms	No arrangement indicated	100	Officers, CPOs, MAAs	Bedrooms w/ shared baths
Typical Layout Diagram for Camouflage Demonstration - Practice Area	614-1602							
Typical Layout Diagrams for WAAC Replacement Training Center	614-703							
Mobilization Buildings WAAC Exchange - Type - WPX - A-M	700-3516							
Mobilization Buildings WAAC Exchange - Type - WPX - A-M	700-3517							
Mobilization Buildings WAAC Exchange - Type - WPX - A-M	700-3518							
Mobilization Buildings WAAC Exchange - Type - WPX - A-M	700-3519							
Mobilization Buildings WAAC Exchange - Type - WPX - A-M	700-3520							
Mobilization Buildings WAAC Exchange - Type - WPX - A-M	700-3521							
Mobilization Buildings WAAC Exchange - Type - WPX - A-M	700-3522							
Mobilization Buildings WAC Barracks	800-425							
Mobilization Buildings WAC Barracks	800-426	50		Open bay	Each floor has 2 rows of single bunks with central aisle	42 EW + 8 NCO	NCO	1st floor: 1 shared room for 2 NCOs. 2nd floor: 1 shared room for 2 NCOs, 2 shared rooms for 3 NCOs each
Mobilization Buildings WAC Barracks	800-427							

Building Type	Drawing Number	Number of Persons Accommodated	Sq. Ft./Person	Floor Plan/Privacy Configuration	Room Configuration	Number of Beds/Bunks	Multi-Rank Capability	Multi-Rank Capability Configuration
See legend or list type of building of not included in legend	Identifying number	How many people is the barrack building designed to accommodate?	How much square footage per person does the design provide for?	How is the barracks sleeping area laid out: open bay, cubicle/partitioned, semi-private, private?	How is the sleeping area configured: what type of beds, how are they arranged, any elements used to define private space, etc.?	How many beds are included in the design?	Does the barracks provide separate area for people of different rank, e.g., Petty Officer in an enlisted barrack?	How is the area for different rank configured?
Mobilization Buildings WAC Barracks	800-428							
Mobilization Buildings WAC Barracks	800-429							
Mobilization Buildings WAC Barracks	800-430							
Mobilization Buildings WAC Barracks	800-431							
Mobilization Buildings WAC Exchange	800-1124							
Mobilization Buildings WAC Exchange	800-1125							
Mobilization Buildings WAC Exchange	800-1126							
Mobilization Buildings WAC Exchange	800-1127							
Mobilization Buildings WAC Exchange	800-1128							
Mobilization Buildings WAC Exchange	800-1129							
Mobilization Buildings WAC Exchange	800-1130							
Barracks for 150 Women WAC Training Center Fort Des Moines, Iowa	193A-49	150 each	indeterminate	Open Squad Room	No furniture or partitions shown	150 each	NO	
Laundry & Toilet Bldg Addition for Barracks Training Center Fort Des Moines, Iowa	193A-22							
Recreation Buildings in connection with Barracks Training Center Fort Des Moines, Iowa	193A-25							
WAC Barracks Training Center Fort Des Moines, Iowa	193A-19	150	Indeterminate	Open squad room	Indeterminate	150	No	
Co. Unit Layout Diagrams for WAAC	614-702							
Training Center Fort Des Moines, Iowa	193A-16							

Building Type	Drawing Number	Number of Persons Accommodated	Sq. Ft./ Person	Floor Plan/Privacy Configuration	Room Configuration	Number of Beds/Bunks	Multi-Rank Capability	Multi-Rank Capability Configuration
See legend or list type of building of not included in legend	Identifying number	How many people is the barrack building designed to accommodate?	How much square footage per person does the design provide for?	How is the barracks sleeping area laid out: open bay, cubicle/ partitioned, semi-private, private?	How is the sleeping area configured: what type of beds, how are they arranged, any elements used to define private space, etc.?	How many beds are included in the design?	Does the barracks provide separate area for people of different rank, e.g., Petty Officer in an enlisted barrack?	How is the area for different rank configured?
Mobilization Buildings WAAC Barracks	700-3525	52	102 sf per person average	Open Squad Room; NCOs have semi-private rooms	Beds are aligned in 2 rows with central aisle. No elements define private space	52	NCOs	NCOs are in rooms of 2 and 3 person
Mobilization Buildings WAAC Barracks (Alt. for sloping site)	700-3526	52	102 sf per person average	Open Squad Room; NCOs have semi-private rooms	Beds are aligned in 2 rows with central aisle. No elements define private space	52	NCOs	NCOs are in rooms of 2 and 3 person
Mobilization Buildings WAAC Barracks	700-3527							
Mobilization Buildings WAAC Barracks	700-3528							
Mobilization Buildings WAAC Barracks	700-3529							
WAC Latrine (Temporary Structure) Training Center Fort Des Moines, Iowa	193A-31							
Mobilization Buildings WAC Recreation, Supply, Co. Admin., & Quarters	700-3540							
Mobilization Buildings WAC Recreation, Supply, Co. Admin., & Quarters	700-3541			3 private bedrooms	Each private room has bed, dressing table, closet	3	1 Bedroom reserved for C.O.	Larger room for C.O.
Mobilization Buildings WAC Recreation, Supply, Co. Admin., & Quarters	700-3542							
Mobilization Buildings WAC Recreation, Supply, Co. Admin., & Quarters	700-3543							
Mobilization Buildings WAC Recreation, Supply, Co. Admin., & Quarters	700-3544							

Building Type	Drawing Number	Number of Persons Accommodated	Sq. Ft./Person	Floor Plan/Privacy Configuration	Room Configuration	Number of Beds/Bunks	Multi-Rank Capability	Multi-Rank Capability Configuration
See legend or list type of building of not included in legend	Identifying number	How many people is the barrack building designed to accommodate?	How much square footage per person does the design provide for?	How is the barracks sleeping area laid out: open bay, cubicle/ partitioned, semi-private, private?	How is the sleeping area configured: what type of beds, how are they arranged, any elements used to define private space, etc.?	How many beds are included in the design?	Does the barracks provide separate area for people of different rank, e.g., Petty Officer in an enlisted barrack?	How is the area for different rank configured?
Mobilization Buildings WAC Recreation, Supply, Co. Admin., & Quarters	700-3545							
Mobilization Buildings WAC Recreation, Supply, Co. Admin., & Quarters	700-3546							
Mobilization Buildings WAC Recreation, Supply, Co. Admin., & Quarters	700-3547			6 private bedrooms	Each private room has bed, dressing table, closet	6	2 Bedrooms reserved for Cos	Larger room for C.O.
Mobilization Buildings WAC Recreation, Supply, Co. Admin., & Quarters	700-3548							
Mobilization Buildings WAC Recreation, Supply, Co. Admin., & Quarters	700-3549							
Mobilization Buildings WAC Recreation, Supply, Co. Admin., & Quarters	700-3550							
Mobilization Buildings WAC Recreation, Supply, Co. Admin., & Quarters	700-3551							
Barracks (30 Men) WAC Training Center Fort Des Moines, Iowa	193A-46	30	68	Open Squad Room	No furniture or partitions shown	30	No	
Mobilization Buildings WAAC Officers' Quarters	700-3532	9	265.5	Private rooms	1 Single bed per room	9	No	
Mobilization Buildings WAAC Officers' Quarters	700-3533							
Office Building of Engineer (Additions & Remodeling) WAC Training Center Fort Des Moines, Iowa	193A-33							
EMB	188660	232	N/A	Open plan	Beds arranged in rows perpendicular to exterior walls	112 double bunks	CPO	1 bedroom on 1st floor for 2 men 1 bedroom on 2nd floor for 6 men

Building Type	Drawing Number	Number of Persons Accommodated	Sq. Ft./Person	Floor Plan/Privacy Configuration	Room Configuration	Number of Beds/Bunks	Multi-Rank Capability	Multi-Rank Capability Configuration
See legend or list type of building of not included in legend	Identifying number	How many people is the barrack building designed to accommodate?	How much square footage per person does the design provide for?	How is the barracks sleeping area laid out: open bay, cubicle/ partitioned, semi-private, private?	How is the sleeping area configured: what type of beds, how are they arranged, any elements used to define private space, etc.?	How many beds are included in the design?	Does the barracks provide separate area for people of different rank, e.g., Petty Officer in an enlisted barrack?	How is the area for different rank configured?
Post Hospital and Drill Hall WAC Training Center Fort Des Moines, Iowa	193A-39							
Nurses' Quarters	1100-361							
Typical Layout Diagrams for WAAC Battalion Organization	614-701							
Mobilization General Hospital Nurses Quarters Officers Quarters	1100-2136							
Mobilization General Hospital Nurses Quarters Officers Quarters	1100-2137							
Mobilization General Hospital Nurses Quarters Officers Quarters	1100-2138							
Mobilization General Hospital Nurses Quarters Officers Quarters	1100-2139							
Mobilization General Hospital Nurses QuartersOfficers Quarters	1100-2140							
Option 1: Mobilization General Hospital Nurses Quarters	1100-2135	56	Varies by room (average of 116 sf)	Private rooms	No bed arrangement is suggested. Each room includes a wardrobe	56	Officer	Officer has private room with closet, and attached bath. Room is located adjacent to office
Option 2: Mobilization General Hospital Officers Quarters	1100-2135 (Same dwg as above, different occupant)	57	Varies by room (average of 116 sf)	Private rooms	No bed arrangement is suggested. Each room includes a wardrobe	57	Higher ranking officer	Private room with closet, and attached bath. Room is located adjacent to office
Mobilization Buildings WAC Barracks	700-3560	50	74 (for enlisted women)	Open Squad Rooms 1st & 2nd floor; NCOs have private rooms	Beds are aligned in 2 rows with central aisle. No elements define private space	15 beds-1st floor (9 single, 3 double); 31 beds-2nd floor (21 single, 5 double)	NCOs and 1st Sgt.	Single private rooms
Mobilization Buildings WAC Barracks	700-3561							

Building Type	Drawing Number	Number of Persons Accommodated	Sq. Ft./Person	Floor Plan/Privacy Configuration	Room Configuration	Number of Beds/Bunks	Multi-Rank Capability	Multi-Rank Capability Configuration
See legend or list type of building of not included in legend	Identifying number	How many people is the barrack building designed to accommodate?	How much square footage per person does the design provide for?	How is the barracks sleeping area laid out: open bay, cubicle/ partitioned, semi-private, private?	How is the sleeping area configured: what type of beds, how are they arranged, any elements used to define private space, etc.?	How many beds are included in the design?	Does the barracks provide separate area for people of different rank, e.g., Petty Officer in an enlisted barrack?	How is the area for different rank configured?
Mobilization Buildings WAC Barracks	700-3562							
Mobilization Buildings WAC Barracks	700-3563							
Nurses' Quarters	1100-360	16	62.5	Semi-private rooms (2 nurses per room)	2 beds & 2 lockers per room	16	No	
W	188697	58	134.7	Private/Semi-Private Rooms	No arrangement indicated	58	none	none
W	188699	58	134.7	Private/Semi-Private Rooms	No arrangement indicated	58	none	none
W	188702	229	67.9	Open Squad Rooms	Double Bunks perpendicular to exterior walls arranged in rows of 3 with center aisle	112 double bunks; 5 single bunks	Petty Officers	2 rooms - 1st floor room: 2 officers 2nd floor room: 3 officers
Mobilization Buildings Conversion of Existing 74 Man Barracks for WAC	700-3570	51	74	Open bay	Single & double bunks in two rows with center aisle (both floors), cabinets used to define bed space from center aisle	1st flr, squad room - 21 (11 single, 5 double), 1 NCO: 2nd flr, squad room - 27 (17 single, 5 double), 2 NCO	NCO	1st floor - private room for 1; 2nd floor - private room for 2
Mobilization Buildings Conversion of Existing 74 Man Barracks for WAC	700-3571							
Mobilization Buildings WAC BOQ	700-3565	17	208	Private rooms along double loaded corridor	Each room has closet; no bed layout is indicated	17	No	
Mobilization Buildings WAC BOQ	700-3566							
Mobilization Buildings WAC BOQ	700-3567							
Mobilization Buildings WAC BOQ	700-3568							
Typical Layout Diagram for Camouflage Demonstration - Practice Area	614-1601							
W	312559	226	N/A	Open plan	No configuration indicated	226	CPO	Private room w/ attached bath

Building Type	Drawing Number	Number of Persons Accommodated	Sq. Ft./ Person	Floor Plan/Privacy Configuration	Room Configuration	Number of Beds/Bunks	Multi-Rank Capability	Multi-Rank Capability Configuration
See legend or list type of building of not included in legend	Identifying number	How many people is the barrack building designed to accommodate?	How much square footage per person does the design provide for?	How is the barracks sleeping area laid out: open bay, cubicle/ partitioned, semi-private, private?	How is the sleeping area configured: what type of beds, how are they arranged, any elements used to define private space, etc.?	How many beds are included in the design?	Does the barracks provide separate area for people of different rank, e.g., Petty Officer in an enlisted barrack?	How is the area for different rank configured?
W	312559-2	N/A	N/A	6-8 person rooms	No bunk configuration indicated; 6-8 closets per room	N/A	Petty Officer	2 man room w/ attached bath
W	188767	156	40.4	Open Squad Rooms	Double Bunks perpendicular to exterior walls arranged in rows of 3 with center aisle	78 Double Bunks	Officer	1 room with attached bath
Symbols for Camouflage - General Plan	614-1603							
Typical Layout Diagrams for one company of WAC	614-t.o.738							
Nurses & WAVE Officers	317319	56	N/A	Single Rooms & 2 bed cubicles	Single rooms: single bunks, closet, sink Cubicles: single bunks perpendicular to exterior wall; lockers	56	Supervising Nurse Senior Officer	3 Private rooms w/ attached baths
MW	256516	448	68.68	Open Squad Rooms	Double bunks perpendicular to exterior walls arranged in 2 rows	224 Double Bunks	NCO	2 rooms - 2 NCOs each room
MW	256517	448	68.68	Open Squad Rooms	Double bunks perpendicular to exterior walls arranged in 2 rows	224 Double Bunks	NCO	2 rooms - 2 NCOs each room
EWB	271541	220	73.6	Open Squad Rooms	Double bunks in rows of 3 parallel to exterior walls with center aisle; lockers used to define space	108 double bunks; 4 single bunks	Petty Officer	2 rooms for 2 Petty Officers each w/ attached bath
SP (Women's Club)	291251							
SP (Women's Club)	291252	112	N/A	Open Dorm Rooms	Double bunks placed in rows with lockers at the foot of each bunk	56 double bunks	none	none
SP (Women's Club)	291254							

Building Type	Drawing Number	Number of Persons Accommodated	Sq. Ft./Person	Floor Plan/Privacy Configuration	Room Configuration	Number of Beds/Bunks	Multi-Rank Capability	Multi-Rank Capability Configuration
See legend or list type of building of not included in legend	Identifying number	How many people is the barrack building designed to accommodate?	How much square footage per person does the design provide for?	How is the barracks sleeping area laid out: open bay, cubicle/ partitioned, semi-private, private?	How is the sleeping area configured: what type of beds, how are they arranged, any elements used to define private space, etc.?	How many beds are included in the design?	Does the barracks provide separate area for people of different rank, e.g., Petty Officer in an enlisted barrack?	How is the area for different rank configured?
BOQ	256638	56	207	Semi-private 2 person bedrooms	No bed configuration indicated	56	none	none
Mobilization Buildings WAC Barracks	700-3560.1	79	1st floor: 55 2nd floor: 53	Open Bay	Double Bunks on both 1st and 2nd floor arranged in rows with central aisle	36 doubles; 12 on 1st flr, 24 on 2nd flr	1st Sgt., NCOs	1st floor: 1 private room for 1st Sgt., 1 shared room for 2 NCOs. 2nd floor: 2 shared rooms for 2 NCOs each
Mobilization Buildings Conversion of Existing Detachment Barracks for WAC	700-3585	68	48.7	Two wings of open bays off central corridor	2 rows of double bunks with center aisle	32 double bunks	NCOs	2 NCO rooms; one at each end of the bldg, each room accommodates 2 NCOs with 2 separate beds in each
Mobilization Buildings Conversion of Existing Detachment Barracks for WAC	700-3586							
W	288273	56	97.5	2 bed cubicles	Double bunks perpendicular to exterior walls; 2 cabinets per cubicle	28 Double Bunks	Petty Officer	1 room with attached bath
Mobilization Buildings Conversion of Hospital Barracks for WAC	700-3580	43	74	2 open bays with centralized restrooms and laundry, 2 NCO rooms at each end	For both squad rooms beds are aligned in 2 rows with center aisle. Beds defined from aisle by cabinets	31 total: Squad room 1-15 single, 4 double; Squad room 2- 7 single, 5 double	NCO	4 private NCO rooms (2 at each end of the building)
Mobilization Buildings Conversion of Hospital Barracks for WAC	700-3581							
W	264793	25	300	Private Rooms	No bed arrangement indicated; each room has closet & sink	25 single bunks	none	none
WB	288273	56	97.5	2 Bed Cubicles	Double bunks perpendicular to exterior wall; storage cabinets	28 Double Bunks	Petty Officer	Private Room w/ closet & attached private bath

Building Type	Drawing Number	Number of Persons Accommodated	Sq. Ft./Person	Floor Plan/Privacy Configuration	Room Configuration	Number of Beds/Bunks	Multi-Rank Capability	Multi-Rank Capability Configuration
See legend or list type of building of not included in legend	Identifying number	How many people is the barrack building designed to accommodate?	How much square footage per person does the design provide for?	How is the barracks sleeping area laid out: open bay, cubicle/ partitioned, semi-private, private?	How is the sleeping area configured: what type of beds, how are they arranged, any elements used to define private space, etc.?	How many beds are included in the design?	Does the barracks provide separate area for people of different rank, e.g., Petty Officer in an enlisted barrack?	How is the area for different rank configured?
W	288280	112	97.5	2 bed cubicles	Double bunks perpendicular to exterior walls; 2 cabinets per cubicle	56 double bunks	Petty Officer	Private room with attached bath
W	288282							
W	288283							
W	320100	192	72	4 Bed Cubicles	Double bunks perpendicular to exterior wall; 8 lockers each cubicle	96 double bunks	M.A.A.	2 person room; 2 closets
W	304236	480 (1st floor)	N/A	2 man cubicles	Double bunks perpendicular to exterior wall; 2 closets each cubicle	240 double bunks	none	none
W	304237	500 (2nd floor)	N/A	2 man cubicles	Double bunks perpendicular to exterior wall; 2 closets each cubicle	250 double bunks	Officers	Officer in Charge: Private room w/ attached bath Petty Officers: 7 private rooms with 2 shared baths
W	257696	144	84.25	4 Bed Cubicles	Double bunks perpendicular to exterior wall; 8 lockers each cubicle	72 double bunks	M.A.A.	2 person room; 2 closets
WB	257055							
SP (Swimming Pool)	304510 - 304511							
W	257698	224	48.9	2 bed cubicles	Double bunks perpendicular to exterior wall; 4 lockers each cubicle	112 double bunks	none	none
W	257701	224	48.9	2 bed cubicles	Double bunks perpendicular to exterior wall; 4 lockers each cubicle	112 double bunks	CPO	Private room with attached bath
W	257669	128	N/A	4 Bed Cubicles	Double bunks perpendicular to exterior wall; 8 lockers each cubicle	64 double bunks	OOD	Double room with 2 closets

Building Type	Drawing Number	Number of Persons Accommodated	Sq. Ft./ Person	Floor Plan/Privacy Configuration	Room Configuration	Number of Beds/Bunks	Multi-Rank Capability	Multi-Rank Capability Configuration
See legend or list type of building of not included in legend	Identifying number	How many people is the barrack building designed to accommodate?	How much square footage per person does the design provide for?	How is the barracks sleeping area laid out: open bay, cubicle/ partitioned, semi-private, private?	How is the sleeping area configured: what type of beds, how are they arranged, any elements used to define private space, etc.?	How many beds are included in the design?	Does the barracks provide separate area for people of different rank, e.g., Petty Officer in an enlisted barrack?	How is the area for different rank configured?
EW & EM	326815	192 (72 women, 120 men)	N/A	Open plan	2 rows of double bunks; partition walls and lockers used to define private space for women	96 double bunks	CPO	3 rooms (2 double rooms on 1st floor w/ attached baths; 1 room on 3rd floor)
W	326814	148	N/A	Open plan	2 rows of double bunks; partition walls and lockers used to define private space	76 (72 double bunks; 4 single for CPOs)	CPO	2 double rooms each w/ attached bath
W	257734	128	N/A	4 Bed Cubicles	Double bunks perpendicular to exterior walls; 8 lockers divide cubicle space in middle	64 double bunks	OOD	1 room with 2 closets
MW	290949	128	161	Open Squad Rooms	Single Bunks perpendicular to exterior wall; 2 rows with center aisle	128	NCO	4 rooms - 2 NCOs each room attached bath (2 rooms)
SP (Office, Lunch, Locker)	364804							
WAC Training Center Fort Des Moines, Iowa	194A-12							
W	342059	112	107.2	2 bed cubicles	Double bunks perpendicular to exterior wall; partition walls divide into 2 bunk spaces	56 double bunks	CPO	Private room w/ attached bath
W	328676	112	100.8	2 bed cubicles	Double bunks perpendicular to exterior wall; 4 lockers each cubicle	56 double bunks	Petty Officer	Private room w/ attached bath
WAVE Mess Hall	328687							
W	328678							
WAVE Clinic	328711							

Building Type	Drawing Number	Number of Persons Accommodated	Sq. Ft./ Person	Floor Plan/Privacy Configuration	Room Configuration	Number of Beds/Bunks	Multi-Rank Capability	Multi-Rank Capability Configuration
See legend or list type of building of not included in legend	Identifying number	How many people is the barrack building designed to accommodate?	How much square footage per person does the design provide for?	How is the barracks sleeping area laid out: open bay, cubicle/ partitioned, semi-private, private?	How is the sleeping area configured: what type of beds, how are they arranged, any elements used to define private space, etc.?	How many beds are included in the design?	Does the barracks provide separate area for people of different rank, e.g., Petty Officer in an enlisted barrack?	How is the area for different rank configured?
EWB	329667 - 329668	256	98.7	2 bed cubicles	Double bunks perpendicular to exterior wall; 4 lockers each cubicle	120 double bunks; 16 single bunks	M.A.A. WAVE Officer NCOs	M.A.A.: private room WAVE Officer: 1 private room; 1 room for 2 officers NCOs: 4 person rooms w/ attached shared bath
W	309299	N/A	N/A	2 bed cubicles	2 beds perpendicular to exterior wall; tables & cabinets included in each cubicle	64 beds (no indication of double or single)	CPO	Private room with attached bath
EWB	347315	224	96.4	2 bed cubicles	Double bunks perpendicular to exterior wall; 4 lockers each cubicle	104 double bunks; 12 single bunks	CPO	4 rooms - 3 CPOs in each room
SP (Lunch, Locker)	309610							
SP Auditorium	360741							
SP (Dispensary)	370691							
SP (Admin.)	342622							
Study for Typical Landscape Development Plan	614-1117							
BOQ	360765	54	N/A	Single & Double Rooms	Single bunks (no configuration indicated) w/ sink and closet in room Single rooms have shared attached baths	54	none	none
SP (Ships Service Bldg)	360764							
SP (Subsistence Building)	360777							
SP Auditorium & Gym	361229							
EWB	339687 - 339688	234	106.8	2 bed cubicles	Double bunks perpendicular to exterior walls; 4 cabinets each cubicle	112 double bunks; 10 single bunks	CPO	2 rooms for 3 CPOs w/ attached bath; 1 room for 4 CPOs w/ attached bath
SP (Dispensary)	373477							

Building Type	Drawing Number	Number of Persons Accommodated	Sq. Ft./Person	Floor Plan/Privacy Configuration	Room Configuration	Number of Beds/Bunks	Multi-Rank Capability	Multi-Rank Capability Configuration
See legend or list type of building of not included in legend	Identifying number	How many people is the barrack building designed to accommodate?	How much square footage per person does the design provide for?	How is the barracks sleeping area laid out: open bay, cubicle/partitioned, semi-private, private?	How is the sleeping area configured: what type of beds, how are they arranged, any elements used to define private space, etc.?	How many beds are included in the design?	Does the barracks provide separate area for people of different rank, e.g., Petty Officer in an enlisted barrack?	How is the area for different rank configured?
W	373486	225	53	2 bed cubicles	Double bunks perpendicular to exterior wall; 4 wardrobes each cubicle	113 (112 double bunks, 1 single)	Lieutenant	Private room w/ attached bath
WAVES Dispensary	409987	30	N/A	Open plan	Single bunks; layouts differ in arrangement; 1st floor ward glass partitions used	30	none	none
BOQ	306882	54	163.3	Single & Double Rooms	No furniture configuration is indicated; double rooms have 2 closets; singles share semi-private bath with adjacent room	54	none	none
BOQ	306883	54	163.3	Single & Double Rooms	No furniture configuration is indicated; double rooms have 2 closets; singles share semi-private bath with adjacent room	54	none	none
SP (Base Site Plan)	401885							
SP Dispensary	401836							
Barrack - WAC - Apartment Type	SK210109	108	180	Shared 4 person units	2 bedrooms with 2 beds in each	108	No	
Barrack - WAC - Hotel Type	SK210108	1-story: 48 2-story: 96 3-story: 144	90	Semi-private rooms	2 single beds per room	48, 96, or 144 (depends on # of floors)	No	
WM	450230	N/A	N/A	Private/Semi-Private Rooms	No room arrangement is indicated	N/A	NCO	5 rooms with shared baths
Emergency Type Construction, EW Barracks	DEFE21020 1-1	64	108	Open squad rooms with partitions (1 opt. w/o partitions)	Single bunks divided into groups of 2 with partitions	64	NCOs	Four partitioned areas for 2 NCOs each
Emergency Type Construction, EW Barracks	DEFE21020 1-2							

Building Type	Drawing Number	Number of Persons Accommodated	Sq. Ft./Person	Floor Plan/Privacy Configuration	Room Configuration	Number of Beds/Bunks	Multi-Rank Capability	Multi-Rank Capability Configuration
See legend or list type of building of not included in legend	Identifying number	How many people is the barrack building designed to accommodate?	How much square footage per person does the design provide for?	How is the barracks sleeping area laid out: open bay, cubicle/ partitioned, semi-private, private?	How is the sleeping area configured: what type of beds, how are they arranged, any elements used to define private space, etc.?	How many beds are included in the design?	Does the barracks provide separate area for people of different rank, e.g., Petty Officer in an enlisted barrack?	How is the area for different rank configured?
Emergency Type Construction, EW Barracks	DEFE250704-1	52		Private & semi-private rooms	Smaller rooms with 1 per room; larger rooms with 2 per room	52	No	
MW	472352	80	106.8	2 bed cubicles	Single bunks; No arrangement is indicated	80	NCO	2 rooms
MW	472353	80	106.8	2 bed cubicles	Single bunks; No arrangement is indicated	80	NCO	2 rooms
MW	472354	112 (1st floor)	185.5	2 bed cubicles	Single bunks; No arrangement is indicated	112	NCO	3 rooms
MW	472355	112 (2nd floor)	185.5	2 bed cubicles	Single bunks; No arrangement is indicated	112	NCO	3 rooms
MW	472366	112 (1st floor)	185.5	2 bed cubicles	Single bunks; No arrangement is indicated	112	NCO	3 rooms
MW	472367	112 (2nd floor)	185.5	2 bed cubicles	Single bunks; No arrangement is indicated	112	NCO	3 rooms
MW	472519	80 (2nd floor)	179.3	2 bed cubicles	Single bunks; No arrangement is indicated	80	NCO	2 rooms
MW	472518	80 (1st floor)	179.3	2 bed cubicles	Single bunks; No arrangement is indicated	80	NCO	2 rooms
BOQ	500363	50	180	Semi-private 2 person bedrooms	No bed configuration indicated	50	Senior Officer	Private rooms; SO lounge
EMB	500359	94		Open Bay	Bunks & Lockers parallel to each other	40 dbl bunks	Petty Officer	Open Bay; 1 single bunk, 3 dbl bunk
EMB	500360	47		Open Bay	Bunks & Lockers parallel to each other	40 Dbl bunks	Petty Officer	Open Bay; 1 single bunk, 3 dbl bunk
EWB	500361	86	104.2	Open plan	Double bunks	39 double bunks; 8 singles	Petty Officers	8 single bunks, 1 toilet, lavatory, shower
EWB	500362	40	112	Open plan	Double bunks	20 double bunks	Petty Officer	1 single bunk, 1 toilet, lavatory, shower

Building Type	Drawing Number	Number of Persons Accommodated	Sq. Ft./Person	Floor Plan/Privacy Configuration	Room Configuration	Number of Beds/Bunks	Multi-Rank Capability	Multi-Rank Capability Configuration
See legend or list type of building of not included in legend	Identifying number	How many people is the barrack building designed to accommodate?	How much square footage per person does the design provide for?	How is the barracks sleeping area laid out: open bay, cubicle/ partitioned, semi-private, private?	How is the sleeping area configured: what type of beds, how are they arranged, any elements used to define private space, etc.?	How many beds are included in the design?	Does the barracks provide separate area for people of different rank, e.g., Petty Officer in an enlisted barrack?	How is the area for different rank configured?
BOQ	496842	50	185.6	Semi-private 2 person bed-rooms	Single bunks arranged perpendicular to exterior wall	50	Senior Officer	Private rooms; SO toilet & lounge on 2nd floor
EWB	496812	86	104.2	Open plan	Double bunks	39 double bunks; 8 singles	Petty Officers	8 single bunks, 1 toilet, lavatory, shower
EWB	496830	40	112	Open plan	Double bunks	20 double bunks	Petty Officer	1 single bunk, 1 toilet, lavatory, shower
Nurses' or WAF Officers' Quarters	DEF250706-1	Indeterminate (Option of 1 or 2 to a room)		58 private or semi-private rooms	Rooms with 1 or 2 beds each; 2 rooms share a bathroom	Indeterminate	No	
Nurses' or WAF Officers' Quarters	DEF250706-2			Unit A: 58 bed rooms Unit B: 50 bed rooms Unit C: 42 bed rooms				
Airmens Dormitory	210171-2	98 or 147 (depends if 2 or 3 person rooms)		Semi-private rooms	Either 2 or 3 to a room. Only 2 beds shown, no indication of double bunk; 3 closets are shown in each room	98; unknown how many single & how many double bunks	No indication of officers' quarters	
Airmens Dormitory	210171-3							
Airmens Dormitory	210171-7							
Airmens Dormitory	210171-8							
Airmens Dormitory	210171-9							
Airmens Dormitory	210171-1							
Airmens Dormitory Modified for Women	210189-1							
Airmens Dormitory Modified for Women	210189-2	98 or 147 (depends if 2 or 3 person rooms)		Semi-private rooms	Either 2 or 3 to a room. Only 2 beds shown, no indication of double bunk; 3 closets are shown in each room	98; unknown how many single & how many double bunks	No indication of officers' quarters	
Airmens Dormitory Modified for Women	210189-3							
Airmens Dormitory Modified for Women	210189-3							
Airmens Dormitory Modified for Women	210189-4							

Building Type	Drawing Number	Number of Persons Accommodated	Sq. Ft./Person	Floor Plan/Privacy Configuration	Room Configuration	Number of Beds/Bunks	Multi-Rank Capability	Multi-Rank Capability Configuration
See legend or list type of building of not included in legend	Identifying number	How many people is the barrack building designed to accommodate?	How much square footage per person does the design provide for?	How is the barracks sleeping area laid out: open bay, cubicle/ partitioned, semi-private, private?	How is the sleeping area configured: what type of beds, how are they arranged, any elements used to define private space, etc.?	How many beds are included in the design?	Does the barracks provide separate area for people of different rank, e.g., Petty Officer in an enlisted barrack?	How is the area for different rank configured?
Airmens Dormitory Modified for Women	210189-5							
Airmens Dormitory Modified for Women	210189-6							
Airmens Dormitory Modified for Women	210189-7							
Airmens Dormitory Modified for Women	210189-8							
Airmens Dormitory Modified for Women	210189-9							
Airmens Dormitory Modified for Women	210189-10							
Airmens Dormitory Modified for Women	210189-11							
Airmens Dormitory Modified for Women	210189-12	96 or 144 (depends if 2 or 3 person rooms)		Semi-private rooms	Either 2 or 3 to a room. Only 2 beds shown, no indication of double bunk; 3 closets are shown in each room	96; unknown how many single & how many double bunks	No indication of officers' quarters	
Airmens Dormitory Modified for Women	210189-13							
Airmens Dormitory Modified for Women	210189-14							
Airmens Dormitory Modified for Women	210189-15	96 or 144 (depends if 2 or 3 person rooms)		Semi-private rooms	Either 2 or 3 to a room. Only 2 beds shown, no indication of double bunk; 3 closets are shown in each room	96; unknown how many single & how many double bunks	No indication of officers' quarters	
Airmens Dormitory Modified for Women	210189-16	96 or 144 (depends if 2 or 3 person rooms)		Semi-private rooms	Either 2 or 3 to a room. Only 2 beds shown, no indication of double bunk; 3 closets are shown in each room	96; unknown how many single & how many double bunks	No indication of officers' quarters	
Airmens Dormitory Modified for Women	210189-17	94 or 141 (depends if 2 or 3 person rooms)		Semi-private rooms	Either 2 or 3 to a room. Only 2 beds shown, no indication of double bunk; 3 closets are shown in each room	94; unknown how many single & how many double bunks	No indication of officers' quarters	
Airmens Dormitory Modified for Women	210189-18							

Building Type	Drawing Number	Number of Persons Accommodated	Sq. Ft./ Person	Floor Plan/Privacy Configuration	Room Configuration	Number of Beds/Bunks	Multi-Rank Capability	Multi-Rank Capability Configuration
See legend or list type of building of not included in legend	Identifying number	How many people is the barrack building designed to accommodate?	How much square footage per person does the design provide for?	How is the barracks sleeping area laid out: open bay, cubicle/ partitioned, semi-private, private?	How is the sleeping area configured: what type of beds, how are they arranged, any elements used to define private space, etc.?	How many beds are included in the design?	Does the barracks provide separate area for people of different rank, e.g., Petty Officer in an enlisted barrack?	How is the area for different rank configured?
Airmens Dormitory Modified for Women	210189-19							
Airmens Dormitory Modified for Women	210189-20							
Airmens Dormitory Modified for Women	210189-21							
Airmens Dormitory Modified for Women	210189-22							
Airmens Dormitory Modified for Women	210189-23							
Airmens Dormitory Modified for Women	210189-24							
Airmens Dormitory Modified for Women	210189-25							
Airmens Dormitory Modified for Women	210189-26							
Airmens Dormitory Modified for Women	210189-27	98 or 147 (depends if 2 or 3 person rooms)		Semi-private rooms	Either 2 or 3 to a room. Only 2 beds shown, no indication of double bunk; 3 closets are shown in each room	98; unknown how many single & how many double bunks	No indication of officers' quarters	
Airmens Dormitory Modified for Women	210189-28							
Airmens Dormitory Modified for Women	210190-1							
Airmens Dormitory Modified for Women	210190-2	98 or 147 (depends if 2 or 3 person rooms)		Semi-private rooms	Either 2 or 3 to a room. Only 2 beds shown, no indication of double bunk; 3 closets are shown in each room	98; unknown how many single & how many double bunks	No indication of officers' quarters	
Airmens Dormitory Modified for Women	210190-3							
Airmens Dormitory Modified for Women	210190-4							
Airmens Dormitory Modified for Women	210190-5							
Airmens Dormitory Modified for Women	210190-6							
Airmens Dormitory Modified for Women	210190-7							
Airmens Dormitory Modified for Women	210190-8							
Airmens Dormitory Modified for Women	210190-9							

Building Type	Drawing Number	Number of Persons Accommodated	Sq. Ft./Person	Floor Plan/Privacy Configuration	Room Configuration	Number of Beds/Bunks	Multi-Rank Capability	Multi-Rank Capability Configuration
See legend or list type of building of not included in legend	Identifying number	How many people is the barrack building designed to accommodate?	How much square footage per person does the design provide for?	How is the barracks sleeping area laid out: open bay, cubicle/ partitioned, semi-private, private?	How is the sleeping area configured: what type of beds, how are they arranged, any elements used to define private space, etc.?	How many beds are included in the design?	Does the barracks provide separate area for people of different rank, e.g., Petty Officer in an enlisted barrack?	How is the area for different rank configured?
Airmens Dormitory Modified for Women	210190-10							
Airmens Dormitory Modified for Women	210190-11							
Airmens Dormitory Modified for Women	210190-12	96 or 144 (depends if 2 or 3 person rooms)		Semi-private rooms	Either 2 or 3 to a room. Only 2 beds shown, no indication of double bunk; 3 closets are shown in each room	96; unknown how many single & how many double bunks	No indication of officers' quarters	
Airmens Dormitory Modified for Women	210190-13							
Airmens Dormitory Modified for Women	210190-14							
Airmens Dormitory Modified for Women	210190-15	96 or 144 (depends if 2 or 3 person rooms)		Semi-private rooms	Either 2 or 3 to a room. Only 2 beds shown, no indication of double bunk; 3 closets are shown in each room	96; unknown how many single & how many double bunks	No indication of officers' quarters	
Airmens Dormitory Modified for Women	210190-16	96 or 144 (depends if 2 or 3 person rooms)		Semi-private rooms	Either 2 or 3 to a room. Only 2 beds shown, no indication of double bunk; 3 closets are shown in each room	96; unknown how many single & how many double bunks	No indication of officers' quarters	
Airmens Dormitory Modified for Women	210190-17	94 or 141 (depends if 2 or 3 person rooms)		Semi-private rooms	Either 2 or 3 to a room. Only 2 beds shown, no indication of double bunk; 3 closets are shown in each room	94; unknown how many single & how many double bunks	No indication of officers' quarters	
Airmens Dormitory Modified for Women	210190-18							
Airmens Dormitory Modified for Women	210190-19							
Airmens Dormitory Modified for Women	210190-20							
Airmens Dormitory Modified for Women	210190-21							
Airmens Dormitory Modified for Women	210190-22							
Airmens Dormitory Modified for Women	210190-23							

Building Type	Drawing Number	Number of Persons Accommodated	Sq. Ft./ Person	Floor Plan/Privacy Configuration	Room Configuration	Number of Beds/Bunks	Multi-Rank Capability	Multi-Rank Capability Configuration
See legend or list type of building of not included in legend	Identifying number	How many people is the barrack building designed to accommodate?	How much square footage per person does the design provide for?	How is the barracks sleeping area laid out: open bay, cubicle/ partitioned, semi-private, private?	How is the sleeping area configured: what type of beds, how are they arranged, any elements used to define private space, etc.?	How many beds are included in the design?	Does the barracks provide separate area for people of different rank, e.g., Petty Officer in an enlisted barrack?	How is the area for different rank configured?
Airmens Dormitory Modified for Women	210190-24							
Airmens Dormitory Modified for Women	210190-25							
Airmens Dormitory Modified for Women	210190-26							
Airmens Dormitory Modified for Women	210190-27	98 or 147 (depends if 2 or 3 person rooms)		Semi-private rooms	Either 2 or 3 to a room. Only 2 beds shown, no indication of double bunk; 3 closets are shown in each room	98; unknown how many single & how many double bunks	No indication of officers' quarters	
Airmens Dormitory Modified for Women	210190-28							
Airmens Dormitory Modified for Women	210193-1							
Airmens Dormitory Modified for Women	210193-2	146 or 219 (depends if 2 or 3 person rooms)		Semi-private rooms	Either 2 or 3 to a room. Only 2 beds shown, no indication of double bunk; 3 closets are shown in each room	146; unknown how many single & how many double bunks	No indication of officers' quarters	
Airmens Dormitory Modified for Women	210193-3	146 or 219 (depends if 2 or 3 person rooms)		Semi-private rooms	Either 2 or 3 to a room. Only 2 beds shown, no indication of double bunk; 3 closets are shown in each room	146; unknown how many single & how many double bunks	No indication of officers' quarters	
Airmens Dormitory Modified for Women	210193-4							
Airmens Dormitory Modified for Women	210193-6							
Airmens Dormitory Modified for Women	210193-7							
Airmens Dormitory Modified for Women	210193-8							
Airmens Dormitory Modified for Women	210193-13	144 or 216 (depends if 2 or 3 person rooms)		Semi-private rooms	Either 2 or 3 to a room. Only 2 beds shown, no indication of double bunk; 3 closets are shown in each room	144; unknown how many single & how many double bunks	No indication of officers' quarters	
Airmens Dormitory Modified for Women	210193-21							

Building Type	Drawing Number	Number of Persons Accommodated	Sq. Ft./Person	Floor Plan/Privacy Configuration	Room Configuration	Number of Beds/Bunks	Multi-Rank Capability	Multi-Rank Capability Configuration
See legend or list type of building of not included in legend	Identifying number	How many people is the barrack building designed to accommodate?	How much square footage per person does the design provide for?	How is the barracks sleeping area laid out: open bay, cubicle/ partitioned, semi-private, private?	How is the sleeping area configured: what type of beds, how are they arranged, any elements used to define private space, etc.?	How many beds are included in the design?	Does the barracks provide separate area for people of different rank, e.g., Petty Officer in an enlisted barrack?	How is the area for different rank configured?
Airmens Dormitory Modified for Women	210193-22							
Airmens Dormitory Modified for Women	210193-23							
Airmens Dormitory Modified for Women	210193-27	146 or 219 (depends if 2 or 3 person rooms)		Semi-private rooms	Either 2 or 3 to a room. Only 2 beds shown, no indication of double bunk; 3 closets are shown in each room	146; unknown how many single & how many double bunks	No indication of officers' quarters	
Nurses or WAF Officers Quarters	SK250706-1	87		29 rooms for 1 woman; 29 rooms for 2 women	Either 1 or 2 beds, desk, drawers, closet, chair	87		
Nurses or WAF Officers Quarters	SK250706-2	Unit A: 87 Unit B: 75 Unit C: 63		Unit A: 58 bed rooms Unit B: 50 bed rooms Unit C: 42 bed rooms	Either 1 or 2 beds, desk, drawers, closet, chair	Unit A: 87 Unit B: 75 Unit C: 63		
Nurses or WAF Officers Quarters	SK250709-1	Unit F: 24 Unit G: 18		Unit F: 16 bedrooms Unit G: 12 bedrooms	Either 1 or 2 beds, desk, drawers, closet, chair	Unit F: 24 Unit G: 18		
Nurses or WAF Officers Quarters	SK250708-1	Unit D: 51 Unit E: 39		Unit D: 34 bed rooms Unit E: 26 bed rooms	Either 1 or 2 beds, desk, drawers, closet, chair	Unit D: 51 Unit E: 39		
EMB	556010	172		Open Bay	2 different configurations provided; adjacent beds divided by 6'6" partition making 4-bed "cubicles"	46 single bunks or 46 single bunks w/ 8 dbl bunks	Petty Officer	Open Bay; 14 single bunks or 7 single bunks w/ 7 dbl bunks; separate lounges; separate restroom with 2 partitioned showers, 2 partitioned toilets (no doors) and 1 partitioned urinal
EMB	556012	172		Open Bay	2 different configurations provided; adjacent beds divided by 6'6" partition making 4-bed "cubicles"	46 single bunks or 46 single bunks w/ 8 dbl bunks	Petty Officer	Open Bay; 14 single bunks or 7 single bunks w/ 7 dbl bunks; separate lounges; separate restroom with 2 partitioned showers, 2 partitioned toilets (no doors) and 1 partitioned urinal

Building Type	Drawing Number	Number of Persons Accommodated	Sq. Ft./ Person	Floor Plan/Privacy Configuration	Room Configuration	Number of Beds/Bunks	Multi-Rank Capability	Multi-Rank Capability Configuration
See legend or list type of building of not included in legend	Identifying number	How many people is the barrack building designed to accommodate?	How much square footage per person does the design provide for?	How is the barracks sleeping area laid out: open bay, cubicle/ partitioned, semi-private, private?	How is the sleeping area configured: what type of beds, how are they arranged, any elements used to define private space, etc.?	How many beds are included in the design?	Does the barracks provide separate area for people of different rank, e.g., Petty Officer in an enlisted barrack?	How is the area for different rank configured?
Air Force Dormitory for Enlisted Women	2101107-1	200	72 (bedroom space)	Semi-private bedrooms	Typical room includes 1 single bed, 1 double bunk, 3 closets, 1 sink	152 (76 single, 76 double)	No indication of officers' quarters	
Air Force Dormitory for Enlisted Women	2101107-2							
Air Force Dormitory for Enlisted Women	2101109-1	133	72 (bedroom space)	Semi-private bedrooms	Typical room includes 1 single bed, 1 double bunk, 3 closets, 1 sink, 2 desks	100 (50 single bunks, 50 double bunks)	No indication of officers' quarters	
Air Force Dormitory for Enlisted Women	2101109-2							
EWB	621844	153	140	Open plan	Double Bunks	74 double bunks; 5 single bunks	Petty Officers	4 single bunks, 4 double bunks, 1 PO restroom
EMB	621843	75					Petty Officer	Open Bay; 4 single bunks & 6 dbl bunks
Women's BOQ	un-numbered	50	202	1 & 2 Bed Rooms	Single bunks perpendicular to exterior wall	50	JO & SO	JO - 2 man rooms; SO - 1 man rooms
BOQ	un-numbered	50	197.2	1 & 2 Bed Rooms	Single bunks perpendicular to exterior wall	50	JO & SO	JO - 2 man rooms; SO - 1 man rooms
EWB	un-numbered	100	94.35	2 bed cubicles	Single & double bunks perpendicular to exterior wall; each cubicle has 4 lockers	68	Petty Officers	Separate room divided into 4 cubicles w/ 2 beds each & attached bathroom
EMB	un-numbered	100	92.8	Open Squad Rooms	2 rows of bunks w/ lockers in between rows; partition walls between every 2 bunks	68	Petty Officers; MAA	PO: Separate room w/ 3 double bunks each & attached bathroom MAA: Private bedroom
CPO Quarters	un-numbered	66	132.1	2 bed cubicles	Double bunks perpendicular to exterior walls; lockers define center aisle	48	none	none
BOQ	539042	50	197.2	Semi-private 2 person bedrooms	Single bunks arranged perpendicular to exterior wall	50	Senior Officer	Private rooms; SO toilet & lounge on 2nd floor

Building Type	Drawing Number	Number of Persons Accommodated	Sq. Ft./ Person	Floor Plan/Privacy Configuration	Room Configuration	Number of Beds/Bunks	Multi-Rank Capability	Multi-Rank Capability Configuration
See legend or list type of building of not included in legend	Identifying number	How many people is the barrack building designed to accommodate?	How much square footage per person does the design provide for?	How is the barracks sleeping area laid out: open bay, cubicle/ partitioned, semi-private, private?	How is the sleeping area configured: what type of beds, how are they arranged, any elements used to define private space, etc.?	How many beds are included in the design?	Does the barracks provide separate area for people of different rank, e.g., Petty Officer in an enlisted barrack?	How is the area for different rank configured?
EMB	539037	47		Open Bay		16 single and 12 dbl bunks	Petty Officer	Open Bay; 1 single bunk, 3 dbl bunks
EMB	539038	94		Open Bay		32 single and 24 dbl bunks	Petty Officer	Open Bay; 1 single bunk, 3 dbl bunks
EWB	539039	40	117.25	Open plan	Single & double bunks	15 single; 12 double	Petty Officer	1 single bunk, 1 toilet, lavatory, shower
EWB	539040	40		Open plan	Single & double bunks			
BOQ	621837	40	211.3	Semi-private rooms	No bed configuration indicated; each room has closet & sink; share bathroom w/ adjacent room	40	none	none
BOQ	621838	75	265.3	Semi-private & private rooms	Single bunks arranged parallel to exterior wall; includes sink, closet, desk, dressers	75	none	none
Standard Components Layout	400140-1							
Standard Components Layout	400140-2	2 per unit & 1 per unit	2 person units: 260 1 person units: 520	Private & semi-private units	2 bedroom units with shared bath; 1 bedroom unit with living room; 2 bedroom, bath, shared living room	1 or 2 per unit (1 per bedroom)		
Standard Components Layout	400140-3							
EMB	658441	14		Open Bay	dormitory style, no privacy partitions	14 single bunks	none	
EWB	658440	11	87.3	Open plan	Single bunks perpendicular to exterior wall w/ central aisle	11	none	none
Air Force Dormitory for Enlisted Women	210204-1	141 (If assume 3 to a room)		Semi-private rooms	Assume 3 to a room. No beds shown; 3 closets are shown in each room	Indeterminate	No indication of officers' quarters	

Building Type	Drawing Number	Number of Persons Accommodated	Sq. Ft./ Person	Floor Plan/Privacy Configuration	Room Configuration	Number of Beds/Bunks	Multi-Rank Capability	Multi-Rank Capability Configuration
See legend or list type of building of not included in legend	Identifying number	How many people is the barrack building designed to accommodate?	How much square footage per person does the design provide for?	How is the barracks sleeping area laid out: open bay, cubicle/ partitioned, semi-private, private?	How is the sleeping area configured: what type of beds, how are they arranged, any elements used to define private space, etc.?	How many beds are included in the design?	Does the barracks provide separate area for people of different rank, e.g., Petty Officer in an enlisted barrack?	How is the area for different rank configured?
Air Force Dormitory for Enlisted Women	210204-2							
Air Force Dormitory for Enlisted Women	210205-1	213 (If assume 3 to a room)	118	Semi-private rooms	Assume 3 to a room. No beds shown; 3 closets are shown in each room	Indeterminate	No indication of officers' quarters	
Air Force Dormitory for Enlisted Women	210205-2							
EMB	665169	252		Open Bay	bunks parallel to exterior walls, two deep on each side of middle aisle; first floor w/longitudinal and transverse dividing partitions for each 4 beds; second and third floors w/transverse partitions only for each 4 beds	240 single bunks	Petty Officer/Non-Commissioned Officer	3 double rooms; 2 single bunks parallel to exterior wall; lockers between bunks
EMB	665171	252		Open Bay	bunks parallel to exterior walls, two deep on each side of middle aisle; first floor w/longitudinal and transverse dividing partitions for each 4 beds; second and third floors w/transverse partitions only for each 4 beds	240 single bunks	Petty Officer/Non-Commissioned Officer	3 double rooms; 2 single bunks parallel to exterior wall; lockers between bunks

Building Type	Drawing Number	Number of Persons Accommodated	Sq. Ft./Person	Floor Plan/Privacy Configuration	Room Configuration	Number of Beds/Bunks	Multi-Rank Capability	Multi-Rank Capability Configuration
See legend or list type of building of not included in legend	Identifying number	How many people is the barrack building designed to accommodate?	How much square footage per person does the design provide for?	How is the barracks sleeping area laid out: open bay, cubicle/ partitioned, semi-private, private?	How is the sleeping area configured: what type of beds, how are they arranged, any elements used to define private space, etc.?	How many beds are included in the design?	Does the barracks provide separate area for people of different rank, e.g., Petty Officer in an enlisted barrack?	How is the area for different rank configured?
EMB	665192	252		Open Bay	bunks parallel to exterior walls, two deep on each side of middle aisle; first floor w/longitudinal and transverse dividing partitions for each 4 beds; second and third floors w/transverse partitions only for each 4 beds	240 single bunks	Petty Officer/Non-Commissioned Officer	3 double rooms; 2 single bunks parallel to exterior wall; lockers between bunks
EMB	665209	252		Open Bay	bunks parallel to exterior walls, two deep on each side of middle aisle; first floor w/longitudinal and transverse dividing partitions for each 4 beds; second and third floors w/transverse partitions only for each 4 beds	240 single bunks	Petty Officer/Non-Commissioned Officer	3 double rooms; 2 single bunks parallel to exterior wall; lockers between bunks
BOQ	723357	10	288	Private Rooms	Private Rooms with a bed, closet, sink, desk, chair, chest, and shared bath with neighboring room	10	none	none
EMB	723347	119		Open Bay	bunks parallel to exterior walls, two deep on each side of middle aisle; longitudinal and transverse dividing partitions for each 4 beds	112 single bunks	Chief Petty Officer	3 double rooms w/2 single bunks parallel to exterior wall; lockers between bunks; 1 single room w/bunk perpendicular to exterior wall

Building Type	Drawing Number	Number of Persons Accommodated	Sq. Ft./Person	Floor Plan/Privacy Configuration	Room Configuration	Number of Beds/Bunks	Multi-Rank Capability	Multi-Rank Capability Configuration
See legend or list type of building of not included in legend	Identifying number	How many people is the barrack building designed to accommodate?	How much square footage per person does the design provide for?	How is the barracks sleeping area laid out: open bay, cubicle/partitioned, semi-private, private?	How is the sleeping area configured: what type of beds, how are they arranged, any elements used to define private space, etc.?	How many beds are included in the design?	Does the barracks provide separate area for people of different rank, e.g., Petty Officer in an enlisted barrack?	How is the area for different rank configured?
EMB	720647	166		Open Bay	bunks parallel to exterior walls, two deep on each side of middle aisle; longitudinal and transverse dividing partitions for each 4 beds	160 single bunks	Petty Officer or Non-Commissioned Officer	3 double rooms w/2 single bunks parallel to exterior wall; lockers between bunks
Battalion Admin. & Classroom Building	Sheet 4							
BOQ	756740	8	302	Private bedrooms	4 private bedrooms per unit; 2 units per building	8	none	none
EMB	788341	250		Open Bay	bunks perpendicular to exterior walls; 4 bunks either side of middle aisle; lockers between each two bunks	120 double bunks	Petty Officer or Non-Commissioned Officer	2 five single bunk rooms w/bunks parallel to exterior wall; lockers between bunks
EMB	795610	100	124	Open Bay	bunks perpendicular to exterior walls; partition between every 2 bunks; 2 bunks either side of middle aisle; lockers/closets at foot of each two bunks	100 single bunks	none	none
EMB	795611	116	123	Double Rooms	bunks perpendicular to exterior walls; two closets and 2 dressers at foot of bunks	116 single bunks	none	none
EMB	795614	166	124	4 Bed Cubicles	Single bunks parallel to exterior wall (1 in each corner); 4 closets, 4 chairs, 1 desk	166 single bunks	3 PO rooms	2 single bunks each room; PO lounge on 2nd floor

Building Type	Drawing Number	Number of Persons Accommodated	Sq. Ft./Person	Floor Plan/Privacy Configuration	Room Configuration	Number of Beds/Bunks	Multi-Rank Capability	Multi-Rank Capability Configuration
See legend or list type of building of not included in legend	Identifying number	How many people is the barrack building designed to accommodate?	How much square footage per person does the design provide for?	How is the barracks sleeping area laid out: open bay, cubicle/ partitioned, semi-private, private?	How is the sleeping area configured: what type of beds, how are they arranged, any elements used to define private space, etc.?	How many beds are included in the design?	Does the barracks provide separate area for people of different rank, e.g., Petty Officer in an enlisted barrack?	How is the area for different rank configured?
EMB	795615	180	124	4 Bed Cubicles	4 Single bunks each cubicle; 4 closets, chairs; desks (2 different layouts for EM Students & EM Ships Company	180 single bunks	none	none
EMB	795616	252	124.5	4 Bed Cubicles	Single bunks parallel to exterior wall (1 in each corner); 4 closets, 4 chairs, 1 desk	252 single bunks	6 PO rooms	2 single bunks each room; PO lounge on 2nd floor
EWB	795612	120	137.5	4 Bed Cubicles	Single bunks; 4 lockers; 2 vanities; arrangement varies	120	3 CPO rooms	2 single bunks each room; CPO restroom on 2nd floor
EMB	795613	152	124.5	Double Rooms	bunks perpendicular to exterior walls; two closets and 2 dressers at foot of bunks	152 single bunks	none	none
EWB	808316	142	87.2	4 Bed Cubicles	Single bunks; 4 lockers; 2 vanities; arrangement varies	142	none	none
EMB	817037	116	124	Double Rooms	Single bunks perpendicular to exterior wall; 2 closets; 2 desks per room	116 single bunks	none	none
EMB	817038	152	124	2 beds per room	Single bunks (2 rooms with 1 double bunk each) perpendicular to exterior wall; 2 closets; 2 desk	150 bunks (2 of which are doubles)	none	none
EMB	817039	166	124	4 Bed Cubicles	Single bunks parallel to exterior wall (1 in each corner); 4 closets, 4 chairs, 1 desk	166	3 PO rooms	2 single bunks each room; PO lounge on 2nd floor

Building Type	Drawing Number	Number of Persons Accommodated	Sq. Ft./ Person	Floor Plan/Privacy Configuration	Room Configuration	Number of Beds/Bunks	Multi-Rank Capability	Multi-Rank Capability Configuration
See legend or list type of building of not included in legend	Identifying number	How many people is the barrack building designed to accommodate?	How much square footage per person does the design provide for?	How is the barracks sleeping area laid out: open bay, cubicle/ partitioned, semi-private, private?	How is the sleeping area configured: what type of beds, how are they arranged, any elements used to define private space, etc.?	How many beds are included in the design?	Does the barracks provide separate area for people of different rank, e.g., Petty Officer in an enlisted barrack?	How is the area for different rank configured?
EMB	817040	180	124.9	4 Bed Cubicles	4 Single bunks each cubicle; 4 closets, chairs; desks (2 different layouts for EM Students & EM Ships Company	180	none	none
EMB	817041	252	124.9	4 Bed Cubicles	Single bunks parallel to exterior wall (1 in each corner); 4 closets, 4 chairs, 1 desk	252	3 PO rooms	2 single bunks each room; PO lounge on 2nd floor
SP	817043	675	130	Open Squad Rooms	Single bunks placed perpendicular to wall in 4 rows with central aisle and lockers in center of squad room	675	D1	9 private rooms with private baths
EWB	817046	120	137.5	4 Bed Cubicles	Single bunks; 4 lockers; 2 vanities; arrangement varies	120	3 CPO rooms	2 single bunks each room; CPO restroom on 2nd floor
SP	817185							
EWB	745932	142	91.9	4 Bed Cubicles	2 single bunks; 2 double bunks; lockers, desk or vanity; arrangement varies	93	none	none
EWB	745933	88	74.1	4 Bed Cubicles	Double bunks; lockers; desks or vanities; arrangement varies	44	none	none
EWB	808224	142	91.3	4 Bed Cubicles	2 single bunks; 2 double bunks; lockers, desk or vanity; arrangement varies	93	none	none
EWB	808326	77-88	72-82	4 Bed Cubicles	2 single bunks; 2 double bunks; lockers, desk or vanity; arrangement varies	44 (varies in amount of singles and doubles)	none	none

Building Type	Drawing Number	Number of Persons Accommodated	Sq. Ft./Person	Floor Plan/Privacy Configuration	Room Configuration	Number of Beds/Bunks	Multi-Rank Capability	Multi-Rank Capability Configuration
See legend or list type of building of not included in legend	Identifying number	How many people is the barrack building designed to accommodate?	How much square footage per person does the design provide for?	How is the barracks sleeping area laid out: open bay, cubicle/ partitioned, semi-private, private?	How is the sleeping area configured: what type of beds, how are they arranged, any elements used to define private space, etc.?	How many beds are included in the design?	Does the barracks provide separate area for people of different rank, e.g., Petty Officer in an enlisted barrack?	How is the area for different rank configured?
EWB	808234	77-88	72-82	4 Bed Cubicles	2 single bunks; 2 double bunks; lockers, desk or vanity; arrangement varies	44 (varies in amount of singles and doubles)	none	none
EWB	836726	142	91.9	4 Bed Cubicles	2 single bunks; 2 double bunks; lockers, desk or vanity; arrangement varies	93	none	none
EWB	836734	77-88	74.1-84.7	4 Bed Cubicles	2 single bunks; 2 double bunks; lockers, desk or vanity; arrangement varies	44 (varies in amount of singles and doubles)	none	none
SP	745934	108	120.8	4 Bed Cubicles	4 single bunks, 2 parallel to exterior wall, 2 perpendicular; 4 lockers; 1 desk	108	none	none
SP	808243	108	120.8	4 Bed Cubicles	4 single bunks, 2 parallel to exterior wall, 2 perpendicular; 4 lockers; 1 desk	108	none	none
SP	808335	108	120.8	4 Bed Cubicles	4 single bunks, 2 parallel to exterior wall, 2 perpendicular; 4 lockers; 1 desk	108	none	none
EMB	745930	250	38.1	Open Bay	Double bunks perpendicular to exterior wall; 4 rows of bunks	250	2 PO or NCO rooms	5 single bunks each room
EMB	745931	125	38.1	Open Bay	Double bunks perpendicular to exterior wall; 4 rows of bunks	125	1 PO or NCO room	5 single bunks each room
BOQ Motel Type	AD250672-1	1 story: 18; 2 story: 36; For Alternate plans: 17 & 34	Unit Type A: 360 Unit Type B: 432	Private "Motel Type" Units	Unit A: 1 room studio Unit B: Separate bedroom	1 story: 18; 2 story: 36; For Alternate plans: 17 & 34		

Building Type	Drawing Number	Number of Persons Accommodated	Sq. Ft./ Person	Floor Plan/Privacy Configuration	Room Configuration	Number of Beds/Bunks	Multi-Rank Capability	Multi-Rank Capability Configuration
See legend or list type of building of not included in legend	Identifying number	How many people is the barrack building designed to accommodate?	How much square footage does the design provide for?	How is the barracks sleeping area laid out: open bay, cubicle/ partitioned, semi-private, private?	How is the sleeping area configured: what type of beds, how are they arranged, any elements used to define private space, etc.?	How many beds are included in the design?	Does the barracks provide separate area for people of different rank, e.g., Petty Officer in an enlisted barrack?	How is the area for different rank configured?
BOQ Motel Type	AD250672-2	40 1st Alt: 39 2nd Alt: 38	Unit Type A: 360 Unit Type B: 432	Private "Motel Type" Units	Unit A: 1 room studio Unit B: Separate bedroom	40 1st Alt: 39 2nd Alt: 38		
EMB	895054	252	121.6	4 Bed Cubicles	Single bunks parallel to exterior wall (1 in each corner); 4 closets, 4 chairs	252	3 PO rooms	2 single bunks each room; PO lounge on 2nd floor
SP	1038068	516	131.5	Open Squad Rooms	Single bunks perpendicular to wall in 4 rows, 2 on each side of center aisle	516	D1	6 private rooms w/ attached baths
BEQ	1038070	varies	1 Man Rms: 142.5 2 Man Rms: 71.25 3 Man Rms: 72.5 4 Man Rms: 73.1	1,2,3, & 4 Man Rooms	Single Bunks; closets; desks; chairs; arrangement varies	varies by room	none	none
BEQ	1038071	varies	TDY: 300 Junior Officer: 450 Senior Officer: 600	Private Suites	TDY: Living Rm/Bedroom & bath JO: Private bedroom & bath, shared living room SO: Private bedroom, bath, living room, kitchen	N/A	TDY, Junior, & Senior Officers	(See room configuration category)
BEQ	1038076	263	124.9	4 Man Rooms	4 single bunks; partition wall divides rooms into 2 sides (2 bunks each side); 4 closets; 2 desks	263	Petty Officer	2 PO single rooms, PO lounge on 2nd floor
Processing Building	380905-3							

Building Type	Drawing Number	Number of Persons Accommodated	Sq. Ft./ Person	Floor Plan/Privacy Configuration	Room Configuration	Number of Beds/Bunks	Multi-Rank Capability	Multi-Rank Capability Configuration
See legend or list type of building of not included in legend	Identifying number	How many people is the barrack building designed to accommodate?	How much square footage per person does the design provide for?	How is the barracks sleeping area laid out: open bay, cubicle/ partitioned, semi-private, private?	How is the sleeping area configured: what type of beds, how are they arranged, any elements used to define private space, etc.?	How many beds are included in the design?	Does the barracks provide separate area for people of different rank, e.g., Petty Officer in an enlisted barrack?	How is the area for different rank configured?
Barracks Reception Station Complex	SK2101153-6	344		Semi-private bedrooms	4 man & 8 man rooms (8 man rooms have partitions that separate it into 2 sections	344	Yes; NCOs, Orderly, 1st Sgt., and CO	Each has private room
Dining Hall	3605118-4							
Enlisted Barracks Reception Station Complex	2101153-6	348		Semi-private bedrooms	4 man & 8 man rooms (8 man rooms have partitions that separate it into 2 sections	Indeterminate	Yes; NCOs, Orderly, 1st Sgt., and CO	Each has private room
Reception Station Complex	1606328-2							
Service Club/ Post Exchange	311847-5							
Service Club/ Post Exchange Reception Station Complex	SK311847-5							
EMB	1038075	252	124.9	4 Bed Cubicles	Single bunks parallel to exterior wall; 4 closets; 4 chairs; 2 desks	252	3 PO rooms	2 single bunks each room; PO lounge on 2nd floor
EWB (Center Hall & Motel Type)	4	61 each	Center Hall: 166.5 Motel Type: 166	Semi-private rooms		61	3 rooms for E5-E6 1 room for E7-E9	E5-E6 & E7-E9: private baths attached to rooms E2-E4: separate restrooms Shared kitchen, lounge, laundry
Officer Personnel Typical Living Units - Center Hall Type	6		O2 & below: 359 O3 & above: 502.6; Cadet 2 man & 4 man: 179.5	Private and semi-private units	1-2 beds per bedroom		O2 & below, O3 & above, Cadets	O2 & below: combined living/bedroom, shared kitchen (one option w/o kitchen); O3 & above: separate living and bedrooms, private kitchen; Cadet: 2 man rooms with bed/studyroom, bath, & 4 man suite with 2 bedrooms, 2 baths, shared living/study room

Building Type	Drawing Number	Number of Persons Accommodated	Sq. Ft./Person	Floor Plan/Privacy Configuration	Room Configuration	Number of Beds/Bunks	Multi-Rank Capability	Multi-Rank Capability Configuration
See legend or list type of building of not included in legend	Identifying number	How many people is the barrack building designed to accommodate?	How much square footage per person does the design provide for?	How is the barracks sleeping area laid out: open bay, cubicle/ partitioned, semi-private, private?	How is the sleeping area configured: what type of beds, how are they arranged, any elements used to define private space, etc.?	How many beds are included in the design?	Does the barracks provide separate area for people of different rank, e.g., Petty Officer in an enlisted barrack?	How is the area for different rank configured?
Officer Personnel Typical Living Units - Motel	5		O2 & below: 359 O3 & above: 502.6	Private rooms	Private sleeping quarters		O2 & below and O3 & above	O2 & below: combined living/bedroom, shared kitchen; O3 & above: separate living and bedrooms, private kitchen
SP (Gym)	1294389 (NAVFAC)							
BOQ	1297661 - 1297662 (FEC)	121	N/A	Private Rooms	Private Rooms w/ closet and attached baths	121	MAA	Private Bedroom w/ attached bath
SP (Gym)	1294390 (NAVFAC)							
BEQ	1403100 (NAVFAC)	12 / module	160	1,2,3 man rooms	1,2, or 3 single bunks; wardrobes used to define private space; arrangements vary	12/ module	none	none
BEQ	1403797 (NAVFAC)	144	160	3 man rooms	3 single bunks; 3 closets; 1 desk; attached private bath	144	none	none
BEQ	1403798 (NAVFAC)	828	160	3 man rooms	3 single bunks; 3 closets; 1 desk; attached private bath	828	none	none
BOQ	1403795 (NAVFAC)	100	N/A	Private Units	Each private unit has living room, bedroom, dining area; kitchen; bathroom	100	Grade 2 & below Grade 3 & above	Grade 2 & below have living/sleeping room Grade 3 & above have separate living room and bedroom
BOQ	1403796 (NAVFAC)	100	N/A	Private Units	Each private unit has living room, bedroom, dining area; kitchen; bathroom	100	Grade 2 & below Grade 3 & above	Grade 2 & below have living/sleeping room Grade 3 & above have separate living room and bedroom
BOQ (Men)	306887 - 306888	104	N/A	Single Rooms	No configuration indicated; each room has 1 closet	104	none	none

Building Type	Drawing Number	Number of Persons Accommodated	Sq. Ft./ Person	Floor Plan/Privacy Configuration	Room Configuration	Number of Beds/Bunks	Multi-Rank Capability	Multi-Rank Capability Configuration
See legend or list type of building of not included in legend	Identifying number	How many people is the barrack building designed to accommodate?	How much square footage per person does the design provide for?	How is the barracks sleeping area laid out: open bay, cubicle/ partitioned, semi-private, private?	How is the sleeping area configured: what type of beds, how are they arranged, any elements used to define private space, etc.?	How many beds are included in the design?	Does the barracks provide separate area for people of different rank, e.g., Petty Officer in an enlisted barrack?	How is the area for different rank configured?
EWB	306869	224	N/A	2 bed cubicles	Double bunks perpendicular to exterior walls with 4 lockers each cubicle	112 double bunks	Petty Officer	Private room w/ attached bath
EWB	306870							
Alterations to Bldg # 268 Training Center Fort Des Moines, Iowa	193A-28							
Alterations to Building # 81 Training Center Fort Des Moines, Iowa	193A-27							
EWB	21-02-06	56	160.5	2 Bed & 4 Bed Rooms	Single bunks parallel to exterior walls	56	none	none
Improved Bachelor Officer Quarters - Women	Sheet 303	16	590	Private units	Separate bedroom	16	No	
Perspective Sketch Drawing	sketch_ reception							
BEQ	1341195 (NAVFAC)	270	142	3 man rooms	3 single bunks; 3 closets; 1 desk; 2 chairs; arrangements vary	270	none	none
EB	731427	180	152.7	Semi-private 3 person bedrooms	Rooms w/ 3 beds each parallel to exterior wall; 3 closets; attached bath (shared with neighboring room)	180	2 MA Rooms	Private rooms with attached private baths
EB	731428	varies	varies	Semi-private suites	6 different room layouts for various grades and type of occupancy	varies	none	none
EB	756735	162	156.9	Semi-private 3 person bedrooms	Rooms w/ 3 beds each; 3 closets; 3 desks; 1 sink	162	none	none

Building Type	Drawing Number	Number of Persons Accommodated	Sq. Ft./ Person	Floor Plan/Privacy Configuration	Room Configuration	Number of Beds/Bunks	Multi-Rank Capability	Multi-Rank Capability Configuration
See legend or list type of building of not included in legend	Identifying number	How many people is the barrack building designed to accommodate?	How much square footage per person does the design provide for?	How is the barracks sleeping area laid out: open bay, cubicle/ partitioned, semi-private, private?	How is the sleeping area configured: what type of beds, how are they arranged, any elements used to define private space, etc.?	How many beds are included in the design?	Does the barracks provide separate area for people of different rank, e.g., Petty Officer in an enlisted barrack?	How is the area for different rank configured?
EB	756736	134	153	Semi-private 2 person bedrooms	Rooms w/ 2 beds each perpendicular to exterior wall; 2 closets; 2 desks	134	1 MA	Private room
EMB	171065	20	N/A	Open Squad Rooms	2 rows of bunks perpendicular to exterior walls; lockers between rows	20	Officer	2 private rooms w/ shared bathroom
SP (Chapel)	367912							
SP (Chapel)	367912							
W	318064	112	N/A	Open plan	Double bunks arranged along angled walls designed to create more privacy	56 double bunks	CPO	Private room w/ attached bath
WB	318064	77-88	N/A	Open Rooms	Double bunks parallel to angled walls; lockers at end of beds	56	CPO	Private Room w/ closet

Restroom Facilities Data

Building Type	Drawing Number	Number of Restrooms	Restroom Configuration	Number of Toilets	Toilet Configuration	Number of Urinals	Urinal Configuration	Number of Showers/ Tubs	Shower Configuration
See legend or list type of building of not included in legend	Identifying number	How many restrooms in building	What type of restroom: guest bath (e.g., men's water closet by date room) and components of each restroom (full--toilet, urinal, washroom, showers; or different combinations thereof)	how many toilets in each restroom	are toilets partitioned; do they have doors	how many urinals in each bathroom	partitioned or not; individual urinals, or trough.	how many showers in each bathroom	partitioned or non-partitioned shower stalls, with or without benches/changing stall; open shower room with central water head, etc.
Typical Landscape Planting for Company Officers' and Double NCO Quarters	630-100								
Typical Landscape Planting for HQ Admin. Bldg, BOQs, Barracks Bldgs	630-101								
Marine Barracks	129241	8	4 Central restrooms (toilets, urinals, sinks, showers) 4 Private baths (toilet, sink, shower)	Central: 6 Private: 1	partitioned w/o doors	Central: 5 Private: 0	Individual, no partitions	Central: 5 Private: 1	Central: Open gang shower room w/ adjacent dressing room Private: Individual shower stall
Marine Barracks	129247		Toilets, urinals, sinks in 1 room; separate shower & dressing rooms	6	partitioned w/o doors	5	individual; no partitions	5 shower heads	Open gang shower room w/ adjacent dressing room
EMB	137497 - 137498	6	2 communal restrooms (toilets, sinks, showers) 1 private bath for CPO 1 shared bath (1st flr bedrooms) 1 restroom for sick bay 1 shared bath for cooks	Communal: 6 Others: 1	partitioned w/o doors	2 each in communal restrooms	2 troughs; no partitions	Communal: 4 shower heads Others: 1 shower	Communal: Open gang shower w/ open changing room w/ bench Others: Individual shower stalls
Mobilization Buildings Hospital (Nurses) Quarters	800-1422 (2)								
Mobilization Buildings Hospital (Nurses) Quarters	800-1421	3	1 Full bath for servants, 1 full bath for nurses, and one private bath for cook	1 for servants; 2 for nurses; 1 for cook	Partitioned with doors (except private bath)	0		1 shower for cook; 1 tub for servants; 2 tubs for nurses	Tubs partitioned with doors and changing space
Mobilization Buildings Hospital (Nurses) Quarters	800-1422								
Mobilization Buildings Hospital (Nurses) Quarters	800-1423								

Building Type	Drawing Number	Number of Restrooms	Restroom Configuration	Number of Toilets	Toilet Configuration	Number of Urinals	Urinal Configuration	Number of Showers/Tubs	Shower Configuration
See legend or list type of building of not included in legend	Identifying number	How many restrooms in building	What type of restroom: guest bath (e.g., men's water closet by date room) and components of each restroom (full--toilet, urinal, washroom, showers; or different combinations thereof)	how many toilets in each restroom	are toilets partitioned; do they have doors	how many urinals in each bathroom	partitioned or not; individual urinals, or trough.	how many showers in each bathroom	partitioned or non-partitioned shower stalls, with or without benches/changing stall; open shower room with central water head, etc.
Mobilization Buildings Nurses (Hospital) Quarters	800-1435	4 (3 on 1st floor)	1 full bath for servants, full bath for nurses, and one private bath for cook	1st flr: servants, 1; nurses, 2; cook,1	Partitioned with doors (except private bath)	0		1st flr: 1 shower - cook; 1 tub each - servants & nurses	Partitioned with doors and changing space
Mobilization Buildings Nurses (Hospital) Quarters	800-1436	4 (1 on 2nd floor)	1 full bath for nurses	2nd flr: nurses, 4	Partitioned with doors	0		2nd flr: 4 tubs	Partitioned with doors and changing space
Mobilization Buildings Hospital (Nurses) Quarters	800-1423.1								
EMB	188167	6	2 Central restrooms (defined spaces for lavatories, showers, urinals, toilets) 1 MAA bath (toilet, sink, shower) 1 restroom near sick bay (separate spaces for toilets, lav, showers) 1 restroom near entry (toilets, sinks) 1 restroom near kitchen (toilets, sinks)	Central: 27 MAA: 1 Sick Bay: 4 restroom near entry: 3 near Kitchen: N/A	partitioned w/o doors	Central: 20 Sick Bay: 3 Near Entry: 4 kitchen: N/A	non-partitioned; individual	Central: 18 MAA: 1 Sick bay: 8	Open shower room w/ partitions between each shower
EMB	184324 - 184325	7	2 Central restrooms (1 per floor) w/ separate rooms for lavatories, toilets, showers 3 semi-private baths for officers 1 CPO restroom 1 restroom next to galley	Central: 12 Officers: 1 CPO: 2 Galley: 1	partitioned w/o doors	Central: 8 CPO: 1 Galley: 1	non-partitioned; individual	Central: 8 Semi-private: 1 CPO: 2 Galley: 1	Central: Partitioned shower stalls w/ common changing area w/ bench CPO: Partitioned shower stalls w/ changing stalls & benches Others: Individual shower stalls
Typical Layout Diagram for Camouflage Demonstration - Practice Area	614-1602								

Building Type	Drawing Number	Number of Restrooms	Restroom Configuration	Number of Toilets	Toilet Configuration	Number of Urinals	Urinal Configuration	Number of Showers/ Tubs	Shower Configuration
See legend or list type of building of not included in legend	Identifying number	How many restrooms in building	What type of restroom: guest bath (e.g., men's water closet by date room) and components of each restroom (full--toilet, urinal, washroom, showers; or different combinations thereof)	how many toilets in each restroom	are toilets partitioned; do they have doors	how many urinals in each bathroom	partitioned or not; individual urinals, or trough.	how many showers in each bathroom	partitioned or non-partitioned shower stalls, with or without benches/changing stall; open shower room with central water head, etc.
Typical Layout Diagrams for WAAC Replacement Training Center	614-703								
Mobilization Buildings WAAC Exchange - Type - WPX - A-M	700-3516								
Mobilization Buildings WAAC Exchange - Type - WPX - A-M	700-3517	3	1 small washroom with toilet and sink, 1 men's restroom, 1 women's restroom	washroom: 1; men's: 1; women's: 4	partitioned with doors	1 in men's restroom	partitioned; individual	0	
Mobilization Buildings WAAC Exchange - Type - WPX - A-M	700-3518								
Mobilization Buildings WAAC Exchange - Type - WPX - A-M	700-3519								
Mobilization Buildings WAAC Exchange - Type - WPX - A-M	700-3520								
Mobilization Buildings WAAC Exchange - Type - WPX - A-M	700-3521								
Mobilization Buildings WAAC Exchange - Type - WPX - A-M	700-3522								
Mobilization Buildings WAC Barracks	800-425								
Mobilization Buildings WAC Barracks	800-426	1	Full restroom with toilets, sinks, showers (divided into 3 sections)	8	Partitioned with doors	0		6 showers 2 bathtubs	Partitioned showers and tubs w/o changing stalls, w/ benches
Mobilization Buildings WAC Barracks	800-427								
Mobilization Buildings WAC Barracks	800-428								
Mobilization Buildings WAC Barracks	800-429								

Building Type	Drawing Number	Number of Restrooms	Restroom Configuration	Number of Toilets	Toilet Configuration	Number of Urinals	Urinal Configuration	Number of Showers/ Tubs	Shower Configuration
See legend or list type of building of not included in legend	Identifying number	How many restrooms in building	What type of restroom: guest bath (e.g., men's water closet by date room) and components of each restroom (full--toilet, urinal, washroom, showers; or different combinations thereof)	how many toilets in each restroom	are toilets partitioned; do they have doors	how many urinals in each bathroom	partitioned or not; individual urinals, or trough.	how many showers in each bathroom	partitioned or non-partitioned shower stalls, with or without benches/changing stall; open shower room with central water head, etc.
Mobilization Buildings WAC Barracks	800-430								
Mobilization Buildings WAC Barracks	800-431								
Mobilization Buildings WAC Exchange	800-1124								
Mobilization Buildings WAC Exchange	800-1125	3	1 small washroom with toilet and sink adjacent to beauty shop, 1 men's restroom, 1 women's restroom	Women: 4 Men: 1	Partitioned with doors	Women: 0 Men: 1	Partitioned individual urinal	0	
Mobilization Buildings WAC Exchange	800-1126								
Mobilization Buildings WAC Exchange	800-1127								
Mobilization Buildings WAC Exchange	800-1128								
Mobilization Buildings WAC Exchange	800-1129								
Mobilization Buildings WAC Exchange	800-1130								
Barracks for 150 Women WAC Training Center Fort Des Moines, Iowa	193A-49	0							
Laundry & Toilet Bldg Addition for Barracks Training Center Fort Des Moines, Iowa	193A-22	2	Full restrooms with toilets, sinks, showers, tubs divided into sections: toilets, showers, washroom	12	Partitioned w/ doors	0		9 showers, 3 tubs	Partitioned with changing stalls and benches
Recreation Buildings in connection with Barracks Training Center Fort Des Moines, Iowa	193A-25								
WAC Barracks Training Center Fort Des Moines, Iowa	193A-19	0 (restrooms in attached bldg)							

Building Type	Drawing Number	Number of Restrooms	Restroom Configuration	Number of Toilets	Toilet Configuration	Number of Urinals	Urinal Configuration	Number of Showers/Tubs	Shower Configuration
See legend or list type of building of not included in legend	Identifying number	How many restrooms in building	What type of restroom: guest bath (e.g., men's water closet by date room) and components of each restroom (full--toilet, urinal, washroom, showers; or different combinations thereof)	how many toilets in each restroom	are toilets partitioned; do they have doors	how many urinals in each bathroom	partitioned or not; individual urinals, or trough.	how many showers in each bathroom	partitioned or non-partitioned shower stalls, with or without benches/changing stall; open shower room with central water head, etc.
Co. Unit Layout Diagrams for WAAC	614-702								
Training Center Fort Des Moines, Iowa	193A-16								
Mobilization Buildings WAAC Barracks	700-3525	1	Bath, lavatory, toilet separated into defined spaces	7	Partitioned with doors	None		4 showers, 2 tubs	Partitioned shower stalls with benches
Mobilization Buildings WAAC Barracks (Alt. for sloping site)	700-3526	1	Bath/showers, sinks, toilets separated into defined spaces	7	Partitioned with doors	None		4 showers, 2 tubs	Partitioned shower stalls with benches
Mobilization Buildings WAAC Barracks	700-3527								
Mobilization Buildings WAAC Barracks	700-3528								
Mobilization Buildings WAAC Barracks	700-3529								
WAC Latrine (Temporary Structure) Training Center Fort Des Moines, Iowa	193A-31	1	Toilet and washroom	12	No partitions, no doors	0		0	
Mobilization Buildings WAC Recreation, Supply, Co. Admin., & Quarters	700-3540								
Mobilization Buildings WAC Recreation, Supply, Co. Admin., & Quarters	700-3541	2	1 small restroom adjacent to rec room with toilet and sink; 1 larger restroom near bedrooms with showers, toilets, sinks	1	Partitioned with door	0		2	Partitioned with changing stalls and benches
Mobilization Buildings WAC Recreation, Supply, Co. Admin., & Quarters	700-3542								

Building Type	Drawing Number	Number of Restrooms	Restroom Configuration	Number of Toilets	Toilet Configuration	Number of Urinals	Urinal Configuration	Number of Showers/ Tubs	Shower Configuration
See legend or list type of building of not included in legend	Identifying number	How many restrooms in building	What type of restroom: guest bath (e.g., men's water closet by date room) and components of each restroom (full--toilet, urinal, washroom, showers; or different combinations thereof)	how many toilets in each restroom	are toilets partitioned; do they have doors	how many urinals in each bathroom	partitioned or not; individual urinals, or trough.	how many showers in each bathroom	partitioned or non-partitioned shower stalls, with or without benches/changing stall; open shower room with central water head, etc.
Mobilization Buildings WAC Recreation, Supply, Co. Admin., & Quarters	700-3543								
Mobilization Buildings WAC Recreation, Supply, Co. Admin., & Quarters	700-3544								
Mobilization Buildings WAC Recreation, Supply, Co. Admin., & Quarters	700-3545								
Mobilization Buildings WAC Recreation, Supply, Co. Admin., & Quarters	700-3546								
Mobilization Buildings WAC Recreation, Supply, Co. Admin., & Quarters	700-3547	3	1 small restroom adjacent to rec room with toilet and sink; 2 larger restrooms near bedrooms with showers, toilets, sinks	1	Partitioned with door	0		2	Partitioned with changing stalls and benches
Mobilization Buildings WAC Recreation, Supply, Co. Admin., & Quarters	700-3548								
Mobilization Buildings WAC Recreation, Supply, Co. Admin., & Quarters	700-3549								
Mobilization Buildings WAC Recreation, Supply, Co. Admin., & Quarters	700-3550								

Building Type	Drawing Number	Number of Restrooms	Restroom Configuration	Number of Toilets	Toilet Configuration	Number of Urinals	Urinal Configuration	Number of Showers/ Tubs	Shower Configuration
See legend or list type of building of not included in legend	Identifying number	How many restrooms in building	What type of restroom: guest bath (e.g., men's water closet by date room) and components of each restroom (full--toilet, urinal, washroom, showers; or different combinations thereof)	how many toilets in each restroom	are toilets partitioned; do they have doors	how many urinals in each bathroom	partitioned or not; individual urinals, or trough.	how many showers in each bathroom	partitioned or non-partitioned shower stalls, with or without benches/changing stall; open shower room with central water head, etc.
Mobilization Buildings WAC Recreation, Supply, Co. Admin., & Quarters	700-3551								
Barracks (30 Men) WAC Training Center Fort Des Moines, Iowa	193A-46	0							
Mobilization Buildings WAAC Officers' Quarters	700-3532	1	Toilets, sinks, shower, tub	2	partitioned with doors	0		1 shower, 1 tub	Partitioned with changing stall, no benches
Mobilization Buildings WAAC Officers' Quarters	700-3533								
Office Building of Engineer (Additions & Remodeling) WAC Training Center Fort Des Moines, Iowa	193A-33	2	Men's restroom, women's restroom	Men's: 3 Women's: 2	Partitioned w/ doors	1 in men's restroom	Individual w/o partition	0	
EMB	188660	2	Communal restrooms (1 per floor with separate rooms for showers, sinks, toilets)	9	partitioned w/o doors	6	individual; no partitions	8 shower heads	Open gang shower w/ open drying/changing room w/ bench
Post Hospital and Drill Hall WAC Training Center Fort Des Moines, Iowa	193A-39	8	Bsmt: Men's restroom (toilets, sink) 1st Flr: 1 men's & 1 women's (toilets, sinks) 2nd Flr: 1 men's, 1 women's (toilets, sinks), additional restroom (sink, toilet, shower) 3rd Flr: 1 men's & 1 womens (full-sinks, toilets, showers)	Bsmt, M: 2 1st flr, M: 2, W: 2 2nd flr, M: 3, W: 2, other: 1 3rd flr, M: 2, W: 1	All partitioned except in restrooms with 1 toilet each; All except men's restrooms on 2nd & 3rd floor have doors	Bsmt, Men's: 1 1st flr, Men's: 2 2nd flr, Men's: 1	Individual w/o partition	2nd flr: 1 each 3rd flr, M: 2, W: 1	Partitioned shower stalls; no benches or changing stalls
Nurses' Quarters	1100-361								
Typical Layout Diagrams for WAAC Battalion Organization	614-701								
Mobilization General Hospital Nurses Quarters Officers Quarters	1100-2136								

Building Type	Drawing Number	Number of Restrooms	Restroom Configuration	Number of Toilets	Toilet Configuration	Number of Urinals	Urinal Configuration	Number of Showers/ Tubs	Shower Configuration
See legend or list type of building of not included in legend	Identifying number	How many restrooms in building	What type of restroom: guest bath (e.g., men's water closet by date room) and components of each restroom (full--toilet, urinal, washroom, showers; or different combinations thereof)	how many toilets in each restroom	are toilets partitioned; do they have doors	how many urinals in each bathroom	partitioned or not; individual urinals, or trough.	how many showers in each bathroom	partitioned or non-partitioned shower stalls, with or without benches/changing stall; open shower room with central water head, etc.
Mobilization General Hospital Nurses Quarters Officers Quarters	1100-2137								
Mobilization General Hospital Nurses Quarters Officers Quarters	1100-2138								
Mobilization General Hospital Nurses Quarters Officers Quarters	1100-2139								
Mobilization General Hospital Nurses Quarters Officers Quarters	1100-2140								
Option 1: Mobilization General Hospital Nurses Quarters	1100-2135	6	4 full restrooms with sinks, toilets, showers, tubs for nurses, 1 private bath for officer, 1 washroom (toilet, sink) for maid	community restrooms: 3; private bath: 1; maid's toilet: 1	Partitioned with doors in community restrooms	0		community restrooms: 1 shower, 1 tub private bath: 1 tub	Partitioned with changing stalls and benches
Option 2: Mobilization General Hospital Officers Quarters	1100-2135 (Same dwg as above, different occupant)	6	4 full restrooms with sinks, toilets, urinals, showers; 1 private bath; 1 washroom (toilet, sink) for maid	community restrooms: 2; private bath: 1; maid's toilet: 1	Partitioned with doors in community restrooms	2 each	Individual urinal; no partition	community restrooms: 2 showers private bath: 1 tub	Partitioned with changing stalls and benches
Mobilization Buildings WAC Barracks	700-3560	1	Bath/showers, sinks, toilets separated into defined spaces	6	Partitioned with doors	0		6	Partitioned w/o benches
Mobilization Buildings WAC Barracks	700-3561								
Mobilization Buildings WAC Barracks	700-3562								
Mobilization Buildings WAC Barracks	700-3563								
Nurses' Quarters	1100-360	2	1 restroom shared by 2 units (8 people). Each includes 2 sinks, 1 toilet, 1 shower	1	Partitioned with door	0		1	Partitioned with doors and changing space

Building Type	Drawing Number	Number of Restrooms	Restroom Configuration	Number of Toilets	Toilet Configuration	Number of Urinals	Urinal Configuration	Number of Showers/Tubs	Shower Configuration
See legend or list type of building of not included in legend	Identifying number	How many restrooms in building	What type of restroom: guest bath (e.g., men's water closet by date room) and components of each restroom (full--toilet, urinal, washroom, showers; or different combinations thereof)	how many toilets in each restroom	are toilets partitioned; do they have doors	how many urinals in each bathroom	partitioned or not; individual urinals, or trough.	how many showers in each bathroom	partitioned or non-partitioned shower stalls, with or without benches/changing stall; open shower room with central water head, etc.
W	188697	4	2 communal restrooms (toilets, sinks, showers) 2 semi-private baths (shared between 2 single rooms)	Communal 1st floor: 3 2nd floor: 5 Semi-private: 1	partitioned w/ doors	0		Communal 1st flr: 3 2nd flr: 4 Semi-private: 1	Partitioned w/ changing stalls (not attached to shower stalls)
W	188699	4	2 communal restrooms (toilets, sinks, showers) 2 semi-private baths (shared between 2 single rooms)	Communal 1st floor: 3 2nd floor: 5 Semi-private: 1	partitioned w/ doors	0		Communal 1st flr: 3 2nd flr: 4 Semi-private: 1	Partitioned w/ changing stalls (not attached to shower stalls)
W	188702	6	2 communal restrooms (toilets, sinks, showers) 2 private baths (attached to PO rooms) 2 small restrooms (toilet, sink)	Communal toilets: 16 others: 1	partitioned w/ doors	0		Communal: 14 Private: 1	Partitioned w/ changing stalls w/ benches (not attached to shower stalls)
Mobilization Buildings Conversion of Existing 74 Man Barracks for WAC	700-3570	2 (one on each floor)	Full restrooms with toilets, sinks, showers	3 3 existing were removed from 1st flr to make room for partitions	Partitions with doors added for conversion	1 (to be removed)	trough	3 (replaced existing gang shower) + 1 on 2nd flr in location of urinal trough	Partitioned shower stalls with changing stalls
Mobilization Buildings Conversion of Existing 74 Man Barracks for WAC	700-3571								
Mobilization Buildings WAC BOQ	700-3565	3	2 full restrooms with toilets, sinks, shower; 1 servants toilet with sink	Full restrooms, 2; Servant's toilet, 1	Partitioned with doors	1 (to be added if occupied by men)	Individual urinal; no partition	1 Shower; 1 tub/shower	Non-partitioned stall & tub
Mobilization Buildings WAC BOQ	700-3566								
Mobilization Buildings WAC BOQ	700-3567								
Mobilization Buildings WAC BOQ	700-3568								
Typical Layout Diagram for Camouflage Demonstration - Practice Area	614-1601								

Building Type	Drawing Number	Number of Restrooms	Restroom Configuration	Number of Toilets	Toilet Configuration	Number of Urinals	Urinal Configuration	Number of Showers/Tubs	Shower Configuration
See legend or list type of building of not included in legend	Identifying number	How many restrooms in building	What type of restroom: guest bath (e.g., men's water closet by date room) and components of each restroom (full--toilet, urinal, washroom, showers; or different combinations thereof)	how many toilets in each restroom	are toilets partitioned; do they have doors	how many urinals in each bathroom	partitioned or not; individual urinals, or trough.	how many showers in each bathroom	partitioned or non-partitioned shower stalls, with or without benches/changing stall; open shower room with central water head, etc.
W	312559	2	Communal restroom w/ toilets, sinks, showers Private bath (CPO)	Communal: 18 Private: 1	partitioned w/o doors	0		Communal: 11 shower heads Private: 1	Open gang showers (2 rooms, 1 w/ 7 showers, 1 w/ 4) Private: shower stall
W	312559-2	4	3 Communal restrooms (toilets, sinks, showers) 1 Private bath	Communal: 2 w/ 5 each; 1 w/ 3 Private: 1	partitioned w/ doors	0		Communal: 3 each Private: 1	Partitioned shower stalls w/ shared drying/changing area
W	188767	3	2 communal restrooms (toilets, sinks, showers) 1 private bath for officer	Communal 1st flr: 11 2nd flr: 13 Private: 1	partitioned w/ doors	0		1st flr: 8 showers, 2 tubs 2nd flr: 10 showers, 2 tubs	Partitioned w/ changing stalls (not attached to shower stalls)
Symbols for Camouflage - General Plan	614-1603								
Typical Layout Diagrams for one company of WAC	614-t.o.738								
Nurses & WAVE Officers	317319	8	4 Central restrooms w/ separate toilet, washrooms, and shower rooms 3 Private baths (toilet sink, shower) 1 visitors toilet (toilet, sink)	Central 1st flr: 2 2nd flr: 4 Others: 1	partitioned w/ doors	0		Central 1st flr: 2 2nd flr: 3 Private: 1	Indvidual shower stalls w/ common drying/changing area
MW	256516	5	2 Shared toilet & washrooms 2 shared shower rooms 1 men's toilet	Shared:16 Men's: 1	Shared: partitioned w/ doors	0		12 showers; 1 tub	Partitioned w/ changing stalls; no benches
MW	256517	5	2 Shared toilet & washrooms 2 shared shower rooms 1 men's toilet	Shared:16 Men's: 1	Shared: partitioned w/ doors	0		12 showers; 1 tub	Partitioned w/ changing stalls; no benches
EWB	271541	8	4 Central Restrooms w/ separate toilet, washrooms, and shower rooms 2 Private baths for POs (toilet sink, shower) 2 Powder Rooms (toilet, sink)	Central: 8 others: 1	partitioned w/ doors	0		Central: 5 PO: 1	Central restrooms: partitioned shower stalls w/ changing stalls and benches PO: Individual shower stall

Building Type	Drawing Number	Number of Restrooms	Restroom Configuration	Number of Toilets	Toilet Configuration	Number of Urinals	Urinal Configuration	Number of Showers/ Tubs	Shower Configuration
See legend or list type of building of not included in legend	Identifying number	How many restrooms in building	What type of restroom: guest bath (e.g., men's water closet by date room) and components of each restroom (full--toilet, urinal, washroom, showers; or different combinations thereof)	how many toilets in each restroom	are toilets partitioned; do they have doors	how many urinals in each bathroom	partitioned or not; individual urinals, or trough.	how many showers in each bathroom	partitioned or non-partitioned shower stalls, with or without benches/changing stall; open shower room with central water head, etc.
SP (Women's Club)	291251								
SP (Women's Club)	291252	2	1 Central Restroom (toilets, sinks, showers) 1 small men's restroom (toilet, sink)	Central: 2 Men's: 1	partitioned w/ doors	0		Central: 12	1 Open shower room w/ 8 shower heads 4 individual shower stalls
SP (Women's Club)	291254	4	1 Women's restroom (number & arrangement of fixtures not indicated) 2 Men's restrooms (toilets, urinals, sinks) 1 toilet room	Women's: not given Men's: 2, 1 other: 1	partitioned w/ doors	Men's: 2, 1	individual; no partitions	0	
BOQ	256638	3	2 Communal restrooms (toilets, sinks, showers) 1 men's lav near lobby	Communal: 5 Private: 1	partitioned w/ doors	0		1st floor: 4 2nd floor: 6	Partitioned shower stalls w/ changing stalls & benches
Mobilization Buildings WAC Barracks	700-3560.1	1	Full restroom with toilets, sinks, showers (divided into 3 sections)	8	Partitioned with doors	0		8	Partitioned shower stalls w/ changing stall, w/o benches
Mobilization Buildings Conversion of Existing Detachment Barracks for WAC	700-3585	3	2 restrooms with lavatory and toilets, 1 separate shower room	4	Partitioned with doors	0		8	Partitioned shower stalls with changing stall; 2 stalls have benches
Mobilization Buildings Conversion of Existing Detachment Barracks for WAC	700-3586								
W	288273	2	1 communal restroom (separate washroom, toilet room, shower room) 1 private bath	Communal toilets: 5 Private: 1	partitioned w/ doors	0		Communal: 6 Private: 1	Communal bath: 4 shower heads in open room, 2 private stalls with changing stalls and benches
Mobilization Buildings Conversion of Hospital Barracks for WAC	700-3580	1	Full restroom with toilets, sinks, showers	5	Partitioned with doors	1 (to be removed)	trough	5	Partitioned with changing stall, no benches

Building Type	Drawing Number	Number of Restrooms	Restroom Configuration	Number of Toilets	Toilet Configuration	Number of Urinals	Urinal Configuration	Number of Showers/Tubs	Shower Configuration
See legend or list type of building of not included in legend	Identifying number	How many restrooms in building	What type of restroom: guest bath (e.g., men's water closet by date room) and components of each restroom (full--toilet, urinal, washroom, showers; or different combinations thereof)	how many toilets in each restroom	are toilets partitioned; do they have doors	how many urinals in each bathroom	partitioned or not; individual urinals, or trough.	how many showers in each bathroom	partitioned or non-partitioned shower stalls, with or without benches/changing stall; open shower room with central water head, etc.
Mobilization Buildings Conversion of Hospital Barracks for WAC	700-3581								
W	264793	13	Baths with toilet and shower shared by 2 rooms	1	No partitions	0		1	Individual shower stall
WB	288273	2	1 shared restroom (separate toilet room, washroom, shower room) 1 private bath (PO)	Shared: 5 PO: 1	Shared: partitioned w/ doors	0		Shared: 6 PO: 1	Shared: 4 shower heads in open room, 2 individual stalls with changing area & bench PO: Individual stall
W	288280	3	Communal restroom (separate washroom, toilet room, shower room) Private bath (PO)	Communal: 5 Private: 1	partitioned w/ doors	0		Communal: 6 Private: 1	Communal: 4 shower heads in open room; 2 private stalls with changing stalls and benches
W	288282								
W	288283								
W	320100	2	Communal restroom (separate washroom, toilet room, shower room)	10	partitioned w/o doors	0 (removed for use by women)		Number of shower heads not indicated	Open shower room with drying room
W	304236	8	6 Communal restrooms (toilets, sinks, showers, tubs) 1 Men's & 1 Women's restroom at entry	Communal restroom: 7 Men & Women not indicated	partitioned w/ doors	0		6 showers; 2 tubs	Showers: Partitioned with changing stalls & benches Tubs: Partitioned w/ changing area
W	304237	10	7 Communal restrooms (toilets, sinks, showers, tubs) 2 PO restrooms (toilets, sinks, shower/tub) 1 OIC bath	Communal restroom: 6 w/ 7 each, 1 w/ 3 each PO: 1, 2 OIC: 1	partitioned w/ doors	0		Communal: 6 w/ 6 showers, 2 tubs; 1 w/ 3 showers PO: 1 w/ 1 shower, 1 tub; 1 w/ 1 tub OIC: 1 tub	Communal and shared restrooms: showers partitioned w/ changing stall & bench; tubs partitioned with changing area

Building Type	Drawing Number	Number of Restrooms	Restroom Configuration	Number of Toilets	Toilet Configuration	Number of Urinals	Urinal Configuration	Number of Showers/ Tubs	Shower Configuration
See legend or list type of building of not included in legend	Identifying number	How many restrooms in building	What type of restroom: guest bath (e.g., men's water closet by date room) and components of each restroom (full--toilet, urinal, washroom, showers; or different combinations thereof)	how many toilets in each restroom	are toilets partitioned; do they have doors	how many urinals in each bathroom	partitioned or not; individual urinals, or trough.	how many showers in each bathroom	partitioned or non-partitioned shower stalls, with or without benches/changing stall; open shower room with central water head, etc.
W	257696	2	2 communal restrooms (1 per floor with separate rooms for showers, sinks, toilets	10	partitioned w/o doors	0		Shower room (number of shower heads not indicated)	Open shower room with drying room with benches
WB	257055								
SP (Swimming Pool)	304510 - 304511	2	1 Enlisted men's 1 WAVES Both have toilets, sinks, showers	WAVES: 3 EM: 5	partitioned w/ doors	EM: 8	individual; no partitions	WAVES: 4 EM: 13	Open gang shower room
W	257698	3	2 communal restrooms (1 per floor with separate rooms for showers, sinks, toilets); 1 private bath	Communal: 10 Private: 1	partitioned w/ doors	0		11	Open shower room with 9 shower heads and attached drying room; 2 individual partitioned showers w/ changing stall and bench
W	257701	3	2 communal restrooms (1 per floor with separate rooms for showers, sinks, toilets); 1 private bath	Communal: 10 Private: 1	partitioned w/ doors	0		11	Open shower room with 9 shower heads and attached drying room; 2 individual partitioned showers w/ changing stall and bench
W	257669	2	Communal restrooms (1 per floor with separate rooms for showers, sinks, toilets)	9	partitioned w/ doors	0		Shower room (number of shower heads not indicated)	Open shower room with drying room with benches
EW & EM	326815	6	2 Women's restrooms 2 Men's restrooms 2 Private baths (CPOs)	Women & Men: 6 each Private: 1	Women: partitioned w/ doors Men: partitioned w/o doors	4	individual; no partitions	4	Open shower room with bench for both men and women
W	326814	6	4 Communal restrooms (toilets, sinks, showers) 2 private baths for CPOs	Communal: 6 Private: 1	partitioned w/ doors	4	individual; no partitions	4	Open shower room with bench

Building Type	Drawing Number	Number of Restrooms	Restroom Configuration	Number of Toilets	Toilet Configuration	Number of Urinals	Urinal Configuration	Number of Showers/Tubs	Shower Configuration
See legend or list type of building of not included in legend	Identifying number	How many restrooms in building	What type of restroom: guest bath (e.g., men's water closet by date room) and components of each restroom (full--toilet, urinal, washroom, showers; or different combinations thereof)	how many toilets in each restroom	are toilets partitioned; do they have doors	how many urinals in each bathroom	partitioned or not; individual urinals, or trough.	how many showers in each bathroom	partitioned or non-partitioned shower stalls, with or without benches/changing stall; open shower room with central water head, etc.
W	257734	2	Communal restrooms (1 per floor with separate rooms for showers, sinks, toilets)	9	partitioned w/ doors	0		Shower room (number of shower heads not indicated)	Open shower room with drying room
MW	290949	7	2 Shared toilet & washrooms 2 shared shower rooms 1 men's toilet 2 private baths (NCO)	Shared: 7 Men's: 1 NCO: 1	partitioned with doors	Men's toilet: 1	individual; no partitions	8	Partitioned with changing stalls & benches
SP (Office, Lunch, Locker)	364804	5	1 restroom near first aid (toilet, sink) 1 colored women's restroom, 1 white women's restroom, 1 colored men's restroom, 1 white men's restroom (all w/ toilets, sinks, showers)	Women's: 5 Men's: 2 Other: 1	partitioned w/ doors	Men's: 1	individual; no partition	Women's: 7 Men's: 2	Women's: Individual partitioned shower stalls Men's: open gang showers
WAC Training Center Fort Des Moines, Iowa	194A-12								
W	342059	2	1 communal restroom (toilets, sinks, showers) 1 private bath	Communal: 10 Private: 1	partitioned w/ doors	0		Communal: 12 Private: 1	2 open shower rooms with 4 shower heads each; 4 individual shower stalls w/ changing stalls & benches
W	328676	3	2 communal restrooms (separate washroom, toilets, shower room) 1 private bath	Communal: 5 Private: 1	partitioned w/ doors	0		Communal: 6 Private: 1	Partitioned stalls w/ changing stalls & benches
WAVE Mess Hall	328687	0							
W	328678								
WAVE Clinic	328711	4	1/2 bath w/ toilet & sink	1 each	1 restroom has partitioned toilet	0		0	

Building Type	Drawing Number	Number of Restrooms	Restroom Configuration	Number of Toilets	Toilet Configuration	Number of Urinals	Urinal Configuration	Number of Showers/ Tubs	Shower Configuration
See legend or list type of building of not included in legend	Identifying number	How many restrooms in building	What type of restroom: guest bath (e.g., men's water closet by date room) and components of each restroom (full--toilet, urinal, washroom, showers; or different combinations thereof)	how many toilets in each restroom	are toilets partitioned; do they have doors	how many urinals in each bathroom	partitioned or not; individual urinals, or trough.	how many showers in each bathroom	partitioned or non-partitioned shower stalls, with or without benches/changing stall; open shower room with central water head, etc.
EWB	329667 - 329668	8	3 Central restrooms w/ separate toilet, washrooms, and shower rooms 4 shared restrooms for officers (toilet, sink, shower) 1 guest restroom	Central: 8 Shared: 1 Guest: 1	partitioned w/ doors	0		Central: 5 Shared: 1	Individual shower stalls w/ common drying/changing area w/ bench
W	309299	2	1 Communal restroom (toilets, sinks, showers) 1 private bath (CPO)	Communal: 10 Private: 1	partitioned w/ doors	0		12	2 gang shower rooms with 4 shower heads each; 4 partitioned shower stalls w/ changing stalls & benches
EWB	347315	2	Central restrooms w/ toilets, sinks, showers, tubs	10	partitioned w/ doors	0		8 showers, 1 tub	Open gang shower room w/ 8 shower heads & separate drying room w/ bench; Bathtub is partitioned w/ door
SP (Lunch, Locker)	309610	6	2 Men's(toilets, sinks, showers); 2 Women's (toilets, sinks, showers); 2 small washrooms (toilet, sink)	Large men's rr: 2 Small men: 1 Large women: 8 Small women: 2 others: 1	partitioned w/ doors	Large men: 3 small men: 2	individual; no partition	Large men: 8 large women: 12 small men: 1 small women: 2	Large men's restroom: open gang shower room Women's & small men's restroom: partitioned shower stalls
SP Auditorium	360741	6	1 ladies restroom 1 men's restroom 2 locker room restrooms 2 small restrooms for each dressing room	Ladies: 2 Men's: 2 LR: 3, 5 DR: 1 each	partitioned w/ doors	Men's: 3	individual w/o partitions	Locker Room restrooms: 1 w/ 11, 1 w/ 8	Partitioned shower stalls; some have changing stalls w/ benches
SP (Dispensary)	370691	15	1 large restroom (toilets, sinks, showers) 6 shared restrooms (2 rooms share w/ toilet, sink, shower) 8 small restrooms w/ toilet & sink	large: 3 shared: 1 small: 1	partitioned w/ doors	0		large: 2 showers, 1 tub shared: 1 shower	Individual shower stalls large restroom: showers & tub partitioned w/ changing area

Building Type	Drawing Number	Number of Restrooms	Restroom Configuration	Number of Toilets	Toilet Configuration	Number of Urinals	Urinal Configuration	Number of Showers/Tubs	Shower Configuration
See legend or list type of building of not included in legend	Identifying number	How many restrooms in building	What type of restroom: guest bath (e.g., men's water closet by date room) and components of each restroom (full--toilet, urinal, washroom, showers; or different combinations thereof)	how many toilets in each restroom	are toilets partitioned; do they have doors	how many urinals in each bathroom	partitioned or not; individual urinals, or trough.	how many showers in each bathroom	partitioned or non-partitioned shower stalls, with or without benches/changing stall; open shower room with central water head, etc.
SP (Admin.)	342622	5	2 Men's; 2 Women's; 1 Private (OD Office)	1	no partitions	0		0	
Study for Typical Landscape Development Plan	614-1117								
BOQ	360765	4	2 Central Restrooms (toilets, sinks, showers) 2 Shared for single rooms (toilet, sink, shower)	Central: 4 Shared: 1	partitioned w/ doors	0		Central: 3 Shared: 1	Central restrooms: partitioned shower stalls w/ separate changing stalls and benches Shared: Individual shower stall
SP (Ships Service Bldg)	360764	3	Officer's Toilet EW Toilet Small restroom near post office	Officers & EW: 2 other: 1	partitioned w/ doors	0		0	
SP (Subsistence Building)	360777	7	1 Men's Restroom 1 Women's Restroom 2 Restrooms (Men's LR) 2 Restrooms (Women's LR) 1 Officers' Restroom	Men's RR: 1 Women's RR: 2 Locker Rooms: 1 Officer's: 2	partitioned w/ doors	Men's RR: 1	individual; no partition	0	
SP Auditorium & Gym	361229	6	1 ladies restroom 1 men's restroom 2 locker room restrooms 2 small restrooms for each dressing room	Ladies: 2 Men's: 2 LR: 3, 5 DR: 1 each	partitioned w/ doors	Men's: 3	individual w/o partitions	Locker Room restrooms: 1 w/ 11, 1 w/ 8	Partitioned shower stalls; some have changing stalls w/ benches
EWB	339687 - 339688	11	4 Central Restrooms (toilets, sinks, showers) 1 Men's restroom 1 Women's restroom 2 Private restrooms (adjacent to offices) 3 CPO restroom	Central: 5 others: 1	partitioned w/ doors	Men's: 1	individual w/ partition	Central: 5 showers, 1 tub CPO: 1	Partitioned shower stalls w/ changing stalls & benches; tub partitioned w/ changing area

Building Type	Drawing Number	Number of Restrooms	Restroom Configuration	Number of Toilets	Toilet Configuration	Number of Urinals	Urinal Configuration	Number of Showers/Tubs	Shower Configuration
See legend or list type of building of not included in legend	Identifying number	How many restrooms in building	What type of restroom: guest bath (e.g., men's water closet by date room) and components of each restroom (full--toilet, urinal, washroom, showers; or different combinations thereof)	how many toilets in each restroom	are toilets partitioned; do they have doors	how many urinals in each bathroom	partitioned or not; individual urinals, or trough.	how many showers in each bathroom	partitioned or non-partitioned shower stalls, with or without benches/changing stall; open shower room with central water head, etc.
SP (Dispensary)	373477	5	1 Men's Restroom (toilet, sink) 1 Women's Restroom (toilet, sink) 3 restrooms attached to wards w/ toilet, sink, shower)	1	partitioned w/ doors	Men's: 1	individual; no partition	Ward bathrooms: 1 each	Individual shower stalls
W	373486	4	2 communal restrooms (separate washroom, toilets, shower room) 1 private bath (lieut.) 1 small toilet room near entry	Communal: 5 others: 1	partitioned w/ doors	0		Communal: 6 showers, 1 tub Private: 1 shower	Showers partitioned w/ changing stalls & benches Tubs partitioned w/ changing space & bench
WAVES Dispensary	409987	6	4 Shared restrooms (toilets, sinks, showers) 2 private restrooms w/ toilet & sink	Shared: 2 Private: 1	partitioned w/ doors	0		1 shower each; 1 first floor bath has tub	Individual shower stalls (1st floor w/ changing area & benches); Tub w/o partition
BOQ	306882	4	2 Central Restrooms (toilets, sinks, showers) 2 Shared for single rooms (toilet, sink, shower)	Central 1st flr: 3 2nd flr: 6 Shared: 1	partitioned w/ doors	0		Central 1st flr: 3 2nd flr: 4 Shared: 1	Partitioned shower stalls w/ changing stalls & benches
BOQ	306883	4	2 Central Restrooms (toilets, sinks, showers) 2 Shared for single rooms (toilet, sink, shower)	Central 1st flr: 3 2nd flr: 6 Shared: 1	partitioned w/ doors	0		Central 1st flr: 3 2nd flr: 4 Shared: 1	Partitioned shower stalls w/ changing stalls & benches
SP (Base Site Plan)	401885								
SP Dispensary	401836	5	2 full restrooms w/ toilets, sinks, showers 3 restrooms in medical office wing; 2 small (toilet, sink), 1 larger w/ toilets, sinks	Full restrooms: 5 Small RR: 1 Large RR: 3	partitioned w/ doors	0		N/A (poor dwg quality)	
Barrack - WAC - Apartment Type	SK210109	27	Full bath with toilet, sink, and shower/tub	1		0		1 tub each	

Building Type	Drawing Number	Number of Restrooms	Restroom Configuration	Number of Toilets	Toilet Configuration	Number of Urinals	Urinal Configuration	Number of Showers/Tubs	Shower Configuration
See legend or list type of building of not included in legend	Identifying number	How many restrooms in building	What type of restroom: guest bath (e.g., men's water closet by date room) and components of each restroom (full--toilet, urinal, washroom, showers; or different combinations thereof)	how many toilets in each restroom	are toilets partitioned; do they have doors	how many urinals in each bathroom	partitioned or not; individual urinals, or trough.	how many showers in each bathroom	partitioned or non-partitioned shower stalls, with or without benches/changing stall; open shower room with central water head, etc.
Barrack - WAC - Hotel Type	SK210108	1 per floor + 1 small restroom off of lobby	Full restrooms with toilets, sinks, showers, and tubs Small guest restroom: toilet & sink	8	Partitioned w/ doors	0		4 showers, 2 tubs	Partitioned with changing area and benches
WM	450230	10 on 1st floor	Private/Shared restrooms (toilets, sinks, showers) 1 men's restroom (toilet, urinal, sink)	1 - 2 each	Restrooms with more than 1 toilet: partitioned w/ doors	Men's toilet: 1	individual; no partitions	1	Individual shower stalls
Emergency Type Construction, EW Barracks	DEFE2102 01-1	2	Full restrooms with toilets, sinks, showers, & tubs	5	Partitioned with doors	0		4 showers, 1 tub	Partitioned with changing area; bench across from shower stalls
Emergency Type Construction, EW Barracks	DEFE2102 01-2								
Emergency Type Construction, EW Barracks	DEFE2507 04-1	2	Full restrooms with toilets, sinks, showers, and tubs	4	Partitioned w/ doors	0		4 showers, 1 tub	Partitioned with changing area and benches
MW	472352	5	2 shared toilet/powder rooms 2 shared shower/drying & washing rooms 1 men's toilet	Shared: 8 Men's: 1	partitioned w/ doors	0		7 showers; 1 tub	Showers: Partitioned w/o changing stalls Bathtub: Partitioned with changing area
MW	472353	5	2 shared toilet/powder rooms 2 shared shower/drying & washing rooms 1 men's toilet	Shared: 8 Men's: 1	partitioned w/ doors	0		7 showers; 1 tub	Showers: Partitioned w/o changing stalls Bathtub: Partitioned with changing area
MW	472354	7	3 shared toilet/powder rooms 3 shared shower/drying & washing rooms 1 men's toilet	Shared: 10 Men's: 1	partitioned w/ doors	0		7 showers; 1 tub	Showers: Partitioned w/o changing stalls Bathtub: Partitioned with changing area
MW	472355	7	3 shared toilet/powder rooms 3 shared shower/drying & washing rooms 1 men's toilet	Shared: 10 Men's: 1	partitioned w/ doors	0		7 showers; 1 tub	Showers: Partitioned w/o changing stalls Bathtub: Partitioned with changing area

Building Type	Drawing Number	Number of Restrooms	Restroom Configuration	Number of Toilets	Toilet Configuration	Number of Urinals	Urinal Configuration	Number of Showers/ Tubs	Shower Configuration
See legend or list type of building of not included in legend	Identifying number	How many restrooms in building	What type of restroom: guest bath (e.g., men's water closet by date room) and components of each restroom (full--toilet, urinal, washroom, showers; or different combinations thereof)	how many toilets in each restroom	are toilets partitioned; do they have doors	how many urinals in each bathroom	partitioned or not; individual urinals, or trough.	how many showers in each bathroom	partitioned or non-partitioned shower stalls, with or without benches/changing stall; open shower room with central water head, etc.
MW	472366	7	3 shared toilet/powder rooms 3 shared shower/drying & washing rooms 1 guest toilet	Shared: 10 Guest: 1	partitioned w/ doors	0		7 showers; 1 tub	Showers: Partitioned w/o changing stalls Bathtub: Partitioned with changing area
MW	472367	7	3 shared toilet/powder rooms 3 shared shower/drying & washing rooms 1 guest toilet	Shared: 10 Guest: 1	partitioned w/ doors	0		7 showers; 1 tub	Showers: Partitioned w/o changing stalls Bathtub: Partitioned with changing area
MW	472519	5	2 shared toilet rooms 2 shared shower/hair drying & washing room 1 guest bath	Shared: 10 Guest: 1	partitioned w/ doors	0		7 showers; 1 tub	Showers: Partitioned w/ changing stalls Bathtubs: Partitioned with changing area
MW	472518	5	2 shared toilet rooms 2 shared shower/hair drying & washing room 1 guest bath	Shared: 10 Guest: 1	partitioned w/ doors	0		7 showers; 1 tub	Showers: Partitioned w/ changing stalls Bathtubs: Partitioned with changing area
BOQ	500363	3	2 large restrooms (toilets, sinks, showers) 1 small restroom (1 toilet, 1 sink, 1 shower)	Large restrooms: 6 Small restroom: 1	partitioned w/ doors	Large RR: 3 Small RR: 0	individual; no partitions	Large RR: 3 Small RR: 1	Partitioned shower stalls w/ shared drying/changing area
EMB	500359	2 (1 on each floor)	Toilets, urinals, washroom, showers in each		partitioned w/o doors		non-partitioned; individual	3	partitioned w/ bench
EMB	500360	1	Toilets, urinals, washroom, showers in each		partitioned w/o doors		non-partitioned; individual	3	partitioned w/ bench
EWB	500361	3	Toilets, sinks, showers, tubs			0		2 tubs, 4 showers	Partitioned w/ benches
EWB	500362	2	Toilets, sinks, showers, tubs			0		2 tubs, 4 showers	Partitioned w/ benches
BOQ	496842	3	2 large restrooms (toilets, sinks, showers) 1 small restroom (for SO's)	Large restrooms: 6 Small restroom: 1	partitioned w/ doors	Large RR: 3 Small RR: 0	individual; no partitions	Large RR: 3 Small RR: 1	Partitioned shower stalls w/ shared drying/changing area
EWB	496812	3	Toilets, sinks, showers, tubs			0		2 tubs, 4 showers	Partitioned w/ benches
EWB	496830	2	Toilets, sinks, showers, tubs			0		2 tubs, 4 showers	Partitioned w/ benches

Building Type	Drawing Number	Number of Restrooms	Restroom Configuration	Number of Toilets	Toilet Configuration	Number of Urinals	Urinal Configuration	Number of Showers/ Tubs	Shower Configuration
See legend or list type of building of not included in legend	Identifying number	How many restrooms in building	What type of restroom: guest bath (e.g., men's water closet by date room) and components of each restroom (full--toilet, urinal, washroom, showers; or different combinations thereof)	how many toilets in each restroom	are toilets partitioned; do they have doors	how many urinals in each bathroom	partitioned or not; individual urinals, or trough.	how many showers in each bathroom	partitioned or non-partitioned shower stalls, with or without benches/changing stall; open shower room with central water head, etc.
Nurses' or WAF Officers' Quarters	DEF250706-1	33 total (28 private, 4 tub rooms, 1 small restroom adjacent to waiting room	Private with toilet, sink, shower Small room with single bathtub Small restroom with toilet & sink	1	No partitions (all private baths)	0		1 shower each private bath; 1 tub in tub rooms	No partitions
Nurses' or WAF Officers' Quarters	DEF250706-2								
Airmens Dormitory	210171-2	4	Full restrooms with toilets, urinals, sinks, and showers	5	Partitioned with doors	3	Individual with no partitions	4	Partitioned shower stalls; no changing stalls; 1 long bench on wall opposite showers
Airmens Dormitory	210171-3								
Airmens Dormitory	210171-7								
Airmens Dormitory	210171-8								
Airmens Dormitory	210171-9								
Airmens Dormitory	210171-1								
Airmens Dormitory Modified for Women	210189-1								
Airmens Dormitory Modified for Women	210189-2	4	Full restrooms with toilets, sinks, and showers	5	Partitioned with doors	0		3 showers, 1 tub	Partitioned shower stalls; no changing stalls for showers or tub; 1 long bench on wall opposite showers
Airmens Dormitory Modified for Women	210189-3								
Airmens Dormitory Modified for Women	210189-3								

Building Type	Drawing Number	Number of Restrooms	Restroom Configuration	Number of Toilets	Toilet Configuration	Number of Urinals	Urinal Configuration	Number of Showers/ Tubs	Shower Configuration
See legend or list type of building of not included in legend	Identifying number	How many restrooms in building	What type of restroom: guest bath (e.g., men's water closet by date room) and components of each restroom (full--toilet, urinal, washroom, showers; or different combinations thereof)	how many toilets in each restroom	are toilets partitioned; do they have doors	how many urinals in each bathroom	partitioned or not; individual urinals, or trough.	how many showers in each bathroom	partitioned or non-partitioned shower stalls, with or without benches/changing stall; open shower room with central water head, etc.
Airmens Dormitory Modified for Women	210189-4								
Airmens Dormitory Modified for Women	210189-5								
Airmens Dormitory Modified for Women	210189-6								
Airmens Dormitory Modified for Women	210189-7								
Airmens Dormitory Modified for Women	210189-8								
Airmens Dormitory Modified for Women	210189-9								
Airmens Dormitory Modified for Women	210189-10								
Airmens Dormitory Modified for Women	210189-11								
Airmens Dormitory Modified for Women	210189-12	4	Full restrooms with toilets, sinks, and showers	5	Partitioned with doors	0		3 showers, 1 tub	Partitioned shower stalls; no changing stalls for showers or tub; 1 long bench on wall opposite showers
Airmens Dormitory Modified for Women	210189-13								
Airmens Dormitory Modified for Women	210189-14								

Building Type	Drawing Number	Number of Restrooms	Restroom Configuration	Number of Toilets	Toilet Configuration	Number of Urinals	Urinal Configuration	Number of Showers/ Tubs	Shower Configuration
See legend or list type of building of not included in legend	Identifying number	How many restrooms in building	What type of restroom: guest bath (e.g., men's water closet by date room) and components of each restroom (full--toilet, urinal, washroom, showers; or different combinations thereof)	how many toilets in each restroom	are toilets partitioned; do they have doors	how many urinals in each bathroom	partitioned or not; individual urinals, or trough.	how many showers in each bathroom	partitioned or non-partitioned shower stalls, with or without benches/changing stall; open shower room with central water head, etc.
Airmens Dormitory Modified for Women	210189-15	4	Full restrooms with toilets, sinks, and showers	5	Partitioned with doors	0		3 showers, 1 tub	Partitioned shower stalls; no changing stalls for showers or tub; 1 long bench on wall opposite showers
Airmens Dormitory Modified for Women	210189-16	4	Full restrooms with toilets, sinks, and showers	5	Partitioned with doors	0		3 showers, 1 tub	Partitioned shower stalls; no changing stalls for showers or tub; 1 long bench on wall opposite showers
Airmens Dormitory Modified for Women	210189-17	4	Full restrooms with toilets, sinks, and showers	5	Partitioned with doors	0		3 showers, 1 tub	Partitioned shower stalls; no changing stalls for showers or tub; 1 long bench on wall opposite showers
Airmens Dormitory Modified for Women	210189-18								
Airmens Dormitory Modified for Women	210189-19								
Airmens Dormitory Modified for Women	210189-20								
Airmens Dormitory Modified for Women	210189-21								
Airmens Dormitory Modified for Women	210189-22								
Airmens Dormitory Modified for Women	210189-23								
Airmens Dormitory Modified for Women	210189-24								

Building Type	Drawing Number	Number of Restrooms	Restroom Configuration	Number of Toilets	Toilet Configuration	Number of Urinals	Urinal Configuration	Number of Showers/ Tubs	Shower Configuration
See legend or list type of building of not included in legend	Identifying number	How many restrooms in building	What type of restroom: guest bath (e.g., men's water closet by date room) and components of each restroom (full--toilet, urinal, washroom, showers; or different combinations thereof)	how many toilets in each restroom	are toilets partitioned; do they have doors	how many urinals in each bathroom	partitioned or not; individual urinals, or trough.	how many showers in each bathroom	partitioned or non-partitioned shower stalls, with or without benches/changing stall; open shower room with central water head, etc.
Airmens Dormitory Modified for Women	210189-25								
Airmens Dormitory Modified for Women	210189-26								
Airmens Dormitory Modified for Women	210189-27	4	Full restrooms with toilets, sinks, and showers	5	Partitioned with doors	0		3 showers, 1 tub	Partitioned shower stalls; no changing stalls for showers or tub; 1 long bench on wall opposite showers
Airmens Dormitory Modified for Women	210189-28								
Airmens Dormitory Modified for Women	210190-1								
Airmens Dormitory Modified for Women	210190-2	4	Full restrooms with toilets, sinks, and showers	5	Partitioned with doors	0		3 showers, 1 tub	Partitioned shower stalls; no changing stalls for showers or tub; 1 long bench on wall opposite showers
Airmens Dormitory Modified for Women	210190-3								
Airmens Dormitory Modified for Women	210190-4								
Airmens Dormitory Modified for Women	210190-5								
Airmens Dormitory Modified for Women	210190-6								
Airmens Dormitory Modified for Women	210190-7								

Building Type	Drawing Number	Number of Restrooms	Restroom Configuration	Number of Toilets	Toilet Configuration	Number of Urinals	Urinal Configuration	Number of Showers/ Tubs	Shower Configuration
See legend or list type of building of not included in legend	Identifying number	How many restrooms in building	What type of restroom: guest bath (e.g., men's water closet by date room) and components of each restroom (full--toilet, urinal, washroom, showers; or different combinations thereof)	how many toilets in each restroom	are toilets partitioned; do they have doors	how many urinals in each bathroom	partitioned or not; individual urinals, or trough.	how many showers in each bathroom	partitioned or non-partitioned shower stalls, with or without benches/changing stall; open shower room with central water head, etc.
Airmens Dormitory Modified for Women	210190-8								
Airmens Dormitory Modified for Women	210190-9								
Airmens Dormitory Modified for Women	210190-10								
Airmens Dormitory Modified for Women	210190-11								
Airmens Dormitory Modified for Women	210190-12	4	Full restrooms with toilets, sinks, and showers	5	Partitioned with doors	0		3 showers, 1 tub	Partitioned shower stalls; no changing stalls for showers or tub; 1 long bench on wall opposite showers
Airmens Dormitory Modified for Women	210190-13								
Airmens Dormitory Modified for Women	210190-14								
Airmens Dormitory Modified for Women	210190-15	4	Full restrooms with toilets, sinks, and showers	5	Partitioned with doors	0		3 showers, 1 tub	Partitioned shower stalls; no changing stalls for showers or tub; 1 long bench on wall opposite showers
Airmens Dormitory Modified for Women	210190-16	4	Full restrooms with toilets, sinks, and showers	5	Partitioned with doors	0		3 showers, 1 tub	Partitioned shower stalls; no changing stalls for showers or tub; 1 long bench on wall opposite showers

Building Type	Drawing Number	Number of Restrooms	Restroom Configuration	Number of Toilets	Toilet Configuration	Number of Urinals	Urinal Configuration	Number of Showers/ Tubs	Shower Configuration
See legend or list type of building of not included in legend	Identifying number	How many restrooms in building	What type of restroom: guest bath (e.g., men's water closet by date room) and components of each restroom (full--toilet, urinal, washroom, showers; or different combinations thereof)	how many toilets in each restroom	are toilets partitioned; do they have doors	how many urinals in each bathroom	partitioned or not; individual urinals, or trough.	how many showers in each bathroom	partitioned or non-partitioned shower stalls, with or without benches/changing stall; open shower room with central water head, etc.
Airmens Dormitory Modified for Women	210190-17	4	Full restrooms with toilets, sinks, and showers	5	Partitioned with doors	0		3 showers, 1 tub	Partitioned shower stalls; no changing stalls for showers or tub; 1 long bench on wall opposite showers
Airmens Dormitory Modified for Women	210190-18								
Airmens Dormitory Modified for Women	210190-19								
Airmens Dormitory Modified for Women	210190-20								
Airmens Dormitory Modified for Women	210190-21								
Airmens Dormitory Modified for Women	210190-22								
Airmens Dormitory Modified for Women	210190-23								
Airmens Dormitory Modified for Women	210190-24								
Airmens Dormitory Modified for Women	210190-25								
Airmens Dormitory Modified for Women	210190-26								
Airmens Dormitory Modified for Women	210190-27	4	Full restrooms with toilets, sinks, and showers	5	Partitioned with doors	0		3 showers, 1 tub	Partitioned shower stalls; no changing stalls for showers or tub; 1 long bench on wall opposite showers

Building Type	Drawing Number	Number of Restrooms	Restroom Configuration	Number of Toilets	Toilet Configuration	Number of Urinals	Urinal Configuration	Number of Showers/ Tubs	Shower Configuration
See legend or list type of building of not included in legend	Identifying number	How many restrooms in building	What type of restroom: guest bath (e.g., men's water closet by date room) and components of each restroom (full--toilet, urinal, washroom, showers; or different combinations thereof)	how many toilets in each restroom	are toilets partitioned; do they have doors	how many urinals in each bathroom	partitioned or not; individual urinals, or trough.	how many showers in each bathroom	partitioned or non-partitioned shower stalls, with or without benches/changing stall; open shower room with central water head, etc.
Airmens Dormitory Modified for Women	210190-28								
Airmens Dormitory Modified for Women	210193-1								
Airmens Dormitory Modified for Women	210193-2	6	Full restrooms with toilets, sinks, and showers	5	Partitioned with doors	0		3 showers, 1 tub	Partitioned shower stalls; no changing stalls for showers or tub; 1 long bench on wall opposite showers
Airmens Dormitory Modified for Women	210193-3	6	Full restrooms with toilets, sinks, and showers	5	Partitioned with doors	0		3 showers, 1 tub	Partitioned shower stalls; no changing stalls for showers or tub; 1 long bench on wall opposite showers
Airmens Dormitory Modified for Women	210193-4								
Airmens Dormitory Modified for Women	210193-6								
Airmens Dormitory Modified for Women	210193-7								
Airmens Dormitory Modified for Women	210193-8								
Airmens Dormitory Modified for Women	210193-13	6	Full restrooms with toilets, sinks, and showers	5	Partitioned with doors	0		3 showers, 1 tub	Partitioned shower stalls; no changing stalls for showers or tub; 1 long bench on wall opposite showers

Building Type	Drawing Number	Number of Restrooms	Restroom Configuration	Number of Toilets	Toilet Configuration	Number of Urinals	Urinal Configuration	Number of Showers/ Tubs	Shower Configuration
See legend or list type of building of not included in legend	Identifying number	How many restrooms in building	What type of restroom: guest bath (e.g., men's water closet by date room) and components of each restroom (full--toilet, urinal, washroom, showers; or different combinations thereof)	how many toilets in each restroom	are toilets partitioned; do they have doors	how many urinals in each bathroom	partitioned or not; individual urinals, or trough.	how many showers in each bathroom	partitioned or non-partitioned shower stalls, with or without benches/changing stall; open shower room with central water head, etc.
Airmens Dormitory Modified for Women	210193-21								
Airmens Dormitory Modified for Women	210193-22								
Airmens Dormitory Modified for Women	210193-23								
Airmens Dormitory Modified for Women	210193-27	6	Full restrooms with toilets, sinks, and showers	5	Partitioned with doors	0		3 showers, 1 tub	Partitioned shower stalls; no changing stalls for showers or tub; 1 long bench on wall opposite showers
Nurses or WAF Officers Quarters	SK250706-1	35	29 shared by 2 rooms 2 (toilet & sink) adjacent to lounge & waiting room 4 tub rooms	1		0		1 shower in shared baths; 1 tub in each tub room	
Nurses or WAF Officers Quarters	SK250706-2	Unit A: 35 Unit B: 31 Unit C: 27	29, 25, or 21 shared by 2 rooms 2 (toilet & sink) adjacent to lounge & waiting room 4 tub rooms	1		0		1 shower in shared baths; 1 tub in each tub room	
Nurses or WAF Officers Quarters	SK250709-1	Unit F: 10 Unit G: 8	6 or 8 shared by 2 rooms 1 (toilet & sink) adjacent to waiting room 1 community bath (toilet, sink, tub)	1	Toilet in community bathroom partitioned	0		1 shower in shared baths; 1 tub in community bath	Tub in community bath partitioned w/ door
Nurses or WAF Officers Quarters	SK250708-1	Unit D: 21 Unit E: 17	17 or 13 shared by 2 rooms 2 (toilet & sink) adjacent to lounge & waiting room 2 tub rooms	1		0		1 shower in shared baths; 1 tub in each tub room	

Building Type	Drawing Number	Number of Restrooms	Restroom Configuration	Number of Toilets	Toilet Configuration	Number of Urinals	Urinal Configuration	Number of Showers/Tubs	Shower Configuration
See legend or list type of building of not included in legend	Identifying number	How many restrooms in building	What type of restroom: guest bath (e.g., men's water closet by date room) and components of each restroom (full--toilet, urinal, washroom, showers; or different combinations thereof)	how many toilets in each restroom	are toilets partitioned; do they have doors	how many urinals in each bathroom	partitioned or not; individual urinals, or trough.	how many showers in each bathroom	partitioned or non-partitioned shower stalls, with or without benches/changing stall; open shower room with central water head, etc.
EMB	556010	5 (1 Enlisted on each floor and 1 Petty Officer on 2nd and 3rd floors)	Toilets, urinals, washroom, showers in each	Enlisted: 5; Petty Officer: 2	partitioned w/o doors	Enlisted: 3; Petty Officer 1	individual; non-partitioned in enlisted; partitioned in officer	2 for enlisted; 2 for officers	non-partitioned, 2 shower heads, 1 common drying space for enlisted; 2 partitioned showers for officer with benches/ changing stalls
EMB	556012	5 (1 Enlisted on each floor and 1 Petty Officer on 2nd and 3rd floors)	Toilets, urinals, washroom, showers in each	Enlisted: 5; Petty Officer: 2	partitioned w/o doors	Enlisted: 3; Petty Officer 1	individual; non-partitioned in enlisted; partitioned in officer	2 for enlisted; 2 for officers	non-partitioned, 2 shower heads, 1 common drying space for enlisted; 2 partitioned showers for officer with benches/ changing stalls
Air Force Dormitory for Enlisted Women	2101107-1	42	Bath with toilet and shower (2 rooms share); visitors toilet first floor; bathroom with 2 tubs (1 on each floor)	1	No partitions (all private baths)	0		1 in private baths; 2 tubs in tub rooms	Tubs are partitioned with changing areas
Air Force Dormitory for Enlisted Women	2101107-2								
Air Force Dormitory for Enlisted Women	2101109-1	28	25 baths (2 rooms share), 2 tub rooms, 1 visitors toilet	1	No partitions (all private baths)	0		1 in private baths; 2 tubs in tub rooms	Tubs are partitioned with changing areas
Air Force Dormitory for Enlisted Women	2101109-2								
EWB	621844								
EMB	621843	5 (1 Enlisted on each floor and 1 Petty Officer on 2nd and 3rd floors)	Toilets, urinals, washroom, showers in each		partitioned w/o doors		individual; non-partitioned in enlisted; partitioned in officer		non-partitioned, 2 shower heads, 1 common drying space for enlisted; 1 partitioned shower for officer

Building Type	Drawing Number	Number of Restrooms	Restroom Configuration	Number of Toilets	Toilet Configuration	Number of Urinals	Urinal Configuration	Number of Showers/Tubs	Shower Configuration
See legend or list type of building of not included in legend	Identifying number	How many restrooms in building	What type of restroom: guest bath (e.g., men's water closet by date room) and components of each restroom (full--toilet, urinal, washroom, showers; or different combinations thereof)	how many toilets in each restroom	are toilets partitioned; do they have doors	how many urinals in each bathroom	partitioned or not; individual urinals, or trough.	how many showers in each bathroom	partitioned or non-partitioned shower stalls, with or without benches/changing stall; open shower room with central water head, etc.
Women's BOQ	un-numbered	2	1 restroom each floor w/ toilets, sinks, showers, tubs	1st flr: 4 2nd flr: 5	partitioned w/ doors	0		2 showers; 1 tub	Showers partitioned w/o changing stall; Tubs partitioned w/ changing area
BOQ	un-numbered	2	1 restroom each floor w/ toilets, urinals, sinks, showers	1st flr: 5 2nd flr: 6	partitioned w/ doors	3 each	individual; no partitions	3	Partitioned shower stalls w/ common changing area w/ bench
EWB	un-numbered	3	2 restrooms for enlisted women (toilets, sinks, showers, tubs) 1 restroom for PO's (toilet, sinks, shower)	EW: 4 PO: 1	partitioned w/ doors	0		EW: 4 showers, 2 tubs PO: 1 shower	Partitioned shower stalls w/ common changing area w/ benches Tubs partitioned w/ changing area
EMB	un-numbered	4	2 restrooms for enlisted men (toilets, urinals, sinks, showers) 2 restrooms for petty officers (toilet, urinal, sink, shower)	EM: 4 PO: 1	partitioned w/ doors	EM: 3 PO: 1	individual; no partitions	EM: 3 PO: 1	Partitioned shower stalls w/ common changing area w/ bench
CPO Quarters	un-numbered	2	1 restroom each floor w/ toilets, urinals, sinks, showers	3	partitioned w/ doors	2	individual; no partitions	1st flr: 1 2nd flr: 2	Partitioned shower stalls w/ common changing area w/ bench
BOQ	539042	3	2 large restrooms (toilets, sinks, showers) 1 small restroom (for SO's)	Large restrooms: 6 Small restroom: 1	partitioned w/ doors	Large RR: 3 Small RR: 0	individual; no partitions	Large RR: 3 Small RR: 1	Partitioned shower stalls w/ shared drying/changing area
EMB	539037	1 Enlisted; 1 Officer	Toilets, urinals, washroom, showers in each		partitioned with doors		individual; non-partitioned in enlisted	3 for enlisted; 1 for officers	partitioned
EMB	539038		Toilets, urinals, washroom, showers in each		partitioned with doors		individual; non-partitioned in enlisted	3 for enlisted; 1 for officers	partitioned
EWB	539039								
EWB	539040								

Building Type	Drawing Number	Number of Restrooms	Restroom Configuration	Number of Toilets	Toilet Configuration	Number of Urinals	Urinal Configuration	Number of Showers/Tubs	Shower Configuration
See legend or list type of building of not included in legend	Identifying number	How many restrooms in building	What type of restroom: guest bath (e.g., men's water closet by date room) and components of each restroom (full--toilet, urinal, washroom, showers; or different combinations thereof)	how many toilets in each restroom	are toilets partitioned; do they have doors	how many urinals in each bathroom	partitioned or not; individual urinals, or trough.	how many showers in each bathroom	partitioned or non-partitioned shower stalls, with or without benches/changing stall; open shower room with central water head, etc.
BOQ	621837	13	10 shared bathrooms (1 for every 2 rooms) 1 men's restroom 1 women's restroom 1 small restroom near kitchen	1 each	men's & women's toilets partitioned w/ door	1 in men's restroom	individual w/ partition	Shared baths: 1 each	Individual shower stalls
BOQ	621838	28	25 shared bathrooms (1 for every 2 rooms) 1 men's restroom 1 women's restroom 1 small restroom near kitchen	1 each	men's & women's toilets partitioned w/ door	1 in men's restroom	individual w/ partition	Shared baths: 1 each	Individual shower stalls
Standard Components Layout	400140-1								
Standard Components Layout	400140-2	1 per unit	Toilet and shower (lavatory located in bedrooms)	1	No (private bath)	0		1	
Standard Components Layout	400140-3		Typical with toilets, sinks, showers, and bathtubs	7	Partitioned with doors	0		4 showers; 2 tubs	Partitioned with changing area & benches
EMB	658441	1	toilets, washroom, showers	2	partitioned w/o doors	none	n/a	2	partitioned; no benches/ changing stalls
EWB	658440	1	Toilets, lavatory, shower, tub	2	partitioned w/o doors	0		1 shower 1 tub	Shower stall; tub has curtain rod
Air Force Dormitory for Enlisted Women	210204-1	4	Full restrooms with toilets, sinks, and showers	5	Partitioned with doors	0		1st Floor: 3 showers, 1 tub 2nd Floor: 4 showers, 1 tub	Partitioned shower and bath stalls with doors and changing areas, no benches
Air Force Dormitory for Enlisted Women	210204-2								
Air Force Dormitory for Enlisted Women	210205-1	6	Full restrooms with toilets, sinks, and showers	1st flr: 5 2nd flr: 6	Partitioned with doors	0		1st flr: 3 showers, 1 tub 2nd flr: 4 showers, 1 tub	Partitioned shower and bath stalls with doors and changing areas, no benches
Air Force Dormitory for Enlisted Women	210205-2								

Building Type	Drawing Number	Number of Restrooms	Restroom Configuration	Number of Toilets	Toilet Configuration	Number of Urinals	Urinal Configuration	Number of Showers/ Tubs	Shower Configuration
See legend or list type of building of not included in legend	Identifying number	How many restrooms in building	What type of restroom: guest bath (e.g., men's water closet by date room) and components of each restroom (full--toilet, urinal, washroom, showers; or different combinations thereof)	how many toilets in each restroom	are toilets partitioned; do they have doors	how many urinals in each bathroom	partitioned or not; individual urinals, or trough.	how many showers in each bathroom	partitioned or non-partitioned shower stalls, with or without benches/changing stall; open shower room with central water head, etc.
EMB	665169	5 (3 enlisted; 2 Officer)	Toilets, urinals, washroom, showers in each	enlisted: 8; Petty Officer: 2	partitioned with doors	enlisted: 6; Petty Officer: none	non-partitioned; individual	6 for enlisted; 2 for officer	enlisted partitioned w/o doors; 2 benches; officer enclosed, no benches
EMB	665171	5 (3 enlisted; 2 Officer)	Toilets, urinals, washroom, showers in each	enlisted: 8; Petty Officer: 2	partitioned with doors	enlisted: 6; Petty Officer: none	non-partitioned; individual	6 for enlisted; 2 for officer	enlisted partitioned w/o doors; 2 benches; officer enclosed, no benches
EMB	665192	5 (3 enlisted; 2 Officer)	Toilets, urinals, washroom, showers in each	enlisted: 8; Petty Officer: 2	partitioned with doors	enlisted: 6; Petty Officer: none	partitioned in groups of 3; individual	6 for enlisted; 2 for officer	enlisted partitioned w/o doors; 2 benches; officer enclosed, no benches
EMB	665209	5 (3 enlisted; 2 Officer)	Toilets, urinals, washroom, showers in each	enlisted: 8; Petty Officer: 2	partitioned w/o doors	enlisted: 6; Petty Officer: none	non-partitioned; individual	6 for enlisted; 2 for officer	enlisted partitioned w/o doors; 2 benches; officer enclosed, no benches
BOQ	723357	6	1 Men's toilet (toilet, sink, urinal) 5 shared baths (toilet, shower)	1	Men's toilet: partitioned with door	Men's toilet: 1	individual w/ partition	1	Individual shower stalls
EMB	723347	4 (2 enlisted, 1 officer, 1 sick bay)	Toilets, urinals, washroom, showers in enlisted; no urinals in officer or sick bay	enlisted 6; officer 2; sick bay 1	partitioned in enlisted and officer w/o doors	enlisted 4; officer none; sick bay none	partitioned in groups of two; individual	2 for enlisted; 2 for officers	non-partitioned, 2 shower heads, no benches/changing rooms for enlisted; partitioned, no benches/ changing rooms in officer and sick bay

Building Type	Drawing Number	Number of Restrooms	Restroom Configuration	Number of Toilets	Toilet Configuration	Number of Urinals	Urinal Configuration	Number of Showers/ Tubs	Shower Configuration
See legend or list type of building of not included in legend	Identifying number	How many restrooms in building	What type of restroom: guest bath (e.g., men's water closet by date room) and components of each restroom (full--toilet, urinal, washroom, showers; or different combinations thereof)	how many toilets in each restroom	are toilets partitioned; do they have doors	how many urinals in each bathroom	partitioned or not; individual urinals, or trough.	how many showers in each bathroom	partitioned or non-partitioned shower stalls, with or without benches/changing stall; open shower room with central water head, etc.
EMB	720647	3 (2 enlisted, 1 officer)	Toilets, urinals, washroom, showers in enlisted; no urinals in officer	enlisted 8,; officer 2	partitioned with doors in enlisted and officer	enlisted 6; officer none	partitioned in groups of three; individual	2 shower rooms for enlisted; 1 for officers	partitioned with 3 shower heads, no doors, no benches/changing rooms in enlisted; partitioned, no benches/changing rooms in officer
Battalion Admin. & Classroom Building	Sheet 4	3	1 men's restroom, 1 women's restroom, 1 small restroom near offices	Men: 8 Women: 2 Small RR: 1	Partitioned w/ doors	Men: 7	Individual w/o partitions	0	
BOQ	756740	4	2 bathrooms (toilet, shower) each unit; 1 bathroom for every 2 bedrooms (sinks in bedrooms)	1	No partitions	0		1	individual shower stalls
EMB	788341	2	unknown	unknown	unknown	unknown	unknown	unknown	unknown
EMB	795610	4	Toilets, urinals, washroom, showers in each	first floor 2; second floor 3	partitioned w/doors	first floor 1; second floor 2	partitioned; individual	first floor 1; second floor 2	partitioned; second floor has one bench
EMB	795611	2	Toilets, urinals, washrooms, showers in each	6	partitioned w/doors	4	partitioned in groups of two; individual	4	partitioned with 1 bench for each two stalls
EMB	795614	5	Toilets, urinals, washrooms, showers in each	4 in EM restrooms 1 in PO restroom	partitioned w/ doors	3 in EM restrooms 1 in PO restroom	individual; no partitions	3 in EM restrooms 1 in PO restroom	partitioned with bench for each 3 stalls; PO bath has changing stall w/ bench
EMB	795615	3 (1 on each floor)	Toilets, urinals, washrooms, showers in each	6	partitioned w/ doors	4	individual; no partitions	4	partitioned w/o benches & changing stalls
EMB	795616	8	Toilets, urinals, washrooms, showers in each	4 in EM restrooms 1 in PO restroom	partitioned w/ doors	3 in EM restrooms 1 in PO restroom	individual; no partitions	3 in EM restrooms 1 in PO restroom	partitioned w/o benches; PO shower has changing stall
EWB	795612	4	1 visitor's toilet (toilet & sink); 1 CPO bathroom (toilets, sinks, shower); 2 central bathrooms (toilets, sinks, showers, tubs)	Visitor's: 1 CPO: 2 EW: 9	partitioned w/ doors	0		CPO: 1 shower EW: 4 showers, 2 tubs	Showers: Partitioned w/ changing stalls & benches Tubs: Partitioned with changing area

Building Type	Drawing Number	Number of Restrooms	Restroom Configuration	Number of Toilets	Toilet Configuration	Number of Urinals	Urinal Configuration	Number of Showers/Tubs	Shower Configuration
See legend or list type of building of not included in legend	Identifying number	How many restrooms in building	What type of restroom: guest bath (e.g., men's water closet by date room) and components of each restroom (full--toilet, urinal, washroom, showers; or different combinations thereof)	how many toilets in each restroom	are toilets partitioned; do they have doors	how many urinals in each bathroom	partitioned or not; individual urinals, or trough.	how many showers in each bathroom	partitioned or non-partitioned shower stalls, with or without benches/changing stall; open shower room with central water head, etc.
EMB	795613	2	Toilets, urinals, washrooms, showers in each	6	partitioned w/doors	4	partitioned in groups of two; individual	4	partitioned with 1 bench for each two stalls
EWB	808316	2 (1 each floor)	Toilets, sinks, showers, tubs	8	partitioned w/doors	0		6 showers, 1 tub	Partitioned w/ changing stalls
EMB	817037	4	Toilets, urinals, washrooms, showers in each	3	partitioned w/doors	2	individual; no partitions	2	partitioned with 1 bench for each two stalls
EMB	817038	6	Toilets, urinals, washrooms, showers in each	3	partitioned w/doors	2	individual; no partitions	2	partitioned with 1 bench for each two stalls
EMB	817039	5	Toilets, urinals, washrooms, showers in each	4 in EM restrooms 1 in PO restroom	partitioned w/doors	3 in EM restrooms 1 in PO restroom	individual; no partitions	3 in EM restrooms 1 in PO restroom	Partitioned w/ 1 drying area for each 3 stalls; PO restroom has changing stall
EMB	817040	3 (1 each floor)	Toilets, urinals, washrooms, showers in each	6	partitioned w/doors	4	individual; no partitions	4	Partitioned w/ 1 bench for every 4 shower stalls
EMB	817041	8	Toilets, urinals, washrooms, showers in each	4 in EM restrooms 1 in PO restroom	partitioned w/doors	3 in EM restrooms 1 in PO restroom	individual; no partitions	3 in EM restrooms 1 in PO restroom	Partitioned stalls; PO restroom has changing stall
SP	817043	20	9 central restrooms (toilets, urinals, sinks, showers) 9 private baths for D1 (toilet, sink, shower) 2 restrooms in administration bldg (toilets, sinks, urinal)	Central: 8 Private: 1 Admin: 1, 2	partitioned w/o doors	Central: 5 Admin: 1	individual; no partitions	Central: 13 Private: 1	Central bathrooms: Open shower room w/ common drying area Private baths: individual shower stalls
EWB	817046	4	1 visitor's toilet (toilet & sink); 1 CPO bathroom (toilets, sinks, shower); 2 central bathrooms (toilets, sinks, showers, tubs)	Visitor's: 1 CPO: 2 EW: 9	partitioned w/doors	0		CPO: 1 shower EW: 4 showers, 2 tubs	Showers: Partitioned w/ changing stalls & benches Tubs: Partitioned with changing area
SP	817185	3	1 women's (w/ powder room) 1 men's 1 adjacent to kitchen	Women & Men: 3 Kitchen RR: 1	partitioned w/doors	Men: 2 Kitchen RR: 1	individual; no partitions	0	

Building Type	Drawing Number	Number of Restrooms	Restroom Configuration	Number of Toilets	Toilet Configuration	Number of Urinals	Urinal Configuration	Number of Showers/Tubs	Shower Configuration
See legend or list type of building of not included in legend	Identifying number	How many restrooms in building	What type of restroom: guest bath (e.g., men's water closet by date room) and components of each restroom (full--toilet, urinal, washroom, showers; or different combinations thereof)	how many toilets in each restroom	are toilets partitioned; do they have doors	how many urinals in each bathroom	partitioned or not; individual urinals, or trough.	how many showers in each bathroom	partitioned or non-partitioned shower stalls, with or without benches/changing stall; open shower room with central water head, etc.
EWB	745932	3	1 visitor's toilet (toilet & sink); 2 central bathrooms (toilets, sinks, showers, tubs)	Visitor's: 1 EW: 8	partitioned w/ doors	0		6 showers, 1 tub	Showers: Partitioned w/ changing stalls & benches Tubs: Partitioned with changing area
EWB	745933	2	1 visitor's toilet (toilet & sink); 1 central bathroom (toilets, sinks, showers, tubs)	Visitor's: 1 EW: 8	partitioned w/o doors	0		6 showers, 1 tub	Showers: Partitioned w/ changing stalls & benches Tubs: Partitioned with changing area
EWB	808224	3	1 visitor's toilet (toilet & sink); 2 central bathrooms (toilets, sinks, showers, tubs)	Visitor's: 1 EW: 8	partitioned w/o doors	0		6 showers, 1 tub	Showers: Partitioned w/ changing stalls & benches Tubs: Partitioned with changing area
EWB	808326	2	1 visitor's toilet (toilet & sink); 1 central bathroom (toilets, sinks, showers, tubs)	Visitor's: 1 EW: 8	partitioned w/o doors	0		6 showers, 1 tub	Showers: Partitioned w/ changing stalls & benches Tubs: Partitioned with changing area
EWB	808234	2	1 visitor's toilet (toilet & sink); 1 central bathroom (toilets, sinks, showers, tubs)	Visitor's: 1 EW: 8	partitioned w/o doors	0		6 showers, 1 tub	Showers: Partitioned w/ changing stalls & benches Tubs: Partitioned with changing area
EWB	836726	3	1 visitor's toilet (toilet & sink); 2 central bathrooms (toilets, sinks, showers, tubs)	Visitor's: 1 EW: 8	partitioned w/o doors	0		6 showers, 1 tub	Showers: Partitioned w/ changing stalls & benches Tubs: Partitioned with changing area
EWB	836734	2	1 visitor's toilet (toilet & sink); 1 central bathroom (toilets, sinks, showers, tubs)	Visitor's: 1 EW: 8	partitioned w/o doors	0		6 showers, 1 tub	Showers: Partitioned w/ changing stalls & benches Tubs: Partitioned with changing area

Building Type	Drawing Number	Number of Restrooms	Restroom Configuration	Number of Toilets	Toilet Configuration	Number of Urinals	Urinal Configuration	Number of Showers/ Tubs	Shower Configuration
See legend or list type of building of not included in legend	Identifying number	How many restrooms in building	What type of restroom: guest bath (e.g., men's water closet by date room) and components of each restroom (full--toilet, urinal, washroom, showers; or different combinations thereof)	how many toilets in each restroom	are toilets partitioned; do they have doors	how many urinals in each bathroom	partitioned or not; individual urinals, or trough.	how many showers in each bathroom	partitioned or non-partitioned shower stalls, with or without benches/changing stall; open shower room with central water head, etc.
SP	745934	2	Full restroom w/ toilets, sinks, showers, urinals	5	partitioned w/ doors	3	individual; no partitions	6 shower heads	Open shower room w/ common drying area
SP	808243	2	Full restroom w/ toilets, sinks, showers, urinals	5	partitioned w/ doors	3	individual; no partitions	6 shower heads	Open shower room w/ common drying area
SP	808335	2	Full restroom w/ toilets, sinks, showers, urinals	5	partitioned w/ doors	3	individual; no partitions	6 shower heads	Open shower room w/ common drying area
EMB	745930	2	Toilets, urinals, washrooms, showers in each	10	partitioned w/o doors	6	individual; no partitions	6	Open shower room w/ common drying area
EMB	745931	1	Toilets, urinals, washrooms, showers in each	10	partitioned w/o doors	6	individual; no partitions	6	Open shower room w/ common drying area
BOQ Motel Type	AD250672-1	17-18, 34-36; Depends on which alternative used; 2nd alt. includes 2 restrooms in lobby	Private with toilet, sink, shower 2nd alt. lobby restrooms: men - toilet, urinal, sink; women - sink, toilet	1	Alt. lobby restrooms partitioned with door	1 in men's restroom	Individual w/ partition	1 tub in each	No partitions
BOQ Motel Type	AD250672-2	(Up to 42 total) 38-40 in private rooms, 2 restrooms in lobby alt.	Private with toilet, sink, shower 2nd alt. lobby restrooms: men - toilet, urinal, sink; women - sink, toilet	1	Alt. lobby restrooms partitioned with door	1 in men's restroom	Individual w/ partition	1 tub in each	No partitions
EMB	895054	8	Toilets, urinals, washrooms, showers in each	4 in EM restrooms 1 in PO restroom	partitioned w/ doors	3 in EM restrooms 1 in PO restroom	individual; no partitions	3 in EM restrooms 1 in PO restroom	Partitioned w/ 1 drying area for each 3 stalls; PO restroom has changing stall

Building Type	Drawing Number	Number of Restrooms	Restroom Configuration	Number of Toilets	Toilet Configuration	Number of Urinals	Urinal Configuration	Number of Showers/Tubs	Shower Configuration
See legend or list type of building of not included in legend	Identifying number	How many restrooms in building	What type of restroom: guest bath (e.g., men's water closet by date room) and components of each restroom (full--toilet, urinal, washroom, showers; or different combinations thereof)	how many toilets in each restroom	are toilets partitioned; do they have doors	how many urinals in each bathroom	partitioned or not; individual urinals, or trough.	how many showers in each bathroom	partitioned or non-partitioned shower stalls, with or without benches/changing stall; open shower room with central water head, etc.
SP	1038068	12	6 Central Restrooms (toilets, urinals, sinks, showers) 6 Private baths (toilet, sink, shower)	Central: 10 Private: 1	partitioned w/o doors	Central: 5 Private: 0	individual; no partitions	Central: 12 Private: 1	Central bathrooms: Open shower room w/ common drying area Private baths: individual shower stalls
BEQ	1038070	1	Full restroom w/ toilets, sinks, showers, urinals	6	partitioned w/o doors	4	individual; no partitions	1 shower room	Open shower room w/ common drying area
BEQ	1038071	1 per suite	Full bath with toilet, sink, shower	1	No partitions	0		1 tub each	No partitions; private bath
BEQ	1038076	4	Full restroom w/ toilets, sinks, showers, urinals	Large restrooms: 12 Small restrooms: 3	partitioned w/o doors	Large RR: 8 Small RR: 2	individual; no partitions	Large RR: 1 open shower room Small RR: 2 showers	Large: Open shower room w/ 2 heads; common drying area w/ bench Small: Individual shower stalls with benches
Processing Building	380905-3	12	7 Men's restrooms, 4 Women's restrooms, 1 additional restroom	2 large men's rr: 16 other men's rr: 3 with 3 each, 1 with 5; Women's: 2 with 3 each, 1 with 4, 1	Partitioned with doors	2 large men's rr: 16 other men's rr: 3 with 3 each, 2 with 2	No partitions	0	
Barracks Reception Station Complex	SK2101153-6	12	Full restrooms with toilets, sinks, showers, urinals	6 restrooms with 5 each 6 restrooms with 3 each	partitioned with doors	6 restrooms with 3 urinals each	Individual with partitions	8 restrooms with 2 each; 4 with 4 each	6 restrooms have 2 partitioned showers, other restrooms have gang showers
Dining Hall	3605118-4	1	Full restrooms with toilets, sinks, urinals (attached to locker room)	3	partitioned with doors	3	Individual with partitions	0	

Building Type	Drawing Number	Number of Restrooms	Restroom Configuration	Number of Toilets	Toilet Configuration	Number of Urinals	Urinal Configuration	Number of Showers/ Tubs	Shower Configuration
See legend or list type of building of not included in legend	Identifying number	How many restrooms in building	What type of restroom: guest bath (e.g., men's water closet by date room) and components of each restroom (full--toilet, urinal, washroom, showers; or different combinations thereof)	how many toilets in each restroom	are toilets partitioned; do they have doors	how many urinals in each bathroom	partitioned or not; individual urinals, or trough.	how many showers in each bathroom	partitioned or non-partitioned shower stalls, with or without benches/changing stall; open shower room with central water head, etc.
Enlisted Barracks Reception Station Complex	2101153-6	12	Full restrooms with toilets, sinks, showers, urinals	6 restrooms with 5 each 6 restrooms with 3 each	partitioned with doors	6 restrooms with 3 urinals each	Individual with partitions	8 restrooms with 2 each; 4 with 4 each	6 restrooms have 2 partitioned showers, other restrooms have gang showers
Reception Station Complex	1606328-2								
Service Club/ Post Exchange	311847-5	7	5 small restrooms (toilet & sink), 2 main restrooms (toilets & sinks), 1 for women (with powder room), 1 for men	Small restrooms: 1 each Large restrooms: 3 for women, 4 for men	Partitioned with doors	4 in men's restroom	Individual w/o partitions	0	
Service Club/ Post Exchange Reception Station Complex	SK311847-5	6	2 small restrooms adjacent to dressing rooms & stage; 2 large restrooms, 1 m 1 w; 2 small restrooms, 1m, 1w, adjacent to post exchange	small restrooms: 1 each large restrooms: men, 4, women, 3	Partitioned w/ doors	4 in men's restroom	Individual w/o partitions	0	
EMB	1038075	8	Toilets, urinals, washrooms, showers in each	4 in EM restrooms 1 in PO restroom	partitioned w/ doors	3 in EM restrooms 1 in PO restroom	individual; no partitions	3 in EM restrooms 1 in PO restroom	Partitioned shower stalls; PO restroom has changing stall
EWB (Center Hall & Motel Type)	4	7	1 Visitors toilet (toilet, sink), 4 private baths for petty officers(toilet, sink, shower), 2 restrooms with sinks, toilets, showers	Visitors: 1 Petty Officer: 1 Shared Restrooms: 5 in each	partitioned w/o doors	0		3 for enlisted; 1 per room for officers	Partitioned shower stalls with changing stall, 1 tub each restroom Private baths for officers
Officer Personnel Typical Living Units - Center Hall Type	6		Private with toilet, sink, shower	1 per bathroom				1 per bathroom	
Officer Personnel Typical Living Units - Motel	5	1 in each unit	1 restroom with toilet, shower, sink for each unit	1 per unit				1 per unit	

Building Type	Drawing Number	Number of Restrooms	Restroom Configuration	Number of Toilets	Toilet Configuration	Number of Urinals	Urinal Configuration	Number of Showers/ Tubs	Shower Configuration
See legend or list type of building of not included in legend	Identifying number	How many restrooms in building	What type of restroom: guest bath (e.g., men's water closet by date room) and components of each restroom (full--toilet, urinal, washroom, showers; or different combinations thereof)	how many toilets in each restroom	are toilets partitioned; do they have doors	how many urinals in each bathroom	partitioned or not; individual urinals, or trough.	how many showers in each bathroom	partitioned or non-partitioned shower stalls, with or without benches/changing stall; open shower room with central water head, etc.
SP (Gym)	1294389 (NAVFAC)	4	1 men's restroom (toilets, sinks) 1 women's restroom (toilets, sinks) 1 restroom in main locker room (toilets, sinks, urinals, showers) 1 restroom in visiting/women's restroom (toilets, sinks, showers)	Men's: 2 Women's: 1	partitioned w/ doors	Men's: 2	individual; no partitions	Men's Locker Room: 4 Women's Locker Room: 2	Men's: open gang shower Women's: partitioned shower stalls w/ changing stall & bench
BOQ	1297661 - 1297662 (FEC)	124	122 Private baths (includes MAA bathroom) 1 men's restroom 1 women's restroom	1	No partitions	0		1	Individual shower stalls
SP (Gym)	1294390 (NAVFAC)	5	1 Men's (toilets, urinals, sinks) 1 Women's (toilets, sinks) 2 Men's locker room restrooms (toilets, urinals, sinks, showers) 1 Visiting/ Women's restroom (toilets, sinks, showers)	Men's restroom: 4 others: 2	partitioned w/ doors	Men's restroom: 4 Men's LR: 2	individual; no partitions	Men's Locker Room: 5 Women's Locker Room: 2	Men's: open gang shower Women's: partitioned shower stalls w/ changing stall & bench
BEQ	1403100 (NAVFAC)	1 per suite; 2 restrooms in core building	Full bath with toilet, sink, shower/tub Core building: 1men's, 1 women's	1	Men's & women's toilets partitioned w/o door	Men's toilet: 1	individual w/ partition	Private baths: 1 tub each	No partitions
BEQ	1403797 (NAVFAC)	48 private (1 per room); 2 (1men, 1 women) in core building	Full bath with toilet, sink, shower/tub Core building: 1men's, 1 women's	1	Men's & women's toilets partitioned w/o door	Men's toilet: 1	individual w/ partition	Private baths: 1 tub each	No partitions
BEQ	1403798 (NAVFAC)	278	276 private baths w/ toilet, sink, shower/tub 2 restrooms (1 men, 1 women) on 1st floor	Private: 1 Men's: 1 Women's: 2	Men's & women's toilets partitioned w/o door	Men's toilet: 1	individual w/ partition	Private baths: 1 tub or shower each	No partitions

Building Type	Drawing Number	Number of Restrooms	Restroom Configuration	Number of Toilets	Toilet Configuration	Number of Urinals	Urinal Configuration	Number of Showers/Tubs	Shower Configuration
See legend or list type of building of not included in legend	Identifying number	How many restrooms in building	What type of restroom: guest bath (e.g., men's water closet by date room) and components of each restroom (full--toilet, urinal, washroom, showers; or different combinations thereof)	how many toilets in each restroom	are toilets partitioned; do they have doors	how many urinals in each bathroom	partitioned or not; individual urinals, or trough.	how many showers in each bathroom	partitioned or non-partitioned shower stalls, with or without benches/changing stall; open shower room with central water head, etc.
BOQ	1403795 (NAVFAC)	100	1 bathroom per unit w/ toilet, sink, shower	1	No partitions	0		1	individual shower stalls
BOQ	1403796 (NAVFAC)	100	1 bathroom per unit w/ toilet, sink, shower	1	No partitions	0		1	individual shower stalls
BOQ (Men)	306887 - 306888	10	All central toilet facilities w/ toilets, urinals, sinks, showers	2	partitioned w/ doors	2	individual; no partitions	2	Partitioned shower stalls w/ changing stalls & benches
EWB	306869	3	2 Central Restrooms (toilets, sinks, showers) 1 Private restroom (PO)	Central: 10 Private: 1	partitioned w/ doors	0		8	Open gang shower room w/ 8 shower heads
EWB	306870								
Alterations to Bldg # 268 Training Center Fort Des Moines, Iowa	193A-28	1	Toilet and washroom	4	Partitioned w/ doors	0		0	
Alterations to Building # 81 Training Center Fort Des Moines, Iowa	193A-27								
EWB	21-02-06	4	2 Central restrooms (toilets, sinks, showers, tubs) 1 Women's toilet (toilet, sink) 1 Men's toilet (toilet, sink)	Central: 5 others: 1	partitioned w/ doors	0		3 showers, 1 tub each	Partitioned shower stalls w/ changing stalls w/ benches; Bathtubs w/ changing area
Improved Bachelor Officer Quarters - Women	Sheet 303	16	Private bath with sink, toilet, & tub	1		0		1 tub	
Perspective Sketch Drawing	sketch_reception								
BEQ	1341195 (NAVFAC)	47	36 private baths (toilet, sink, shower) 9 central restrooms (toilets, sinks, urinals, showers) 2 restrooms by lobby (1 men, 1 women)	Private: 1 Central: 2 Men: 1 Women: 1	Partitioned with doors	Central: 2 Men's: 1	individual; no partitions	Private baths: 1 each Central baths: 2 each	Individual shower stalls; central baths have shared bench for 2 showers

Building Type	Drawing Number	Number of Restrooms	Restroom Configuration	Number of Toilets	Toilet Configuration	Number of Urinals	Urinal Configuration	Number of Showers/Tubs	Shower Configuration
See legend or list type of building of not included in legend	Identifying number	How many restrooms in building	What type of restroom: guest bath (e.g., men's water closet by date room) and components of each restroom (full--toilet, urinal, washroom, showers; or different combinations thereof)	how many toilets in each restroom	are toilets partitioned; do they have doors	how many urinals in each bathroom	partitioned or not; individual urinals, or trough.	how many showers in each bathroom	partitioned or non-partitioned shower stalls, with or without benches/changing stall; open shower room with central water head, etc.
EB	731427	36	1 visitor's restroom (toilet, sink) 30 shared baths (toilet, sink, shower) 3 central restrooms (toilets, sinks, showers) 2 MA private baths (toilet, sink)	visitor: 1 shared: 1 central: 2 MA bath: 1	Central toilets: partitioned w/ doors	6 (2 each in central restrooms)	individual; no partitions	shared: 1 central: 3	Individual shower stalls
EB	731428	varies	Shared with 2 rooms (toilet, sink, shower)	1	No partitions	0		1	Individual shower stalls
EB	756735	4	1 visitor's toilet 3 central restrooms (toilets, sinks, showers)	visitor: 1 central: 7	partitioned w/ doors	visitor: 1 central: 4	individual; no partitions	4	Partitioned shower stalls
EB	756736	6	Central restrooms w/ toilets, sinks, showers	2	partitioned w/ doors	2	individual; no partitions	2	Partitioned shower stalls
EMB	171065	3	1 Central Restroom (toilets, urinals, sinks in one room; separate shower & dressing room) 1 Shared bath (toilet, sink, shower) between 2 officer rooms 1 restroom near kitchen w/ toilet & sink	Central: 2 Others: 1	partitioned w/o doors	Central: 3 Others: 0`	individual; no partitions	Number of shower heads not indicated	Central restroom: Open gang shower room w/ adjacent dressing room Officers restroom: Individual shower stall
SP (Chapel)	367912	2	Small restroom w/ toilet & sink	1	partitioned w/ doors	0		0	
SP (Chapel)	367912								
W	318064	3	2 Communal restrooms (separate room for showers) 1 private bath (CPO)	Communal: 5 Private: 1	partitioned w/ doors	0		Communal: 6 Private: 1	Partitioned shower stalls w/ changing stalls & benches
WB	318064	4	2 restrooms with toilets and lavatory 2 shower rooms	5	partitioned w/ doors	0		6 showers each room	Partitioned w/ changing stalls & benches

Appendix B: Copies of Plans and Drawings

Not for Public Release. Unattached.

Contact the Legacy Resource Management Program Office for availability information.

www.ingramcontent.com/pod-product-compliance
Lightning Source LLC
Chambersburg PA
CBHW082110230426
43671CB00015B/2659